Robert Winder was literary e̶   [D0779022]   years and deputy editor of *Gr*   of *Bloody Foreigners: The Story of Immigration to Britain and three* novels, the most recent being *The Final Act of Mr Shakespeare*.

'Spirited, provocative, wise, hugely entertaining' Dominic Sandbrook, *Sunday Times*

'Winder, who in 2004 wrote a compelling book about immigration called *Bloody Foreigners*, expertly navigates his subject without mentioning Brexit. Yet it has a pertinent lesson for some of the more excitable Brexiteers – we have never been an island nation' *Prospect*

'A glorious romp through more than eight centuries, told with humour and charm, with the same themes recurring over the ages. Highly recommended' William Hartston, *Daily Express*

'A provocative and lively look at what has made the English who they are' *Sunday Times*

'*The Last Wolf* is an engaging ramble through the wool towns and open ranges of medieval England' *Spectator*

'An entertainingly discursive anatomy of the English character' Jane Shilling, *Mail on Sunday*

'This is digestible, friendly, whimsical history: Winder is clearly allergic to boring history books and makes it his business not to write one' Ysenda Maxtone Graham, author of *Terms & Conditions*, *Times Literary Supplement*

'I will return to its insights again and again' *Country Life*

The
Last Wolf

The Hidden Springs
of Englishness

ROBERT WINDER

ABACUS

First published in Great Britain in 2017 by Little, Brown
This paperback edition published in 2018 by Abacus

3 5 7 9 10 8 6 4 2

A CIP catalogue record for this book
is available from the British Library.

ISBN 978-0-349-14186-2

Typeset in Bembo by M Rules
Printed and bound in Great Britain
by Clays Ltd, Elcograf S.p.A.

Papers used by Abacus are from well-managed forests
and other responsible sources.

Abacus
An imprint of
Little, Brown Book Group
Carmelite House
50 Victoria Embankment
London EC4Y 0DZ

An Hachette UK Company
www.hachette.co.uk

www.littlebrown.co.uk

To H. D.

What seest thou else
In the dark backward and abysm of time?

William Shakespeare, *The Tempest*

Contents

Introduction

Peter and the Wolf

When the Shropshire knight Peter Corbet raised his goblet of Christmas wine at the end of the year 1290, he may well have permitted himself a contented smile. The scion of a notable Norman family who had been granted fine lands near Shrewsbury, he was basking in the glow of a job well done. He had added lustre to his already famous name by ridding England's western shires – Gloucestershire, Herefordshire, Shropshire, Staffordshire and Worcestershire – of a grim scourge: the wolf.

The King himself had given Peter this task in a royal edict of 1281: 'Know ye that we have enjoined our dear and faithful Peter Corbet that he take and destroy Wolves with his men, dogs and devices, in all ways in which he shall deem expedient.' Corbet had risen to the challenge with a will, becoming a fearsome wolf killer. Ranging across the royal forests with his pack of hounds, he was known as 'the Mighty Hunter'. His crest featured two ravens on a gold shield, echoing the ravening banners of the Viking hunters who had stormed across northern England only two centuries earlier.

And now, it seemed, he had done it.

The countryside held its breath.

In truth, he may have culled no great number of the beasts. The thirteenth century did not keep detailed records: there were no electronic tags or radio collars available to monitor the lupine community. But we can tell that the wolf population was already thin. As far back as the tenth century King Edgar had craftily exacted tribute from his vassals in the form of wolf skins; and the number of sheep in the Domesday Book (they outnumbered cattle, goats and pigs combined) suggests that wolves were already on the rare side a century later. By the time of Magna Carta, King John was offering a sizeable reward for their capture (five shillings a pelt – too high a sum for easy prey), which suggests that they were genuinely uncommon in the early 1200s. The pell-mell destruction of England's forests had eroded their habitat and exposed them to predators like Corbet.

But a few continued to roam the land under Edward I, slipping out of the woods above Hereford or Evesham to take a lamb, a calf or even a child. And since they also showed a treasonous taste for royal venison (on the bone) a new war was declared. Death sentences could be waived if men agreed to harvest wolf tongues – a perilous duty, no question. January was declared to be the official wolf-hunting month.

And now, after almost a decade of diligent stalking, it seemed that Corbet had prevailed. There had been a report of wolves savaging deer in the Forest of Dean in early 1290, but since then ... nothing. Not a single howl had been heard in the hills and woods of the West Country; not a single royal deer had barked out its death-throes in the Shropshire night.

Whether this meant the end of wolves in the kingdom as a whole is open to debate. Half a dozen calves were mauled in Lancashire in 1295, and in the years to come there were occasional glimpses in the northern wilds – a gleaming eye here, a shadow there, a glimpse on the Cumbrian shore near Barrow-in-Furness as late as Tudor times. But these undocumented sightings have the shimmering quality of the Loch Ness legend or the Beast of Bodmin. The fear of wolves certainly outlasted their actual presence.[1]

---

1 A reporter from the *Darlington and Stockton Times* spotted a group of wild dogs in a bus shelter in the spring of 2015 ... and they were indeed genuine Canadian timber wolves. But they had escaped from a nearby zoo, and were swiftly returned.

In the latter half of the fourteenth century, Edward III granted land near Kettering to the Engaine family as a reward for their ridding the shires of Buckingham, Huntingdon, Northampton and Oxford of wolves, foxes and other vermin.[2]

© Wolves Attacking Sheep (Rein de Trop II) 1732 (pen & ink with wash and gouache on paper), Oudry, Jean-Baptiste (1686–1755)/The Art Institute of Chicago, IL, USA/Restricted gift of the Joseph and Helen Regenstein Foundation/Bridgeman Images

What big teeth you have. The eradication of the wolf allowed England to become something unique: a giant sheep estate.

But this was a generalised enjoinder not nearly so precise as the one addressed to Peter Corbet. Similarly, though the lantern tower atop the church of All Saints Pavement in York (erected in 1400) is said to have guided travellers through the

2 The family crest shows a running wolf trapped between a spear and an axe. And the Engaines seem to have been successful. Pytchley, where they hunted, is now home to a golf range and a lot of pylons.

'wolf-infested' forest to the north of the city walls, there is no evidence to suggest that wolves posed anything like so grave a danger to the weary medieval traveller as the human predators in those woods.

These were misty times. But while it may be that the odd wolf did continue to lope through the English forest, unseen and unheard, for years, the determined efforts of Peter Corbet signalled at least the beginning of the end. Indeed, even if all the subsequent sightings are 24-carat authentic, their most striking feature is their scarcity. To all intents and purposes, when Peter killed his last wolf, that was it.

His reward was a place in Edward I's Parliament.

Mighty consequences often flow from modest alterations, but the after-effects of Corbet's handiwork (or at least the centuries-long cull in which he played a part) were radical indeed. It involved a certain loss of glamour: England became a tamed terrain, scoured of exciting wild animals. But the new-born peacefulness of the rural scene made possible a form of landholding – the enormous sheep estate – that was beyond contemplation in the wolf-haunted woods of the European mainland, where livestock had to be ushered into pens at night by watchful shepherds.

Nothing could be done about this: the wolves padded into Germany and France from the endless Russian forest in numbers too great to control. But in the centuries that followed the completion of Corbet's handiwork, England, an Anglo-Saxon–Viking–Celtic witch's brew of an island governed by Norman occupiers, would turn into the biggest sheep farm in the world, and become the source of its finest wool.

It is this – the growth of sheep farms even in remote parts of the country – that most persuasively describes England as a land cleansed of wolves.

The nation stood on the brink of a tremendous agricultural revolution.

*

As often happens, I came upon the story of Peter Corbet in the course of looking for something else. Going out after sheep, I stumbled on wolves.

Why sheep? Because I was minded to trace the origins of Englishness. Since narrating the story of immigration to this country in *Bloody Foreigners* (2004), I had taken part in quite a few discussions on the so-called 'national identity', and kept butting up against the assumption that this must be a matter of ideas and principles – fair play, tolerance, law, equality, diversity, democracy and so on. It flowed, ran the argument, from a native 'culture' that had matured over many centuries of progressive ideas.

I chafed against this assumption, for two reasons.

First, it seemed hard to maintain that such 'values' were exclusively English. They were also Swiss, Indian, Japanese, Cuban, Kenyan or Portuguese aspirations: standard-issue social dreams shared by everyone. Second, I was pretty sure that Englishness was no innate quality, but had been shaped by migration from elsewhere ever since the first people tiptoed into this cold island when the ice retreated all those aeons ago.

The English language was a blend of German, French and Latin, spiced with exotic notes from further afield ... and so was the English population. Even the much and rightly vaunted legal system had its origins, in the age of Henry II, in an England that conducted its affairs in Norman French, and recorded its rulings in Latin.

I knew, in other words, that Englishness was not some ancient genetic miracle that had somehow weathered the storms of history, but a broad river with many tributaries. There was no aboriginal germ that could be emblazoned on a banner; the national character was not a matter of blood. Quite the opposite: it was a mongrel, the hybrid product of many identities. And the local culture could drip its influence over anyone. England's weather, England's food and all the other textures that grew out of its unique (by definition) geographical place in the world shaped everything.

Of the 180 'tenants-in-chief' installed after the Norman Conquest, only half a dozen were English. The rest were French. A few generations later, they had all gone native.

If we really wanted to search for the national identity, I thought, the real place to look was in the natural heritage of hills, valleys, rivers, stones and mists – the raw materials that had, over time, moulded the way we were. Landscape and history – the past and the elemental backdrop – were the only things we could truly claim as our own. Just as some plants thrive in sand and others in clay, so a national character is fed by nutrients it cannot alter. We are not passive creatures living out dim destinies assigned long ago, but our formative years were shaped by nature as well as nurture.

Englishness, in this context, was the product not of racial or political factors, but the tantalising outcome of many natural forces: the island location, its mild marine climate, the well-defined seasons and the fertile soil, along with lush grass, plentiful timber, deep seams of coal and excellent stone. Geography, in effect, was destiny. It was not native guile that fed and watered our crops but an unusual combination of topographical forces, notably the warm Gulf Stream, which even in this northerly latitude delivered the temperate winters that shaped our agricultural tradition.

This is not to say we were wholly different from our neighbours. Indeed, there were many similarities. We had the same sort of rain as Wales, the same lush grass as Ireland, an intricate coast rather like Scotland's, hills and rivers that were not so different from those of France and Germany. We had the same low marshes as Holland, the same stone quarries as Italy and Spain, and timber forests that resembled those in Scandinavia. Our bird life migrated hither and thither, our soil supported many of the same crops as continental Europe, and we were not the only place to send fishing boats out to sea.

But slight variations, magnified over time, produce profound differences. And, in England's case – indeed in all these cases – it was the idiosyncratic way in which all these elements combined that produced the singular effect.

We were a land of sheep, wheat and apples, not goats, rice and vines. Oak and beech, not palm and olive. We had little choice in the matter; it was in our nature.

I was interested in sheep because in the Middle Ages they were the beating heart of the national wealth. One only had to think of the grand heritage spun from wool: the defining swathe of cathedrals, churches, guild halls, villages, fields, markets, mills and manor houses that remain the poster children of British tourism to this day.

It did not seem odd that English wool reigned supreme. We had the best rain, and therefore the best grass, in Europe. We were a natural wool farm.

That was where Peter Corbet made his entrance. He was only a footnote, a squiggle in the margins of medieval history. But as soon as I came upon his story, a light bulb flashed above my head. It wasn't only the rain and the grass – though both were essential. The decisive element in England's wool supremacy, the magic ingredient, was the fact that it could maintain enormous flocks of sheep, secure in the knowledge that they would not be decimated by the exciting hazards of tooth and claw.

I was well aware of the confusion that tends to beset any discussion of Englishness and Britishness. Though they are not the same thing, they are often taken to be. In this case, my focus was on England partly because, in medieval times, Britain did not exist (the Act of Union between England and Scotland was signed in 1707) and partly because, at the time of writing, it was looking as though the British Union might well be approaching its sell-by date. The Scottish referendum had been a close-run thing. The lure of nationalism could not be wished away. A Disunited Kingdom was very much on the cards.

In the course of that campaign, however, there was a notable absentee, a rather strident ghost at the feast. Englishness. What was it? And what did it want?

It felt like a good time to think about those questions. But of what might Englishness consist? The national character was too variegated to be reduced to a single definition. Even the briefest summary would have to include tea, beef, gardening, beer, curry, cricket, Shakespeare, toast, royal pageantry, military bands, washing the car, banging on about the war, stiff upper lips, Chinese takeaways, whingeing, saying 'sorry', home-made jam, queuing, road rage, stand-up comedians, tabloid headlines, plastic bags in trees, post offices, Big Ben, pillar boxes, supermarket trolleys, choral evensong, poppies, village greens, brass bands, football hooligans, carols, dog mess, broken umbrellas, chewing gum, 'Order! Order!' and a thousand other resonant things.

Identities are cartoons: they always leave things out. Many writers have tried to encapsulate Englishness, and some of their attempts have been extremely alluring. But all fall short in the end; something is always omitted. How could it be otherwise?

It mattered, though. In 1801 England contributed only half the population of the United Kingdom. Today, it is more like four-fifths. It has often acted like the fattest cat in the federation and, increasingly, that is what it is.

Perhaps we should begin with the basic facts of England's natural inheritance. And the first of these was the climate. It was rain that sculpted the landscape and established the pattern of settlement; rain that fed the grass that filled the sheep that produced the wool that built the churches; rain that watered the fields of wheat and the endless lawns, parks and greens; rain that filled the rivers and canals that carried English freight; rain that drove the mills and made the beer. Finally, it was rain that hissed on red-hot coals to create the head of steam that drove the turbines of the industrial age.

Coal. That was a natural resource too, lying deep in the earth beneath England's feet. It was as natural as grass, in its way. And if the merger of rain and grass created sheep, then the alliance between rain and coal made something even more powerful: steam.

Was it possible to shed light on Englishness based on these raw facts of life?

At this point, something else happened: Britain voted to leave the European Union.

There was no need to sift through the poll data to understand that this was a victory for English rather than British sentiment. It was England, not Britain, that seemed happy to risk returning to the wintry political atmosphere of the 1970s. It was England that wanted to raise the drawbridge, paddle its own canoe, abandon its allies, emphasise 'sovereignty' over cooperation, and withdraw from an experiment that had (though imperfect) brought peace to a warring continent and turned thirteen dictatorships into democracies.

In one way it was misleading to call it Brexit. If anything, it was Exit. And it made it even more urgent to think about what England once was, and might soon become.

Like the Scottish referendum, the European vote was emphatic, but close. Nearly half the country was dismayed. Whatever the rights and wrongs of the decision – and time would be the only judge – it left England looking lonely. Even its own Union was fraying. Britain, once a byword for imperturbable continuity, was no longer a steady ship.

Until these upheavals, Englishness had long seemed a rather low-throttle beast. This may have been because England had only rarely existed as an independent nation – in Tudor times and under Cromwell – but it was also because, as the dominant, swaggering party in the British federation, it had not often needed to puff out its chest. Scotland, Wales and Ireland all had vivid identities formed partly by the *contrast* with Englishness. Englishness, more heavily implicated in the federal project, was more evasive. Few people even claimed it, except for sports fans;

and that wasn't always a pretty sight. Most English people preferred to take cover under the British flag.

The result was a world of fuzzy lines. We had the British
Library, British Airways, the British Museum, the BBC and
British passports; we wished each other the 'best of British' and
took pride in the Battle of Britain. It was Britannia, not Albion,
that ruled the waves. Yet we spoke English, studied English literature, ate full English breakfasts, supported England in the World
Cup and subsidised the English National Opera. No one ever sang
about mad dogs and Britishmen going out in the midday sun; it
was England, not Britain, that was the green and pleasant land.

In these and other ways the English had learned to live with
contradictions – a trait that was always obvious to foreign
visitors, who found the natives purposeful, but blockheaded.
Goethe said they were 'complete men' even when they were
being 'complete fools'; Emerson felt that 'no nation was ever so
rich in able men', but added that they had a 'saving stupidity'.
Walter Page, US ambassador to the Court of St James in the
Second World War, claimed: 'I could write a book in worship of them … and another book damning them.' George
Santayana added that Anglo-Saxons were 'the most disliked
of men … except when people need someone they can trust'.

Perhaps we have always been a two-tone people: half eccentric, half pedestrian. There is a materialistic streak, to be sure,
and a famous suspicion of ideas. But England has also produced
lofty theorists such as Newton, Locke, Paine and Darwin.
Long celebrated as the home of fair play, it has tolerated amazing extremes of cruelty. Every time we are tempted to identify
an English quirk, we sense that the opposite may also be true.
England prizes individualism, yet is conformist; is polite, yet
rude; stuck-up, yet plain-speaking; repressed, yet exuberant;
moderate, yet unconventional; peaceful, yet combative. Perhaps
this is why cricket has for so long been its symbolic game,
being both the slowest sport in the world and (when you are
facing a fast bowler) one of the quickest.

Though rarely in the van of the avant-garde, the English have long been proud non-conformists. Eccentricity is not just tolerated but cherished. Never so highly as the calm, undemonstrative middle way, however. In a land of extremes, the best course was always the safe passage between them.

As Joseph Conrad once remarked, the highest praise in England was the restrained yet heartfelt signal to a ship of the line that had done its duty: 'Well done'.

That may be a poetic rather than a historical observation, but it is a way of saying that we must look not only to the past; we should also explore the landscape from which we sprang, the ground that shaped us in ways we can barely fathom. If history is nurture, then landscape is nature; and civilisations, like individuals, need both.

It is possible that history plays too heated a role in contemporary life. The world might be more peaceful if the troubled narratives of the Middle East, the Balkans, Sri Lanka, Northern Ireland and half a dozen African countries could be magically erased. The past can be a lethal weapon, and grubbing around in it sometimes does no more than breathe life into grievances that have no remedy. But while we may agree that history only ever offers a partial glimpse of the past, we should at least accept that the past *did* happen, and that its echoes reach into the present whether we like it or not.[3]

Tradition matters too, however much we try to ignore it. As G. K. Chesterton once quipped, to dismiss the past is to give undue weight to a mere accident of death. It is the ground on which we stand, and it has an interesting way of surviving down the generations. Posterity operates like natural selection, favouring only the moments in our past that pass the test of time. Even with memories, only the fittest survive.

---

3 For a wider discussion of the way historians have dealt with geographical and environmental factors, see Historical Note on page 426.

One

A Tale of Three Townships

The village of Great Dunmow, in northern Essex, has all the time-honoured features of modern English country life. There are traces of ancient Rome, medieval accents, a sixteenth-century town hall, Georgian and Victorian villas, a tranquil green, fine old cottages around a pond, a stately home, a Grade II-listed hotel, a museum, a cricket club, a heritage brewery, a clutch of shops and a riverside church. To complete the set of traditional charms, the village was also host to an RAF base in the Second World War.

All of this is overlaid by more contemporary flavours. The main road is a crowded thoroughfare of banks, estate agencies, chemists' shops, electronics outlets and chain stores, along with the usual range of British restaurants – Italian, Chinese, Bangladeshi and Thai. Meanwhile, the surrounding fields have been colonised by housing estates.

The fact that Great Dunmow cowers within a loop of ring road beneath the flight path to Stansted Airport casts a slight pall over the scene, but does not ruin it altogether. Children in purple school uniforms swarm outside sweet shops on the way home, while cherry blossom falls on the new models outside car showrooms on the perimeter road.

In the 1940s the village was part of the so-called General Headquarters Line, a redoubt of concrete pillboxes built to repel a German invasion. H. G. Wells lived here for a while, but these days it is better known as the home of 'The Flitch'. Dating back to the Middle Ages, this ceremony takes the form of an open court (a temporary marquee is installed on the village green) in which married couples claim to have enjoyed a year and a day of domestic bliss without 'repenting' of their union. If their claim is upheld by an impressive jury – a panel of local dignitaries dressed as off-duty morris men – they win a side (or 'flitch') of bacon.

The event was devised to reward newlyweds' good behaviour, and soon became well known. Langland casually alluded to the 'flicche' of 'Donemowe' in *Piers Plowman* as if it were general knowledge, as did Chaucer in the prologue to the *Wife of Bath's Tale*.[1] In the middle of the eighteenth century it lapsed, but a Victorian author named William Harrison Ainsworth (a friend of Dickens and quite famous in his day) made it the premise of a novel.

It is tempting to see The Flitch as no more than a quaint, olde-worlde excuse for a pint and a boisterous runaround – like those cheese-rolling races in the Cotswolds. But it is also the source of the saying 'bringing home the bacon', a familiar aphorism for making a living (putting food on the family table). Until I visited Great Dunmow, I had assumed this to be figurative; it had not occurred to me that the bacon might be real, or that 'bringing it home' might signal victory in a heritage-themed pub competition.

Like many a modern saying, however, its ancestry is older than we might think.

Plenty of everyday phrases have deep roots of this sort.

---

[1] The *Wife of Bath*'s prologue is a blunt discourse on medieval marriage, brazen in the way it urges wives to marshal their sexual resources in order to manipulate their husbands. Such gambits do not always make for domestic peace, and, at one point, speaking about her five turbulent marriages, the Wife of Bath declares:

> *I sette hem so a-weke, by my fey*
> *That many a night they songen Weilaway.*
> *The bacon was nat for hem, I trow*
> *That some men have in Essex at Dunmow.*

Sometimes they have lost their original meaning: 'making hay while the sun shines' was not at first a call to have a party while the coast was clear, but the opposite – a commandment to work hard while conditions were propitious. And sometimes the origins are apocryphal, as in the idea that 'going round the bend' refers to the Victorian habit of building lunatic asylums on curved drives, so they could not be seen from the road (hence the way we speak of being 'driven round the bend' or going 'loopy'). This, sadly, is too good to be true. But 'bringing home the bacon' really does come from a twelfth-century ceremony to reward harmony in the home. And it lives on to this day.

A lengthy walk (or half an hour's drive) north-east of Great Dunmow stands the village of Lavenham. It is one of England's most photographed beauty spots, and the first-time visitor can quickly see why. Once the wool capital of Tudor Suffolk, this timber-framed antique generates a dizzy sense of *déjà vu*. As with one's first glimpse of Venice, it seems immediately familiar. Yes, you catch yourself thinking, it is precisely like the image on the fudge box, place mat, tea towel, calendar or jigsaw puzzle. It seems implausible that so classic a piece of heritage could have survived intact: you half expect to see a shepherd nudging his ewes across the square, a monk leading a donkey to the well for a drink, or a jester jingling out of the local hostelry, dragging a bear by the nose.

It is so picturesque, so awash with faded plaster, grey oak, tidy hedges and jutting windows, that it takes a firm effort to imagine how it might have struck a medieval visitor. Back then, it was surely not so captivating. On the contrary, it was an ugly factory town, blighted by stinking animals, whirring looms, wicked get-rich-quick merchants and horrible modern buildings that were ruining a former rural idyll. Just look at those executive homes for the fat-cat wool merchants – tasteless eyesores stuffed with vulgar mouldings, show-off porches and overhanging eaves.

Modern Lavenham is vintage England. But in its medieval heyday it might have struck visitors as an ugly new factory town.

This hideous modernisation made Lavenham a force to be reckoned with in the fourteenth century. Indeed, it was the pumping heart of England's most important commercial enterprise. The 1327 tax survey confirms that this was no serene farming community but a full-on wool manufactory, with a complete set of dyers, fullers, shearers, shepherds and weavers. These are all wool-related trades, of course, and most would become common English surnames. If we add Mercer, Tucker, Walker, Webb, Webster (or even Winder) to the list, we have a vivid indication of the senior position of wool-working in the historic economy.

The high point of Lavenham's prosperity came in the six-teenth century, but it was a grand estate long before then. It was granted to Aubrey de Vere, William the Conqueror's brother-in-law, right after the Norman Conquest, along with other enviable properties (such as Kensington), and there were vineyards here at the time of the Domesday Book. One hundred and fifty years later it was already a formidable wool exchange, and in 1290 Edward III granted the parish the right to hold a Whitsun Fair. This paved the way for its emergence as a boom town: by 1524 it was ranked the fourteenth-richest parish in the kingdom.

It has an oak-aged guild hall, a quaint museum, time-cured cottages (all immaculate) and a distinguished hotel – once a coaching inn on the road from Ipswich to Bury St Edmunds. There are so many ancient beams that it feels as if an extensive forest has been carved into the very fabric of the place, and the village seems to slumber in the cosy heart of an area so hallowed you could spend weeks sleeping only in rooms that pre-date Shakespeare and Raleigh. It is possible, whenever you duck under yet another lintel hewn from salvaged Armada struts, to feel cheated by the nouveau décor.

More grand than any of these, however, is the church of St Peter and St Paul, on a rise to the west of the town. Far too substantial for the small community it serves, it was built at the end of the fifteenth century thanks to the largesse of two men. The first was John de Vere, the 13th Earl of Oxford, who led Henry VII's rebel army to victory at Bosworth Field in 1485.[2] His title was purely honorific: the family seat was in East Anglia (Hedingham Castle in Essex). Like every other earl from this family, in official portraits he wears a bold shade of blue: Lavenham broadcloth, dyed with the same vivid woad that was once daubed on Boudica's warriors. The de Vere house in Lavenham, with its extraordinary carved door, is one of the wonders of the village.

The second great benefactor was Thomas Spring III, a wealthy wool merchant who inherited his father's business just as Suffolk was becoming the wool and textile capital of England. Spring emerged as Lavenham's leading cloth baron,

2 One of his descendants, the Elizabethan courtier Edward de Vere, 17th Earl of Oxford, is often hailed as the secret author of Shakespeare's plays. However, since he died before many of the greatest works were written, he is a rather less plausible candidate than Shakespeare himself.

then ploughed the proceeds back into the land. He owned six thousand acres by the time of his death and was widely supposed to be the richest non-nobleman in England. He may have spoiled his bid for divine favour, however, by having his initials carved into the church thirty-two times. The needle's eye through which rich men struggled to pass may have narrowed further in the face of such brazen self-glorification. But there is no gainsaying the beauty of the church. It is a mini-cathedral in delicious pale stone, with towering windows in the finest Perpendicular style and a magnificent oak ceiling. The interior is full of elaborate carvings, and the gaunt tower – the tallest in the county – can be seen from miles around.

Lavenham differs from Great Dunmow in that, by changing less, it has in one way changed more. What was once a wool factory is now a visitor attraction with more than three hundred historic buildings. But both exude the pungent aroma of medieval culture.

There are few finer places to order a cup of tea and a scone, and think of England.

Jarrow lies some three hundred miles to the north of Lavenham, but the aesthetic gap is even wider. There are no picture-book Tudor tea-rooms here. The promontory overlooking the point where the River Don curls into the Tyne affords a sweeping view of industrial England: the Nissan factory with its fleet of hatchbacks waiting to go; the hill of coal rising in the distance; the dockyard cranes; the gantries of an oil rig; the funnel of a passing tanker; the sheds and warehouses of South Shields.

Even in the summer the North Sea wind can cut through your clothes like a knife.

It was from the banks of this muddy estuary in 1936 that two hundred unemployed shipbuilders struck out for London, carrying a petition against the closures. It was a modern peasants' revolt, and it went down in history as a byword for dignified civil disobedience. When the marchers were fobbed off with tea in the House of Commons, Jarrow – a great capital of coal and ships that had been brought to its knees – became synonymous with industrial decline.

Yet in the field behind the promontory there are hints of a quieter world ... frail echoes of an earlier, agricultural time cling on, like stubborn weeds, even here. A cluster of thatched huts has been constructed on the site of a famous monastery: the first stone-built religious house in all England. A fragment of that building still stands beside the parish church, and though the huts resemble a toy village – or a medieval theme park – they comprise a serious museum dedicated to the memory of an extraordinary man.

He is internationally famous, and has been for thirteen hundred years. Schools are named after him in every time zone, and his legacy is incalculable. Yet we know little about him, since the monastery was destroyed by Viking raiders in 875. It is clear he was a monk and a scholar, but the only record of his birth is his own remark that he was born in 672. There are hints that he may have been married,[3] but we have no idea what he looked or sounded like. We do not even know his Christian name – quite an irony, since he is one of the most celebrated Christians in history.

We remember him only as the Venerable Bede.

It is likely that he was born into a significant family of local priests, since a couple of other Bedes are recorded in the lists at Durham Cathedral. He entered the sister house in Monkwearmouth at the age of seven, then moved to Jarrow in 685. He may even have helped to lug stones around the site during the monastery's construction, and he possibly survived a bout of plague in 686 to become a senior member of the brotherhood. An eighth-century manuscript mentions that

---

3 In one of his works he explains that doing his 'conjugal duty' interfered with his religious duties, and elsewhere he admits to having 'the lustful passion of desire'.

only two Jarrow monks were able to sing the liturgy, one of whom was a mere stripling. Few have been able to resist the temptation to identify the unnamed boy as the not-yet-venerable Bede.

He wrote his first book, a poetry primer, in the first year of the eighth century, and went on to produce sixty more. The library at Jarrow was a wonder of the world, boasting two hundred precious volumes, all beautifully copied by hand. Bede found himself in a rare centre of learning.

The cultural impact of his own work is hard to overstate. For instance, it is chiefly thanks to him that England is so called, as a different monk might have seen things from a Jutish or Saxon perspective, rather than the Anglian angle. And it was Bede's use of *anno domini* to describe the years after the birth of Christ that established this as the accepted notation. But there are some keen ironies here. We think of Bede as one of the first great English authors, yet he wrote in Latin. He is notably fussy about facts, yet believed fervently in miracles. And though we think of him as a literary pioneer, he was preoccupied with the past and took history as his theme.

To an extent easy for modern readers to overlook, he felt he was living through the conclusion to a story, not its beginning. He was very interested in dates, puzzling over the age of the world and the timing of Easter. His most famous work, *An Ecclesiastical History of the English People*, begins by describing Caesar's invasion before narrating what, for Bede, was the more significant incursion – St Augustine's introduction of Christianity to England in 597. The five-line song he wrote on his death bed was the most copied poem in Old English.

It is hard, staring over the Tyne today, to visualise what the area must have been like back then, when lonely, windswept Jarrow was a haunting beacon of scholarship and spiritual purity in the wilderness. But there are hints of the industrial roar to come even in Bede's work. On the second page of his history he comments on the plentiful supply of jet – 'a black jewel which can be set on fire'. The ink-dark rocks that the North Sea deposited on the beach were known as 'sea coal' (in part to distinguish them from 'coal', which in those days meant charcoal). The Romans had used them to heat their baths.

We do not always think of coal as part of 'nature'. Nowadays, indeed, since the last English mine closed in 2016, we rarely think of it at all. But ever since Blake shuddered at the 'dark satanic mills' that were polluting England's dells and dales, and Ruskin warned of the 'plague cloud' gushing from the nation's chimneys, there has been a tendency to see industrial progress as a blight – the enemy of natural beauty. So it is salutary to think of coal as something that simply lay on the beach.

That is all it was, however: a fossil of carboniferous forest ripened underwater for millennia and hidden in the ground on which our forefathers walked. As coal historians are quick to remind us, it is not a 'mineral' but a rock – a seam of geological nature threaded into our techno-industrial world.

England's earth produced not just grass, wool and wheat (not to mention milk and honey), but coal, iron, salt, stone and tin. And the nation drew its identity from all of them.

They have quite a lot in common, these three old villages. It is not by chance that Lavenham's and Jarrow's principal churches share the name St Peter and St Paul, for they share a religious heritage. Nor is it coincidental that the first coal shipment bobbed down the Tyne past Jarrow in 1291, just a year after Peter Corbet slew the last wolf in Shropshire, and only months after Edward I granted Lavenham the right to hold its annual fair (and thereby guaranteed its prosperity). Moreover, all of this took place only a few decades after Little Dunmow had awarded its first haunch of bacon to a happily married couple. All over England, similar forces were stirring much the same ingredients at much the same time.

And they were not abstract, these forces; they grew out of qualities embedded in the natural, inherited landscape. Thus, in Great Dunmow, we can glimpse flashes of a native language and diet. In the pastel shades of Lavenham we can admire oak monuments to the terrific wealth that flowed from wool – a boon that would eventually give England the flood of capital that allowed it to dominate first the British Isles and then an immense overseas empire. And in Jarrow we see not just the shimmer of the religious culture that would light our national path for more than a millennium, but the first glow of a later inspiration: coal.

Close your eyes, and the entire history of England seems to dance in the light of this magic lantern: the thousands of villages, each with its own church spire and unique folk traditions; the poetry and drama; the pies and cakes; the green hills full of sheep; the factories; the Victorian ships and railways; the smoke and smog of urban life in the 1950s.

If you can find infinity in a grain of sand, why not Englishness in a spot of time?

The tale of The Flitch seemed to confirm my sense that English culture was to a large extent a product of its natural geography. It was quite logical that the prize should involve bacon (rather than bananas, say, or ostrich), since pigs were an intrinsic part of the English annual cycle long before the Norman Conquest. In common with the Germanic territories from which the Angles and Saxons had emigrated, English pigs were fattened over the summer in acorn-rich woods and slaughtered in the autumn for their meat. Since that meat was perishable, it had to be preserved. However, English air was too damp to create the dry-cured *saucissons* and *salami* of sunnier climes, so this could be done only with salt and smoke.

Bacon, in other words, is as English as an April shower.

It is often said that we are what we eat, and it follows that national diets are shaped by what the land produces. Coastal people eat fish, mountain people cheese; low-country people live on grains, tropical people fruit. The long English winter left people in permanent need of calories, so the taste for bacon was partly created by cold weather. The inhabitants of the Arabian desert developed a religious injunction against pig meat in part because their climate could not support it – it was unnatural before it became a religious taboo. If the notion of The Flitch had appealed to an Egyptian, the prize might have been a bunch of dates or a pomegranate. It would never have been half a pig.

The picture has been broadened and coloured by the modern world, but not as much as we might think, because the past was multicultural too. English medieval fairs were full of foreign merchants, and many observers viewed London as a 'global village' long before the term was coined. Englishness has always been multifaceted.

One of the most durable English myths is that we are insular hermits, wanting nothing so much as to close the door on the outside world. Indeed, this was one of the widely touted explanations for Brexit: our rough old island nature was merely asserting itself once again. It seems to make sense: we inhabit an island – therefore we are insular.

This has been the received wisdom for a long time. The sea is a rampart, a defensive wall, 'a fortress built by nature'. It is the moat around our English home, which, as everyone knows, is a castle.[4] It was also a curtain wall, keeping the continental wolf at bay, and allowing England to become a sheep farm.

The emerging nation of England had secure marine boundaries, which provided a rare degree of continuity in a millennium of European turmoil. The saltwater moat created a haven safe from the schisms, wars and holocausts that afflicted the rest of the continent. Even the medieval Crusades – which drew in most of Christendom – felt marginal within this western outpost. For the most part, they were a series of French and

4 In Napoleonic times many French observers felt that England was *all* coast, and its people wholly nautical. And at least one American, Ralph Waldo Emerson, believed that, as with the topography, so with the people: 'Every one of the islanders is an island, safe, tranquil, incommunicable.'

papal campaigns waged on the unimaginably distant shores of the Mediterranean.

Jerusalem was an awfully long way from Chester. England, by and large, could stand aloof.

Yet are we really so insular? Stop the clock at any point in the last few hundred years and you will find English men and women trudging through polar regions, crossing deserts, penetrating jungles, storming citadels, mapping rivers or haggling for coffee in faraway souks. The country is unimaginable without tea, sugar, chocolate, tobacco and curry spice. England is addicted to all of them, but these are not native tastes – they reflect a craving for the unusual, the exotic and the distant.

We hail from piratical stock (all those Roman, Saxon, Danish and Norman adventurers) and have the travel bug in our genes. A land of negligible snow, whose highest hill can be climbed in a morning, we virtually invented Alpine skiing and mountaineering.

Even thoroughly English people have mixed origins. The most fragrant of English roses – Audrey Hepburn – was born Audrey van Heemstra in Brussels. The nation's favourite engineer, Isambard Kingdom Brunel, was the son of a French refugee. Even our fictional heroes have twisted roots. Robinson Crusoe seems a classic English archetype. He responds to his predicament not by moaning about injustice but by getting on with his chores – building a shelter, calculating a calendar and tending a garden. But he is not English. On the novel's first page, Daniel Defoe tells us that he was born Robinson Kreutznaer – the son of a merchant from Bremen.

Even the quintessentially English townships that are the subject of this chapter have foreign shadings. Lavenham's Shilling Street was not named after the English coin but to honour John Schylling, a Flemish weaver. It was French glaziers who moulded England's first stained-glass windows for Bede's monastery. And one Thomas LeFuller brought home Dunmow's bacon in 1510, along with his friends De Chatelain and Devereaux. Meanwhile, nearby Braintree was home not only to Flemish weavers but, later, to a famous Huguenot silk family – the Courtaulds.

These locales are not exceptional. Englishness has complicated roots.

In the Middle Ages, especially, it was a complex coat of many colours, not an isolated, monochrome fortress. None of the invading tribes killed the locals; they mingled with them. As a result, England was a loose society. We might call it the 'America of the Middle Ages' – a new world in the west, home to at least half a dozen languages (Latin, French, Anglo-Saxon, Norse, Flemish and Old English) and a sappy, can-do frontier spirit. Migration was no threat to the English way of life because newcomers became English simply by living in England.

It could take a while – perhaps centuries. But the landscape would drip into their souls eventually.

The English did not become Norman; the Normans became English.

Given the primitive nature of transport in medieval times, it is remarkable how energetically Europeans travelled. There were twenty thousand people of foreign birth in England in 1440: Swedish students in Cambridge; German servants in Huntingdon; Spanish doctors in Suffolk; Dutch painters in Lincoln; as well as those Flemish weavers in Essex. Englishness – not to mention the English language – was formed by this rich broth. England was the end of the line for anyone heading west, towards the setting sun. And they were arriving in a land already settled by many generations of previous adventurers. The earliest settlers faltered when they reached the wilder fastnesses of Scotland or Wales, and this is where England planted itself behind man-made barriers – Offa's Dyke in the west and Hadrian's Wall in the north. As a result, these lands were only lightly touched by the migratory forces that shaped English life for centuries.

These walls completed the fortifications offered by the sea to the east and south. Englishness was a cosmopolitan compound, but isolation gave it time to set.

This is not to say that there is no connective tissue in English life. No matter how great are the contrasts between white van man and Cumbrian hill farmer, Home Counties golfer and Geordie ironworker, Essex girl and Worcester woman, Birmingham curry magnate and Sussex polo player, London money trader and Cornish nurse, all share an elusive range of qualities and sympathies that distinguish them from, say, Russians or Palestinians. They have something in common with each other which derives partly from the natural landscape, and partly from the past.

History strikes some as arid – a raking over of the ashes. But for others it is the source of the hidden springs of modern life. The past is never done and dusted, but always pushing into the present. As T. S. Eliot put it in 'Tradition and the Individual Talent', history was by no means a matter of mere 'pastness' but a living presence. This is ancient wisdom – *finis origine pendet* (conclusions depend on beginnings) – but to sniff the thousand-year-old air in places like Great Dunmow, Lavenham and Jarrow is to feel once again the power of the old insight: the aroma of history rises through the ancient streets like mist through reeds.

The present is hectic and indecipherable; the future is unknowable. Only in the past can we discern the grooves in which we are stuck. And while much has been lost, plenty survives. The English have been living and loving, working and ageing, dreaming and sinning, drinking and driving for as long as they have lived on this land. The outward show may have been refashioned, but the underlying forms are familiar.

In wondering whether Englishness might derive from its geography, however, we will clash with the modern sense that nations are abstract entities – or 'imagined communities' – bound by nothing more than cultural and political norms. This has been the prevailing view more or less since the time of Bede. The sage of Jarrow saw England primarily as an ecclesiastical construct: his England was mired in Dark Age ignorance until the Christian flame was reignited by European holy men.

Generations of intruders arrived as colonists and settlers – clearing forests, lighting candles and planting native culture.

Victorian thinkers shared a similar view. Painting themselves as guardians of an ancient flame, they depicted Englishness as a rare, superior quality of a rare, superior people, and argued that the land bore the tell-tale stamp of this blessed, masterful race. Their conceit, which looks comical today, was understandable. After all, who else was building steam engines, railways, ships and guns on England's scale. How could we *not* be a race apart?

But what if it was the other way round? What if it was not people that made the landscape, but landscape that made the people?

It is easy for us to see patterns that Bede could not. Modern archaeology (supported by the aerial view) has revealed that England in the Dark Ages was far from dark. Indeed, the many traces of Iron Age farming, Bronze Age burial sites and forest clearances remind us that English culture dates back to long before the Roman invasion. Nor did the Vikings decimate English society. They may have had warlike names like Thorkell the Skullsplitter, but they were farmers and fishermen too. Like all the European peoples who barged their way up England's estuaries and inlets, they were moulded by the unique rhythms of the new land, its seasons and traditions, everything that held sway in this temperate realm.

So even when we are talking about England's past, we are talking about its natural geography – its shape, location, weather, soil and raw materials. These set in motion the forces that shaped its history. And it is telling that we can glimpse these resonant pressures as far back as 1290: the farms bursting with sheep and wheat; the wisps of smoke drifting above the trees; the glow of coal; and the torrents of water falling from the sky.

All of these ingredients were buried in the native habitat: the ocean setting with its temperate climate (just enough heat, just enough light, and shires where hurricanes hardly ever happened); year-round rain that filled the rivers, streams and wells; forests full of deer and other game; cool lakes jumping with fish; sheep-nibbled hills; rich soil and every sort of rock, from limestone to granite; seams of coal, iron, salt, tin and copper. Had any one of these ingredients been absent, England's character would have baked in a different way, and produced a different result.

We could even, in a playful spirit, reduce Englishness to a simple formula. If we began with *wool* (the founding father of the national wealth), added *wheat* and topped it off with the explosive marriage between *rain* and *coal* . . . what then? Might that be some sort of essential oil or sap? And if we reduced it down to a simple equation

$$e = cw^4 \text{ (Englishness is coal} \times \text{wool, wheat and wet weather)}$$

we might uncover a rough recipe for the national character.

Just as the rich vocabulary of our language rests on a modest alphabet of individual letters, so perhaps our national identity might have grown from a surprisingly simple set of primary characteristics.

We cannot be categorical about the precise effect of such a varied set of factors. But perhaps we can speculate that they contributed at least something to the prevailing mood. If nothing else, they may have engendered a fatalistic approach to life's ups and downs (it never rains but it pours; any port in a storm; and always put something aside for a rainy day) while also encouraging us to be watchful, alive to tell-tale signs. We know that red sky at night means shepherds' delight, because it tells us that the rain clouds are clearing. And we know that it probably won't rain if the morning grass is thick with dew, for a similar meteorological reason: dew condenses best on fine, dry nights. But we also know that things can change fast: rain before seven, fine by eleven. So we have learned to smile or shrug in the face of life's adversities. This also explains the English taste for slapstick: earthquakes and volcanoes are no laughing matter, but a gust of

The English landscape is not 'natural' or even 'man-made'. It was created by sheep. The rain that nourished the grass that fed the animals turned medieval England into a great wool power.

wind that blows a hat into a puddle is a hoot, and being caught in a downpour is downright hilarious.

It is well understood that Christianity took one – Catholic – form on the sun-drenched littoral of the Mediterranean, and quite another in the gloomy forests of the north, and that this contrast led to markedly different traditions. The Protestant work ethic is as much a product of snowy woods as it is of religious doctrine, so we should not be surprised that England's geography has shaped its social culture, too. Just as each vineyard (or *terroir*) produces its own unique wine, so human beings are conditioned by their local landscape. We move around more now, so the lines are blurred, but the underlying skeleton of English culture – the bare bones of the national psyche – may have changed less than we think.

Geography did not define everything, of course, but it did provide the template. It gave us the grass that nourished the sheep that grew the wool that made the wealth that built the castles, cathedrals, towns and cities. It generated the rain that fed the streams that drove the mills. It supplied the raw materials from which the engineering miracles of the future were forged. And its coast provided the transport system that fostered the trading habits that stoked the desire to explore the wider world. This combination of natural assets gave English men and women the means to build new forms of agriculture, industry, trade, finance, religion, politics and society. And its first green shoots were visible at the end of the thirteenth century, in the flocks of sheep being urged through Lavenham, or the pair of newlyweds bringing home the bacon in Essex.

That is why our story begins in 1290. There was an intriguing convergence of English causes and effects at that precise moment – when sheep first started to spread over the hillsides like a blanket.

There was even, in the summer of 1290, that most English phenomenon of all: an endless downpour. It led to a catastrophic harvest, but what could anyone do? This was England.

Two

Lords and Shepherds

S heep were hardly a novelty. Ever since they were tamed in Mesopotamia ('Babylon' means 'Land of Wool') they had been central to human life. It was hard to conceive of a more useful animal: they produced milk, cheese, meat and clothes. They were docile and easy to manage, with a well-developed flocking instinct. They were wonderfully unadventurous, grazing all day and ruminating all night. And though they were somewhat accident prone (a single dog could spook them into a frenzy), they were happy to follow a leader. Shepherds had only to train one of the beasts with a bell around its neck – a 'bellwether' – and the rest of the flock would fall into line.

There is no written record of the time when human beings first noticed the wonderful properties of wool – although modern archaeologists estimate that it was some ten thousand years ago – so we are left to imagine that the story starts with an early man or woman finding a clump of fleece on a thorn. It was soft and yielding, and anyone could think of a hundred ways in which it might be used. Since these people were gatherers as well as hunters, they collected the wild tufts and laid them on the floors of their caves to create primitive mattresses.

There was no way to shear a whole coat of wool at this time, but the animals were simple to catch and herd into pens, and their hair could be pulled out in clumps. Even more miraculously, the wool grew back quickly, so it could be harvested many times over.

During the Bronze Age, a few cunning humans learned how to twist threads of wool and knot them into rough cloth using sharpened sticks. Then the discovery of iron gave people stronger tools, farming was transformed, and the entire enterprise of fabricating clothes from wool, rather than wearing pelts and furs, began to take shape. It was rudimentary – subsistence weaving – but it was the kernel in which the textile industries of the future began to be hatched.

Some fifteen hundred years later, in Anglo-Saxon England, sheep were kept for their milk, not their fleeces, but the variable English climate was having a magical effect on the quality of the local wool. The process of evolution and natural selection made it unusually long and strong, yet also soft and thick. It was the finest raw material for cloth in the world, so it was hardly surprising that Norman England decided to harry the wolf population to extinction and turn the kingdom into a giant sheep farm.

Europe was unable to follow suit. Wolves remained a danger to everyday life for centuries, and were constantly demonised in folk tales and nursery rhymes, clinging on in Denmark until 1772, in Bavaria until 1847[1] and in France until the twentieth century.[2] Everyone, in children's stories, was afraid of the big bad wolf.

England was different. The wolf still loomed large in the

---

1 Adolf Hitler gave the German wolf official protection in 1934, and a few years later he dubbed his military hideaway in East Prussia the Wolf's Lair. In 2011 a lone wolf killed fifteen sheep in one night in the northern German province of Pomerania.

2 A total of 1,386 wolves were killed in France in 1883. Although officially eradicated in 1930, wolves have recently returned to the Hautes-Alpes – so much so that in July 2015 a ten-man task force was created to hunt them down. According to government figures, the national pack, numbering some three hundred animals, had killed more than nine thousand sheep the previous year. One farm in the Alpine village of Roquebillière lost twenty-one in a single raid. And in 2016 wolves were spotted in woods on the edge of Paris.

collective imagination as a fearful hunter, thanks to depictions in Aesop's fables and the Bible.[3] But while 'Wolf' is a common name in Germany today, it has not featured in English nomenclature since the time of Beowulf. The efforts of Peter Corbet and his colleagues allowed England to become a new sort of farm, a new sort of economy, a new sort of society.

Sheep plus grass equalled gold. Who needed alchemists?

The rural culture that grew out of this involved much more than hand-to-mouth farming. It was agriculture on an industrial scale: agribusiness. There was fine wool in Spain, shorn from the country's Merino sheep; and the Duchy of Burgundy was a significant producer, too. Sheep nibbled the rocky hills of Italy and Greece, as well. But not in these numbers. It was England that became Europe's pre-eminent wool producer, and then its leading cloth manufactory.

The consequences of this were sizeable. Wool fostered the growth of ports like Hull, King's Lynn and Southampton, from which the fleeces could be shipped to the cloth-working centres of Flanders and Italy. It introduced England to large-scale commerce, to fairs and markets, and it financed the construction of fine churches, guild halls and granaries in towns and villages. In short, it was the foundation stone of all subsequent English history.

Wool changed England's countryside for ever, creating what now seems to be its 'natural' character. Alongside the traditional subsistence cropping and dairy farming, the landscape became a giant pasture. Vast tracts of forest were felled and turned into meadows for the wealth-producers, while thousands of acres of common land were 'enclosed' to make sheep runs. By Tudor times, sheep outnumbered people by three to one.

England still treads in the footprints of those long-lost times.

---

3 Aesop told the tale of a wolf in sheep's clothing some five hundred years before St Matthew recorded a similar parable in his Gospel. But the latter version probably reached English ears first, since Aesop was not translated until 1484, more than a century after John Wycliffe produced his English Bible.

Its fields have evolved over the centuries, but it remains a land whose hills swarm with sheep.

Wool gathering was not an industrial revolution in itself, although it did inspire the first flashes of the skills and crafts that would prove vital several centuries later. The most important consequence of sheep-rearing, however, was that it created the first solid accumulation of wealth. As always, it was the merchants, rather than the shepherds, who grew fat on the proceeds of the wool trade, but the residue is still there for all to see in the cathedrals, abbeys, castles, gate-houses, dovecotes, tithe barns and chapels that adorn the English countryside to this day. The fact that the windfall was concentrated in only a few noble hands created pools of capital that would eventually be invested in the next phases of commercial enterprise: manufacturing, slavery, industry and empire.

Clearly, not everything about the early wool trade was glorious. But it did provide the foundation for England's rise to prominence. It created the conditions that supported the social and commercial edifices of later English life: systems of landownership and law, mechanisms for settling disputes, political institutions, schools (to produce an educated middle class of administrators, scientists and financiers) and all the ancillary trades and services (such as transport and storage) that were needed to keep the show on the road.

It may even have helped to shape the stereotypical national temperament, since the rearing of sheep called for patience, flexibility, practicality and the ability to withstand misfor-tune. And since it took half a day to gather up a flock of sheep on a damp hillside, footpaths began to criss-cross our countryside, along with the habit of mind that wanted to ramble across the country on long-distance tracks, whatever the weather.

Unsurprisingly, such qualities eventually insinuated their way into every aspect of England's language, literature, art, architecture and philosophy. Indeed, they continue to colour our daily life. No one talks of spinsters any more, and sheep-skin coats are no longer quite the thing, but plenty of the old allusions remain. We still speak of sacrificial lambs and pastures new; and the Lord is still our shepherd, watching over his flock by night. We still separate the sheep from the goats when deciding what to keep and what to throw away; we can be on tenterhooks or may as well be hung for a sheep as a lamb; we ridicule mutton dressed as lamb; sigh over the black sheep of the family; have the wool pulled over our eyes;[4] tuck into a shepherd's pie; or weave a narrative thread. We are forever tipping our hats to wool's prominent role in our sheepish past.

These are not merely sayings. Christianity and sheep-minding have always gone hand in hand. Caedmon, one of the earliest English poets, was a lay brother who cared for the flocks at Whitby Abbey, while St Cuthbert, the supreme bishop of the north-east whose miracle-strewn life and even more miraculous death are enshrined at Durham Cathedral, was also a shepherd. He was tending his sheep in the wilds of Northumbria when he received the first of his divine visions.

Cricket, a defining national pastime, was invented by play-ful shepherds. And these shepherds were sufficiently important citizens to officiate at weddings.

We may no longer be sons or daughters of the soil, but many of our habits, customs and aphorisms can be traced back to a collection of sheep-like associations, all of them inspired by the well-watered downlands and wolds of medieval England.

Historical periods rarely have neat beginnings or endings, but it is at least possible to argue that Englishness truly started to coalesce, like the threads in a tapestry, at the end of the

4 In Restoration times it was obligatory for the deceased to be buried in a woollen shroud. So anyone who had the wool pulled over their eyes had, figuratively, been left for dead.

thirteenth century, not least because the age of the last wolf was also when the English language first emerged from its Anglo-Saxon, Latin and Norman French antecedents. It would not become the official language until Henry V's reign, but it is no coincidence that the earliest works of the national literature (Layamon's *Brut*, the *Ancrene Wisse* and *The Owl and the Nightingale*) all date from this time. While to a modern eye these texts are not easy reading, they are recognisably English rather than Saxon-German.

Other strands in the national story support the notion that this was a formative period. When Peter hung up his traps, and England became a rich sheep terrain, it was the final piece in a jigsaw. English patriotism was already alive and kicking; and, as so often, it took warlike form. After quelling Simon de Montfort's uprising (a protest against foreigners led by an English noble of French descent), Edward I raised the blood-red cross of St George over castles at Beaumaris, Harlech and Caernarfon. In an often-forgotten irony, one of his captains in Wales was Robert the Bruce, whose son of the same name would lead the rout at Bannockburn two decades later.[5]

This was ironic not only because both Roberts, when they denounced Sassenachs, probably did so in Norman French, but also because the English assault on Scotland was already gathering pace in 1290. The death (at sea) of the seven-year-old Maid of Norway, the Scottish princess who had been betrothed to Edward I's son[6] led to a bitter feud over the succession; Edward

---

5 There were other odd bedfellows, too. One of the King's fiercest opponents was the Bishop of Hereford, who was excommunicated by the Archbishop of Canterbury in 1282 for standing firm against the Welsh campaign. But he was no ordinary Welsh nationalist: his name was Thomas de Cantelupe, and he was born in Buckinghamshire and educated in Orléans before becoming Chancellor of Oxford University.

6 Of course, if the marriage had proceeded as planned, England and Scotland would have been united in 1290, Edward would have felt no need to hammer the Scots, there would have been no Bannockburn, and the long history of Britain might have followed a very different course.

reached for his famous hammer, rode north, sacked Berwick, and defeated a Scottish army at Dunbar.

This was just one of many signs that England already saw itself as noticeably different from (and senior to) its neighbours. It is commonly suggested that the warlike idea of Englishness as a coherent nationality rose to the fore when England invaded France in 1337, setting in motion the Hundred Years War and the nation-building triumphs of Crécy and Agincourt. But the same pressure is evident in its much earlier attacks on Wales and Scotland.

England was already heavily implicated in French territories. One of Edward's predecessors, Henry II, had been King of England, but also Count of Anjou, Duke of Normandy, Duc d'Aquitaine and Lord of Brittany. Born in Le Mans, he claimed the English throne by invasion in 1154, then spent most of his life at Chinon. So when he begged his courtiers to 'rid him' of a 'turbulent priest' – Thomas Becket – he was to some extent hoping to crush an infuriating English rebel.

A hundred years later, the emphasis had shifted. Edward I sought to enhance English, not French, prestige. If anything, his kingdom bridled at the overweening power of foreigners. In a hint of what was to come under Henry VIII, a ground-breaking edict of 1286 restricted the power of papal courts. Then, four years later, the famous *Quia Emptores* statute ('In favour of buyers') broke with Norman tradition by allowing people to sell their land to anyone they chose, rather than just to the feudal next in line. A triumph for the country's emerging merchant class, this gave rise to one of the deepest English reflexes of all: property speculation.

Two hundred years of Crusading zeal took its toll in angrier ways, because it wasn't only wolves that were expelled in 1290. Following anti-Semitic riots in London, Norwich and York, this was also the year when England's entire Jewish population was deported. It marked the culmination of a dismaying programme. Having acted as bankers to both the Crown and the growing merchant class, the Jews were herded into ghettos, obliged to wear a cloth patch as a badge of their heritage and taxed almost to the bone before being finally banished.

Such assaults on 'strangers' were often fuelled by the age-old desire to renege on debts, but they also signalled the emergence of a new force in the world: Englishness. Two centuries of Norman and Angevin rule had dissolved into a single national consciousness. Scots, Jews and all other foreigners were ... *different*. 'We' didn't want 'them' here any more.

The following year, work began on the nave at York Minster. It was planned on a scale that would make it the largest in Europe. Something new and significant was stirring.

There was another sign that a recognisable English identity was emerging around this time. England was becoming a powerful kingdom with possessions in France, rather than a conquered dominion of Norman dukes, and the whispers of what would develop into the Hundred Years War were growing louder. Although most English aristocrats still spoke French and had French names, they increasingly viewed France as England's principal enemy. When Edward's queen, Eleanor of Castile, took ill and died in November 1290, it was a resonant event. Her body was taken from Lincoln on a ceremonial journey south to London, and twelve 'crosses' were erected at the twelve places where the cortège paused for the night.[7] A foreign princess, she was the subject of nationwide mourning.

And this too was in 1290, the year that Peter killed the wolf.

As it happened, fate had a twist in store for Corbet. A few years after he killed his last wolf and was enjoying the comforts of his manor, he learned that his daughter was dallying with a humble suitor from the neighbourhood. The chosen rendezvous for their trysts was the tunnel he had built beneath his own moat. In a rage, he unleashed his wolf-hounds, sent them

---

7 Only three of these crosses have survived – two in the Northamptonshire villages of Geddington and Hardingstone, and one at Waltham Cross. The most famous, Charing Cross, is a reconstruction; the original was destroyed in the Civil War.

Mighty hunters: a ferocious footrest (on the tomb of the fourth Baron) from the Corbet family church in Shropshire.

into the tunnel and let them tear the poor man to pieces. His daughter came up with an operatic response, drowning herself in the moat. Grief-stricken, her father hanged his hounds and flung them into that accursed stretch of water before entering the *Penguin Book of Ghosts* as an eternally vexed spirit, tormenting the Corbet castle for centuries.

He is not much remembered now. On the thirteenth-century oak entrance to a church at Abbey Dore, near Hereford, there is an iron wolf's head in the leaf design which, it has been claimed, is a memorial to his work. But otherwise he is forgotten.

His legacy was an England of large sheep estates, the properties of noble families whose wealth, power and status rested on the land they owned and farmed. Naturally, they wanted to keep these intact, 'whole and entire', when the time came to pass them on to the next generation. So the custom of primogeniture – inheritance by the first born – became official law.

Inheritance is a deep and imperfectly documented topic, but it is known that while most of the Holy Roman Empire favoured dividing estates (and indeed kingdoms) equally among siblings, England's aristocracy (along with Scandinavia and some north German duchies) preferred to pass them on to a single child – usually the first-born son.[8] The system was undoubtedly unjust (a junior twin might miss out on a princely life by a couple of minutes),[9] but it meant that most disputes over who should inherit were easily resolved. Hence, it promoted stability and order; and, most importantly, left the family business with the large-scale footprint it needed to thrive.

For evidence, England had only to look at its own recent royal history. When William the Conqueror died he left Normandy to his oldest son, Robert, and England to the next in line, William. When the latter himself was killed (that shooting incident in the New Forest) the third son, Henry, had to go to war against his own brother (now Robert of Normandy) to secure the crown. No one wanted to go through *that* again.

The mountains of capital generated by primogeniture could be poured into building projects or new business schemes. It thus helped to usher in a world of new markets in money and goods, innovative legal procedures, and countless other commercial mechanisms.

It was a powerful agent of social change. The bourgeoisie was not populated solely by hard-working strivers from the lower orders who managed to grab a shard of valuable property for themselves. It was also the natural home of aristocratic younger sons with high expectations and something to prove.

8 In light of this, the plot of Shakespeare's *King Lear*, which echoes this disastrous division, seems to be decidedly un-English. Perhaps it was intended as a cautionary tale about the folly of dividing kingdoms.

9 It was not only younger sons and daughters who had cause to criticise primogeniture. Cardinal Pole denounced the custom as 'plain against reason' and 'a disorder in our politic rule'.

Capital needed middle men, and – thanks to the property laws – there were plenty of them in England.

This was conservative in the deepest way: it gave land ownership a sacred role in the national life. It also bound England to the earth, and realm, that underpinned its life and symbolised its traditions.

As Burke put it, continuity in the landscape connected people both to the past and to the future, to the generations that came before and the generations not yet born.

It may even have invented a new class of person: the landless younger son.

Not all of these younger sons prospered, and that was the point. In marked contrast to the rest of Europe, the country was full of penniless but well-born children who gave society a snakes-and-ladders character: the younger son of a duke who had to fend for himself might slide down the social scale, while a pretty lass from the village might catch the eye of an earl-in-waiting and rise accordingly.

Medieval England is sufficiently full of rags-to-riches stories to suggest that the feudal obstacles to social advancement were not quite as unyielding as we tend to think. The head of the Plantagenet royal kitchen, Flambard, became a bishop, while Richard I's most fêted nobleman, William the Marshal (Langton called him 'the greatest knight who ever lived'), rose from modest beginnings to become the 1st Earl of Pembroke and holder of the Cartmel Estate in Cumberland. Sir Richard Sturry was a valet in the 1340s, but a knight by 1353. The Church offered a pathway to success for the humble-born. William of Ockham, who rose from obscurity in Surrey to become a prominent theologian, was famed for his useful razor, which could settle complicated arguments with one slice. Walter Langton entered royal service as a mere youth and became Bishop of Lichfield as well as Master of the King's Treasury. Even immigrants could prosper: Christopher Ambrose, a merchant from Southampton, was twice mayor of that town, yet he was Cristoforo Ambruogi when he arrived. Later, two of the great men of Tudor times had plain origins: Cardinal Wolsey was the son of a butcher; Thomas Cromwell's father was a blacksmith.

Richard Whittington ('Dick' in the pantomime version of his career) was another penniless younger son. Born to a Gloucestershire knight, in the 1370s he famously walked all the way to London, where he became a mercer, clothier, money-lender and four-time mayor of the city. Having sold more than £3400 of silken draperies to Richard II, he was made London's official 'Collector' of wool duties. Finally, he helped to finance the expedition that carried Henry V to Agincourt.

Whittington had no interest in purchasing a country estate. Instead, he spent a fortune on philanthropic ventures: alms-houses, refuges for 'yong wemen that hadde done a-mysse' and hospitals. He even built a 128-seat toilet block which used the Thames's tidal flow as a flushing mechanism. He is immor-talised in Highgate's Whittington Hospital, near to the spot where he supposedly heard the bells of London and vowed to escape the humdrum life of a scullery servant.

In Tudor times it was well understood that men could rise and fall in the blink of an eye: Shakespeare's plays are full of people climbing fortune's ladder or being crushed by fortune's wheel. So when foreigners cite class-consciousness as an indel-ible English trait, it might not be a sign that England's class barriers have always been impenetrable. On the contrary, our keen consciousness of class may have its roots in the fact that those barriers were once rather porous. In Europe, Cinderella's slipper really did have to be back by midnight, but England was a land where people could switch social stations. In later times the pressures of pride, prejudice and financial advantage tended to keep people pinned to their backgrounds, but there was a surprising amount of hurly-burly mobility in the Middle Ages.

It is even possible that some deep-rooted English characteris-tics – individualism, self-reliance, a rugged preference for small private realms – developed in response to the way land was used and transferred in medieval times. Equally, our national attitude to property, inheritance and marriage was formed by a political culture that was responding to the world of grass and sheep – in short, to the natural facts of English life.

This is a chicken-and-egg conundrum. Which came first: liberty or wealth? We all know that the Magna Carta set in stone certain ideas about individual rights. But perhaps it was a symptom, not a cause; a flowering of an English tradition, not its fountainhead. It may have seemed ahead of its time to the rest of the world, but perhaps it was the product of principles that had been congealing in English veins for decades.

Three

Coals from Newcastle

In 1291, as the monks of Yorkshire and Northamptonshire were exchanging contracts with wool merchants from Lucca and Bruges, something equally surprising was stirring in Newcastle. Carts full of coal were being dragged down to the quays on the Tyne and heaved on to a ship bound for the south coast. The plan was to catch the morning tide and reach Hartlepool by nightfall. If the weather held, the crew might reach Dorset in a week or so.

We know little about this voyage beyond the fact that it happened. We can only guess at the course it took, the conditions it encountered, the nature of life on board. We know that such a venture would have taken a long time – even if the weather held, which it rarely did in these parts. But the crew knew nothing, because this was a historic voyage: the first consignment of coal ever to leave Newcastle.

We usually think of coal as part of modern England's story – the black gold that drove the steam-fuelled Victorian rush of iron, steel and rail. Ask people to guess the date of that first shipment from Newcastle and they usually venture that it was in the eighteenth century, in the first shudders of industrial progress and scientific discovery. They might add that it surely did not grow into a truly significant enterprise until the engineering uproar of the Victorian era.

In fact, the first cargo of coal to leave Newcastle set sail hundreds of years earlier than that. It was bound for the royal fireplace at Corfe, in Dorset, a haughty English fortress where the Crown Jewels had once been kept.

None of the men had sailed that far in their lives. They might have criss-crossed the North Sea, hauling cargoes of wool, salt and lead to Hamburg, Antwerp, Bruges or London. Some may have gone as far as Lübeck, on the Baltic coast. The older hands probably knew those foreign ports more intimately than they did their own land. Yet the prospect of sailing due south, then west along England's south coast, into the teeth of the prevailing wind, might well have made them edgy. In all likelihood, they would spend long days idling in the Cinque Ports, waiting for a favourable breeze. Or they would have to offload the coal on to smaller boats and barges, then row them through the waves.

Their ship – we do not know the name, but let's name her the *St Hilda*, after the holy woman of Whitby[1] – was a cog, sturdier and chubbier than a Viking longship but otherwise similar. She was clinker built (with curved planks laid over one another like clapperboard), with a fixed rudder on the stern and castles fore and aft, partly for shelter, partly for self-defence. From a distance, her single sail must have caused shivers in onlookers, since it was reminiscent of the terrifying Viking sails that had haunted these waters in earlier times. But the *St Hilda* was a plough-horse compared to those rakish warships – a rough-and-ready beast of burden. She made up in strength what she lacked in agility: she could carry a big load below the oak-timbered deck, and cope with heavy seas.

The crew loaded barrels of bread, cheese, onions, beer and water, and intended to supplement their meagre rations by catching mackerel and herring on lines and nets cast from a hatch in the stern. They would not sail at night, but there were plenty of harbours on England's eastern coast that they could

1 Hilda founded the abbey there, but her greatest claim to fame (and sainthood) was that she turned snakes into stone.

keep in almost constant sight. It was July, so the days were long. The swell was heavy once they left the harbour and on two occasions the coal pile slipped. The *St Hilda* listed so fearfully that the men had to clamber down into the hold and shovel it back into place.

After that, they made good progress and put into Hart le Pool[2] early. They spent the evening securing their filthy cargo with ropes and canvas sheets, but still had time to walk around the town and take a drink in the fishermen's rest house on the strand. There they heard that a local aristocrat named Robert de Brus had recently been granted a licence to make salt by heating pans of seawater over burning coal. Times were certainly changing.

The next morning, the captain announced that they ought to be able to make it to Grimsby by sunset. Out at sea, as the *St Hilda* skimmed on the crest of the swell before a brisk northerly wind, the crew realised that their securely fastened cargo had improved their sea-worthiness – the ship was moving with a previously unsuspected balance and grace. They raced past Whitby, saluting their patroness with a rousing cheer and a flagon of ale, and soon left Scarborough far behind, too. But off Flamborough the sky darkened, the swell rose and the wind veered to the south, slowing their pace to a crawl.

When they finally entered the wide Humber estuary they had to fight an obstinate current that kept pushing them back out to sea. Grimsby lay ahead in the gloom for many hours as they inched towards it, before at last they arrived for the night.

Even then it was barely like being on shore: Grimsby was virtually an island, surrounded by marshy fens, and its relations with the outside world were entirely maritime. Goods arrived from overseas and were then dispatched upriver into the heart of Yorkshire. Yet plenty of the port's denizens – many of whom had explored the fjord at Bergen and ridden the swell

2 Named after a long-vanished (even in 1291) island of stags.

off the Hook of Holland – had never been as far inland as York. Marine life alone was enough to make Grimsby rich, however, and the town generated high tax revenues for the King.

The following day the *St Hilda* made good progress all the way to Yarmouth, a big, bustling town on a finger of land at the mouth of the River Yare. It was the principal trading post in this part of the country: the perfect place to stretch your legs and take on supplies. The great city of Norwich was only twenty miles inland, and a fine guild house presided over the port's busy trade in herring and oysters. The beach was stacked with boats from Sandwich and Deal, selling their catches before turning for home. But they would not be leaving any time soon: dark clouds were rising over the steeple of the church of St Nicholas, and everyone in Yarmouth knew that there was no going to sea once rain touched the head of the saint.

Yarmouth's other striking feature was that it was full of foreigners. As the crew of the *St Hilda* wandered through the 'Rows' – the cramped alleyways where hundreds had died in the floods of 1286 and 1287 – they could hear German, Norwegian, Flemish and Italian accents.

The only English voice was the cry from a ground-level grille in the wall of the guild hall, where a prisoner was pleading with passers-by for a fish head or a crust of bread.

On they went the next day, pressing through mild waves as they pushed south, cheerfully saluting the church turrets that poked above the trees at Southwold and Blythburgh. But as they rolled past Dunwich the men fell silent; one or two snatched the caps from their heads and clasped them to their chests in a solemn gesture. They all knew what had happened here. This had once been the foremost city in the whole kingdom, a thriving port, capital of the East Angles, a place of fine churches, rich monastic houses and hospitals. But the storms of 1286 and 1287 had caused even more damage here. Almost half of the town had been swept away, and the harbour, once the finest on the coast, was now a silted-up maze of dangerous sandbanks

and shingle spurs. At a stroke, Dunwich had lost its *raison d'être*.
From a mile out to sea, the broken arch of the monastery looked
like a tombstone, a mournful echo of a once-great settlement.[3]

Even the irreligious souls among the crew were sobered
by this stark reminder of the fragility of human life in the
face of God and His frightful weather demons. So there was
no appetite for braving the elements when the wind fresh-
ened into a sharp gale and hard waves began to hammer the
dunes of Pegwell Bay. The *St Hilda* remained in the shelter of
Sandwich's harbour for two nights, waiting for the wind to
ease. When she finally departed it was with a sense of trepida-
tion, as if the sea had evil purposes.

This remained the dominant emotion in the days that followed, because many of the resting points on the *St Hilda*'s
route – including New Romney and Hastings – had been battered by the same cruel seas, and the wreckage was still visible.
Only Winchelsea, which Edward I had declared a new town
in 1288, seemed to be reviving. The crew spent a day there,
shivering in the rain, then lost another in Portsmouth, where
they put in for water and were trapped by the low tide. The
crescent on the town's banner was a reminder that one of King
Richard's Crusader fleets had set sail from here. When the *St
Hilda* finally left the crew felt a little like warriors themselves,
as they battled the wind, heaving and barging their way down
the Solent to their destination – Poole.

They unloaded their cargo of Newcastle coal on to a convoy of
mule-drawn barges on the western edge of the shallow harbour

---

3 There is even less of Dunwich now than there was in 1291. Another deluge, in 1326,
turned what was left of the town into an underwater ruin. Seven centuries of further
erosion drowned its once-proud lintels and rooftops. Half a dozen churches lie stranded
in the murky depths, along with the chapel of the Knights Templar, a toll house, the
market place, a mint, a guild hall and the shipyard. Divers can nose around the remains
and reflect on this medieval Atlantis, and strain their ears to catch a sound of the bell
that supposedly still chimes to this day. This lost city once sent two members to the
King's Parliament. One of its early bishops – Felix – gave his name to another harbour
just down the coast: Felixstowe.

and waved it farewell. Then they took it in turns to climb the mast, which offered a better view of Corfe Castle, which stood on a looming mound a few miles to the south. Its lofty stone turrets and curtain wall, built from local Purbeck stone, were recent constructions – insurance against potential French attack – but it was a place of ancient mystery as well, a hill fort that had been an important Norman stronghold. The high keep was whitewashed, and shone like a Pennine fell in winter.

This may be an imaginary description of the first coal ever to leave Newcastle, but we do know that a vessel similar to the *St Hilda* would have made the trip, since cogs were the standard North Sea freighters at the time. They had a daily range of some seventy-two miles, and their single sail was not as manoeuvrable as those on modern craft, so a journey on this scale would have taken at least a week, and probably longer.

Sailing at night was out of the question. Although experienced mariners could steer by the stars, there were no accurate charts of the shoreline, no lighthouses, no coastguards, no radios, no weather forecasts ... and an awful lot of rocks. The North Sea sky often blotted out the stars, in any case.

The point of narrating the *St Hilda*'s voyage is not simply to have some speculative fun, however. First, the importance of coal in English history can hardly be overstated. Something mighty grew from this small beginning, so when the steam age finally came Britain found itself with an immense competitive advantage over its European rivals. It had ten times the exploitable coal reserves of France,[4] and while the German lands had a rich lode, they did not unite as a single nation until 1866, by which time Britain had been a joint venture for 150 years.

---

4 Nearly all of France's coal was in the far north, so it was vulnerable to German seizure. In the first year of the First World War France lost 75 per cent of its coal field (and 80 per cent of its iron). And note the use of 'Britain' here, rather than 'England': Scotland and Wales were also very rich in coal. Indeed, we might easily think of the United Kingdom as an Organisation of Coal Exporting Countries.

England alone had many times more coal than Prussia, the coming force in European affairs.

It has been estimated that Britain could call on an energy resource of 35,000 horsepower (not counting actual horses, of course) by 1800. A century later, it had more than 9 million, thanks almost entirely to the demand created by the need to haul coal. And all this can be glimpsed, as if in the flashlight of an imaginary photograph, in that first shipment down the medieval Tyne.

The Romans had used coal as fuel for their underfloor heating (hypocausts) and thermal baths in chilly Britain, but it became a dormant resource when they left in 410. This first shipment was only a faint streak, in the medieval sky, of the tremendous power to come. But we can see it as a beacon, lighting a path to the future.

The fact that the voyage began in Newcastle is important, since the location of England's richest coal fields would in due course determine many other aspects of the national life – not least the balance between its northern and southern halves. The division between these was starting to emerge as early as the thirteenth century, as coal from the North was burned in the South. There was a 'Sea Coal Lane' in London in 1228, and twenty-nine years later Queen Eleanor was much distressed by the malodorous fumes that blighted her visit to Nottingham.

The first coal shipment from Newcastle was significant in another way. The east coast down which the *St Hilda* sailed was itself a momentous part of England's natural inheritance, central to its island character. Nothing could more obviously showcase the vital role of landscape in human affairs than the simple fact that the English were, from their earliest days, a seagoing people.

And, despite vigorous attempts to enlist it as a bastion, the sea was not particularly good at repelling boarders. Yes, England's location may have forged the incurious mentality best summed up in the old headline: 'Fog in Channel; Europe Isolated'. This enduring national characteristic still finds sharp expression in the modern lack of interest in learning foreign languages (earlier generations were more eager students); and the sense that we prefer our own company, thank you very much, was surely a contributory factor in the Brexit vote. But while the medieval sea was occasionally a shield, protecting us from invasion, much more often it was the exact opposite: a gateway, a transport system, a perimeter ring road. Thanks to the sea, England was open to the outside world, and the outside world was open to England.

Only a few decades after that first coal shipment, Chaucer's shipman knew every port from Sweden to Finisterre, and every creek in Brittany and Spain.

The sea even opened England up to *itself*. It was not easy for coastal settlements to reach one another by land. Who wanted to walk or ride from Hull to Dartmouth? So the seaside towns were not only trading posts but refuelling stations, ideal spots for a break, a rest and a bite to eat.[5]

This simple topographical feature turned England's modest size into an asset. In a neat paradox, the nation was small enough to be big – with the assistance of its formidable transport infrastructure, it was able to unite more swiftly than the French, German or Italian lands, all of which continued to be swirls of small, warring duchies and principalities for many centuries to come. In *A History of the English Speaking Peoples*, Winston Churchill suggested that the French elite that seized England in 1066, and then trampled over its regional distinctions, was a unifying force because it acted against 'the tendency towards provincialisation'. But it was able to achieve this only

---

5 Of course, we know far more about this coastline than our ancestors did. When Bede wrote his *History*, he calculated that the coast of 'Albion' stretched for 3600 miles – a sign that he was well aware of its importance. But this was not a very good guess. According to the British Cartographical Survey, it actually runs (including islands) for some 20,000 miles!

Ships in the Tyne. The sea around England is often seen as a barrier, a moat. But it was also a perimeter road, an open highway to the entire known world.

because of England's modest size and maritime location.

These same attributes also helped England to forge trading links with distant lands. England had long been a land of natural harbours, ideal for the domestic trade. But now it became a land of international ports, too. By the end of the thirteenth century, King's Lynn[6] was already an important hub in the Hanseatic League, dealing in wool, timber, salt and grain with numerous Baltic ports. (It granted special privileges to Hamburg merchants in 1271.) And Boston, which is not even mentioned in the Domesday Book, was a thriving international trading post in 1205. In King John's famous levy on England's merchants it coughed up £780 – more than any town in the kingdom, aside from London (£836).

Half a century later, it was sending lead to Westminster and ferrying Lincolnshire's wool to Flanders. In 1227, Sandwich, in Kent, was importing wine from Gascony, and twenty-eight years later the town was the point of entry for one of the first elephants ever to arrive in England – a gift from the King

---

6 Although it was then known as Bishop's Lynn. The town changed allegiance from Church to Crown only after the Reformation.

of France. Wine from Bordeaux came ashore at Dartmouth, while the Hanseatic League established offices in London's Steelyard (the site of Cannon Street station today). The latter subsequently became a walled-in community with its own warehouses, offices and dormitories.

Edward I's *Carta Mercatoria* of 1303, which gave foreign merchants tax concessions in return for financial support, was an early sign of the free-trade mentality that would later dominate English life, but in truth it was a symptom of trade as much as a cause.

Nineteen years later, Newcastle had 122 merchants who specialised in wool, hides and skin, while in 1327 a long registry of licences granted to the port revealed the full breadth of the North Sea trade. Wool and coal were on the list, of course, but so were almonds, alum, ash, butter, charcoal, cheese, cloth, corn, cows, figs, garlic, grease, herring, horses, hides, lead, millstones, nets, oars, onions, peas, peat, pepper, pigs, pitch, raisins, salmon, salt, sheep, skins (fox, rabbit and squirrel), steel, tallow, wax, wine and (naturally) woad.

This was no peasant economy. The cold sea that lapped England's coast may have been an effective defensive shield, but it was also a powerful modernising agent. The nautical ring road was every bit as significant as the wolf cull. The great rivers of France and Germany were in some ways mightier – broader and longer than England's gentle streams – but they lacked the connective tissue, the arterial saltwater highway. Southampton could trade with Coventry, and Gloucester with Ipswich. A merchant could send wool and cheese from York to Henley by sailing down the Ouse, south along the east coast, and up the Thames. A Warwick priest could glide down one Avon as far as Bristol, then up another to Bath. When monks sailed from Exeter to Canterbury they had a grand view of the whole south coast to inspire their prayers.

The navigable sea was useful in another way, in that it created new allegiances. As the East Anglian fringe looked out over its own *mare nostrum* – the cold and grouchy North Sea – it forged closer ties with foreign ports than it did with its own inland neighbours. Those who lived on the North Sea rim formed a nation of their own, an 'imagined community' of coastal settlements humming with half a dozen languages. A Wiltshire man might seem stranger than a Dane to the residents of Hull or Harwich. The fishermen of Deal could see the smudged shore of Flanders as soon as they put out to sea, and often unloaded their catches in its muddy creeks. Yet they would narrow their eyes at the sight of a visitor from Warwickshire.

The East Anglian topography may even have acted as a cradle for some distinctive English traits. The marshy fenland in the north (there were ditches, but the land was not properly drained until the seventeenth century) was a strange, misty, lawless zone of poachers and pioneers set in watery flats away from the national mainstream – a peninsular realm beyond the reach of the ruling class. East Anglia was a destination, not a route to anywhere else – an island within an island. Many of its villages – Aldeburgh, Southwold, Cromer – were literally at the end of the road. This was the mysterious world from which Boudica emerged to taunt the Romans, and it was in the watery wilderness of the fens that Hereward the Wake hid from the Normans.

It was a land of big skies, bracing winds and featureless views; it suited only the intrepid. In due course it would kindle the buccaneering frontier spirit that was needed to topple kings (Oliver Cromwell), overthrow prevailing wisdom (Isaac Newton) and inspire naval zeal (Horatio Nelson).

If England was the America of the Middle Ages, its Wild West was East Anglia, a tough, lawless zone of migrants and pioneers.

This is not to say that the region was uniform. Even today, a visitor who dropped in by parachute would know immediately whether he had landed in the low-lying, soggy, wind-scoured, treeless expanse of the 'north folk' (Norfolk) or the copses, dells, hedgerows and streams of Suffolk and Essex. It has always been a land of two halves. Norfolk, isolated by bogs and with its gaze fixed firmly on the sea, had wide horizons, ruler-straight lines and edges, Baltic gales, windmills over ditches, sluice gates set in rich black mud – all features it shared with its trading partners across the water. It evolved a herring-tinted, salt-scoured North Sea life.

The southern portion, in contrast, was near enough to London to acquire metropolitan tastes and habits.

This regional north–south divide was every bit as striking as the larger one that would later split the whole of England into the industrial north (where money was made) and the well-favoured south (where it was spent). It is a division with a long natural history.

The demise of the shipping industry, the decay of England's wharves and docks, the disappearance of the subcultures that supported maritime trade and the decline of the nation's nautical towns mean that modern English sensibilities are no longer defined by the sea. To the dismay of old-timers, England is now almost entirely 'sea-blind'. Only a handful of people still lead lives that are regulated by the ebb and flow of the tide.

But the sea had already done much of its most important work. Far from being trapped or isolated by it, a people with salt water in their veins, and a good feeling for hidden shallows, became a nation of explorers and adventurers, ranging far and wide. They returned with silk, furs, porcelain, spices, tea, sugar, coffee, chocolate, roses, wine, vanilla, citrus fruits, bananas, tobacco, cotton ... all of which became integral to English life. In building a world-spanning transport system to meet the clamour for these products, England became a realm of trade.

The country's marine adventuring steeped other aspects of English life in sea lore. There was a 'tide in the affairs of men' long before Shakespeare's Brutus spoke of such things. The immensity of the ocean, its constant perils and storms, promoted a thrilling sense of nature's grand indifference to human endeavour. This is why the national storybook overflows with

voyages, and why so many of its leading characters are ships –
whether they represent triumph (the *Golden Hind*), disaster (the
Titanic), war (HMS *Victory*), horror (the *Zong*), adventure (the
Mayflower), science (the *Beagle*), empire (the *Cutty Sark*), industry
(the *Great Western*) or luxury (the *Queen Mary*).

There is an equally celebrated pantheon of nautical heroes –
from Drake, Cook and Nelson to the little ships of Dunkirk,
the fishing smacks, coal freighters and round-the-world sailors.
Confronted by Viking invaders, King Alfred understood that
he would have to meet them at sea, so he built a navy. When
Canute wanted to show his courtiers that even kings could not
rule the waves, he used the placid English water to prove the
point. And when Elizabeth's captains routed the Armada she
knew that her most important ally was the divinely ordained
storm that delivered England from the galleons.[7]

Since the sea was one of the few ways in which an ordinary man might become rich – whether by discovering new
lands or through plunder – it engendered a surprising degree
of social mobility. In Elizabethan times the country's inns
and taverns were full of enterprising sailors gossiping about
the treasure waiting for any man brave enough to aim for
the setting sun. One of them, Sir Walter Raleigh, had a
keen understanding of how England's future might develop:
'Whoever commands the sea commands the trade,' he wrote.
'Whoever commands the trade commands the riches of the
world, and consequently the world itself.'

The outline of the colonial system was clearly evident – at
least to some – as early as the sixteenth century.

The rising-falling sea, and the way it flowed up and down
England's beaches and estuaries twice a day, regular as clockwork, seeped into the English soul in less exhilarating ways
too. The to-and-fro rhythm of the tide regulated the pulse of

---

7 As the Armada Medal put it: *Flavit Jehovah et dissipati sunt* (God blew, and they were
scattered). This was not the only favourable breeze in the annals of English history:
William of Orange was said to have been blown west by a 'Protestant wind'.

daily life, and its relentless tick-tock attuned the population to the concept of timetables – the non-negotiable sense that everything must advance in an orderly and methodical way. This made English life highly structured, but also chimed with other polar contrasts – between light and shade, sun and cloud, day and night, summer and winter. Perhaps this helped to inspire England's long-standing distaste for absolute remedies – and its corresponding faith in the idea that two contrary propositions can both be true.

What goes up must come down. Absence makes the heart grow fonder. The short cut might be the long way round.

The sea's many dangers – its sudden squalls and storms – may also have fostered that familiar English stoicism. For the devout, the sea was a mirror for God's fickle moods, while for the non-believer it was a stirring metaphor for the untameable power of the elements. It encouraged an austere approach to religious observance (if only to be on the safe side) as well as a prayerful mentality. Church spires were not only upstanding emblems of faith but navigational landmarks. No wonder the seafarers and fishermen despised the soft citizens who lived up on the heathlands . . . and called them heathens.

Many other countries have coasts, but England is one of the few that is nearly *all* coast. 'There is no place on earth,' wrote Tacitus, 'where the sea has a greater dominion.' And the daily, endless battle with its winds, waves and tides produced a special kind of civilisation that demanded bravery, resilience, hard physical endeavour and humility. It was impossible to defeat a storm; one merely had to sit it out. If the English needed a strong drink to see them through a cold night – or a barrel full of strong drink to celebrate a safe homecoming after a perilous voyage – then so be it. The infamous pugnacity of the English sailor, which has enlivened the nation's history with a thousand brawls, most likely crystallised in the ports and dockyards long before it spread inland. It was born in a high wind on a rough night, or in the dockyard settings where press gangs roamed the streets looking for men who could be forced to haul rope in the dark before dawn.

In these and other ways, the water around England's coast nursed into life a nautical tradition that soon saw a thousand English ships jostling for space in a hundred foreign harbours. They rode the sea lanes to distant ports, and many of them never returned. Some brought foreign seamen back home. There were many facets to the imperial impulse – including the obvious yearning for money and power – but another lies in the simple fact that the world's oceans are *huge*.

It took months to sail to Sydney or Calcutta. It was only natural to stay for a while . . . or indeed a lifetime.

If the sea's immensity fed into centuries of global adventuring, it also nurtured the English fondness for messing about in boats. Until the twentieth century, England's seafarers did not regard sailing as a leisure activity – it was too dangerous for that. So there is a nostalgic aspect to the yacht clubs that line the coast today: they are playing with a tradition, rather than maintaining it. They are not shipping coal from Newcastle, exporting wool from Ipswich or bringing tea from China. They are simply testing the water.

Something similar lies behind the suburban dream of a sea view: it offers a glimpse not just of worlds beyond the horizon but of our nation's distant past.

But in 1290 all of that lay far ahead. While the sea lanes around England's coast played their part in the formation of a nation entirely at ease on the ocean waves, something very different was happening on the inland hillsides, where most people had never even seen salt water.

Yet the sea played a part in that story too, since it began with a dozen monks travelling from Burgundy to England's northern wilderness in search of a quiet place where they might develop their holy ambitions.

Four

Quarries and Quarrels

B efore going any further, I should say that dating the birth of modern England to the heart of the Middle Ages – beside those fresh springs of wool, wheat, water and coal – is considered somewhat crude these days. The prevailing wisdom is that it began several hundred years later, in the eighteenth century, when a feudal, agrarian society was convulsed by industrial and financial novelties to produce the nation we know today. This, with a few variations, is the standard academic line as well as the popular view, merging as it does with the idea that English history has been a perpetual tussle between competing class interests. In this analysis, the country was a feudal realm of squires and serfs until the raw energy of capitalism shook it by the throat and laid it open to dissident new ideas.

There are some dissenting voices to this view (see the Historical Note at the end of this book), but for the most part it is axiomatic that the Industrial Revolution landed 'like a thunderbolt from a clear sky' in the soft, green heart of a blissful, rural, timeless England.

This is not the place for a detailed survey of a large, scholarly and (as modern historians say) 'problematised' field, but we should note in passing that it is always worth taking historical 'periods' with a pinch of salt, because they have a habit of slipping their bounds. Even times of intense change have traces of continuity. So, while it is tempting to divide English history into sharply defined chunks – Norman, Tudor, Hanoverian, Victorian – we should not be too categorical. No one came over all Tudor the morning after Bosworth; no one attending the funeral of Queen Victoria turned to their neighbour and said that they were suddenly feeling strangely Edwardian, don'tcha know?

By the same token, much of what is thought to have arrived with the Normans (feudalism, Gothic architecture) had been stirring in England for decades. And the people of the so-called Dark Ages surely thought of them as anything but. Entrepreneurs were coming up with new gadgets all the time – mills, boats, keys, glass. So far as they were concerned, it was a period of hectic change.

Nor do individual people always align themselves with the period in which they happen to live. In 1898, a Cornish fisherman had little in common with a road-sweeper in Westminster – one mended his nets by candlelight, had never used a postage stamp and could not imagine a photograph, while the other saw horseless carriages, steamships and electric lights every day. Yet they were both 'Victorians'.

Dividing the past into neat slices is convenient, but puts it into a straitjacket.

The important thing is that everyone in 1290, 1920 or any of the years in between believed themselves to be ... *modern*. Whenever they thought about the past, they did so with a slightly superior smile.

One of the unfortunate side-effects of viewing the Industrial Revolution as a conclusive break with the past has been to push medieval England into the shadows. We have little difficulty finding parallels between ourselves and the ancient Greeks or Romans – the classical world seems oddly familiar. And the Elizabethans were *exactly* like us, in Shakespeare. But it is hard to feel any such connection with the Middle Ages. Those years are a deep pit of despair peopled by brutal kings, cackling witches, gap-toothed peasants and scheming bishops, with only the occasional knight in shining armour to lift our spirits.

Primary schools narrate the whole period as a fairy tale peopled by wicked barons and hapless villagers. 'Medieval' has become little more than a synonym for 'cruel'.

It doesn't help that the documentary record is thin, but it takes only a glance at the *Canterbury Tales* to see that the squire–peasant axis in English society was dissolving long before the 'revolution' ignited by industrial change. Chaucer's fourteenth-century pilgrims are drawn from a wide social base, and reveal an England that is no longer feudal but rather home to a chattering bourgeoisie of merchants, reeves, franklins, millers, clothiers and lawyers. Those talkative travellers (who clearly share a language) behave like early package tourists, using official coin to pay for room and board in the inns where they pause. England, even then, was a commercial power with advanced patterns of trade and finance, a legal system, wages, property rights, mining, engineering skills and transport links.

When steam engines appeared on the scene, many centuries later, they would supply power to a society well-placed to advance full-throttle.

If today's historians dislike this notion, they give even shorter shrift to the idea that Englishness might have been forged by mere geography. The suggestion that the nation was shaped not (or not solely) by conflicts between power blocs – Church, Crown, Parliament, aristocracy – but by basic facts of landscape and climate ... this strays perilously close to theories of racial supremacy. It feels tantamount to saying that England hit the ethnic jackpot. Surely, they say, we have moved on from the idea that nationhood is a folkloric matter of blood and soil.

Indeed we have. But in doing so we may have left something of value behind. When we stand in places like Great Dunmow, Lavenham and Jarrow, and reflect on the men who hunted wolves in Shropshire and sailed down England's east coast, it is hard not to feel that the national history was written not only

by royal whim and political change but also by the water dripping from the sky, the rocks, the grass, the hills. It was wild
features like these that governed how people lived.

It is common to talk about the landscape as if it was a natural
paradise until greedy humanity came along and ruined everything. But England's fabled scenery has not been 'natural' for
thousands of years. It has been brushed, drained, scrubbed and
groomed by centuries of human history, human 'nature' and
human hands.

Even its wildlife is not primordial. Agriculture has virtually
eliminated some species (skylarks, turtle doves, water voles
and red squirrels as well as wolves) while many once-common
sights are now rare (nightingales, cowslips, beetles and butterflies). Human intervention has allowed rhododendrons, roses,
crayfish, grey squirrels, urban foxes, red kites and a hundred
other migrant species to replace the original inhabitants.

Nature moves in mysterious ways, not all of them natural.

That said, while people have shaped the environment, the
environment has shaped people, too. Wet skies and fertile soil
made England an ideal place to rear sheep and grow wheat,
creating a land of wool and bread. But English culture also
rested on what lay beneath its feet. The ground contained
ample seams of metals, minerals and other useful substances.
Nature provided England with more than a larder; it was a
hardware store, too. Millions of years of sedimentary geology
left it with young, soft rock (chalk, shale and limestone) in the
south and east, while the north and west were defined by their
igneous granite, gneiss and heavy sandstone.

When we say that northerners are grittier or more rugged
than their soft southern cousins, we are not speaking figuratively: it is a geological fact.

It may have taken aeons for the rain, wind and frost to carve
the cliffs, valleys, coves, gullies, bluffs and hollows that comprise England's scenery, but the result is unique to this island,
not least in its variety. Scafell Pike used to be twice its present

height before thousands of years of drizzle and downpour, freeze and thaw, rubbed those Wagnerian chasms down to size. When we gasp at the beauty of the Yorkshire Dales, we may be struck by drystone walls, barns, churches and cottages, but mostly we are admiring 350 million years of natural bio-chemistry. Nature made the bones and added the flesh; humans merely applied the make-up.

The consequences of geology's defining power are visible everywhere. The primary division in English culture, for instance, falls between the regions that lie north and west of a line from Exeter to Lincoln (the route of the Roman Fosse Way), and the land to the south and east. The former sits on hard Palaeozoic rock; the latter on Triassic clay, sand and chalk. The impact of this contrast is not uniform, but it is marked.[1]

Sometimes these variegations can create noticeable differences within the confines of a single area. It may be true that dairy herds thrive on plains and in valleys, whereas sheep prefer the grass on hillsides, but each area has its own twist on the theme. The Peak District, for example, has grassy limestone pastures in the south, perfect for sheep, and tough gritstone in the north, all gloomy cliffs and bogs. Stand on the ridge over-looking Castleton and you can still see the curved hump of what was once an underwater reef – a spur of coral on which ancient lime-secreting organisms laid down the deposits that have become spectacular countryside.

It took millions of years to create this view. How could it not be breathtaking?

At the other end of the country, falling from the south coast like a teardrop, hangs the 'isle' of Portland. From Weymouth it looks like a rugged offshore mountain, with a naval base at its

---

1 Not the least of its consequences was that the early settlers – Romans, Angles, Saxons, Danes and Normans – all stayed overwhelmingly in the south and east, which made Englishness a more amalgamated nationality than either Welshness or Scottishness. This remains the case today. If the United Kingdom ever did break up, England would be by a long way the most cosmopolitan of the new nation states.

foot and a prison on top. But as soon as one climbs the hill and looks south towards the lighthouse, its true nature is revealed. A proud slab of limestone, home to three ancient castles with commanding views of the western approaches, Portland is a plateau that tilts to the sea (from 500 to 20 feet) between steep flanks of grey stone. Fragments of rock litter the slopes and coves.

It is as if a giant's fist pounded the headland until its teeth fell out.

The truth is not so different. William Rufus (the Conqueror's son) built a castle on the eastern cliff, and ever since Portland has been famous for its stone. At first the limestone was harvested simply because of its accessibility: it could be hacked out of the cliffs and hoisted directly on to barges (England's saltwater ring road proving useful again). But before long it was the stone's rare combination of softness and strength, as well as its fine grey-white colour, that led to the founding of dozens of quarries. In the fourteenth century Portland stone was used in Westminster Abbey, the Tower of London, London Bridge and Exeter Cathedral; and when Christopher Wren used it for St Paul's Cathedral and many other City churches it became the signature building material of upper-class England.

The Royal Naval College at Greenwich, Buckingham Palace (that balcony overlooking the Mall), the Cenotaph (as well as the gravestones of those who perished in both world wars), Somerset House, the Port of Liverpool, major municipal buildings in Bristol, Manchester and Leeds, the Bank of England and the National Gallery are other grand examples. One area of Portland is known as Whitehall because the stone for so many government buildings was quarried there. There was quite a fracas in 2000 when the British Museum – having ordered the classic soft-toned Dorset rock for its restored courtyard – was fobbed off with some shocking-white rock from France instead.

The papers called it a 'pale imitation' of the real thing.

Portland rock is only the most famous of England's building

materials. The Taynton quarry, near Burford, produced a mellow form of limestone that along with the local Headington material was used to build the colleges and chapels of Oxford University and Blenheim Palace. The honey-tinted limestone from Ham Hill in Somerset went into Sherborne, Beaminster, Montacute and other Dorset villages. Canterbury Cathedral's russet building blocks were hoisted out of the ground at nearby Maidstone. And the Cotswolds have a palette all their own: pale-cream Bath stone in the south (from the quarries at Corsham); straw-coloured Minchinhampton in the west; and buttercup-gold in the north, at Broadway.

Winston Churchill once remarked that we shape our houses and then they shape us. He was thinking of the layout of the House of Commons – two rows of benches facing each other – which turned the debates into adversarial contests (other nations have opted for circular chambers). But something similar is evident in the way that England's regions have all developed distinct vernacular architectures which are rooted in the materials that lay close to hand. After all, New York does not have more skyscrapers than London because it has a preference for them. It merely has granite for the foundations, rather than soft Thames clay.

The limestone belt that runs from Portland, through the Cotswolds, and up to the Pennines produced the weathered stone villages and farmhouses of those areas, while the absence of quarries in East Anglia and the Midlands encouraged such regions to build in brick instead. By the same token coastal Norfolk uses flint, whereas Kent and Sussex prefer wood and tile. Roofs are thatched in Dorset and made of slate in Cumbria, and some have timber beams while others do not. Builders use whatever materials the local landscape has to offer.

This is why Lancashire differs from Kent, why England differs from Scotland – and why both differ from Egypt or China. It is also why so many northern houses are whitewashed. The intention is not to reflect the heat of the midday sun – as in the

Aegean – but to make the buildings visible from miles away (useful when walking home on a dark winter's night).

England's weather has shaped its buildings in other ways. Some have large windows and lightwells to make the most of the limited daylight; others have pitched rather than flat roofs to divert the rain. In Tudor times it was said that Hardwick Hall in Derbyshire was 'more glass than wall', and it continues to stand as a brilliant reminder that meteorology drove architectural advances. The thickness of walls, the height of doors, the width of windows, the size and shape of rooms – these are not purely aesthetic features. They were all dictated by mundane climatic facts. Few English houses had cellars – they were rarely necessary in our moderate climate – and English plumbers felt there was no real need to lag pipes. So when the ground froze, as it did occasionally, they burst. One could thus say that geography – as well as modern politics – has played a role in the rise and rise of the Polish plumber. Plumbing has never been an English skill.

The globalised, metropolitan modern mind rarely thinks that natural history might be a branch of political science.[2] But if we are searching for the raw materials of our national identity, it makes no sense to overlook the inescapable facts of rock, rain and vegetation. Vast sheep ranges were inconceivable in central Europe, thanks to the wolf. But the climates of Arabia and the tropics made them unimaginable there, too. By the same token, if a seam of coal had been discovered in ancient Crete, people might have fashioned it into jewellery, but they would not have dreamed of setting it on fire. It was too hot already. And while a religious ritual like a month-long fast found a receptive audience in desert lands, it had little chance

2 Abstractions such as 'globalisation' can be slippery. Here, I am using it in its most literal form, in reference to the world-shrinking advance of transport and communications – from Drake's circumnavigation of the globe to mass air travel. It is the homogenising tendency that gives us strawberries in winter, air-conditioned comfort in the summer, and Indonesian shopping malls that resemble their equivalents in Sweden or Switzerland.

of catching on in northern Europe, where the population needed calories all year round.

It would be surprising if the English subconscious were *not* influenced by such fundamental concerns. Even in the glass towers of today's corporate world people still nurse familiar fantasies – a place in the country, a stroll by a river, a plough-man's lunch in a meadow.

Some of them may forget that the ploughman's lunch is not traditional English fare, but the brainchild of an advertising agency in the 1950s, designed to boost sales of cheese. Once again, what seems 'natural' turns out to be man-made.

A few mavericks have resisted the prevailing view that history is shaped primarily by religious, constitutional, economic and ideological patterns. In 1951 Jaquetta Hawkes, in her classic *A Land*, blended history, science, nature, archaeology, art history and personal reflection into a notion that English culture grew out of its various substrata. She liked to lie on the grass at night and feel the weight of millennia pressing into her shoulder blades. And in his famous 1960 essay 'Spirit of Place' Lawrence Durrell argued that national temperaments were shaped by such forces. 'I believe you could exterminate the French at a blow,' he wrote, 'and resettle the land with Tatars, and within two generations discover that the national characteristics were back at norm – the relentless metaphysical curiosity, the tenderness for good living and passionate individualism.' In his view, a Cypriot who settled in London would in time become English, simply because human customs owe just as much to the local environment as do trees and flowers. Greece was governed by its raw elements – sun, sea, rock – just as Scotland was shaped by its mists and heather. Durrell was not suggesting that children were influenced only or immediately by their surroundings. He was observing that the landscape would stealthily impose its will over the course of generations. Humans have hinterlands; nations have memories.

In this he was echoing George Orwell in *The Lion and the*

Unicorn. Orwell argued that, even if England were to be conquered (he was writing in 1941), its sturdy island personality,
formed like granite over the ages, would surely endure: 'The
Stock Exchange will be pulled down, the horse plough will
give way to the tractor, the country houses will be turned into
children's holiday camps, the Eton and Harrow match will be forgotten, but England will still be England, an everlasting animal.'

It is unfashionable to suggest that complex historical events
can have simple causes. There are a thousand nuances that help
explain the Viking assault on England. But the Norsemen *did*
abandon a freezing and inhospitable strip of rocky coastline
in favour of a temperate and fertile land of (literally) milk and
honey. And the brief Norwegian summer favoured barley,
which produced a dark, tough loaf – no fun in an age of rotten
and aching teeth.

Those raids across the North Sea were spurred in part by a
longing for soft white bread.

Geography cannot construct a national temperament overnight;
nor can it do so alone. National identities are always works in
progress, evolving throughout history. And in England especially,
history and geography are as closely entwined as a crumbling
garden wall matted with ivy and bramble. Turn a corner almost
anywhere and you will step on ground that is hallowed by both
geographical and historical events. In Tewkesbury, for example,
which makes the front pages every time the Severn bursts its
banks and sloshes through the town, both traditions drip from
the eaves of the abbey, which is pictured like a miraculous ark,
a foot above the flood.

Tewkesbury was once a monastic town on the River Severn.
But on 4 May 1471 the field in front of its famous church was
the setting for one of the grimmest battles in the War of the
Roses, when Margaret of Anjou's Lancastrians met the Yorkist
army of Edward IV. Margaret may well have watched the
combat from the abbey's tower. If so, she would have witnessed

the death of her son, Edward, Prince of Wales. The King's army won the day, and the retreating Lancastrians sought sanctuary behind the abbey's stone walls. But the Yorkists forced their way in and hacked them to pieces. (Medieval knights were not always chivalrous.)

One of the abbey's doors is enamelled with armour removed from the fallen warriors, complete with crossbow-bolt and arrow holes. The field is still known as Bloody Meadow.

An aroma of that brutal day still clings to these walls. Most of England's Gothic buildings have a gracious air, a sense of choirs and candlelight, but something thicker and more sanguinary clouds these massive Romanesque precincts, with their elephantine columns, something to do with swords and dynasties. The visitor glimpses not a sacred spirit but a sleeping monster, a rough reminder of old England.

This barely audible cry hints at something important – the deep bass note of savagery and tragedy in our national past. It is as English as the lilting music of larks and the blood-dark tang of blackberries plucked from hedgerows.

A contrasting note sounds through the fog of time, however. When the monasteries were seized seventy years later, the residents of Tewkesbury saved their ancient abbey by buying it (for the princely sum of £453). As so often, Englishness can be glimpsed in a clash of opposites. The storybook drama of princes and queens has an amiable thread as well: the everyday persistence of ordinary people – determined, self-reliant and not easily parted from their local treasures.

Generalisations, they say, are always wrong. We should not give too much weight to the role of monasteries in medieval life, because their prominence might signify no more than that monks left better written records than washerwomen. Yet a remarkable number of tender green shoots – fragile intimations of what would become Englishness – did seem to rise through the earth at the end of the thirteenth century. And, while identifying a precise starting point is always moot – the patriotic equivalent of wondering how many angels might stand on the head of a pin – the convergence of so many strands is highly suggestive.

This era marked the beginning of a specific way of rural life, based on large estates that were full of sheep. It led to a land-owning structure in which aristocratic property rights created concentrations of wealth that laid the foundations of industrial capitalism.[3] The social and economic edifices that would come to dominate English life started to emerge at this time.

Modern economic models suggest that national prosperity rests on four main pillars: financial strength (the ability to invest in new enterprises); human capital (the presence of an educated and motivated population); infrastructure (transport links); and political institutions (to enforce the rule of law). These four elements are highly interdependent, of course, and probably not the whole story. But there is surely room for a fifth: the underlying geographical features that made thirteenth-century England a land of ships and sheep, wheat and beef.

A heavy wash of ancillary enterprise grew on the back of these simple stirrings: carters, saddlers, weavers, brewers, ostlers, grooms, bakers, stable-boys and tavern keepers, but also lawyers, merchants, millers, clerks and money-lenders. A recognisable new society was emerging, whose growing prosperity rested entirely on wool. And it was only in its infancy.

---

3 The famous legal achievements of Henry II grew out of the dispute between Church and State: wool carried them forward into the all-important arena of property.

Five

The White Monks

The young stonemason rubbed his eyes in disbelief. It had taken him a week to walk to this secluded spot. In Lincoln he had chiselled niches on the memorial to the late Queen, whose cold remains lay entombed beneath the cathedral floor. Then he had trudged through a deep, dark forest, with only brief glimpses of the sky. More than once he had fancied he could hear the pant and rustle of a nearby wolf, and quickened his step, though he had been assured that none remained in these parts.

He had seen impressive religious buildings before, of course, having worked on the cloister at Bedford and the nave at Bath. He was fond of saying that, oh yes, he had seen a fair bit of this old world. But nothing had prepared him for this first sight of Rievaulx. Rounding the last curve in the river, he felt the air grow warm until, all of a sudden, he stepped into a bright clearing in the forest. Ahead lay a stretch of pasture glistening with dew, while on a ledge above the valley an amazing stone structure soared to the sky. He could see that the platform on which the abbey stood had been levelled and cut into the slope by hand. He could also see that the river had been diverted to make room for the building: the former watercourse was still visible beneath the stone arches, like the grassy echo of a moat. It gave the building an immodest air – a hint of fortifications and ramparts. This was a divine castle.

The abbey towered above the trees, kissing the clouds in a swirl of columns, vaults, arches, cornices, pediments, buttresses and stairs, all lightened by tracery that made the massive building blocks seem as light as silk. But what made the mason whistle was the sheer scale. The church itself was no bigger than the great minster at York, where he had stopped for a night; indeed, it might have been smaller. But it was only one of many such buildings – dormitories, refectories, kitchens, libraries, chapter houses, infirmaries and cloisters.

He knew that the abbey's name referred to its location in the Rye valley, and that the hay-coloured sandstone had been hacked from a quarry just three miles downriver. There was nothing magical about its construction, no matter how astonishing it seemed. He could almost smell the sweat of the men who had built it. But he could not suppress a supernatural shiver. What kind of divine will could have inspired something on such a wondrous scale? What sort of people had conceived of such things? He could only gasp at their audacity – the soaring stone ribs, the steep roof, the tremendous limbs and windows. He had heard that was home to more than a hundred monks, as well as several hundred lay brothers (who did the heavy lifting). And here it was, soaring up to the trees in the summery dale.

The mason tightened his grip on his bag of chisels and hammers, and took a breath. It might not be easy to grasp the magnificence of the concept, but in one sense he felt at home. He knew how to carve stone, so there would be plenty of work for him here. And the sight of those shapely towers rising from the forest left him feeling that he was in the presence of something truly divine. It felt like a place of miracles.

Rievaulx, founded in 1132, was the first of the great Cistercian monasteries to appear in the wilds of Yorkshire in the twelfth century. Over the course of the next twenty-five years the White Monks – so named because of the colour of their cloaks – also founded Fountains Abbey, Kirkstall, Meaux, Sawley, Byland and finally Jervaulx.[1] For centuries, this had been a bleak and sparsely populated area of the country, scoured by wintry storms.[2] But the Cistercians discovered something profound in this remote wilderness – their flocks were not devoured by wolves. God Himself seemed to be smiling on their enterprise. The emptiness of the land became a commercial as well as a spiritual boon – they could fill the hills with sheep on a previously unimagined scale.

Rievaulx Abbey. In seeking holy solitude in the wilderness, the Cistercians found agricultural wealth and power.

1 It was at Jervaulx that monks first made the distinctive ewes'-milk cheese – Wensleydale – that eventually became famous around the world, especially after being enthusiastically promoted by Wallace and Gromit.

2 In fact, the landscape in which the Cistercians settled was not quite so empty as was once thought. The villagers of East Witton, in Wensleydale, were relocated a mile or so along the valley to keep them at a respectable distance from Jervaulx.

The Cistercians had their origins in Burgundy and owed their name to a mother foundation at Citeaux – once a swamp near the regal vineyards of Chambolle-Musigny, Gevrey Chambertin and Vosne-Romanée. They did not seek to be original; on the contrary, they strove to imitate the holy example of St Benedict himself, whose followers, the black-robed Benedictines, had strayed from the path of righteousness. They were disciples of austerity, disgusted by the venality and corruption of Europe's priesthood. (As John Wycliffe said, the medieval Church was 'drunk with simony and avarice'.) In modern terminology, they were fundamentalists – they saw solitude and simplicity as holy virtues, and hard graft as a religious duty. Their churches, consecrated to the Virgin, were free from all adornment, and they had no possessions, relying instead on gifts from benefactors.

They drifted to England from Burgundy in the twelfth century in search of lonely spots where they might withdraw from the world and practise their spiritual ideals: manual labour and self-sufficiency. So what followed was a paradox: in seeking isolation, they built society; in seeking seclusion, they cultivated trade; in seeking simplicity, they generated wealth. Supported by armies of lay brethren, they raised huge flocks of sheep on the gentle wolf-free slopes of Lincolnshire, Yorkshire and the Cotswolds ('cotswold' literally means 'sheep pen on the hill').

Their most original innovation turned out to be the secret of their success. Rejecting the old concept of tithes – which local people tended to view as an imposition – they vowed instead to be self-supporting through agriculture. Nevertheless, they were still in a good position to offer access to immortal life to any generous souls who offered to help, and indeed many rich men were happy to provide land in return for a quiet word in high places. The abbeys grew bigger and better with every passing year.

There was nothing superficial about the Cistercians' devotion to a Spartan lifestyle, however. As one novice at Rievaulx wrote: 'Our food is scanty, our garments rough; our drink is from the stream and our sleep is upon our book; under our tired limbs is a hard mat.' He and his holy brothers wore untreated wool and fleece to highlight their humble status. But the harder they worked to fulfil their self-sufficient vision, the more expert they became in matters pertaining to land management. In an especially inspired move, they invited secular farmhands (lay brethren) to do the hard work in return for food and shelter, leaving the monks free to devote themselves to strict religious observance.

Their prayers were soon answered, and the money started pouring in.

Before long, all of Yorkshire's abbeys had huge flocks: Rievaulx itself had 14,000 sheep; Fountains (the largest), 18,000. Merchants sailed to England from the cloth-making centres of Flanders and Tuscany, where the demand for high-quality English fleeces was relentless. Fountains even had its own ship to carry wool downriver to the North Sea and the wider world.

The profound influence of foreigners – French monks, Flemish traders, Italian merchants and Norman patrons – in this story is striking, but the essentials of English topography played a decisive role, too. While the sheltered and fertile Vale of York was ideal land for wheat, barley, oats and beans, and its streams could be diverted into fish ponds, the higher Pennine slopes were perfectly suited to the hardier breeds of sheep.

Large-scale sheep-rearing was not a complete novelty. The Benedictine nuns of Minchinhampton, in the Cotswolds, tended some two thousand sheep,[3] while the abbeys at Canterbury, Glastonbury and Winchester, and the salt marshes of Romney and Somerset, had similarly large flocks. But it was the Cistercians, alone in their wilderness, who took sheep farming to a new level.

When Bede outlined the features of the country in his *History*, he noted that it was 'rich in grain and timber', had

3 They produced a ewes'-milk cheese that is still marketed, in their memory, as 'Nuns of Caen'.

'good pasturage for cattle and draught animals', and had abundant salmon, eels and shellfish. He did not even mention sheep. By the end of the twelfth century, however, they were a precious national resource. When a king's ransom was required to liberate Richard I in 1195, it was wool that came to the rescue. Fountains alone contributed a year's worth of wool revenue to the cause. The Crown was so mindful of the material's terrific value as a source of tax that it actively encouraged the creation of more abbeys. Indeed, one of the leading benefactors of Rievaulx itself was King Henry II.

By the end of the thirteenth century the Cistercian houses of Yorkshire were a power in the realm. And they were part of an international family, a network of brother and sister houses that were all bound to the mother ship in Citeaux. By this time there were more than three hundred of them in Europe, and they were not much less than Europe's first multinational corporation. Until this time, grain – barley in the north, wheat in the milder south – had dominated rural life, but these were grown to be eaten, not sold. By contrast, wool became England's first significant cash crop.

The Cistercians prospered in part because they were devout and conscientious, but also because they learned, through long experience and reflection, how to turn virgin land into gold. This quality was noticed by their contemporaries. Gerald of Wales – the son of an Anglo-Norman baron who, as Archdeacon of Brecon, became the travelling chaplain to Henry II before devoting his life to study in Lincoln – wrote: 'Settle the Cistercians in some barren retreat ... hidden away in an overgrown forest. A year or two later you will find there splendid churches and fine monastic buildings, with a great amount of property and all the wealth you can imagine.'

It is tempting to see the monks' pragmatic spirit as hypocritical, cutting against the grain of their theology. But there is no reason to believe that they were, at least in these early days, in any way cynical. It simply turned out that their keen religious faith gave them a couple of telling advantages. It equipped them with the fiery zeal needed to withstand the long Yorkshire winters, and gave them a useful, long-term view of human endeavour. No one could build an abbey overnight. Those who laid the foundations needed a loving belief in a brighter future and a patient sense of self-sacrifice, since they knew they would never see the end product of their labours. Their keen sense of the endless, fluctuating passage of time gave them immortal longings, and made them unusually industrious. They took extensive tracts of marshland around Pickering (once a glacial lake) and set about draining it to create a thousand acres of sweet pasture for their sheep, but it was decades before they completed the project.

We have already noted the coincidence of several significant events in 1290 and 1291, and Cistercian Yorkshire had its share of these, too. Its flocks fell victim to an unpleasant disease – sheep scab – so the wool harvest was poor. But there was no slowdown in the building schedule: churches and chapter houses appeared all across the region. These projects were not cheap, and Fountains, for one, was forced to borrow heavily from the best-known Jewish merchant in the north – Aaron of Lincoln.

Jewish financiers had arrived with the Normans in the eleventh century, and ever since they had performed a vital function – providing capital to the new aristocracy so that good Christians could observe the biblical injunction against usury. They helped England to build its castles and cathedrals, and Aaron of Lincoln – supposedly the wealthiest man in the kingdom – bankrolled a total of nine Cistercian monasteries. There were Jewish financiers in every town; they benefited from royal warrants and other exemptions, and to all intents and purposes they were agents of the Crown.

Naturally, though, the more they prospered, the more they were resented. They also suffered as a result of the Crusading frenzy that was gripping England at the time. Why trek to the

Holy Land when foreigners could be baited or lynched just round the corner? It was asking a lot of a medieval patriot to understand the difference between a Muslim and a Jew.

In the latter half of the thirteenth century the Crown, sensing a possible solution to the aristocracy's spiralling indebtedness, turned a blind eye to mob uprisings against Jewish creditors. The King himself turned out to be an unreliable business partner, reneging on many of his debts and then, as we have seen, ordering England's Jews to be herded into ghettos. Mob rule did the rest: 400 Jews were killed in a single London massacre on Palm Sunday 1263; and twelve years later Edward I forbade them, by statute, from charging interest on loans. Finally, in 1290, they were all deported in a terrible eruption of nationalist wrath. Another facet of Englishness – the victimisation of others – had emerged.

The deportation of the Jews was bad news for Fountains Abbey. The monks had been selling wool on credit, and in 1289 they faced bankruptcy, with debts to foreign merchants totalling £6373. Two years later, the General Chapter disbanded the abbey for three years, leaving only a skeleton staff in place. The King, vexed that one of his biggest money wells had run dry, appointed the Bishop of Durham to set matters straight. John of Berwick was dispatched to cast his eye over the monastic accounts.

This was by no means the only example of financial irregularities in the wool trade. The whole business was built on paper money and fine distinctions were common. Back in 1231, a legal dispute over grazing rights between the Abbot of Rievaulx and a local landowner had ended with one side agreeing to take game – but not birds – from the land in question. Similar arrangements were struck over rights to charcoal, copper, lead and iron, not to mention the fish in the icy waters of the Swale and the Ure. In these and other documents we can see the way in which England's land played a pivotal role in this new business culture. As more sheep grazed on the wolf-free land, with its well-watered soil, even-tempered climate and reliable transport routes, the demand for other pieces of commercial infrastructure grew. England had ample raw materials for such a task, and built bridges, roads, drainage systems and irrigation channels. It also developed a wide range of associated crafts, a network of markets and something like a merchant navy.

The Cistercians may not have sparked 'the first industrial revolution' (though some have said so) since the machines they installed were made of wood, rope and leather – but they did spin its wheels.

The burgeoning realm of sheep and wool had another knock-on effect: it fostered the creation of sophisticated financial instruments designed to smooth out the traditional peaks and troughs of rural life. As a wool monoculture, England's economy was vulnerable to boom-and-bust price fluctuations caused by bad weather or disease. Now, with monastic estates in the vanguard, a new regime of legal and administrative routines evolved: the world of financial planning.

A glance at the arrangement struck by Pipewell Monastery with Cahors in 1291 reveals how well developed this had become by this date. The document was drafted by lawyers, not dreamers. There are even some clauses on the care of livestock:

> It is ... ordained that 900 of the common two-tooth sheep (*bidentibus*) of the Abbey shall be separated, half of which shall be ewes and the other males, by the view of the merchants before mid-Lent next, which sheep the monks shall hold of the merchants, and they shall be signed with the mark of both parties, and then shall remain in divers places with the two-tooth sheep of the monks in as good pasture as the monks' own two-tooth sheep.

The same agreement specifies that Pipewell's wool should be 'well washed, dry and cleaned'. Furthermore, 'Neither party shall have the power to refuse or reject any part of the wool against his deed, or challenge his proceedings in any way.' No doubt the proceeds were intended to fund God's work, but

Welcome to Pipewell: water, sheep, monks, and financial instruments.

this document does not read like the work of holy men whose minds were fixed on higher things. Nor was it an isolated example. In 1292, Kirkstall Abbey, near Leeds, showed itself to have a sophisticated grasp of worldly affairs when it signed a bulk-buy agreement with the merchants of Lucca, promising all of its wool for a decade. Such contracts reveal that clammy legalese is nothing new. Indeed, they suggest that the towering financial castles that would one day fill the City's Square Mile were born, like so much else, in the long-lost days of monks and sheep.

England's Jews would not have been expelled had there not been an alternative source of ready capital, and their position in England's commercial life was soon filled by a group of Tuscan merchants – Bardi, Frescobaldi, Mozzi and Riccardi – who were already seasoned players in the country's wool markets. It was a rule of the Florentine guilds that only English wool could be used for their fine fabrics and tapestries, so their agents were always roaming the shires in search of the best fleeces. At first they headed due north from Italy, using the Rhine as a highway, but by the fifteenth century they were able to sail around the Iberian peninsula and pick up their consignments in bulk.

In Cynthia Harnett's novel *The Woolpack* (1951), set in Burford, these foreign merchants are regarded as a menace: 'They ride the country, stealing trade out of honest men's hands . . . they are the curse of this modern world.' As so often, migrants were depicted as draining the country's wealth when, if anything, they were boosting it.

One such agent, Francesco Balducci Pelogotti, left a list of his dealings between 1318 and 1321 which shows that he bought wool in many Cotswold towns: Boriforte (Burford), Sirisestri (Cirencester), Norleccio (Northleach) and many others. The wool from Cistercian monasteries was pricier (presumably of finer quality) than Benedictine thread: a sack of the latter might cost just £8, while premium Cistercian wool commanded £25 or more. But the most notable aspect of Pelogotti's record is the sheer scale of the wool network it describes.

Medieval England was well aware of the importance of these sacks, so it was only natural for Edward III to order his Lord

Chancellor to sit on one in Parliament.[4] It has been estimated that the wool tax accounted for a third of the Crown's total income during his reign. No wonder the authorities termed it the 'great and ancient custom' ... while those who had to pay it called it the 'evil toll'.

It was a natural step for the wool merchants to become money-lenders too, since they were expected to extend credit when necessary, as the Jews had done. However, as they also served as papal tax collectors, they introduced England to the subtle arts of high finance – letters of credit, bills of exchange, debentures, promissory notes, currency swaps and other monetary instruments. They became, quite literally, merchant bankers, and left an indelible imprint on English finance. From the *lire*, *soldi* and *denarii* that gave us our pounds,[5] shillings and pence to London landmarks such as Lombard Street, through the Latin terms for 'debit' and 'credit', and even our word for 'bank' (from *banco* – a money-lender's bench), their impact was broad and deep. Ever since, a ruined trader has been disdained as a 'broken bench' or *banca rotta* – a bankrupt.

The emergence of this fledgling financial system was significant because it not only lubricated but accelerated the nation's commercial activity. To put it crudely, it was not the capital markets that created England's wealth, but the wealth that created the capital markets. The fact that those markets allowed the already wealthy to grow richer still, is one of those winner takes all truths with which England has lived ever since. Theologians even found support for it in the Gospels: 'For to whomsoever hath, more shall be given, and he shall have more abundance ... For he that hath, to him shall be given.'[6]

4 The Woolsack has been the symbolic seat of English government ever since, so it came as a surprise when, during repair work in 1938, it was found to be stuffed not with English wool but with horsehair.

5 It is a rarely noticed irony that anyone who denounces the euro in favour of the 'dear old pound' is in fact rallying to a traditional, revered, but undeniably *Italian* symbol.

6 Matthew 13:12.

Nearly all of this burgeoning commercial activity could be traced back to the fortuitous marriage of grass and rain that made England such a matchless source of high-quality wool. By the early years of the fourteenth century, the kingdom was exporting an enormous amount of wool through an increasingly intricate web of trading connections. Parallel markets then developed in grain, tin, salt, cheese, leather, metal, seafood and scores of other products. And a new sort of organisation sprang into existence to preside over such matters: the guild.

Guilds were hardly liberal-minded self-help organisations; rather, they were cartels, elite clubs, determined to capture and defend monopolies, and quick to suppress any competition. The benefits of forming one were obvious, and there were soon guilds and livery companies for every sort of trade: butchers, brewers, fishmongers, bakers, cobblers, goldsmiths, furriers, apothecaries, saddlers, vintners and many more. More than a hundred were established in London alone. But they did also function as fraternities, awarding apprenticeships, settling disputes and providing mutual insurance. In short, for all their faults, they established a pattern for the great institutions of cooperative endeavour that lay ahead – the trades unions and non-conformist societies.

The grandest guilds were those with links to the wool trade: the clothworkers, mercers, drapers and merchant taylors. Once again, England's great sheep ranch was helping to form the institutions that would shape the nation's future.

The fact that a single abbey could own vast tracts of land, stretching a day's walk in any direction, gave birth to an enduring feature of England's scenery. Anxious to mark the borders of their estates, and to prevent their flocks from straying on to neighbours' land, the landowners walled in the remote moors with sinuous lines of local stone. To this day, there are five thousand miles of stone walls in the Yorkshire Dales alone. They have become a cherished aspect of the area's character,

snaking over the hills, with stiles cut into them. Some date
back only as far as the nineteenth century, but many were built
in the Middle Ages to define the boundaries of the great ecclesiastical holdings.

But it was the mercantile machinery that wool ushered into
existence that proved to be its greatest legacy. All of those
woolsacks gave England purchasing power ... and a taste for
luxury. Previously, only monarchs and bishops could entertain
the idea of trading in gold, silver, gemstones and other rich
ornaments. But now, thanks to sheep, a new class of person had
the means to 'live like a king'. That meant much more work
for goldsmiths, jewellers and artists. After all, the art world –
like the financial markets – did not pre-date wealth creation; it
relied on it. Florence was not the world's leading cloth-maker
because it was home to Giotto and Dante; rather, the artists
lived there because the town's cloth barons, merchants and
bankers were eager patrons of their work.

It is no longer controversial to cite the Cistercians' agrarian
achievement as a major fact of medieval life, but quite a few
classic histories mention it only in passing, as ornamentation.
They prefer to focus on ecclesiastical and doctrinal matters. Such accounts tend to assume that the daily grind of a
labourer was dominated by spiritual concerns. As Jacques le
Goff put it in his celebrated *Medieval Civilisation* (1964): 'The
aim of work was not economic progress ... it had religious
and moral ends.'

Yet even if the wealth generated by the wool trade was
merely a by-product of this prayerful mentality, its consequences were immense. Estimates vary, but there were
probably five million sheep in England between 1270 and 1290,
producing some 30,000 sacks a year. This rose to eight million
animals in the first decade of the fourteenth century, when
exports of woolsacks hit 40,000 per annum. A century later, in
the reign of Henry V, £35,000 out of the Crown's income of
£55,750 came from the tax on wool. As the medieval historian

Michael Postan once noted, the wool era was 'the great breeding season of English capitalism'.

The first great basis of England's wealth, in other words, was
down to a few unremarkable facts of landscape.

The monasteries led the way in other businesslike arenas.
They built fisheries, dug wells, cut ditches, reclaimed land,
brewed ale, baked bread, diverted rivers into mills, and signed
deals with landowners to secure hunting rights.[7] There were
even early glimmers of industry. In 1195 Fountains Abbey
paid ten shillings a year for the right to drag dead wood out of
Knaresborough forest; this was then turned into charcoal for
the monastery's forge (like many religious houses, Fountains
made its own bells). It also sought permission to mine iron and
copper. In 1309 it secured the right to take millstones from
Huddersfield, partly to grind the corn that flowed through its
water mills and partly to sharpen its knives.

These were only murmurs of what was to come. At this
stage, it was just the ring of a hammer on molten iron in a
forest clearing, the bronze glow from a furnace on an abbey
estate, the scream of a blade on whirring stone, the creak of
a wooden cog. It would be an exaggeration to call it a technological revolution. But all of the ingredients for industrial
advance were being nudged into place by England's flocks of
dumb sheep.

Nothing highlights the Cistercian monks' commercial
instincts more clearly than the fact that their founder – Bernard
of Clairvaux – also played a prominent role in the formation
of the Knights Templar (or, in full, the Poor Fellow-Soldiers
of Christ and the Temple of Solomon). With their white
tunics and bold red crosses, the Templars were holy icons of
the Crusades. They built frontier castles from Portugal to the
Holy Land, then established themselves as charity officers and
international bankers. St Bernard wrote their official code of

---

7 In 1181 Rievaulx was granted permission to take six stags a year from Nidderdale.

conduct, the so-called 'Latin Rule', which covered not just the order's spiritual obligations but eating habits, the number of horses a knight could own and plenty more besides.

No one needed to look any further to understand the power of prayer.

Six

It Never Rains

If you walk around the southern shore of Derwentwater in the Lake District, then follow the beck up Borrowdale, you soon come to the head of the valley, where the fells cast shadowy frowns across the green fields. At the end of the road stands a cluster of buildings, some in grey stone, others washed white. One of them is an inn. The hills glow green in the summer but are rust-brown in January, when snow drifts like icing sugar on the bracken.

There is not much here. A few wooden signposts and a circle of tents suggest that it may be a popular rambling route, but that's about it. Up by the lake, oak trees stand ankle-deep in water, while to the south, behind the bulk of Seathwaite Fell, sits Scafell Pike, England's tallest summit. Apart from the odd rumble from the nearby slate mine, there is nothing to hear but the rustle of the wind, the cry of a lapwing, the bleating of invisible sheep or the moan of a distant cow. From Elizabethan times these hills yielded graphite for the Keswick's pencil manufactory, but today this patch of cold, damp grass is little more than a marker post on a Lakeland hike.

It is, however, notorious as the wettest place in England. The mild wind from the west sucks up moisture from the Atlantic and dumps it on these hills at a rate of 140 inches per year, according to a plaque in the village. This soggy fact emerged as long ago as 1845, when rain gauges were set up across the Lake District for the first time. Keswick collected 62 inches of rain that year, while Grasmere, Wordsworth's village, ten miles to the south, recorded almost twice as much – 121 inches. But Seathwaite was in a league of its own, registering a staggering 151 inches – nearly half an inch per day. Three years later it was doused by 160 inches.

These dizzy readings made headlines even in far-off London.

Not much has changed. Five inches fell in a single hour in 1966, washing away the packhorse bridge, while a foot was recorded in the space of twenty-four hours in 2009 – a record-breaking deluge. The rain gauge on Seathwaite Fell is still the busiest in the land.

In 1845 it was a zinc tube; today it is made of plastic. But it is still full of water.

The Rainfall Survey of 1895 explained that the frequent downpours in these parts were triggered by the topography of the surrounding hills, which lifted the damp south-westerly air stream up to 1500 feet before funnelling it over Wastwater, where it tumbled into Scafell Pike and broke over the narrow neck of the Sty Head Pass. So when we call this the wettest spot in England, we really mean that it is the wettest *inhabited* spot. Walk for an hour up to Styhead Tarn and you find your-self in a sodden, empty hollow which is the prime target for any passing cloud. If a rain gauge had been placed here in 1845, it almost certainly would have put Seathwaite in the shade. No one wants to live here. The water may have floated on a warm breeze all the way from Bermuda, but that is not enough to attract holiday homes. Yet it has allowed Seathwaite to play a starring role in one of England's favourite pastimes: grumbling about the weather.

The building blocks of English life – the geological inheri-tance, the sea-washed island location, the hills crawling with sheep, the seams of coal, the rich soil – needed one more crucial ingredient to bring them to life: water. This, indeed, was the most basic resource of all.

England's wet climate is probably its best-known feature. The seemingly endless spatter of rain is the first thing that impresses – or depresses – most visitors, and with good reason. As the old maxim says, if you can't see the hills, it's raining; and if you can, it's about to. Water sluices down in predictable patterns – heavy in the north and west, lighter in the 'rain shadow' cast by the Pennines. This makes the west good for grass-munching livestock, and the east better for crops. Either way, there is an ever-present cloud on the horizon.

It makes sense, in this context, that small talk about the weather is the default setting of most English conversations. According to surveys, some 40 per cent of us admit to having talked about the weather within the last *hour*. It has often been pointed out that this is a mere social convenience, a convenient way for strangers to break the ice, nothing more than a superficial rhetorical convention. But it may be that all of this casual weather talk ('turned out nice', and so on) has left a deeper imprint on our national personality than this might suggest. It is well understood that it was rain that sculpted the underlying contours of the landscape, creating its lattice of valleys and lakes, ridges and marshes, but our prime position as the lucky recipient of Atlantic rainfall has also been the invisible hand behind our taste in everyday essentials such as clothes, food, and working patterns.

Meteorologists like to talk about the 'hydrological cycle', but there is more to this watery realm than mere chemistry. England's rain has played a major role in the country's history. First of all, when it froze into ice and formed glaciers (as it did periodically for 450,000 years), it had the power to carve out England's scenery. When the ice sheet melted for the last time, nine thousand years ago, it left a land etched with ridges and dales, and not long afterwards the land bridge that had linked

England to continental Europe was submerged. This was when England officially became 'insular' and migrants could no longer stroll in as they pleased. However, the narrow Channel was not enough to keep out some delightful 'native' species (pine, birch, elm, oak, elder, lime and so on), which continued to creep up from the warm south to blossom in the island's new temperate climate.

English society has been ruled by its weather ever since. It determines where people live and how they use the land. We can talk about constitutional, intellectual and social change as much as we like, but underpinning it all lies the straightforward fact of England's position at the meeting point of three weather systems: the Arctic, the African and the North Atlantic. Why would we want to talk about anything else?

The capricious weather created by the fluctuations of these massive air masses has played a starring role in several iconic battles. It was not wind alone that scattered the Armada in 1588, but it certainly played its part. Bad weather kept a French fleet in port in 1798, which gave the Royal Navy just enough time to assemble a much larger force. Dark clouds persuaded Hitler to call off his planned invasion in 1940, while clear skies gave the RAF a clear view of his lumbering bombers. And a fortunate break in the clouds permitted D-Day to go ahead four years later.

One storm had a telling impact in another way. In 1789 a ship called the *Adventure* was stranded half a mile off Tynemouth, and the violent sea drowned the passengers and crew even as spectators watched, helpless, from the shore. Those people resolved to build a special boat for such crises, and launched a design competition, which Henry Greathead won with an unsinkable craft he named *Original*. It was the first purpose-built lifeboat in the world, and the start of a long and heroic story.

The weather is also the reason why English people have tended to congregate in the bottom right-hand corner of the

map. It is often argued that the congestion in the south-east
is due to the magnetic appeal of London as a hub; sometimes
it is attributed to the complacency of the metropolitan elite.
But the early English clustered in precisely the same region
chiefly because it was the most habitable spot – just as Europe's
earliest civilisations flowered in the warm climates of Greece
and Rome, where it was easy to keep warm and dry. The
Domesday Book estimated that there were fewer than five
people per square mile in the northern half of England. Only
in East Anglia, Kent and a few patches of Lincolnshire did the
number exceed fifteen. As late as Tudor times, three-quarters
of the population lived below the line that stretches from the
Severn estuary to the Humber.

Today, it is easy to forget the extent to which central heating, constant hot water, air-conditioning and electric light have
enlarged the zones where people can live in comfort. Similarly,
it is hard to imagine a time when London was a mild and
peaceful paradise, nestling in the woods beside its broad river,
brimful of fish and shining through the trees.

Back then, there was nothing to keep a person warm except
a burning log and a wolf's pelt.

Rainfall provokes a range of contradictory emotions. It is
bounty, refreshing the grass that feeds our wildlife and plants,
warding off drought and famine, cleansing the air of fire and
dust. It is the principal source of almost all life, and it is a lucky
land that has plenty of it. We know this. Yet we dread it, struggle to avoid it, and complain when it catches us out.

As it happens, the last time I visited Seathwaite the sky was
bright and the air was clear. But I could not forget a previous
ramble across the fells, when I spent a long day getting soaked.
It was already pelting down before we set out, so we hummed
and hawed, inspected forecasts, glared at the clouds, consulted
bus timetables and fished out waterproofs before admitting that
we'd just have to grin and bear it. Then we found ourselves

squelching through mud as soft as pudding. Somewhere near Seathwaite I fished a cheese roll from my rucksack, wrung out a long stream of water, then tossed the squishy remains to the ducks that were crouching in the reeds.

On we marched, teeth gritted against a rain that stung our cheeks, seeped into our boots and flowed down our necks.

But after a while, all of a sudden, I stopped hating it, stopped sweeping it from my hair and blinking it out of my eyes. I even stopped wishing it would end. Instead, I experienced the elation of passing a point of no return. All of this dismal water became a splendid balm.

It was exhilarating, and the rugged fells, which until then had seemed menacing, now felt amiable. The lake was pimpled by raindrops and bubbles; leaves glinted; bracken hung dark; birds shivered spray from their tails. The scenery felt drained of its vibrant colours, but the muted palette seemed to glow. The landscape felt like a watercolour softened by a sponge; the earth gave off the aroma of cold stew; a hush settled over the hills. Nothing waved in the breeze; even the sheep were motionless. The water dripped from the trees, plinked on the stones and gurgled in the rills.

At one point we fell in step with some other walkers. One of the fields had become a lake, and there was nothing for it but to wade across. The water was knee deep and the grass streamed like seaweed. I was glad that we would soon be drying out in a pub, but when I shared this thought with one of our new companions and congratulated him for bravely camping (he had a tent on his back), he merely sighed, 'It adds to the difficulty. It adds to the difficulty.' I realised that I was a feeble amateur compared to these hardy souls. Then another thought struck me: I didn't mind *being* wet. Most of my holidays involved swimming; I was a regular in the local pool; and I wallowed in hot baths like a hippo. Being wet was fine by me. What I hated was *getting* wet, and the dread of getting wet.

But at that moment, amid the tranquillity of those sodden hills, I stopped seeing wet weather as 'bad'. How often had I squinted at the sky to see if rain might be approaching, like a meerkat sniffing for predators? I had pored over weather maps, changed plans, fiddled with umbrellas, sprinted for shelter. But as I splashed across that Cumbrian field/lake, dripping like a dog, the metaphorical clouds lifted. I took off my hat and let the rain drum down.

Of course, the pleasures of sunshine and fine scenery are so delightful that we are always dismayed when clouds get in the way. But we should reserve a little reverence for rain, too. Like all things that we take for granted, we would be lost without it. If rain were rare, we would honour it, pray for it, dance in it whenever it arrived. As it is, we brace ourselves against it like ungrateful children.

The most obvious benefit of a rainy climate is that the soil is well watered. But there is a flip side: floods. A land geared up for rain goes into convulsions when it falls too fast or for too long. Rivers swell and burst their banks – and crops drown.

This has been a perpetual feature of English life. There is a media outcry when it happens today, as if someone in the Department of Agriculture has forgotten to place an order for sunshine. But as long ago as 1257 a monk named Matthew Paris observed that rain had ruined that year's crop of wheat, leading to widespread suffering and hunger: 'Whatever had been sown in winter, had budded in spring, and grown ripe in summer, was stifled and destroyed by the autumnal inundations.' Almost seven centuries later, in 1947, England's rivers overflowed in the thaw that followed a particularly snowy winter. Windsor, Gloucester, Shrewsbury and London were all waist deep; the East Anglian fens became a lake, as did the Thames valley; Nottinghamshire was a marsh. The army delivered supplies to upstairs windows by boat, and Canada (which faces the effects of a thaw every year) sent food parcels. No one was surprised – it was typical English weather. Some old-timers said it was nothing compared to the floods of 1894 or 1915. Now *that* was rain.

Holy water: in Tewkesbury (and elsewhere in England) it never rains but it pours.

Rain can be destructive, to be sure. But it has created a priceless by-product: a wonderful transport system. If the sea was England's arterial ring road in medieval times, then the rivers were its veins. Glance at a map and the first things you see are the wriggling lines of water fanning out to estuaries. These rivers are expressions of the land through which they flow – its changing aspects, gradients and geology. The Severn is muddy and the Test clear because the former passes through clay and the latter through chalk. Each brings with it a particular ecology that defines the surrounding countryside: it is said that there are two hundred chalk streams in the world, and half of them are in southern England. But they all share a single element: England's rain. And while some rivers have presented sturdy obstacles, for the most part they have served as silky means of communication. England's small size meant that they formed a close-knit and effective network, even in early times.

They have certainly helped to determine the locations of half the country's towns. Some are positioned near vital raw materials (coal, iron, lead, sheep, salt – the numerous -*wiches* of Cheshire – or seawater). A few are transport hubs. A handful are defensive redoubts. All, however, need fresh running water, whether it is for drinking, irrigating crops or carrying ships. Modern urban planners, with easy access to ring mains, taps and pumps, prefer to emphasise the human factors that drive settlement patterns. But if we run a finger down England's major river systems (on the east the Thames, Humber and Tees; on the west the Severn, Avon[1] and Mersey), we find almost every historic town.

When the Romans elected to fortify Londinium, for instance, they had one eye on its topographical advantages. The original walled settlement was bordered by the uncrossable Thames to the south, the marshes of Moorfields to the north, and several smaller streams, such as the Fleet, which tumbled down from Hampstead Heath to Blackfriars, and the Walbrook, which entered the Thames where Tower Bridge stands today. But these were not merely defensive moats: they provided drinking water, sanitation, power for mills and tanneries; and they were vital highways.

Most of London's smaller rivers are now buried and forgotten, but echoes of the aquatic past linger in place names: Bays*water*, Kil*burn*, Knights*bridge*, Stamford *Brook*, Ty*burn*, Wal*brook* and *Wands*worth (where the River Wandle flowed through Huguenot cloth mills in the seventeenth century). Glance up in Sloane Square underground station and you will see a broad metal tube set into the ceiling. It carries the last trickle of the Westbourne to the Thames at Chelsea, where at low tide the pipe still gapes like a gargoyle in the mud.

1 It is not by chance that there are so many English Avons – *afon* is the Celtic word for river.

This river died when Queen Caroline, the wife of George II, dammed it to create the Serpentine, but there is still a bump in the Bayswater Road where it once passed beneath a bridge. A plaque on St Pancras Old Church, meanwhile, reminds us that Londoners once bathed in the nearby Fleet River, before it became a foul and fetid ditch.

The fact that human settlement requires fresh water is the most obvious of all geographical principles. Every cathedral city has a river running through it, and many of England's county borders follow the lines of waterways. Surrey and Middlesex stand on either side of the Thames, as do Berkshire and Oxfordshire, while the Tees serves as the boundary between Yorkshire and Durham, and the Mersey marks the ancient frontier between Mercia and Northumbria. The old course of the Westbourne still divides two London boroughs, Westminster and Kensington & Chelsea. Indeed, the road that was built above it now has residential parking for one borough on its eastern side and the other on the west.

Many towns began life as inland river ports, including Boston, Chester, Gloucester, Ipswich, Lancaster and York. Others stand on estuaries, among them Bristol, Harwich, Hull, Liverpool, London, Newcastle and Southampton. The drowned valleys of Falmouth, Plymouth, Dartmouth and Grimsby made fine harbours, while river crossings could also grow into historic cities (Ox*ford* and Cam*bridge* spring to mind). In one way or another, England's rivers were a sorting hat, placing people in artful clumps around the country.

Some of them were important sources of energy. The wool-weaving industry could not stray far from running water. Meanwhile, Sheffield grew into the steel capital of the world not only because it was close to a good supply of iron, but because five punchy Pennine streams – the Don, the Loxley, the Porter, the Rivelin and the Sheaf (which gave its name to the city) – delivered all the water the foundries could possibly need. These watercourses were diverted into reservoirs, but they also turned wheels and drove forges. Throw in the fact that a cliff of millstone grit (perfect for knife-grinding) rises nearby and it is clear to see why Sheffield developed in the way that it did. Robert le Coteler was making sharp blades in the town as early as 1297, and Edward III had a Sheffield knife in his apartment in the Tower of London in 1340. Half a century later they were widely celebrated: a character in Chaucer's *Reeve's Tale* keeps one tucked in his belt. There was a Company of Cutlers during the Civil War, by which time Sheffield was manufacturing not just knives but bladed tools of every description: shears, scissors, scythes, sickles ... even ice skates.

The town prospered as the cutlers' reputation grew. A fraternity of craftsmen and merchants – forgers, smiths, grinders, sharpeners, coal men, engravers, handle-makers and so on – honed their skills over several hundred years of small-scale knife-making, so the town was perfectly placed to take full advantage when the Industrial Revolution started to gather pace. In 1743 a local cutler named Thomas Boulsover chanced upon the concept of silver plate. He was struggling to fix the handle of a knife, spilled molten silver on to a patch of exposed copper, watched it fuse and – *bingo!* – Sheffield plate was born.

A single accident put silver spoons into the mouths of England's middle class.

We can trace the importance of water as a location scout in many other places. The highest market town in England, Buxton, stands on a river and is also home to a famous thermal well. These features attracted both the Romans and the Georgians, who turned the place into a spa town (they did the same in Harrogate, Leamington, Cheltenham and elsewhere). As for the cathedral at Wells ... well, the clue is in the name. Meanwhile, some cities have migrated in search of a better supply of water. Roman Salisbury (Sarum) was a hilltop fort, and the Normans occupied the same site, but in the thirteenth century it was decided to build the cathedral at the foot of the hill, where five rivers flowed south. Legend has it that the exact location of the new site was dictated by an arrow shot from the top of Old Sarum; but that is two miles away, so the archer must have had a mighty strong arm. It is rather more likely that a ready supply of clear water was the deciding factor.

York, the country's second city for most of the Middle Ages, straddled the Ouse, and other towns, including Bedford, Boston, Derby, Nottingham, Shrewsbury, Stamford, Warwick and Winchester, achieved prosperity because they were easily accessible by river. The banks of the Severn were thick with monasteries, while Henley could supply London with fruit and vegetables by sending boatloads down the Thames.

The extent to which England's rivers were navigable in the Middle Ages has been much disputed. Some have investigated the numerous conflicts over the obstruction of waterways (with mills, nets and weirs) and concluded that they must have been mostly open prior to human interference, while others have interpreted the same evidence as proof of the exact opposite – that they must have been mostly blocked. What is clear is that while some people wanted the waterways open to river traffic, others wanted to dam or divert them. Nevertheless, although the exact mileage cannot be measured, England certainly had a functioning river network long before it had a good road system, let alone railways.

The English are inclined to disparage sogginess. They look down on anyone deemed 'wet' or a 'drip', and prize 'dry' humour over anything that is 'watered down'. Gardeners and farmers may cheer when the clouds open, but most of us grumble. *Bloody typical!* The poets who write so lyrically about west winds, icicles, autumn mists and shafts of sunlight have little to say about rain. It has never been a muse.

Yet the English are famous for their incessant preoccupation with the subject – to the extent of becoming something of a laughing stock. In truth, though, this is a tribute to the whims and moods of the prevailing climate.[2] Our weather is not actually unpredictable – it follows clear and reliable patterns within the parameters set by winter, spring, summer and autumn – but it is variable. It can rain on one side of a road while the other is bathed in sunshine, be nippy at breakfast and warm at lunch. As the saying goes, we often get all four seasons in one day.

We are so accustomed to the weather's sudden mood swings that we rarely reflect on the ways in which they can affect us, especially as most us now occupy urban areas and spend most of our life indoors.

This has not gone unnoticed. In *England: An Elegy*, Roger Scruton bemoans the way that metropolitan people idealise the countryside without having any great experience of it: 'The landscape where their ancestors dwelled is one they are merely passing through.' England's rural heartland, he complains, has become the domain of weekenders from the city, who hold their noses as they park their sports cars outside the pub. Similarly, Jeremy Paxman, in *The English*, dismisses 'pseudo-cottageyness' – malls tricked up as manors, countryside reduced to mere 'scenery', and commuters who keep their windows shut against the smells and sounds of actual country life. The English rural idyll is a fantasy, a nostalgic delusion. To metropolitan England, the farmer's most important task is to keep the footpaths clear.

One might add that there has often been an ideological component to the veneration of the countryside. It has been sufficiently powerful to persuade young men to sacrifice their lives in its defence. First World War recruiting posters steeled the nation's resolve with images of rural bliss. And when railways and roads allowed the masses to take excursions into the ancient shires, the guidebooks invariably stressed that they were entering the 'real' England. This was a realm of hidden byways, charming – if mystifying – customs, and enchanting hamlets

2 As Dr Johnson said: 'When two Englishmen meet their first talk is of the weather.'

that had lain undisturbed for centuries. The visitors did not care that this was to a great extent a myth. As H. V. Morton's *In Search of England* (1934) put it: 'The village that symbolises England sleeps in the consciousness of many a townsman.'

And yet this remembered England, this rose-tinted ideal, draws on a powerful set of images that continue to cast a stirring spell. The modern urban population may no longer chop its own firewood, help a neighbour deliver a lamb or gather in the harvest, but it knows without thinking to expect blossom in April, cricket in May and strawberries in June. Come autumn there will be dew-lapped mornings and long afternoon shadows, swirls of migrating swallows and bonfires. In winter there will be frost, carol singers in the streets, mince pies and holly. And in the new year we all wait in eager anticipation for the first daffodil.

There may well be joy in the spring when the birds begin to sing in an English country garden . . . but the same is true in suburban gardens too.

Nature may be a church we no longer attend, but its rhythms move us still. ''Tis the hard grey English weather,' wrote Charles Kingsley, author of *The Water Babies*, 'breeds hard English men.' Even now, when we have severed most of our links with the natural world (to the extent that some young Britons no longer know that bacon comes from pigs), the old customs continue to ring through. We only have to glimpse a patch of blue sky between the office blocks, notice blossom from a train, hear birdsong in the back yard, catch the flash of crocuses in the park or the scent of grass on a freshly mown roundabout to feel the stir of something older and more persistent than modern life.

Of all the features of our geographical inheritance, the shape of England's four-season year might be the most influential. It is far from unique (Japan's climate is almost identical, to name just one), but the texture of England's landscape and weather produces flavours that are seen nowhere else. In Tuscany autumn has the heady scent of truffles; in Bordeaux it smells of wine; in Sweden the lingonberries ripen in the woods; in New England the fall enflames the leaves; while Alpine farms collect the last of the year's honey and make cheese for the winter. The English autumn is different from all of these: it is a season of bonfires and windfall apples, pheasants, chestnuts (a Roman import that went native) and blackberries.

The seasons no longer dictate what we eat, what we wear, and what we do. But though we have only a remote connection to such things, the relentless rural obligations of the past – ploughing, feeding and harvesting – designed our mental furniture and continue to affect us even now. Much has been handed down, not least the proverbial sense that we reap what we sow, that to everything there is a season, and that every cloud has a silver lining. The four English seasons planted the winter of our discontent and the darling buds of May deep in the national psyche. They are the reason why we compare people to a summer's day and relish the season of mists and mellow fruitfulness. If it weren't for spring, autumn, summer and winter, we might not plant ideas or wait until the time was ripe before seeing if they have borne fruit. We might not shower each other with gifts, either.

The study of natural rhythms – the emergence of butterflies, the glow of autumn leaves, the ripening of elderberries, the first snowdrop – is called phenology. Its pioneer was Robert Marsham, who in 1736 started to record 'indications of spring' on his estate at Stratton Strawless, north of Norwich. For the rest of his life, he kept a tireless eye out for new foliage and fresh insects, and when he died his family continued his work. One of their findings – that oak trees came into leaf a week earlier in 1950 than they had in 1850 – became one of the founding facts of a new scientific field: climate change. Marsham planted two million trees on his land, many of which were felled for timber in the two world wars. However, one – a great cedar he planted in 1747 – provides a living connection with that first patient attempt to tabulate the seasons.

Marsham is not much known today, though there is a memorial to him in the village church. He is the kind of determined eccentric for which England is known the world over: one of his diary entries records the fact that 'the urine in my chamber-pot froze to a cake under my bed four nights successively'. But the millions of viewers who settle down to watch *Springwatch* each year are in a quiet way honouring the memory of his first, earnest researches and connecting with nature in a broadly similar way. Even urbanites revel in the knowledge that rain is on the way when the swallows are swooping low or the petals of the scarlet pimpernel are closing.

John Ruskin once remarked that there is no such thing as bad weather, only different sorts of good weather. This has recently been updated into the assertion that there is no such thing as bad weather, only the wrong clothes. Either way, the changeable nature of our skies remains a central feature of England's everyday life.

In the old days, a wise man always carried a cloak in fair weather. Today, we carry umbrellas, just in case.

Is it going too far to suggest that England's particular climate and landscape had such detailed consequences? Perhaps. But it is hard not to feel that the moody climate did inculcate certain reflexes in the English mind. Our ancestors had to keep a 'weather' eye on the sky, since no one could be sure, from one hour to the next, what it might bring. People knew they had to be flexible, since the weather would decide which chore was most pressing. Only when the sun shone could farmers even think of making hay.

Yet we were stoic too, because we knew that into each life a little rain must fall. So the wheat was harvested when it was dry, the fields were ploughed and seed scattered when the earth was damp, and the roof was fixed before the winter storms arrived.

The sheer changeability of our weather meant that previous generations had little time for – or faith in – absolutes or generalities. A farmer on one side of a hill might be harvesting while one on the other was drenched by a deluge.

English men and women had to pay close attention to the shifting rural scene. They knew that there would be no frost when the corn was higher than a crow, that one swallow did not make a summer, and that rain was on the way if cows slapped their tails, bulls licked their hooves, dogs ate grass, donkeys rubbed gates, spiders fell from their webs or pigs' tails straightened. Even today, shopkeepers stock up with beef when the barometer dips, prawns when sunshine is on the horizon.

But though the weather was scarcely ever stable enough to promote idle confidence that a task could be left till tomorrow, it was not so extreme that people viewed the elements as angry gods. The English seasons inspired neither resignation nor terror. Our ancestors may have developed a passion for grumbling, but they only rarely had cause to panic. The famous English *sang-froid* or stiff upper lip may well have developed out of a meteorological tic.

Our ancestors were seasonal beings: they slept longer and worked less in the dark winter months, emulating the hibernating creatures in their fields and woods. Of course, today we are better insulated against changes in the weather, but vestiges of the old reflexes linger on.

The weather may even have played a part in colouring the English attitude to financial risk: the misery of the long, cold, wet winter months was usually recouped the following summer in an annual cycle of investment and return.

And it has certainly dripped into the famous English sense of humour. In *Watching the English*, Kate Fox suggests that comedy has long been valued as a central plank of English culture – she calls it 'the importance of not being earnest' – and charts the ways in which irony, understatement and self-deprecation have been revered down the generations. This has had some surprising consequences: in England, poking fun has become a highly respected form of truth-telling, while sincerity is rendered a pose. Would we have evolved in this way if the weather had not continually made a mockery of our best-laid plans? A sudden downpour does not discriminate between a fishwife and a duchess – they both get soaked, while the rest of us laugh. The weather pricks pomposity and brings braggarts 'down to earth'. Fox goes so far as to suggest that the national catchphrase could be 'Oh, come off it!', but she might have mentioned that another common expression – 'Typical!' – performs the opposite function. The English may chuckle at what divides them, but they are equally likely to raise a comradely eyebrow in the face of life's little mishaps.

England's climate may have moulded the emotional life of its people in a larger sense, too. The mutable seasons and local micro-climates have combined to create a nuanced world that encourages flexibility. But beneath those minor variations the insistent drumbeat of an annual cycle promoted a powerful awareness of mortality and fate. Time, in England, has always moved on, with a scythe in its hand and a wallet at its back.

The symmetrical rhythm of country life, meanwhile, swinging every six months between winter and summer, presented people with constant parables of life and death. This was true in every European country, of course, but it was especially pronounced in England due to the incessant lapping of the sea against its long and sinuous coast. Anyone who lived near the shore, as most English men and women did, had a deep sense of the rise and fall of the tide, coming and going, ebbing and flowing, growing and dying.

The real surprise would be if the landscape and climate had *not* had a lasting impact on English manners. In *The Mayor of Casterbridge*, Thomas Hardy had this to say of Wessex folk: 'The farmer's income was ruled by the wheat crop, and the wheat crop by the weather.' He was 'a sort of flesh barometer, with feelings always directed to the sky and wind'. George Santayana agreed, adding that the Englishman always carried his weather with him, and somehow managed even to make his own 'cool spot in the desert'.

Mercury continues to run through English veins. We still sense dark clouds in even the sunniest sky.

Seven

Our Daily Bread

O ne can tell a lot about a nation's culture by looking at its preferred carbohydrate. And the English have always been flour people (rice and maize are relatively recent interlopers). Ever since the first gatherers ground grains between rocks, or noticed the way leftovers cooked on hot stones, wheat has been the basis of the national diet. The combination of English soil and Atlantic weather, so perfect for sheep-rearing, was ideal for growing wheat, too. The repercussions have been immense. Bread, pastry, cakes, tarts, pies, puddings, biscuits and scones: cooked wheat has been our soul food for centuries. Modern England gets through ten million loaves every day, and its favourite television programme is a baking contest.

Carbohydrates are important because, compared to protein-rich meat and dairy, they are cheap, providing cost-effective bulk for hungry mouths. England's population stood at just over a million at the time of the Domesday Book.[1] Today it is sixty times that, and wheat – mostly kneaded and baked into bread, the staff of life – has fuelled the increase. In 1762 the Earl of Sandwich gave his name to a new snack by slapping a wedge of meat between two slices of bread during a card game. This

---

1 This is not a scientific figure, merely the best guess. The Domesday Book is a precious survey, but not a census. Significant parts of the country were overlooked, and the methodology, though impressive for the time, was rough and ready by today's standards. Some estimates put the population at a million, others at closer to two.

was not mere ingenuity. It was a gambit inspired by the nature of English loaves, which could be easily carved. A French duke with his baguette, an Italian count with his focaccia, or a German prince with his pumpernickel, would have struggled to do such a thing no matter how hungry he was.

Ancient England was covered with thick forest, with smoke curling out of the few small clearings where people lived, and not much space for arable farming. But the clearings began to grow as the trees were felled for timber, the woodland receded, and the open countryside we know today was born. Much of this work had been done by the Middle Ages, and steady rain on the old forest floor had created strong, rich soil. England did not produce a uniform grain on endless, sun-kissed prairies. Only in the south was the weather warm enough for the gluten-rich wheat that made the softest bread. The area to the north and west of the Severn-Humber line was dominated by shorter, tougher crops, such as barley and oats, which needed less sunlight and were not so vulnerable to wind.

But the country was made for grass. Even in Roman times, while Scotland and Wales remained wild, it was a granary.

The Romans favoured spelt, a low-gluten crop (not that they knew it) that was common in ancient Greece and thrived on the well-drained chalk fields of Sussex and Wiltshire. The grain was kept dry in well-ventilated granaries, then transported on fine, straight roads. However, it produced a relatively low yield of flour, so it gradually gave way to wheat, in the mild southern regions at least. Otherwise, though, the land-use map of England changed little in the next two thousand years.

Wheat, along with water and wool, became the third great 'w' in English life.

Wheat is one of nature's miracles. It contains sixteen billion pairs of DNA, forty times more than rice, and this has allowed it to evolve from the early Mesopotamian strains – einkorn and emmer – into the numerous varieties we eat today. There were many hybrids of wheat, barley, rye and millet even by the time of the pharaohs, and they spread rapidly to Europe. The early farmers favoured emmer because the grains were tightly packed at the top of each stalk, making them easy to harvest.

It is extremely adaptable: it can be pounded, kneaded and cooked in a hundred different ways.

No one knows when the first wheat germinated in England. Marine archaeologists have found traces of wheat DNA on the seabed off the Isle of Wight, and other scientists believe it may have arrived in England up to eight thousand years ago, just before the land that connected Kent to Europe flooded. Whenever and wherever wheat arrived, though, it flourished. It needed both water and sunshine, so it adored England's variable weather; the tall stalks made it simple to harvest; it could be mashed into food with ease; and the straw was useful too. Over time, English wheat developed larger ears, with swollen grains that could be threshed and winnowed even more efficiently. Then the simple addition of water transformed the flour into dough. Early English bread was dark and barley based (and used as a semi-edible plate), but the bran was sieved out as soon as milling techniques improved. The result was the white, fluffy loaf that has been a national favourite ever since.

And once England discovered pie crust, a flour-based future was assured.

The most important of wheat's qualities was the length of its growing season. This had a direct impact on English society. Life in primitive times was semi-nomadic – people lived off their sheep and goats, moving around as the mood and the weather took them, foraging for fish and fruit as they went. But wheat turned England into a land of stay-at-homes. As has been said, people may have domesticated animals, but wheat domesticated people – by encouraging them to put down roots. England became a land of villages, with crops grown around huts and barns that were built to last (a novel idea in itself). The villagers began to plan ahead, too. They would plough the fields and scatter in winter, then harvest the wheat in summer. An air of permanence began to colonise the nation's psyche, as well as its waistline. England has been a nation of millers and bakers ever since; a land of pork pies, apple turnovers, suet puddings, cakes, rolls and tarts. Wheat has long been the central ingredient in our cuisine. It symbolises our countryside, and plays an important ceremonial role in many of our cherished rituals – christenings, birthdays, weddings. When we celebrate, we say it in wheat.

Some wheat products have names that betray their origins: Cornish pasties, Eccles cakes, Bakewell tarts, Cumberland pies, Bath buns and Yorkshire pudding. Other names are more fluid. The hot cross bun, for instance, dates back to the Middle Ages, when a monk in St Albans decided to make a sacred Easter roll – the 'one-a-penny, two-a-penny, hot cross buns' immortalised in the nursery rhyme. But in Victorian times that cake became known as a 'Good Friday bun', after the day on which it was baked. The latter name clung on well into the twentieth century, but in 1972 the *Daily Telegraph* received a grumpy letter complaining that the 'traditional' Good Friday bun had been cruelly stripped of its one-a-penny, two-a-penny *raison d'être* because it would now cost two and a half 'new pence'.[2] A pun-minded sub-editor ran the letter under the headline 'Hot and Cross', and in one quick thud of a printing press the traditional name was reborn.

Bread's principal ingredients (grain and water) were so plentiful in England that they could almost be taken for granted. Moreover, as luck would have it, the third vital component – yeast – grew naturally on leftover broth. It had a miraculous aerating effect on heavy dough, transforming it into wonderfully light bread. And that was not the end of its magical properties. Crumble a few dots of yeast into a jar of grain-flavoured water and a few days later you had a morale-boosting

2 Britain had adopted decimalisation the previous year.

drink: ale. Then skim the yeasty scum off that jar of ale and you could raise bread all over again. It was like the beans in Jack and the Beanstalk: the more yeast you used, the more you had.

There could hardly have been a more momentous coincidence of English flavours. The yeast that grew on old grain, mixed with fresh-milled wheat and the bright water that gushed from England's springs, created not just the daily wedge of bread, but the national drink. When Sir Toby Belch railed against the puritanical idea that there might be 'no more cakes and ale' in the world envisioned by Malvolio, he was giving voice to a profound English conviction that these were staples, not treats. He was also sketching out the silhouette of everyday English conviviality, which has always relied on the same humble trinity of raw ingredients: wheat, water and yeast.

The fruits of this alliance have inspired endless English nights out, many swift pints on the way home, and a thousand beery heroes from Falstaff to Flintoff.

They also gave birth to that most English setting: the pub.

It is no coincidence that the first food regulations in English history concerned bread and ale. Henry III's Assize of 1266 established a law governing the size of a standard loaf (measured in multiples of fourteen ounces) that survived until 2008. In the Middle Ages most English subjects could count on two pounds of wheat (enough for a single loaf) and a gallon of ale (brewed with malted barley) every day. If this sounds a lot, we must remember that the ale was weak (small beer) and fresh water not always easy to come by. There were clear class differences in the English diet, however: only the wealthy could afford moist white bread; the poor had to make do with heavy rye loaves lightened with chalk. But bread and ale, along with bakeries and breweries, were ubiquitous.

In Chaucer's day yeast was known as 'goddisgoode' – a mysterious gift from the Almighty. Earlier, the Anglo-Saxon word for it had been *gist* – the hidden meaning at the heart of baking and brewing.[3] Its actual properties were not fully understood until Louis Pasteur established that it lived in the bloom on the skin of grapes. But long before then bakers knew from experience that they should keep back one lump of sour dough to raise the next batch. Theirs not to reason why: it may have been baffling, but it worked every time.

Wheat, like wool, is central to England's sense of itself. It is the root of many familiar surnames (Baker, Miller, Granger, Hay and so on), while the hay rick, the corn dolly, the harvest festival and the crop circle have long been archetypes of our pastoral world. Our kitchens, our stomachs, our food and our drink are all founded squarely on the annual wheat crop.

It has also inspired a host of everyday sayings: when we are not bringing home Great Dunmow's bacon we might earn a crust or hope to make some dough. We acknowledge the folly of the biblical sower, who cast his seed on stony ground, while knowing how to value a grain of truth, how to search for a needle in a haystack, and we understand that half a loaf is better than no bread. We mock the upper crust, look askance at half-baked plans, and depict Death as the 'Grim Reaper', harvesting souls with his sharpened scythe. For centuries, English Christians asked God to give them this day their daily bread. Wheat put not just consecrated food in their mouths, but sacred language too.[4] Open Gilbert White's *Natural History of Selborne* at almost any page and you will find plenty of crop news: 'The ears are very long ... sweet harvest weather ... much wheat still abroad ... wheat spoiled' and so forth.

Arable farming is often seen as an idyllic contrast to the Industrial Revolution, a traditional way of life not yet

3 It is only thanks to an orthographic shift that we do not ask long-winded speakers to stop rambling and get to the yeast of the matter.

4 Just as there were class differences in the gulf between white and dark bread, so there was a theological schism over which bread to use during the sacrament. The Eastern Churches insisted on leavened bread, while the Catholic Church preferred an unleavened 'wafer'. Protestant Churches were happy to use either.

supplanted by machinery. But it did much to 'sow the seeds' of the changes that lay ahead. Grinding wheat by hand was painful, tedious work, so people had long employed beasts of burden to turn their mills. But, as luck would have it, England had an even better source of power rushing through the countryside every day, in the form of its rivers and streams; and the hills were full of boulders that could be turned into millstones.

With one spin of the wheel, England became a land powered by water.

At the time of the Norman Conquest there were already some 5624 water mills in the southern region alone. By 1300, there were twice as many. They were not an English invention – they were common in Byzantium, Egypt, Greece and Rome (Tunisia had one in the third century), but England was so awash with trickling water that mills were soon a common sight: every village dipped a wheel or two into the stream to harness nature, and turn wheat into flour.

One of England's oldest working water mills is in Eskdale, not far from Seathwaite, on the edge of a village called Boot. Corn has been ground in this green valley for two thousand years, but the 'new' mill, like so much else in this story, dates to the last decade of the thirteenth century – 1294. Standing on a beck that begins its journey on Scafell Pike, the mill is driven by the 'overshot' method – water flows along a narrow flume to the top of the wheel, so gravity accelerates the flow. One of the original stones, a five-foot monster hewn from a quarry near Lancaster, remains, but it has not been used for centuries. Finer-grained stones were imported from France and Germany to produce lighter flour.

This fact implies another. The transport system must have been highly sophisticated when the decision was made to order these new stones from the continent. A five-foot millstone weighs at least a ton, and it has to be carefully 'dressed' (scored with grooves) to produce the required grind. Importing them was a major project, impossible on the roads of the day.

Once again, we see the value of England's navigable rivers and saltwater ring road. Not to mention the lengths the English would go to for a soft, white loaf.

On the southern edge of the New Forest, not far from Corfe Castle, stands another old mill. In Norman times this area was a royal park – William Rufus was killed hunting here – and echoes linger of the foggy days when people could graze cattle, horses and pigs in the woods. But though the New Forest feels unspoiled, it is actually a monument to human interference. It was turned into a heath by foresters. The mill touches Southampton Water near the village of Totton. With its shopping precinct, marina, sixth-form college, cricket club and industrial estate, the village feels more like a suburb these days, part of the Southampton sprawl. And yet, like everywhere else in England, history lies just beneath the surface. New Forest ponies roamed through Totton's streets until 1967, when a fence was installed to keep them out, and the tidal mill is one of only two that still turns (the other is in Woodbridge, Suffolk). Housed in a row of brick cottages on a causeway over the water, it has become a local tourist attraction – a working museum.

There was a mill here in the Domesday account, and today's incarnation uses the same system to turn its twelve-foot wheel. Twice a day the tide surges up the estuary, forcing water into a holding pond, then a sluice releases the jet that spins the wheel. Governed by the tides, it turns for two five-hour bursts each day, but that was sufficient for Winchester College, which used it for centuries. On a good day it could produce ten tons of flour, more than enough to keep the school well fed.

There were 200 of these tide mills in medieval England. The £1.3 billion project to extract tidal power from Swansea Bay, announced in 2016, works on very much the same principle.

But if mills were an essential feature of English life, millers were not universally loved. The one who appears in the *Canterbury Tales* is a slobbering oaf with a red beard, black nostrils, gaping jaws and a hairy wart on his nose. A wrestler, he bashes down doors with his head, adulterates his flour with cheap ballast, then overcharges for it. It is sometimes argued that this is no more than a patronising depiction of working-class manners, but the miller actually stood a rung or two above those on which his customers laboured, so Chaucer probably had a different intention: he wanted to portray his miller as a villain, not an oik. Millers took a percentage of every sack of grain they turned into flour, which made them richer than most of the farmers they served. So, while they were not quite in the merchants' league, they were certainly much better off than peasants.

The miller also ran the village bakery. This monopoly position allowed him to 'add value' to his flour by turning it into bread. Setting himself up as a middleman, he was able to pocket a tidy sum. The principles of capitalism began to weave their way into English life, and the miller gained an entry into the modern economy of cash and coins. Unsurprisingly, he was often resented, and rarely trusted. He could not even count to twelve: a baker's dozen often contained an extra roll. Chaucer pressed the point home by making another crooked miller the villain of his next story, the *Reeve's Tale*. A boastful trickster who skims off his customers' grain, he finally gets his comeuppance at the hands of a pair of lusty students from Cambridge.

But a miller's life was by no means easy. In fact, it was hot and dangerous. Those whirling stones could tear off a careless arm at any moment; that racing wheel could dash a man's brains out. In those superstitious days it was easy to see the mill as a living creature, and if anyone died in a milling accident the guilty stone was retired – cut into a tablet to commemorate the man it had killed. Yet within that swirl of sweat and dust lay a force that would change the world. Millers supervised a roaring chaos of cogs, wheels, rods, camshafts, gears, pulleys, ropes and couplings. They lived among contraptions made from wood, stone, iron and leather, all of which demanded constant maintenance. Milling therefore served as a broad introduction to almost all the engineering challenges that lay ahead.

It also opened England's eyes to the awesome power of water, whether in the form of a bright river, an irresistible tide or a divine force. Some of the biggest mills were operated by monasteries – Tewkesbury Abbey's was especially grand – and Bernard of Clairvaux observed that the rivers which ran through *his* abbeys were instruments of God, surging past mills, sloshing into brew houses, and driving the hammers of the cloth-working yard and the blacksmith's shed. Wherever it gushed, this torrent of holy water left 'a blessing behind for its faithful service'. In time, people learned that this miracle could be channelled and deployed in other ways, too: it could smash limestone into powdery cement, crunch animal feed, chop wood or blow air through bellows into forges.

Chaucer's pilgrims rode through a country that had as many mills as villages; the larger settlements often boasted several. There were more mills than churches. So, while it is hard to imagine what medieval England felt like, we can at least imagine what it sounded like – the whirring creak of a water mill was the background music in every valley, all day, every day, as integral to the English scene as birdsong or the bleating of lambs. It was as if the whole country were gearing up, like some giant clockwork toy, for the industrial trials ahead.

One small example: English bread may have created the English bread knife. It had a serrated edge that could carve clean slices from a soft, white loaf, a quality not needed in lands where bread was broken rather than sliced. London's Victoria and Albert Museum has one of these knives in its collection. More than 120 years old, the handle is shaped like a head of maize, and the blade is engraved with an image of children sowing wheat.

England's water was not always benevolent. Although the country was spared nature's most violent catastrophes – earthquakes or tsunamis – rain could wreck a harvest if it fell too heavily or at the wrong time. When Edward II visited St Albans in 1315 there was no bread in the town, even for the royal table. The entire wheat crop had been lost, leading to the Great Famine.

There were other calamitous failures, but the occasional country-wide write-off did not affect English farming as much as the smaller, local fluctuations – the seasonal or daily variations. These obliged growers and traders to develop supple reflexes. They had to adjust both their expectations and their prices in line with every twist and turn of barometric pressure. A late frost, an early heatwave, a sudden downpour or a furious gale might send tremors through the market. The mills, granaries, bake houses, delivery systems and shops were all active players in the formation of a dynamic new economy.

A shortage of milk might mean no fancy cakes; a poor wheat harvest might result in chalky loaves; a high wind might ruin the apple crop. But the teeming variety of England's rural scene meant there were usually alternatives. Most villagers knew how to catch a fish, trap a rabbit, poach a deer or forage for berries. England was a bountiful larder, well stocked in any weather.

And it was small enough to survive most setbacks. A drought in one region might be offset by a shower elsewhere. Even individual farms had shadings: the low field might be flooded while the top one was as dry as a bone. To live in England, you had to be adaptable.

Let us briefly jump forward seven hundred years, to a modern miller's tale on the edge of London, at Chorleywood. The name suggests a vanished forest, and the golf club has a deer on its crest, but there are not many trees here now. This is the buckle of the commuter belt. Its most prominent feature is the M25, a six-lane monster that howls past west London. The town centre is the familiar blend of budget grocers', estate agents, charity shops and Chinese restaurants. It lies at the end of John Betjeman's much-loved Metropolitan Line, and

William Penn was married here before heading west to give his name to a whole new colony – Pennsylvania.[5]

Push a little further, however, and there is something more significant. For this was once the home of the British Baking Industries Research Association. This august organisation no longer exists, but in 1960 it was the beating heart of a major revolution. In an initiative funded jointly by the post-war government and three milling and baking conglomerates (Allied Bakeries, Rank–Hovis–Macdougall and Spillers), a crack team of 130 food scientists were brought to Chorleywood and told to invent a new sort of bread.

During the Second World War England had been forced to survive on the so-called 'national loaf' – a weak pudding beefed up with calcium and vitamins. There was no alternative even in the years of austerity that followed, when bacon, butter, potatoes, sugar and meat all continued to be tightly rationed, and the only cheese was 'government cheddar'. As English society returned to something approaching normality, there was a pressing need for a mass-produced bread that was tasty, reliable and cheap. This was where Chorleywood came in.

In retrospect, the venture seems mock-heroic. While America was assembling its best brains to shoot for the moon, England was inviting its boffins to come up with a cheaper slice of toast. Yet in some ways the Chorleywood experiment did resemble NASA, or the code-breaking mathematicians on the other side of the Chilterns at Bletchley Park. The scientists shared data and pursued their quest tirelessly, testing new ingredients in new combinations, using innovative machines, and formulating novel ideas.

In the end, they solved the puzzle by turning to the greatest English commodity of all – extra water. They added yeast, slipped in a few additives, then mixed the dough at high speed

5 It is not the town that time forgot, however. On the contrary, a 2016 study judged nearby Amersham to be the most ethnically integrated and multicultural community in England.

with strong paddles. Instead of taking all night to prove, the dough could be whipped into shape in a matter of minutes. Indeed, the boffins boasted that they could turn a sack of wheat into a loaf of bread in less than four hours. The end result was a scientific miracle: a white loaf that was light, springy, could be delivered ready-sliced, and lasted for ever.

Even more amazing, the process required less flour than the old method. And it seemed to work well with English wheat.[6] The loaves were a bit tough at first, but the boffins solved that by adding ascorbic acid (vitamin C). This gave the bread a squishy quality that mimicked freshness. It was an illusion, but who cared?

Just add water: essence of England, ready-sliced.
© Shutterstock

The fact that the bread was of dubious nutritional value was beside the point. It was perfect mass-market fodder – ideal for the shelves of the supermarkets that were springing up all over the land. Coinciding as it did with the emergence of the electric toaster, Chorleywood's sliced white bread soon spread across England like a blanket of snow.

Sliced bread, went the joke, was the best thing since bread!

By 1965, a quarter of England's bread was made in this way.

6 One motivation for the project was to reduce Britain's reliance on imported North American wheat.

Today, despite a recent rise in the number of artisan bakeries, more than three-quarters of our loaves are still produced using the Chorleywood method. It is a dazzling success story.

The bread itself never impressed the elite, though. The food writer Elizabeth David called the scientists 'make-believe bakers', while medical experts went even further and said that their product was 'harmful to the body ... not even fit to be given away'. As a result, the men who led the task force – Norman Chamberlain and Bill Collins – were never hailed as heroes; no one said they had the 'right stuff'. On the contrary, their new technique was not seen as a breakthrough but as a reckless short cut. Indeed, ever since, there have been whispers that the boom in gluten intolerance may be related to the amount of Chorleywood bread that the nation consumes.

The day when the first batch emerged from a commercial oven was certainly a bad one for the small baker. There were 24,000 such businesses in 1918, but only 4500 by 1982. Progress doesn't take prisoners.

We can skip over the history of English bread, although it is a good one: the crusts that were used as 'trenchers' (or plates) in the Middle Ages; the fact that the Great Fire of London began in a bakery on Pudding Lane; the brick ovens of the eighteenth century; the Victorians' penny loaves; the rise of fancy treats before the First World War. But there is no denying the pivotal role that Chorleywood's scientists played in this story, for they transformed England's most basic foodstuff.

Yet few of the millions of people who spread butter on their Chorleywood toast, bite into Chorleywood sandwiches and dip Chorleywood soldiers into boiled eggs have the least idea where it all began.

Whether bread begat beer or beer begat bread is an archaeological conundrum that goes back thousands of years, long before anyone was taking notes. But we do know that the natives of what became England enjoyed a drink well before the English arrived as migrant settlers from Central Europe and Scandinavia. The Viking mead hall fitted snugly into the island lifestyle – King Edgar ordered the closure of the kingdom's ale houses in a bid to encourage temperance, but few of his subjects listened – and William of Malmesbury was asserting that the English drank too much as early as the twelfth century. Beer bellies have been a national characteristic for well over a thousand years.

The English have long had a taste for other drinks, too. In 1374, when Edward III was casting around for the perfect birthday gift for Geoffrey Chaucer, he settled on just the thing: a gallon of wine a day for the rest of the poet's life. No wonder he never got round to finishing the *Canterbury Tales*.

But ale was the favoured tipple, because it was a by-product of the barley that filled England's fields. Grain was left to rot for a while ('malted'), then fermented in water. It could be either strong or weak and soon became the nation's standard, everyday drink, slaking thirsts at breakfast, lunch, tea and any point in between.

As with wool, the monasteries led the way, establishing brew houses in their marvellous compounds. It goes without saying that they did not have to look far for water, and the temperate climate was ideal for storing grain without it drying out.

The ale they produced not only quenched thirsts; it also provided much-needed calories. And apothecaries swore by it.

As with every large-scale business, the Crown soon demanded a share of the proceeds. At first the money was raised by 'granting' (i.e. selling) brewing licences, but this proved unworkable – there were too many small brew houses to operate it as a state monopoly. So in 1267 tax-collecting 'assizes' were introduced for both bread and ale. By 1309, London alone had 354 registered taverners and 1330 ale suppliers. Oxford was a brewing capital, too. Indeed, the city's trade was supervised by the university. Even then, drinking and scholarship went hand in hand.

As did ale and bread. Stale bread was toasted on a fire, then dipped in ale to soften it again. And hey presto – a toast!

Ale became beer when Dutch weavers brought a strange sour fruit across the Channel and introduced England to the process of 'hopping'. As well as adding a distinctive 'bitter' flavour, the hops acted as a preservative: they kept beer fresh for weeks, allowing it to be brewed and transported in bulk. This transforming development in English brewing retained its foreign accent for quite a while. At the end of the fourteenth century hopped beer was imported from Bremen and Hamburg, and immigrants continued to play a major role in domestic brewing. In 1574, before Shakespeare arrived in London, half of the city's breweries were said to be run by 'aliens'. By the next decade, the twenty-six largest breweries in the capital were producing some twenty-two million gallons every year. It wasn't only the navy, or the wind, that saw off the Armada – it was beer, and drunken sailors.

And it didn't stop there. The development of intensive farming techniques, the diversion of ever more rivers to feed the mills' booming demand for power, the rapid growth of the population and new outbreaks of plague made fresh drinking water increasingly hard to find. Small beer was the answer. In 1695 perhaps a quarter of England's total spending went on beer. By 1700 the country's 200 breweries were producing a total of 180,000 barrels each year. A century later just five London breweries churned out 3.5 million barrels.

As the Prince Regent (the future George IV) remarked: 'Beer and beef have made us what we are.' His words live on today in the nation's enthusiasm for roast beef lunches, steak and ale pies and beefburgers.

Prince George should really have mentioned gin, too. In an attempt to persuade the people of England to give up French brandy, William III actively encouraged the manufacture of a home-grown alternative. The Dutch were noted gin wizards at the end of the seventeenth century, but England was well supplied with the crucial ingredient: juniper berries. One of the first plants to colonise England when the glaciers retreated after the last Ice

Age, juniper is a small, hardy conifer, and its bluish berries can be distilled with water to make a bright and spicy spirit.

Unfortunately, William's strategy worked almost too well. Within a few generations the drink had earned the nickname 'mother's ruin' because the English were downing it by the pint, if not the gallon. William Hogarth depicted its depraved effects in his etchings of London's Gin Lane (near Tottenham Court Road). The following century, it was discovered that the spirit mixed particularly well with quinine-flavoured sparkling water to make a very palatable defence against malaria. A world-famous English cliché was born: the gin and tonic.

Nowhere was England's water sweeter than in Burton-on-Trent. The layer of sand and gravel in this part of the Trent valley filtered the river as it flowed through the Midlands, so the water was unusually rich in magnesium, sulphates and other minerals. Ale was first brewed at the nearby abbey in 1295 (that vigorous decade yet again). But the magic had begun far earlier, when the cool waters of the upper Trent had supposedly effected a famous cure. The story was that an Irish nun named Modwen paused on her pilgrimage to Rome, took a liking to an island in the river, and ended up staying for seven years. When a dying boy was brought to see her she revived him with water from the island's spring; and when that boy grew up to become Alfred the Great the nun's magical grotto became Modwen's Well. The abbey was founded in her honour, and the monks began to make beer there. Before long, many more travellers were breaking their journeys in Burton. There were forty-six brewers in the town by 1604, and their beer was drunk as far afield as London.

When industry came, it lifted brewing in Burton to a different level. Coke's emergence as a cleaner form of coal produced a beer that was lighter and fresher than before. The upper reaches of the Trent had never been navigable – there were too many weirs and mill races for barges to make their way so far upstream. But in 1712 the river was opened up with a new system of locks and cuts, and suddenly Burton could trade directly with Nottingham, Hull and all points east. After the completion of the Trent–Mersey canal a few decades later Burton beer began to make its way to Liverpool and Bristol, too. Before long, the whole world was its oyster.

And it was all thanks to the flood of water flowing from Stoke to Hull. England's third-longest river brought Burton barley from Norfolk and hops from Kent and Worcestershire; it provided the main ingredient for the beer itself;[7] and it was the route along which the end product was sent to many markets. In 1750, a mere 740 barrels were dispatched in this way; twenty-five years later, it was more than 11,000. Burton ale was said to be especially popular in St Petersburg.

The biggest character in the Burton success story was William Bass. A Leicester man who inherited his father's carting business, lugging freight around the Midlands, his rise up the commercial ladder began in 1756 when he married the daughter of a London publican. Nine years later, the haulage business had done well enough for the couple to buy a spacious brick house on the High Street. Fortunately, a malthouse was included in the sale, and Bass decided to try his hand at brewing. He clearly had a knack for it. A hundred years later the brewery that bore his name was churning out a million barrels a year. The top brand, Pale Ale, was the British Empire's favourite drink. Its emblem, a red triangle, became the nation's first ever registered trademark.

A few bottles of Bass even made their way on to the marble counter in Manet's *A Bar at the Folies-Bergère*. It was fashionable, even in Paris, to sip English beer.

The fast-flowing water that spun the medieval water mills began to play an even bigger role in England's economy after

7 The water was not lifted straight from the river, but sucked from boreholes. This was just as well, because pollution from the Potteries upriver made Trent water undrinkable for decades.

the mercantile class had a bright idea. Why settle for being mere fleece suppliers, vulnerable to price fluctuations in Italy and Flanders, when England had all it needed to manufacture cloth itself and profit from both sides of the wool trade? After the expulsion of the Jews in 1290 – and the instant evaporation of what had been a reliable cache of taxable wealth – the Crown also began to see the wisdom of encouraging a domestic textile industry.

English people had been spinning and weaving in their own homes for centuries, but now the plan was to turn their endeavours into a thriving cottage industry that would generate bolts of cloth for export as well as healthy tax revenues for Edward I (he needed funds for his military campaigns in Wales, Scotland and France). The Flemish weavers who crossed the Channel with their hops did not wander to England by accident. Edward made a point of inviting 'divers foreign craftsmen' to teach his compatriots the necessary skills and boost the domestic industry. The migrants from Bruges and Ypres received royal protection and settled in the towns of Kent and East Anglia, where they produced fine cloth with the help of local apprentices.

Edward III extended his grandfather's policy when he came to the throne. He may have been prompted by his Flemish wife (Philippa of Hainault), but above all he wanted to fund his martial ambitions. War with France was looming, and though no one thought it would continue for more than a hundred years, it would clearly be costly. So more skilled weavers were lured from Flanders to 'exercise their mysteries' in England. One of them, John Kempe, arrived in 1331 with the King's guarantee and a statute promising 'fair treating'. The 'letters patent' attaching to this case still feature in legal textbooks as ground-breaking examples of patent law.

Not everyone was delighted by the new arrivals – Londoners happily smashed Flemish looms – but they kept coming, drawn by the commercial opportunities in England. They followed their predecessors to East Anglia and Kent and started making 'new draperies'. In Norwich some four thousand 'aliens' set about turning the town into a world-class cloth capital. By 1350, its market had a busy, cosmopolitan, multilingual flavour, as continental merchants jostled for business in the alleyways.

England would never be the same again. That cosmopolitan flavour would remain a notable national characteristic, however often and how keenly it was denied or resented. Up to the end of the thirteenth century, the country had primarily been a pastoral realm of sheep and shepherds. Now it was fast becoming the weaving heart of Europe.[8] By the end of the fifteenth century, English cloth production had increased ninefold – surely the most significant economic development in the late medieval world.

Across the Channel in Flanders, the disappearance of so much talent and expertise was a severe blow – it was a medieval brain drain. Ypres had three to four thousand weavers in 1400; a century later it had fewer than a hundred. And the migration of the town's artisans represented not just a transfer of labour but the departure of a significant social class – cottage industrialists. The Flemish weavers were calculating business people who moved to England to make the most of a golden opportunity. English fleeces were more expensive in Antwerp than they were in Norwich (due to the taxes levied on wool exports), so it made perfect sense to cross the sea with a loom and get weaving.

The wool trade with Flanders had another potent ramification: it was one of the chief causes of the Hundred Years War. In 1337 the Flanders wool lobby asked England to protect it from possible French assault. Edward III needed no second invitation. The resulting conflict then persuaded many more cloth workers from both Flanders and indeed northern France

---

8 The arrival of the Flemish weavers is the subject of a substantial work by the Pre-Raphaelite artist Ford Madox Brown. Appropriately, it is one of a series of murals in Manchester Town Hall, a city which profited enormously from the textile industry.

to head for England. No doubt there were plenty of grouchy comments from the locals about these swarms of bloody foreigners stealing our jobs, but in fact they were just what England needed. The country became a major textile manufacturer. As fleece exports continued to fall – from 30,000 sacks a year in the 1340s to just 5,000 sacks in 1540 – cloth exports went in the opposite direction. In the 1340s only 5,000 rolls of English cloth went overseas; by the 1540s the export trade was touching 120,000 rolls a year. It was very big business.

The boom in East Anglian wool-working turned out to be short lived, however, because textile manufacture made heavy demands on the environment. It needed clean, fast-flowing streams for washing, fulling and dyeing, and to drive the mills that powered the looms. The flatlands of the east could not meet those requirements, so there was a shift in the regional shape of the wool trade. Suffolk was better supplied with running water than Norfolk, so the golden triangle of Lavenham, Sudbury and Long Melford continued to thrive, as did the towns at the foot of the Lincolnshire escarpment. But the best land for the new textile mills lay in the West Country – in the hills that ran through Gloucestershire and Oxfordshire. The undulating countryside was cross-hatched by rushing rivers and streams, and the open downs were already famous for a remarkable breed of sheep. There was a good supply of fuller's earth (ideal for softening and disinfecting the wool), and the quarries were rich in gorgeous stone.

It was the nearest thing to an oil strike. The Cotswolds were about to get rich.

Eight

Heart of England

History quiz: what connects King Charles II, the Conservative Party, the National Trust, the Magna Carta, the House of Commons, HMS *Victory*, the wooden walls of England, and a pair of riding boots?

Answer: the oak tree.

Charles hid in an oak after fleeing the lost battlefield of Worcester in 1651. Then merely a prince, he took refuge in the branches of the tree in the grounds of Boscobel House, Shropshire. Without the protection of those famous boughs he would not have been able to regain the throne in 1660 and England might have remained a republic; Nell Gwynn might have remained unknown for ever.

The 'Royal Oak' has been recalled in pub signs and battleships ever since.

The Conservative Party uses the silhouette of an oak as its logo. The National Trust uses a leaf cluster as a symbol of stately conservation – the nearest thing in nature to a country house.[1] The Magna Carta was written in ink distilled from the gall in oak bark (as were Darwin's letters, and a good deal of English literature).

1 The oak leaf was selected in a design competition in 1935. The Yorkshire-born artist, Joseph Armitage, had previously worked on St George's Chapel, Windsor, the Bank of England and the relief of W. G. Grace at Lord's, so he was something of a specialist when it came to designing national symbols. He was rewarded with the princely sum of thirty pounds.

The House of Commons is coated in oak panelling, as are many great houses across the country. *Victory* is the product of some five thousand oak trees; and two centuries before Trafalgar the ships that saw off the Armada were made of oak, too. While tough, oak wood has the wonderful quality of not splintering when hit by cannonballs (the fibres yield a little, like a glove). This made it a priceless military asset, and explains why eighteenth-century England planted thousands of acres of oak woods.

Finally, oak tannins were used to dye millions of leather boots, shoes, reins and saddles. Truly it has been a bountiful tree.

You could make a case for willow. Cricket would not be cricket were it not for *Salix alba*, which grows only in the rain-soaked English wetlands. Some 'English willow' is now grown overseas, but every cricketer knows that there is no substitute for the genuine article. The sound of leather on willow has traditionally been the music of the English summer.

But it would take more than this to displace the oak as England's national tree. Japan has its ginkgo, China its rose, Lebanon its cedar, Scotland its pine, Canada its maple, Indonesia its banyan. In Russia the birch forest, full of light, birds, berries and snow, occupies centre stage. That nation's literature began with words written on birch bark, which also provided roofs, baskets, brooms, boats, and the supreme essential: fire. Its sap was a tonic. But in England the oak was always sovereign.

It is not unique to this habitat: it is common across Europe. Indeed, it is also the national tree of Germany, where it was used to adorn military medals, just as its leaves once garlanded Roman foreheads. But the benign combination of geology, soil and climate has allowed the oak to flourish in England long enough for it to become emblematic – the most common tree as well as the best loved, whether in dense woods or standing heroically alone, in a field.

It is a strong, silent type – tubby yet tough – and can live for a thousand years (the Bowthorpe Oak in Lincolnshire is said to have witnessed the Norman Conquest). It provides bed and board for 284 native species: magpies, squirrels, woodpeckers, owls, moths and beetles. Its acorns nourish pigs, badgers, mice, deer and many other woodland creatures. And it is perfect for furniture – the antique shops of England groan with oak tables, chairs, chests, sideboards and bookshelves.

Merlin performed his best magic beneath a spreading oak tangled with mistletoe, perpetuating an ancient Celtic tradition (the original word for 'druid' meant 'oak'). Ever since, the tree has been a burly presence in English life. The Yule log was an oak limb, decorated with holly and ivy, then dragged around like a slain hero. And in 2016 one of the Queen's ninetieth-birthday presents was a bronze replica (achieved by 3-D printing) of an ancient oak that stands in Windsor Great Park, complete with metallic acorns.

In 1763 Roger Fisher, a Liverpool shipwright, gave due credit to this mighty tree in *Heart of Oak: The British Bulwark*. Written to highlight the dwindling oak forest – tree loss was the eighteenth-century equivalent of our hole in the ozone layer – Fisher's prime concern was national security. If the nascent British Empire did not protect this providential resource, he declared, it would wither like the empires of Greece, Persia and Rome. Oak was the nation's maritime shield. His greatest fear was 'supineness' – a lack of respect for this supreme resource. 'Let us remember,' he warned, 'all things have their mutations ... we are preying on our very vitals'. He went on to paint a grim picture of an oakless island and asked: 'What will become of the glory of this realm?'

Fisher chose a fine phrase for his title, for it was 'hearts of oak' that beat in the chests of Nelson's sailors at Trafalgar, and within the empire builders who followed them. It has become an evocative term for English bravery. Whether as a single, majestic tree in an abbey cloister or university quadrangle, or sprinkled through a lavish green park, it always suggests doughty and implacable resolve.

As such, it has acquired semi-mystical status as an emblem of continuity. The power of the proverb 'Great oaks from little acorns grow' – a line from Chaucer's *Troilus and Criseyde* – hints at the extent of England's faith in the idea that monumental achievements have modest beginnings, and that small islands can achieve greatness. The oak is a force of nurture as well as nature; it offers both shelter and defence. No wonder Edmund Burke saw it as the essence of England – rooted, eternal and venerated for its 'greatness ... shade ... stability'.

It is another reminder of the way England's natural inheritance has sent tendrils into the emotional subsoil of its people.

Nowhere, perhaps, does the oak flourish as vividly as in the Robin Hood stories. Just as Maid Marian incarnates the figure of the May Queen, so Robin is the spirit of the greenwood. Scholars have connected him with Woden, the German tree god, and this is echoed in popular tales. His earliest appearance, in a Lincoln Cathedral manuscript, begins: 'Robyn Hod in Schereword stod' – as if he himself were a forest sprite. In the 1938 film, Errol Flynn assembles his outlaws at the trunk of a tremendous tree; and later, in a famous image, the branches dissolve as Merry Men leap from their hiding-places in the canopy.[2]

Not much survives of Robin Hood's fabled home in Sherwood Forest. In those days it was a great English wood: eight thousand acres of thick forest, a deciduous swirl of oak and sycamore, dappled with light and shade and alive with deer, rabbits and birds. Today it is still lovely, but a tiny fragment of its former self, a small oasis of protected woodland on the road between Nottingham and Doncaster. Well-kept footpaths wind through glades, rare cattle breeds potter in the clearings, and ancient trees throw shadows on the grass.

2 In the film, when Robin Hood comes across Friar Tuck, dozing by a river with a leg of mutton in his hand, he is told to be careful, because that man is a friar from Fountains Abbey. With typical confidence, Hollywood thus slides Sherwood Forest about a hundred miles north, towards the Yorkshire Dales.

The Major Oak in Sherwood Forest, one of England's oldest and fattest trees. In Robin Hood's day it was only a couple of hundred years old.

There are still a few connections to the good old days, though. For instance, one immensely grand tree called the Major Oak is thought to be at least eight hundred years old. Robin himself is said to have hidden in the hole at its base. Standing not far from the Visitor Centre, its twenty-three tons are supported by a trunk with a circumference of thirty-three feet, but it is a battle-weary veteran these days, its aged limbs propped up on crutches. Even so, it has been named 'Tree of the Year' by several of the committees that judge such things.

Edward I, en route to Scotland in 1290, summoned his government in the shade of another award-winner, the nearby Parliament Tree. Believed to be a thousand years old, it now lives in reduced circumstances next to a lay-by on the A6075. Plastic bags float across what was once a royal hunting ground.

It was not far from here, in the autumn of that year, that the King's wife, Eleanor of Castile, fell ill and died.

Richard I also passed through, in 1195, and his brother King John loved hunting in these parts. It is a living link to the beginning of England.

Robin of Sherwood has often been called on to give modern Nottinghamshire a merry past – and for understandable reasons, because this part of the county was utterly colonised by the industrial age. In *Sons and Lovers*, D. H. Lawrence noted that the terraced cottages of his home town stood beside a railway that ran near 'the ruined priory of the Carthusians and past Robin Hood's well'. This was not a coincidence: the coal mines were on the edge of Sherwood Forest, and the spoil heap at Silverhill was one of the biggest in the country. Heavy industry buried ancient heroics in a drift of soot.

Tourist Board Robin continues to throw modern Nottinghamshire into bruised relief. And he is not the only medieval hero to be commemorated in the county, for the market town of Newark was home to another legendary figure: Lady Godiva. Famous for riding naked through the streets of nearby Coventry, she is a salutary reminder that medieval women were not always as subservient as we like to think. After her marriage to Leofric, Lord of Coventry (one of Canute's most powerful noblemen), Godiva donated her title in Newark to the Bishop of Lincoln, but she did not surrender her spirit. According to legend, she proposed her famous ride as a gambit to persuade her husband to lighten the tax burden on his subjects. Leofric thought she was bluffing, but she was not. Somewhat protected by her long tresses of golden hair, she duly stripped off and rode her white horse through the centre of Coventry. The people of the town were ordered to close their doors and avert their eyes.

Her husband, chastened, suspended the tax. It was a great and popular victory.

Like Robin Hood, Godiva owes her fame to her willingness to stand up for the common people. Both stories reveal that this was a winning idea as early as the eleventh century.

Another stock figure first appeared in this same tale. Although most of the townsfolk obeyed the command to look the other way, a local tailor could not resist taking a peek. He went so far as to drill a hole in his shutters so he could enjoy a better view. In the blink of an eye, he became an immortal English character: Peeping Tom.

He was punished for his sauciness by being struck blind. But by then he had entered the national mythology.

There are many resonances in this story: the clumsy patriarch outflanked by female virtue (or womanly wiles); the greedy elite; the plight of the poor; the shock of bare flesh; the humbling of a nobleman. All of these are English archetypes. And Peeping Tom even gives the episode a cheeky seaside-postcard twist. He lives on as a statuette in the Coventry Lanes Shopping Centre, still leering at a nearby sculpture of the naked lady herself.

We may not be able to see Lady Godiva and Peeping Tom as expressions of Midlands geography in the same way as we can identify Robin Hood as an emanation of Sherwood Forest. But they do connect us to the medieval period and many of its themes. They are aspects of a world created by water, sheep and wheat. They express the ideas of an England that was starting to see itself as a wool-working empire, one that sought to enrich itself further by expanding overseas.

As home to a bridge across the Trent, Newark was an important inland port for the wool trade – and thus played a significant role in generating the common wealth. The fact that it (like Great Dunmow) still has a historic inn called the Saracen's Head reminds us that was the period when the Crusading spirit had infiltrated large parts of English life.[3] It also created a yearning for native heroes. Robin Hood is

3 A number of English towns share this echo, though few boast about it. There are Saracen's Heads in Amersham, Beaconsfield, Chelmsford, Dunstable, Henley, Hertford and many other old settlements.

sometimes held to have been returning from the Crusades himself, but he is always a partisan renegade who remains loyal to the one true King. It doesn't quite make sense for Lady Godiva to have been the model for Robin's beloved Maid Marian, but they did grow up in the same landscape. Newark was in those days the gateway to Sherwood Forest, and in 1227 Henry III gave six Sherwood oaks to its church, St Mary Magdalene – a church that had been endowed by Lady Godiva herself. The town has many half-timbered houses supported by boughs from which Will Scarlet may once have swung.

As a river town, Newark was a major crossroads even in Roman times: it was the point where the Fosse Way, running from Exeter to Lincoln (now the A46), crossed Ermine Street (now the A1). A millennium later it hosted a twice-weekly wool market, and there were still plenty of soldiers to taunt: William the Marshal mustered 400 knights and 250 bowmen in Newark during the First Barons' War. In short, it was exactly the sort of town Robin Hood would have wanted to raid, especially in 1216, when King John contracted dysentery there. It was whispered the King may have been poisoned by a Cistercian monk from Swineshead. All the great medieval ingredients – wool, stone, oak, water, wealth and myth – are in evidence here.

Not that this made the place special. England is a country where many such things have happened.

Newark has modernised. It is home to various electronic concerns. But there is still, as so often in England, a sense of ruin. The visitor who leaves the railway station and looks across the river at the castle sees only a hollowed-out shell. Built from timber for the Bishop of Lincoln in the twelfth century, it became a stone fortress under Edward I, boasting England's biggest gateway. It once housed dungeons and a mint, and in Tudor times it became a manor house, with superb tall windows. But it was razed – or 'slighted' – in 1648 on the grounds that it was a Royalist stronghold, and though it has been revived as a tourist attraction – slender wooden walkways wind through the broken battlements – the dominant note is still one of destruction and decay.

The afternoon sun shines on the western wall, but this is the only piece that is standing: the rest is a shattered remnant of former glories. The tourist literature admits you can 'do' the whole place in ten minutes.

It is not an unusual sight. England is awash with such ruins. Some were castles – Kenilworth in Warwickshire, Dunstanburgh in Northumberland, Corfe and Portchester on the south coast. Some date from the industrial era – Battersea Power Station and Millennium Wharf (the towering East London grain depot that is often used as a film set). There are ruined walls, villages, mills, road, barracks and barns. And there are religious leftovers – the abbeys of Glastonbury, Fountains, Rievaulx, Whitby and many others. In all these places, the strongest presence is the past.

Wherever we look, we find broken stones of this sort, haunted parables of decline and fall. This is history told by the losers, and it grips us still.

England is so studded with these evocative skeletons that it is easy to forget how unusual and characteristic they are. It was only in England that the early Church took such a determined battering. Nowhere else in Europe were the monuments of Catholicism so roughly dismantled; nowhere else has lived for so long with the wreckage. The dissolution of the monasteries was a destructive act, as the name implies (we could even call it the Final Dissolution). But if we put theological issues to one side for a moment, we can see that it was also a creative force. And what it created was ruins.

Another thought comes to mind as one loiters in these ancient grounds. When Henry VIII's vandals – and Oliver Cromwell's puritan zealots a century later – smashed their way into these compounds, scattering their libraries[4] and altars to the four winds, hardly a hand was raised to defend them.[5] There was the Pilgrimage of Grace, which raised its banners in Yorkshire, where so many of the rich monasteries were situated, in 1536. But this meek uprising was easily crushed. The hanging of a handful of abbots was enough to nip it in the bud. Such was the esteem in which the old Church was held: hardly anyone leapt to its aid.

At a stroke, England became a land decorated with sad relics of what it once had been. Wild flowers grew through sacred stones; people wandered among the groves and graves of the past. But as the monasteries fell, other institutions rose, sometimes using the same stones for their walls and foundations. Cardinal Wolsey himself used the dissolved priory of St Frideswide (along with twenty other monastic houses) to build Christ Church, Oxford. In a single convulsion, old England – the land of a thousand churches – gave way to something new. But it was so richly laden with hidden treasures that it would always nurse a sneaking suspicion that its glory days lay in the past.

There is one more special – and specifically English – feature of these monastic ruins. They celebrate England's disobedience – its refusal to accept the authority of remote rule. We cannot call the break with Rome a medieval Brexit, however, because Britain did not yet exist. It was a purely English act, driven by English obduracy and pride. Pondering it at a time when the same national feelings have just achieved a similar coup – the break with the Treaty of Rome – obliges us to see both ruptures as expressions of deep English emotions.

---

4 Worcester Priory had a library of six hundred books before the break with Rome; only six have survived.

5 No one tried to stop the thuggish clergyman Richard Culmer, for instance, who demolished the magnificent (by all accounts) stained glass of Canterbury Cathedral with visible glee. But we should not read too much into the fact that an anti-papist crowd gathered to cheer him on. The people who hated such violence probably stayed at home that day.

Either way, the dissolution of the monasteries turned England into a land of wracks and ruins. Taken as a whole, they symbolise an abiding strand in the national life – the faint but rock-solid belief that greatness fades, and empires fall.

It takes different forms, this belief. The gaunt bones of Whitby Abbey glower from a cliff like a storm-tossed mariner (often featuring on front pages, to illustrate sunsets or rainbows). Kirkstall lords it over the suburbs of Leeds like a heron in a thicket of willow. Cleeve perches in its Somerset nest like a tree house, full of staircases and carvings. And Bolton Abbey reclines in its fold of Wharfedale like a deposed king.

Such monuments are sometimes at their most evocative when little remains. As grave souvenirs of past conflicts, they have a particular charm. At Guisborough, North Yorkshire, a single wall with one high arch is all that survives of a medieval priory (barring a fragment of the porch). It pokes out of the fields near Redcar like a rocky ghost. Sometimes there is snow, sometimes daffodils rise through the grass, sometimes a rosy sky shines through the silhouette, sometimes a storm is gathering. It is the kind of place that would have had Turner reaching for his watercolours. Once the fourth-richest religious house in Yorkshire, Henry VIII marked it for destruction in 1541. The tower was induced to collapse on to the building, pulverising it to rubble. It is a sad reminder of the squalls of violence that blasted England for so many centuries.

Modern England is so strewn with the debris of the past that we may be forgiven for ignoring it. Walk along the Thames path at Rotherhithe and you pass the outline of an Edwardian manor house – a stone building that once overlooked the river. It belonged to Edward *III*, not Edward VII. Yet it does not feel out of place between the wings of a modern housing estate.

Sometimes, though, we overlook these echoes because they are so faint. For example, on the South Downs north of Chichester, down a grassy valley that adjoins the Monkton

estate north of Chilgrove, you would never know that a village
once stood on this spot. It was a proper settlement in 1348, but
only a single farmhouse by 1605. The Black Death was probably responsible for its demise, but there may have been other
factors, too. It could have been something as simple as the
stream drying up.

Whatever the cause, the village is no more. But if you look
very carefully, a few humps and banks begin to emerge out
of the gentle slopes of the land; and it is possible to imagine a
little lane, a handful of thatched huts, a few rows of beans and
a gaggle of medieval geese.

England boasts two thousand vanished villages of this sort.
And when we factor in Henry VIII's assault of the monasteries,
as well as the more mundane ravages of time, we stumble again
on the notion that England is not just rich in ruins – it is rich
in the *sense* of ruin. Elizabethan England was already littered
with broken stones. It is not easy for us to see the sixteenth
century as modern, but England was *old* even then. Even before
America was settled by Europeans, England thought of itself as
a land of ghosts and former glories.

It makes perfect sense that Shakespeare set his seventy-third
sonnet against this melancholy backdrop:

> *That time of year thou mayst in me behold*
> *When yellow leaves, or none, or few, do hang*
> *Upon those boughs which shake against the cold,*
> *Bare ruin'd choirs where late the sweet birds sang.*

This note has chimed through countless elegies ever since:
a glint of mortality, the failing light of autumn days and the
pathos of old walls. It informs the literature we usually take
to be classic – from the sunken bowers and broken stones ('in
shapeless ruin all') of Oliver Goldsmith's 'Deserted Village' to
the 'still, sad music of humanity' William Wordsworth felt he
could detect at Tintern Abbey. It haunts the shadows of Gothic

fantasy and the poetry of Samuel Taylor Coleridge. When
T. S. Eliot surveyed the wreckage of England after the Great
War, he combed the Arthurian legends for dolorous strokes and
allusions to the creation of a cursed waste land.

Rose Macaulay traced the history of this aesthetic in her
1953 essay 'Pleasure of Ruins' and pointed out that it was a very
old story. As one of the Jacobean characters in John Webster's
The Duchess of Malfi says:

> *I do love these ancient ruins.*
> *We never tread upon them but we set*
> *Our foot upon some reverend stone.*

His use of the word 'reverend' may have been a witty
reference to the monastic origins of the stones he was contem-
plating, but it also catches the way in which those ruins are
themselves sacred – sanctified by time. The same reflex may
have informed England's stoic response to the bombs that fell
in the Blitz. We were a people half in love with fallen masonry.

There is a similar strand in our architecture. During the aesthetic ferment of the eighteenth century, the stately houses of
England became home to brand-new follies that were carefully
constructed to resemble classical temples. In effect, they were
fake ruins. Some of the dissolved monasteries became atmospheric backdrops. When John Aislabie built a new property
at Fountains Abbey, he and his MP son physically rearranged
the scenery so that the abandoned arches of the old Cistercian
monastery could be seen from the terrace.

England has tried valiantly to modernise, but it has long
been accused of living in the past. Indeed, it is often satirised
for replaying the military highlights of yesteryear, wallow-
ing in period dramas and indulging endless dreams of life in a
stately home. As Gilbert and Sullivan put it: 'There's a fascination frantic / In a ruin that's romantic'.

This tendency is itself old. It has been stirring since at least the days of Robin Hood. One Anglo-Saxon poem, 'The Ruin', begins (in modern language): 'Wondrous is the stone of this wall, shattered by fate.' Such thoughts arise naturally in England's landscape; they are buttressed by a thousand seasonal intimations of death and birth. The whole country can seem like the ruins of a great house, with bats in the belfry and mice in the cellar.

As Shelley put it, describing the broken statue of Ozymandias, whose 'vast and trunkless legs' were all that remained of a great empire:

> *Nothing beside remains. Round the decay*
> *Of that colossal wreck, boundless and bare*
> *The lone and level sands stretch far away.*

This has been a constant, sorrowful hum in England's literary voice. One of the things that gave W. G. Hoskins's *The Making of the English Landscape* (1955) its power was the heartfelt way it lamented the 'decline' of the historic countryside: 'Since the year 1914, every single change in the English landscape has either uglified it or destroyed its meaning, or both ... let us turn away and contemplate the past before all is lost.'

What he would make of today's England is anyone's guess. Hoskins did not have to reckon with aircraft noise, motorway jams, roadworks, pneumatic drills, neon lights, shopping malls, enterprise parks, leisure centres, muzak, plastic bags, pinging phones, rows of wheelie bins, satellite dishes, car alarms, round-the-clock television and all the other luminous features of modern civilisation. Compared to all this, his England looks both Merrie and Olde.

Yet Hoskins was being dyed-in-the-wool English in bemoaning the loss of the country he loved, for few national reflexes are as sharp as the urge to sing anthems to our glorious past. We adore narratives of decline: they feel true. Despite recent bounding leaps in national prosperity, and the relative ease of modern life, we still prefer to think that England is on the slide, drowning in decay. It is in our nature to feel that everything turns to dust. As Tennyson put it (in *In Memoriam*): 'Our little systems have their day / They have their day and cease to be.'

Shakespeare's 'bare ruin'd choirs' bring us back to Sherwood Forest by eliding the idea of ruined buildings with the texture of oak – the wood from which the choir stalls were made. Two motifs entwine themselves in one modest phrase. Close your eyes, and you can make out cowled figures hurrying through a cloister, distant singers raising their bright voices to rainbows cast by stained glass, vales fat with sheep, men inching through fields with scythes, and stooped women gleaning.

Nine

Ploughing and Sharing

A few miles south-east of Sherwood Forest lies another historic locale. At first sight it appears to be an unremarkable row of red-brick buildings set in muddy countryside that is not quite flat yet not quite hilly. But the time-honoured village of Laxton is an unspoiled slice of medieval England. It is listed in the Domesday Book as Laxintone,[1] and there are hints of a Norman motte-and-bailey mound (with views over Robin Hood country), ancient fish ponds and mill platforms, and a twelfth-century parish church. But an even simpler feature has kept Laxton in the guidebooks: this is the only place in the land where the tradition of open field farming is still practised to this day.

The terrain around the village is a living reminder of the way in which England was farmed before it was chopped into smaller parcels by thousands of walls and hedges. The open field, which is shared by the villagers, is not as extensive as it once was, but it has managed to survive both the Tudor land grab and the much later programme of 'prairie-isation' which urged England's farmers to clear the ground for heavy machinery. Today it is protected and run by the Crown Estate. In 1999 it even featured on a commemorative stamp.

This is a large and nuanced subject. But broadly speaking, open field farming was the system by which manorial land was

1 It may have been the inspiration for Lexington, Massachusetts.

divided into three huge spaces which ran on a cycle – one field for wheat or barley, another for beans and peas, and the third left fallow for animal grazing and replenishment (the animals fertilised the soil with their droppings). These fields were subdivided into one-acre strips, but there were no barriers. The villagers contributed some of their labour or a portion of their produce to the lord of the manor, but the rest of the time they worked the land on their own behalf.

Echoes of this system are visible to anyone flying over the farming plains of Europe. There the fields are still smooth, level strips. But in England only Laxton remains.

The open field was not a free-for-all: it was closely regulated. In the interests of fairness – to ensure that one farmer did not always claim the patch nearest to the village, for instance, or the best drained – the strips themselves were rotated annually. Villagers ploughed a different furrow every year.

Not all terrains were suited to this approach. The dry and rocky soils of southern Europe, for instance, were good for olives, vines and other fruiting trees, but there were few large expanses of workable soil for potatoes and cabbages. So they favoured smaller plots. In England, too, the regions took on agricultural accents determined by variations in the lie of the land. The clay soil in the Midlands made it hard for oxen to turn around, so it made sense to create long, slim parcels. With no wolves, and winters cold enough to kill pests, there was little need for fences: a farmer merely had to leave a thin line of grass on the edge of his strip to mark his territory.

The system had some straightforward physical consequences. The ridge-and-furrow pattern that is still visible in many English fields was caused by many years of ploughing the same narrow lane. In due course these long furrows became known as 'furlongs'. They represented a day's ploughing and were standardised at 220 yards in length (and were 22 yards wide). These measurements are still used in horseracing, and they remain the dimensions of the most basic English unit of land: the acre

(4840 square yards). There is another archetypal English echo: the length of a modern cricket wicket is 22 yards – exactly the width of a medieval 'furlong'.[2]

The open fields had social consequences, too: they made villagers watchful, wary of trespassers. Neighbourly snooping became a routine fact of life. By forcing people together, the arrangement made them somewhat guarded and suspicious of one another.

On the other hand, it did make them receptive to a simple Christian message: do as you would be done by.

Laxton's open field is no medieval theme park. It is real farmland worked by real farmers who grow real crops. There is a notice on the church door that reads: 'Welcome – but please, no muddy boots'. Nor is the village stuck in the distant past: it boasts, of all things, a Holocaust Museum. But the thousand-year-old structure of its arable farming is its primary claim to fame. In memory of a time when the individual farmers' plots of land were allocated each year during village meetings, today's residents operate a similar system of governance, and the layout of the farms (sideways on to the road) is aligned with the breadth of the strips their ancestors once tended.

In Piers Plowman's day a typical open field would have occupied several hundred acres (and would have been the scene of endless despair and back-breaking toil), so Laxton offers only a glimpse of the original pattern.[3] But it does let us see how the tradition worked. One of its side-effects was that it encouraged farmers to live not in isolated farmsteads but in neighbourly groups (what geographers call 'nucleated settlements'). So this is where the underlying pattern of English village life was born – a cluster of cottages looping around a granary, a church, a blacksmith's forge and a mill.

2 This may be why a cricket wicket is known as a 'strip'. Few modern batsmen are on top of the medieval allusions in their sport, but they are there all right.

3 William Langland's work was a gripping departure from the traditional literary formula because it placed a ploughman, rather than a warrior-prince, at the centre of the story, then invited us to marvel at his anguish.

This model remains alive to this day. As W. G. Hoskins made clear, the majority of England's settlements already existed at the time of the Domesday Book (most of the exceptions were created during the Industrial Revolution). Over time, many of the villages developed into towns, and some of the towns mushroomed into cities. This explains their higgledy-piggledy shapes and locations: the underlying pattern was laid down at a time when access to a well was more important than bus routes or high-speed internet connections.

We tend to think of early England as dangerous, a time of Viking raiders sweeping up England's rivers – 350 longships astonished the natives when they appeared in the Thames in 842 – but for most of England's history, its people did not live in daily fear of violent attack. The defensive hilltop village – so striking a feature of France, Spain, Italy and even Switzerland – is rare in England. Durham Cathedral occupies one of the few locations where defence was a major consideration, because it remained vulnerable to Scottish assault throughout this period. And while the Normans built many castles, most of them were designed to intimidate the locals, not repel invaders. On the whole, the English preferred to put down roots in low-lying land.

There was a meteorological aspect to this, too. In hot countries, people settled on high ground, where the air was cool. No one in England felt the need to do that.

An even more important legacy of the open field system was the textured civic culture it inspired. It was not adopted throughout the country: the south-eastern shires of Essex and Kent retained the Roman pattern of manorial estates with smaller fields; and in other areas the terrain was too rocky, steep, sandy, dry or wet for big plots. But in Laxton (and across the Midlands) the system gave people a degree of independence. They were more than mere vassals: with access to their own strips of land, they could feed and fend for themselves, and even produce a surplus that they could sell for real money.

It gave them an early taste of *laissez-faire* – the freedom to sink or swim.

This is not to say that England's farmers were a free bourgeoisie, or well off. But they were not serfs. Elsewhere in Europe, the peasantry was a disposable army, but the Atlantic weather made English farming so varied – it did not lend itself to monocultures, such as vines; it had to adapt to wheat one day, cabbages the next, dairy farming the next – that it rarely made sense for all hands to be engaged on a single task at exactly the same time. So when we describe an 'average' manor or an 'average' farm, we must remember that it might not resemble anything that existed on the ground. Medieval England was a land of surprising range.

The open field required a high degree of cooperation. It made no sense for each farmer to have his own plough and oxen, so such resources were pooled. And it was important that every member of the village behaved responsibly. It was not the done thing to have more animals than your neighbour, graze your sheep next to his corn, or take more than your fair share of timber from the wood.

Over time, a set of rules evolved to govern this sort of thing, which in due course gave rise to a judicial system to deal with any disputes: the first 'keepers of the peace' were appointed during the reign of Richard I; they became 'justices' – in effect, magistrates – under Edward III. Moreover, since the open field was a cooperative venture, it helped to inspire the communal spirit that would later inform many English voluntary associations and trades unions. Quarrels affected everyone, so everyone had an interest in settling them peacefully. In 1296, in Leicestershire, a tenant was fined twelve pence for 'unjustly' ploughing the wrong plot. Fifty-six years later, in Sedgefield, it was established that 'one third of the fields ... shall lie fallow every third year'; thereafter, sowing on the wrong soil would incur a fine.

It didn't take long for this cooperative spirit to express itself in institutions. The earliest craft guilds (many of which came out of the wool trade, as we have seen) grew out of the procedures that operated on manorial estates – the unwritten rules by which reeves, stewards and bailiffs had always supervised production and laid down the law. Increasingly, these rules were formalised into legal contracts. In our favourite year of 1290, in Newton Longville, Buckinghamshire, it was 'granted and ordered by the community of the village that no one henceforth shall be allowed to glean who is able to earn a penny a day'. Gleaning was the custom that allowed poor people to scavenge for leftover corn, so this may have been the first political move against 'benefit cheats' in English history.

The guilds quickly became quasi-legal bodies, with their own vested interests. By the fourteenth century, there were powerful guilds for butchers, bakers, candlestick-makers and many other trades and professions along with the wool-related fraternities – a total of forty-eight corporations, each with a head office in London and branches all over the kingdom.

Though they were set up with the best of intentions – to offer mutual support and even insurance protection to their members – some of them became closed shops, dedicated to the exclusion of outsiders. A fuller could not shear, a shearer could not weave, and a weaver must on no account dye. The power of these monopolies – and the attendant wealth that was accruing to the country's merchants – started to vex the Crown. So, in 1335, Edward III sought to undermine the guilds by decreeing that all merchants, aliens and denizens alike must be permitted to trade 'freely without interruption ... to what persons it shall please them'. The effect was minimal: the guilds continued to rule the roost. Their lavish halls were usually the most prominent buildings in the parish, after the church.

It is a typical English story: an innovative self-help movement for independent craftsmen grew into a stalwart defender of the status quo.

*

The spirit of cooperation kindled by this agricultural tradition may even have had a significant influence on the development of another great national tradition. In most respects England has a weaker musical tradition than the rest of Europe, and especially Germany and Italy. But it can claim to excel in one sphere: choral music. From the great works of Handel to the televised choirs of Gareth Malone, England has always been a land of communal singalongs.[4] In churches, pubs and village halls, group singing has been a vibrant part of English civilisation for longer than anyone cares to recall. We may have no Bach, Mozart, Beethoven or Wagner, but we have few peers when it comes to choirs.

It is said that St Augustine brought choristers with him when he moved from Rome to England in 597. Both the new faith and the singing thrived. In Canterbury, Augustine created a school that in time became The King's School, and which at first taught only two subjects – Latin and music.

Similar establishments – known as 'song schools' – were subsequently founded in Westminster, Chichester, Norwich, Salisbury, Winchester, Wells (where Aelfric heard a chorister singing nocturnes) and elsewhere. In the biographical note at the end of his *History*, Bede noted that he 'sang the choir offices daily'. In those days all of the music would have been plainchant (every voice in the choir sings the same line), but by the twelfth century York Minster was introducing polyphony, with the boys singing vibrant descants of their own devising.[5]

---

4 Can we call Handel English? Obviously there is no hiding the fact that he was German: born in Halle, he was Kapellmeister in Hanover before arriving in London with George I. Yet he had a shrewd understanding of his new audience – 'What the English like is something that hits them straight on the eardrum' – and his music certainly sounds English. He pretty much wrote the musical accompaniment to the British Empire, and was buried with full honours in Westminster Abbey. One of his finest works – 'Zadok the Priest' – has been played at the coronation of every British monarch since its first performance. No one has a greater claim to be the master of English choral music.

5 A monk named 'Hugh the Chanter' is given some of the credit for this innovation.

It is not going too far to say that the main purpose of the abbey schools – which marked the first stirrings of formal education in England – was to keep the church choirs well stocked with junior choristers.[6] In 1236 there were fourteen boy singers in Exeter; and in 1265 it was decreed that a dozen should be retained as choristers in Lincoln. The architecture in such cities' cathedrals created acoustics that were ideal for choral music. Right across the country, the voices of English boys swirled up to delicate stone vaulting.

When Winchester College was founded in 1382, it was stipulated that scholarships must be awarded to twelve paupers; in 1443 Eton's statutes insisted that the boys must sing an anthem every night (evensong); and in 1446 Henry VI decreed that a choir of sixteen boys must be maintained at King's College, Cambridge (Eton's sister foundation), to accompany daily mass and vespers. The latter's descendants are among the star turns of Christmas to this day.

As early as the thirteenth century English singers were mastering the six-part roundelay 'Summer is a-comen in' ('Sing cuckoo! Sing cuckoo!'), launching a rich tradition that would one day produce Thomas Tallis's forty-voice Tudor masterwork, *Spem in Alium*.[7]

Between times, England was swayed by communal singing of all kinds. When Erasmus visited England in 1510, he was struck by the 'agile throats of the choristers'. From Tallis to Britten, nothing brought England to mind so much as a stately melody sung by a choir.

It has often been said that architecture is 'frozen music', and in England they certainly go together. It is hard to say which came first: the soaring harmonies of a cathedral choir, or the fan vaulting above their heads.

It should come as no surprise that English education has its

---

6 The boys were obliged to leave both choir and school the moment their voices broke.

7 As featured, to popular acclaim, in the 2015 film version of *Fifty Shades of Grey*.

© Robert Winder

Even when deserted, the sound of ancient choirs in England's churches (as here, in Southwold, Suffolk) echoes into the present day.

origins in the production of choristers, because the Church was by far the most powerful cultural patron in the Middle Ages. Schooling began as an ecclesiastical, rather than a social, idea. But the speed with which England adopted choral singing as its favoured musical form reveals the extent to which the people enjoyed acting in unison. And the rural traditions which inculcated that spirit of cooperation did not die when people drifted from the countryside to towns and cities in the nineteenth century. On the contrary, in an attempt to keep their traditions alive in the potentially soulless confines of the urban slums, they formed brass bands, temperance societies, mutual funds, scout groups, friendly societies, cadet corps, pony clubs and innumerable other cooperative associations.

More than anything else, they formed themselves into teams and played sports – cricket, football, rugby and the rest. We can trace that love of teamwork all the way back to villagers getting together to sing and pull bell ropes in medieval churches.

It is common knowledge that many sports began in the countryside: Shrovetide football matches between neighbouring villages have been a fact of country life for centuries,[8] and cricket grew as a rustic pursuit, too. Sport's ecclesiastical roots are less often mentioned, yet choristers in fourteenth-century Wells would play 'kick-ball' in their off-duty moments, and a medieval carving at Gloucester Cathedral shows two boys hoofing a ball about.

Other sports – rowing eights, tennis fours, rugby fifteens, relay squads – also demand a communal approach. Although in their modern forms these were mostly shaped by the leisure needs of the industrialised workforce, they still drew strength from instincts that were planted many centuries earlier. The urge to work together in teams – an urge that linked harvesters and choristers with bell-ringers and cricketers – had held sway in England long before French musketeers trumpeted the idea of 'all for one and one for all'. Victorian evangelists were quick to promote the benefits of team sport – the way it improved moral fibre by frowning on sharp practice and adhering to the rules.[9] But

8 The rules of the annual contest at Ashbourne in Derbyshire stress that murder and manslaughter are not permitted . . . but otherwise just about anything goes.

9 As Vita Sackville-West once put it: 'The English man is never seen in a better light than when another man starts throwing a ball at him.'

this was nothing new. English villages had been booting bladders from one end of the parish to the other, pulling ropes in tugs of war, or singing madrigals, since the days of Robin Hood (and his team of outlaws).

Some other typical facets of Englishness emerged from all this teamwork. Fitting in as an act of self-interest rather than a gesture of 'sheep-like' obedience generated a culture of conformity for which the English have long been well-known. The demands of agriculture made it impossible to escape the daily round of tasks, and since every farmer on an open field had to get up, sow his plot and sharpen his scythe at the same time, all of them could police each other.

They had to plough in March, shear in May, harvest in August, pick fruit in September, then gather some winter fuel. They had to take it in turns to scare off the crows. Nosy neighbours were quick to denounce anyone who broke the rules – mavericks were scorned. Gossip was an entertaining way to keep everyone on the straight and narrow – no one wanted to be sniggered about behind their back. Englishness, from this time onwards, was all about singing from the same hymn sheet, forming an orderly queue, and never stepping out of line. A characteristic conservatism had its roots in the routines and traditions of village life.

It is hard to say that the natural landscape made England uniquely receptive to the Christian message, since the same religious spirit animated the whole of Europe. But Christianity's distinctive English accent certainly owed something to the prevailing conditions. Rural culture fostered both the patience and the spirit of readiness demanded by Christian observance. While the land lacked a desert's power to inspire awe, or a Mediterranean sky's ability to encourage carefree sensuality, it did call for a Job-like fortitude in the face of suffering, perhaps combined with confidence that there would be light at the end of the tunnel.

Either way, it was not a complete accident that Christian wisdom came to be expressed in all those famous proverbs inspired by the local weather. The new faith was able to curl in its new home like a hedgehog in someone else's nest. This was why the Christian calendar was able to slip so easily into the footprint of pagan English society. It was only natural to place Christmas in the depths of winter; and Eastertide merged well with notions of rebirth and spring – with the annual cycle of sap rising in woods, meadows ... and lusty young people. The golden precepts of Christianity – love thy neighbour, turn the other cheek, do (unto others) as you would be done by – resonated with people whose daily routines forced them to be neighbourly.

The historic town of Southwell lies a few miles south of Laxton, nestling in a bowl of shallow hills near Nottingham. Its spectacular minster, with its lead-capped pepperpot turrets towering over the rooftops, carries a rare – for England – hint of the Romanesque, and it has a Norman nave. In the twelfth century it had a bishop too, but the religious college is now a lovely ruin.

Visitors often pronounce the place to rhyme with *mother*, but natives prefer to retain the echo of the south well, emphasising the importance of fresh water in the town's origins. The Romans built a bridge over the Trent near here, so it served as a pit stop on the Fosse Way. Royal visitors such as Richard I, John and James VI of Scotland all passed through, the latter en route to becoming James I of England. In 1646 Charles I spent his last night as a free man in the inn before surrendering to Scottish Presbyterian troops. Byron lived in the local manor house during school holidays from Harrow in between 1803 and 1808 (he called the place 'detestable'). Later in the nineteenth century, just down the road, a woman named Mary Brailsford planted some apple pips in her garden, but she had sold the cottage by the time the resulting tree bore fruit. So it was the new owner – a butcher named Matthew Bramley – who gave his name to the famous cooking apple.

Unsurprisingly, given this sort of history, Southwell enjoys a vibrant modern life: race meetings and an arts festival attract visitors to its pretty high street. The prevailing tone is Georgian – for Southwell became a prosperous market town in the eighteenth century – but the medieval origins still shine brightly in the minster's chapter house.

Several powerful English forces converge in this decorated stone hall, where monks once met to discuss monastic affairs. First, its octagonal shape was consciously egalitarian (as was true of the polygonal chapter houses at Salisbury and Wells): the monks would sit around the edges on stone benches, with none taking precedence. It is a striking echo of King Arthur's round table. Second, the echoes of Robin Hood are particularly strong. The pillars are decorated with intricately carved foliage – exquisite sculptures of oak, maple, mulberry, vines, hops, ivy and roses. It is as if the leaves of nearby Sherwood Forest have just blown through the door. Men's faces peep out too, looking like Will Scarlett or Much the Miller's son. Third, this medieval masterpiece was created just as Peter Corbet was accepting the King's congratulations for a job well done, and as a Tyne freighter bobbed down England's east coast for the first time, carrying coals from Newcastle. It coincides perfectly with the moment when Englishness started to find its voice.

Finally, the minster invites us to marvel anew at the sheer scale of the endeavour required to raise such an edifice. As at Winchester and Salisbury, as in Norwich and York, it took a large, well-organised army of workers to dig, drag, heave, hoist, carve, climb, scheme, sing and bicker these masterworks into life.

We can see how the medieval zeitgeist acted on an individual Englishman by considering the career of a certain William Long. Born in the 1320s to an ordinary farming family in the village of Wickham, Hampshire, he rose to become an architect–builder at Windsor Castle under Edward III. In due course he became Bishop of Winchester and Lord Chancellor of England. In 1382 he founded Winchester College to provide choristers for the city's cathedral, and also founded New College, Oxford, to support poor scholars such as he had been. By this time he had taken the title of his birthplace and was known as William of Wykeham.

This unusual but not unprecedented rise to prominence reminds us that social mobility is an older concept than we often imagine. Medieval England was a little more fluid than the set-in-stone feudal archetype suggests. Indeed, the country's relative stability – certainly in comparison with continental Europe – may well have rested on its pragmatic openness to self-improvement.

Wykeham's career affords an insight into another famous English quality: politeness. The school he founded bore the motto 'Manners Makyth Man', and he expanded on this by writing: 'It is by politeness, etiquette and charity, that society is saved from falling into a heap of savagery.' Today this may be read as nothing more than a bossy injunction to mind one's Ps and Qs, or a defence of upper-class polish, but Wykeham had something more robust in mind. His motto was in part a plea for people to be judged not by their background but by their personal qualities, and in part a suggestion that if people wanted to get on in life, well, it never hurt to be polite. It was a self-help manual.

We celebrate Robin Hood as a common-man hero who stood against tyranny. But the founder of Winchester College was a meritocrat, too. In cloaking his educational projects in ecclesiastical garb – stone quadrangles, cloisters, libraries, chapels and refectories – he established a tone that still rings through schools and universities to this day.[10] Today, England's public schools and Oxbridge colleges strike most people

10 The great quadrangles of Christ Church, Oxford, and King's College, Cambridge, certainly resemble the solemn precincts of a cathedral. In the case of the former, that is exactly what it is.

as exclusive and expensive luxuries rather than beacons of scholarship. But rooted as they are in the monastic ideals and ceremonial manners of the Middle Ages, they continue to transmit a sense that learning thrives best in the robes of ancient fellowship. And their *modus operandi* has been imitated in other walks of life, including the law and politics. Like it or not, these bookish medieval traditions continue to pervade English society and culture.

The 'fellows' still wear cloaks, gowns and mortar boards, they recite Latin oaths, and they dine together like knights of old, connected by ancient rigmaroles to the wisdom (and folly) of the past.

Wykeham is said to have etched a boast into Windsor Castle when he worked there: '*Hoc fecit Wykeham*'. Years later, when he met the King, he explained that he had not meant to imply that he personally had made the castle; on the contrary, the castle had been the making of *him*. That's manners for you. They can be polite, but they can also be weasely.

Certainly, English politeness often strikes others as evasive: the art of not saying what one means. 'One for the road?' actually means 'Close the door on your way out'; 'Please don't go' means 'On your bike'. The English are often accused of a compulsion to preserve distance without causing offence, which is why courtesy may be interpreted as the forked tongue of perfidious Albion – a charade, an exclusive code. Even our apologies can seem two-faced, especially as we deliver them so lightly. We damn with faint praise, boast with false modesty, give high marks to people who merely keep up appearances, let others down gently, and put on a good show. Even our love of queuing is dubious: it tranquil-lises the hostility we feel towards queue-jumpers.

There may be a well-intentioned streak to such evasions, but it is easily missed.

It was eighteenth-century French idealists who first charac-terised England as *la perfide Albion*. They were outraged that it sided with Europe's autocratic royal houses to crush France's revolution, despite its own democratic history. This was a diplomatic assessment – indeed, it may be why 'diplomatic' often means 'sparing with the truth' (as one definition put it, an English diplomat was an honest man sent to lie abroad for his country). But what could one expect from a people who lived with such untrustworthy weather – one moment sun, the next rain? Surely no one could imagine that what was true yesterday would still hold today?

The open field system lives on in England in one last, unobtrusive way: the allotment. It is an entrenched national habit for English people to maintain small plots of communal land in urban areas for vegetables and flowers.

The concept was born almost as soon as they started congregating in towns, in the early days of the Industrial Revolution. The grim reality of their new existence left people longing for green realms, and the government agreed to compensate them (a little) for the common ground they had lost through the relentless advance of land enclosure. An 1819 Act of Parliament gave parishes the right to set aside 'lots' of earth so that the labouring poor could grow vegetables, and in 1908 the Allotment Act obliged local councils to provide such resources.

More recently, after a notable spike during the Second World War (when it was a patriotic duty to grow carrots, and there were one and a half million active allotments), the number has fallen dramatically: by 2008, a mere 330,000 of them were in regular use. Yet the spirit of the allotment lives on in the English love affair with the back garden. All across the country, every day, people reap and sow, prune and mow, seed and dig their little patches of well-watered ground. The very word 'garden' comes from the Old English *garth*, meaning a plot of enclosed land.

The open field system did not long survive the medieval period, for a variety of reasons. One of the simplest was the fickle English weather.

The feudal arrangement by which continental serfs paid dues to their lord by giving up a regular portion of their time – two days a week working on his demesne – was never well suited to the English climate, because it was hardly ever possible to know in advance when crops would ripen, whether the hay would dry, or when a field might be ploughed. Consequently, English lords increasingly preferred to charge rent in lieu of their subjects' time, then use the money to hire their own permanent labour force – workers who had no other duties and could be called into action at a moment's notice. The theoretical structure remained – the peasant class was still subjugated to the whim of the lord. But in practice the system led to glimmers of independence in the fields of England, visible in the emergence of a yeoman class which occupied a position in society some way above the humble mass.

Nudged by the treacherous skies over England's fields, the binary system of class hostility – peasant and squire glaring at each other across an unbridgeable chasm – began to take on its distinctive English character.

Ten

Wool: A Good Yarn

The Cotswolds is chock-full of picture-perfect villages, but few places are quite so picturesque as Chipping Campden. Situated at the northern margin of the range, this golden town has changed only superficially over the last five hundred years – a road sign here, a shop front there. It is a whirl of butterscotch walls, arches, doorways, pillars, gables, towers, chimneys and mullions, all clad in stone from a quarry only a mile up the hill.

There are 170 listed buildings in the High Street alone – official residences, barns, workers' cottages and almshouses – and they ooze history like butter from a crumpet. The oldest, the Grevel House, was built in 1380. The nearby market hall, a relative newcomer in comparison (it was completed in 1627), is crowned by a spectacular timber roof. Towering above both is the fifteenth-century church of St James, which was modelled on Gloucester Cathedral. It is a colossal structure for such a modest town, with stunning tall windows and a lavish set of pinnacles on the parapet.

Small wonder that Nikolaus Pevsner, in his *Architectural Guide*, described Chipping Campden as 'the best piece of townscape in Gloucestershire, arguably one of the best in England'. In this he was merely echoing what the historian G. M. Trevelyan said when he referred to the curving High Street as 'the most beautiful village street now left on the island'.

But the most important feature of Chipping Campden is the fact that every single stone, every architectural delicacy, every pretty cornice and buttress, every mossy slate on every time-ripened roof, every oak support was paid for by wool. Thanks to the bountiful local breed – the 'Cotswold lion', so-called because of its rich, shaggy coat – the town became a commercial powerhouse.[1] 'Chipping' derives from the Old English word for fair – *ceping* – and there was a weekly market here from 1247 onwards.

There is even an antique stone sheep dip set into a grass verge in the town centre, although the sign on it now says 'Cart Wash', so it may have had more than one use.

In the Middle Ages the village lacked only one thing – running water. The River Cam trickled through the middle of the settlement, but it was a piddling stream, lacking the power needed to drive a textile mill. So this was old Cotswolds: a sheep farm. The people who lived here were wool merchants, not cloth dealers. They did not complain, however, because these rolling hills produced the best wool in England ... and therefore the world.[2] As William Camden (no relation) wrote in 1610: 'In these woulds there feed in great numbers flockes of sheepe, long necked and square of bulk and bone, by reason (as it is commonly thought) of the weally and hilly situation of their pasturage; whose wool being so fine and soft is had in passing great account among all nations.'

The most prominent of numerous local merchants was William Grevel, the man whose house dominated the High Street. It was the first building in these parts to boast stone

---

1 The precise origins of the Cotswold breed are unclear, which makes it likely that a combination of topography and climate played some part in its evolution. There was, as the saying goes, something in the water.

2 This is not a truth universally acknowledged. Rivals include the famous 'Lemster Ore' from Leominster (Elizabeth I would wear nothing else), and the shepherds of Lincoln and Stamford have always claimed that the most lustrous wool of all is that produced around the Wash.

chimneys rather than a simple hole in the roof, and one of the first in England to be fitted with large windows. The memorial brass in the church calls Grevel the 'flower of the wool merchants of all England'. And he was no aristocrat who inherited his estate from a Norman forebear, but a London trader (a financier to Richard II) who decided to set up shop in the town. As such, he is further proof that it was possible for a commoner to make it in trade. He was also a pathfinder for that enduring English fantasy – ownership of a country retreat. By the end of his life he possessed fourteen houses in Chipping Campden, and grew fat on the rent. But he never forgot his woolly origins: his crest depicts a swan holding a lamb.

Chipping Campden stands at the northern end of the Cotswold Way, a long-distance footpath that starts at Bath Abbey. In November 2014 a stone was unveiled at the water fountain near the middle of the village to mark the spot where it ends. It is a round medallion with an acorn in the centre and some well-chosen lines from T. S. Eliot's 'East Coker', about light falling on a gloomy afternoon, etched around the rim.

The hills above Chipping Campden may have been rich in sheep, but this was not, as we have seen, a cloth manufactory. As England turned to weaving in addition to shearing, the wool trade migrated to better-placed villages – in the valleys of the Windrush, the Leach, the Evenlode, the Coln and all the other tributaries of the Severn and the Thames that bubbled through these splendid hills.

To Castle Combe, for instance.

It lies at the opposite – southern – end of the Cotswolds, near Bath and Chippenham. And while it is now ideal for car-spotters (it lies a stone's throw from the M4, and there is a motor-racing circuit on the edge of the village, on a disused airfield that was used by Polish pilots in the Second World War), it is also a place that time forgot: no one has built a house here since 1617. It is gorgeous enough to be favoured by filmmakers

(*Doctor Dolittle*, *Robin Hood* and *War Horse* were shot in its narrow lanes) but, like Lavenham, it was once a hive of industry.

Unlike the Cam, the By Brook had enough energy to wash wool and drive the hammers that pounded it into thread. (In its modest twenty-mile course it falls more than six hundred feet before joining the Avon at Bath.) Castle Combe was already a Norman manor, a sheep estate and a market – a weathered cross still marks the spot where three roads meet at a water pump, and where the fair was held. John Aubrey called it 'the most celebrated faire in North Wiltshire for sheep', but in the first half of the fifteenth century it became a textiles centre too.

Much of the village's success was due to the work of a single remarkable man. Sir John Fastolf was an East Anglian

Castle Combe: an icon of the English countryside, made by sheep.

knight who in 1408 married a widow who had inherited Castle Combe manor. His family hailed from Great Yarmouth – his father was Sheriff of Norfolk – and he ended his life by building a great brick tower at Caister Castle on the east coast. But for four decades he lavished most of his energy on Wiltshire.

Fastolf owned a house in Southwark and a tavern called the Boar's Head. But he was no stay-at-home farmer–landlord. In 1415 he and his troop of thirty archers fought alongside Henry V at Agincourt, and the King knighted him two years later. In his time he was also appointed Governor of Harfleur, Bastille and Anjou. But then his fortunes started to turn. In 1429 he led an army of reinforcements to join the siege of Orléans, only for Joan of Arc to defeat his forces on the battlefield. Fastolf fled and was subsequently accused of cowardice on account of the fact that he was the only English officer to remain on horseback during the battle. He was acquitted, but the mud stuck. A century later, when looking for a name fit for a cowardly braggart, Shakespeare plumped for Sir John 'Falstaff'.[3]

And where did he hold court, in *Henry IV Part I*? Why, in the Boar's Head tavern, of course.

Returning from Orléans with his military reputation in tatters, Fastolf found refuge in Castle Combe, putting mills and weavers' cottages where kingfishers swooped over the shallow, fast-flowing river, otters played in the shade of willow trees, and rooks built great nests of twigs in the trees on the hill that sheltered the village from the north wind. It was an ideal location. First, it enjoyed easy access to wool from the markets of Cirencester and Tetbury; second, there was rich local stone for building; and third, it was a long way from the wearisome regulatory hands of the city guilds.

There was one more attraction. Even with vigorous

3 'If I fought not with fifty of them, I am a bunch of radish,' he boasts in *Henry IV Part I*, after running away from just two assailants.

scrubbing in fresh running water, it was not easy to extract all of the oil and grease from wool. Years of patient trial and error had revealed that the best agent for the task was palygoskite, which (as everyone surely knows) is found in hydrous aluminium silicates, along with kaolinite, montmorillonite, attapulgite and other active ingredients. Medieval weavers did not use any of these terms, of course, but they knew that this unusual soil could soften and clean fleeces. They called it 'fuller's earth', and as luck would have it there was a ready supply in Combe Hay, near Bath. It was another gift from the bounteous English soil.

There had been mills in the region since Roman times, crushing grain into flour, but by the middle of the fifteenth century there were twenty water-driven wheels in the valley, and some fifty weavers' cottages. A pair of brothers, billeted in a mill-side home that was icy on winter nights, started to produce a thick red cloth that was used to make 'redcoats' for the British army (it is still worn today by the Guards at Buckingham Palace). But this was not their chief claim to fame. Their surname was Blanquet, and before long they had become synonymous with the humble – but soon ubiquitous – English blanket.[4]

Another everyday item may have grown out of this landscape. In the meadows beside the rushing river (by the By, if you will) stand wild flowers known as teasels (*Dipsacus fullonum*), whose spiky heads were dragged over cloth to raise the nap. These rapidly became the fuller's best friend, and we have been teasing out threads ever since.

For his services to the wool trade, Sir John Fastolf was named a Knight of the Golden Fleece – a chivalrous order in

---

4 This story is disputed in Bristol, where it is claimed that a Flemish migrant weaver named Thomas Blanket invented the item that bears *his* name. It may be that he was related to the Blanquet brothers, but it is equally possible that a number of weavers, not called Blanket, all had the idea of producing a thick cloth that would keep them warm on chilly nights.

Bruges to which few Englishmen have ever been admitted.[5] And he continued to support Castle Combe after his death. In his will he left £4000 – an immense sum – for additions and improvements to the Norman church. The result – in 1434 – was a new clock tower that is now home to one of the country's oldest working timepieces. It is decorated with carvings of a shuttle and scissors – emblems of the trade that paid for it. The fan vaulting in the nave was modelled on the superb ceiling of Bath Abbey.

Castle Combe is one of many Cotswold villages where clothworking developed as a cottage industry. More than a few of the others – including Shipton, Washbrook, Sheepscombe and Sherborne (from 'shearing') – owe their names to the trade; and the area is full of Sheep Streets and Ram Alleys. Others have continued to reap the benefits of the trade by becoming renowned heritage sites. When foreigners close their eyes and think of England, they see the Cotswolds. That might not be the best thing, though, because Castle Combe – with its two pubs, tea shop and country house hotel (with adjacent golf course) – now resembles a butterfly pinned on velvet.

Other nearby villages have enjoyed – or suffered – similar fates. Lacock, for example, was an affluent wool centre when its lands were held by Shaftesbury Abbey, but Henry VIII turned its monastery into a manor house – albeit one with a cloister to remind visitors of bygone days. In 1944 it was bequeathed to the National Trust, and it is now a period piece: tithe barn, granary, church, abbey, gift shop, museum, pottery, inn. Huge crowds wander through its atmospheric streets every year, and millions saw it as a backdrop in the Harry Potter films. It has also appeared in *Pride and Prejudice*, *Emma*, *Moll Flanders* and *Downton Abbey*.

5 The order still exists. Among its living members are King Juan Carlos I of Spain, Queen Elizabeth II, the Emperor of Japan, Tsar Simeone II of Bulgaria, the Grand Duke of Luxembourg and Princess Beatrix of the Netherlands. Unlike Fastolf, none of them could quite be called a textile magnate.

Much the same can be said about Bibury. The stone cottages in Arlington Row are now a world-famous tourist destination. Originally a monastic wool store, then a line of weavers' homes, they overlook a bright stream where trout twist in the crystal-clear water. Throw in a time-encrusted church, parts of which date back to Saxon times, and a skein of other buildings carved from the same delicious lemon-grey stone, and you have another chocolate-box image of English country life.

William Morris called it 'the most beautiful village in England', and in 2014 it was voted the 'most charming in Europe', outdoing even Castle Combe, which in 1961 was declared 'England's prettiest village'. These awards were gratefully received, even if they did choke the villages with more visitors than they can easily handle (Bibury welcomes 40,000 a year, and Castle Combe five times that). In 2010 Arlington Row was engraved in the British passport (along with Ben Nevis and the White Cliffs of Dover) as a national emblem. Yet it is not only British convoys that intrude on this rural idyll. Bibury is a must-see for American, Chinese and Japanese visitors too.[6]

Taken together, these age-encrusted places form the most celebrated man-made scenery in the country. They may not reflect – or even hint at – the cosmopolitan reality of modern English life, but they are an evocative part of the country's skeleton, a living link to its past. And nearly all of them have monuments to the weighty role they played in the economy in the form of parish churches that are much too grand for the communities they serve. There is no castle of note in the Cotswolds, but you can hardly move for medieval pulpits. The wool churches of Lechlade, Moreton-in-the-Marsh, Burford, Painswick, Bourton on the Water, Stow-on-the-Wold and Cirencester are among the glories of England – 'the cathedrals of the Cotswolds'. All of them bear witness to the immense power of sheep in English culture.

6 Henry Ford once tried to buy the whole place, lock stock and barrel, for his museum in Michigan.

© Stephen Sykes/Alamy Stock Photo

St Peter and St Paul, Northleach. A shrine to wool wealth. There are not many castles in the Cotswolds – but you can hardly move for medieval pulpits.

Winchcombe is famed far and wide for its impish gargoyles, which leer and grimace at the people below. Northleach is known for its brass engravings, set into the stones beneath a hundred-foot tower which, like the one at Chipping Campden, bristles with high battlements that can be seen for miles. But it is impossible to miss the allusions to sheep and wool in these sanctuaries. In the stately church of St Peter and St Paul in Northleach, a stained-glass window features John Fortey, the merchant whose largesse made the church 'lightsome and splendid'. He is depicted carrying the source of this bounty – a sheep – in his arms, and the engraving on his memorial features his woolmark. His fellow merchants are immortalised in similar ways – with shears, woolsacks and crooks.

Northleach was one of Europe's richest towns, yet fewer than five hundred people lived there in the Middle Ages. Its power lay in the pastures that surrounded it.

It would be a mistake to think of these wool merchants as twinkly-eyed philanthropists, endowing their local churches with a generous smile. Medieval theology was loud in its condemnation of avarice: Thomas Aquinas and John Wycliffe were both adamant that wealth was a form of wickedness.[7] So the only way for the merchants to enjoy their ill-gotten gains (in the unforgiving eyes of God, all profits were the wages of sin) was to recycle them into ecclesiastical good works. They were not the only benefactors: everyday people paid their tithes too, so the churches were communal projects, not simply upper-class trophies. But the building programme would never have been so ambitious had it not been for textile money.

The most glorious expression of this impulse can be found

7 As R. H. Tawney noted in *Religion and the Rise of Capitalism*, the seemingly radical labour theory of value proposed by Ricardo and Marx was not much of an advance on Aquinas's concept of the 'just price' – a fee that reflected the work that went into something, and would not be boosted by extra demand.

at St Mary's in Fairford. The town is now known as an air force base (in 2003 it thundered to the sound of USAF bombers heading for sorties over Iraq), but it was once a sheep capital, and its church contains a high point of English art. There are the usual allusions to the trade that buttressed its construction, but its outstanding feature – a genuine national treasure – is the largest expanse of medieval stained glass in the country.

The church was funded by John Tame and his son Edmund, wool merchants from Cirencester who moved to Fairford in 1491. It is an acknowledged classic of the Perpendicular style – a new engineering method in the fifteenth century which allowed lofty walls and extravagant windows. Tame's London connections – he made a splash at the court of Henry VII – gave him access to the King's Glazier, a noted artist who had already worked on the chapel in Westminster Abbey, King's College, Cambridge, Winchester Cathedral and St George's, Windsor. When Tame invited him to decorate St Mary's, the result was an extraordinary rendition of the whole biblical story, from Adam and Eve to the Last Judgement, in twenty-eight huge, colourful frames.[8]

These windows are famous, but perhaps not famous enough. A historic piece of storytelling in sunlight, glass and lead, replete with demons and monsters, they are the nearest thing in England to the Sistine Chapel ceiling. Indeed, the two works are contemporaries: Michelangelo put the finishing touches to his magnum opus in 1512, and the Fairford glass was completed five years later. Even in a land so rich in such artefacts they are a supreme work: *Paradise Lost* brought to life by sunlight.

Yet, in marked contrast to the Italian genius, the Fairford artist is forgotten today.

---

8 The involvement of the King's Glazier meant that there were secular elements, too. The designer acknowledged his royal patronage (he received a retainer of £24 per year from the Crown) by sprinkling Fairford's windows with allusions to Henry VII. The woman accompanying the Magi in the Nativity scene was a royal princess.

His name was Barnard Flower, and he was a maestro. But he was not English. The first foreigner to be appointed King's Glazier, he was one of a large group of Flemish glaziers who lived in Southwark (to the angry displeasure of the native craftsmen).[9] The migrants worked on almost all

© Colin Underhill/Alamy Stock Photo

The stained glass at Fairford tells the complete
Bible story in coloured light.

the magnificent works of this medieval high noon. Twenty or more realised Flower's designs for St Mary's. As a consequence, in the early years of the sixteenth century the tiny village of Fairford was vibrant with Flemish craftsmen,

9 In 1500 a Venetian visitor wrote of the English: 'they have an antipathy towards foreigners, and imagine that they never come into their island except to make themselves masters of it and usurp their goods'. Some things do not change.

chattering and muttering as they polished Flower's images into glowing walls of art.[10]

Like everything in English life, in time the windows fell victim to the weather: parts of the south-west window felt the full fury of a gale in 1703 and were broken. Some of the fragments were lost – or deliberately discarded – in a nineteenth-century restoration programme (although they turned up many years later in the Victoria and Albert Museum). The 'restored' sections are a Victorian blot on the medieval glass-scape, but they cannot detract from the power of the whole. The great window depicting the Last Judgement, for instance, is a masterpiece in its own right: the golden figure of St Michael stands with fragile scales in the centre (for weighing souls) with the virtuous being guided heavenwards on one side and the sinful consigned to a pit of flames and snapping jaws on the other.

In the window celebrating Jesus's birth two shepherds hasten towards the cradle, while in the glass above Mary's head during the Annunciation a pair of sheep look down with benign expressions, as if this were all their handiwork – which in a way, of course, it was. Meanwhile, the sophistication of the artistry can be glimpsed in the way the image of Adam, Eve and a serpent-entwined tree echoes the depiction of the same event in John Lydgate's *Fall of Princes* (1431–8) – an epic meditation on decline that was based on a French translation of Boccaccio's original Italian work.

By some sort of miracle Flower's work survived the anticlerical wrath of two Cromwells (Thomas and Oliver) as well as a long civil war. In 1939 the glass was stored in the cellar of Fairford's manor house to keep it safe from enemy bombs. Today, it sits quietly once again in an expanse of English

10 After the Second World War Fairford was home to another migrant community, when some twelve hundred Poles, displaced by the conflict, were lodged in Nissen huts on the empty air force base as part of the Polish Resettlement Scheme. Almost half of them settled permanently in nearby Swindon.

farmland half an hour north of Swindon. A few people visit it, but not many.

The Cotswolds may have been the beating heart of the English weaving industry, but, as we have seen, large swathes of the rest of the country were also devoted to sheep-rearing. By 1300 there were approximately two sheep for every human being in the kingdom. The Bishop of Winchester kept thirty thousand on Salisbury Plain, and the other ecclesiastical centres – Bath, Exeter, Canterbury, Lincoln, Norwich and Gloucester – tended similarly vast flocks. Crowland and Peterborough had sixteen thousand each – similar to the Yorkshire granges of Fountains and Rievaulx – while a hundred thousand chewed their way through the grass of the South Downs. Medieval England was one huge pasture – from see to shining see.

Even poets noticed. John Gower was inspired to call wool 'that noble lady, goddess of the merchants', while John Lydgate named it the 'cheeff tresour in this land'. As a medieval maxim put it: 'the foot of the sheep turns sand into gold'.

The various breeds acquired names which suggested that they were rooted in the land itself, responsive to the gradations of the English rural scene: Cheviot, Herdwick, Sussex Downs, Herefordshire, Wiltshire, Leicester, Suffolk, Swaledale and Dorset. Some had more exotic names: Northumberland Muggs, Cheshire Delameres, Exmoor Horn. Other countries had wines and cheeses; England had sheep, each of which produced a unique sort of wool. Merchants could choose between the 'lustres' of Lincolnshire, the softer threads from the Cotswolds, short Leominster wool or tough Yorkshire fibres.

The towns that grew rich on the back of the trade were happy to acknowledge the fact: Leeds, Halifax, Preston, Wolverhampton, Malvern and many others added sheep to their civic coats of arms. Meanwhile, innumerable inns and pubs were named after the land's greatest resource: the Lamb and Flag (emblem of the Knights Templar), the Lamb and the Leg of Mutton were all popular places to have a pint.

As we have seen, tending sheep nurtured a love of the outdoors that now seems innate, along with a preoccupation with weather that is stereotypically English, and an adaptable outlook. It entailed herding, rescuing, feeding, healing, watching, waiting, driving, washing and shearing. It promoted responsibility, since sheep are notoriously accident-prone, and it promoted thoughtfulness, thanks to those long days and nights on lonely hills. It inspired play, and fostered a national love of dogs – initially to work the flocks, but then as trusted companions. Anyone who takes their collie-cross for a stroll around the boundary of a village field is evoking the earliest days of sheep husbandry in England's grassy countryside.

The qualities that sheep-rearing teased to the surface spread rapidly, because almost everyone had some sort of link to the wool trade. Although the large estates remained the dominant players (the monasteries alone may have held 25 per cent of all the land in medieval England), smallholders were important too. As much as half of England's wool output may have been produced by individual farmers, who found that owning a few sheep liberated them from feudal subsistence and might, if they were lucky, propel them into the ranks of the bourgeoisie. You didn't have to be rich to graze a small flock on common land and build a nest egg of your own.

This had a trickle-down effect in other areas. It wasn't only the merchant class who made the most of early commerce: villagers also profited from the cash economy, the financial industry (for loans and credit) and the increasingly busy market in land.

The wool trade did not create England's ports, but they would not have grown so fast without it. The harbours on the east coast grew rich on the trade with continental Europe, but the rise of the Cotswolds helped to turn Southampton and Bristol into ocean-going terminals as well. After 1337, when

Italian galleys began to navigate a route past Gibraltar and up through the Bay of Biscay (their ships had large sails as well as three decks of oars[11]), Southampton became the preferred port for Florentine merchants. The King forged a deal with the Bardi and Peruzzi families that gave them duty-free access to English wool, and their hungry fleets sailed up the Solent to collect fleeces brought down by cart and barge from the Cotswolds and the Salisbury Plain.

By the middle of the century the port was handling a fifth of England's wool trade.

A similar pattern was repeated across England. No other country had the same serendipitous mixture of natural features. Having laboured through the Dark Ages, medieval and then Tudor England found itself in possession of a woolly gold mine.

The wealth was not evenly distributed, of course; quite the opposite. But for those who were in the right place, it was certainly the right time. The investiture of the Archbishop of York in 1467, for instance, involved 300 tons of ale, 100 tons of wine, 2000 geese, 1000 capons, 2000 pigs, 104 oxen, 100 peacocks, 13,500 other birds, 500 deer, 600 fish (pike and bream) and 13,000 jellies. Oh ... and 12 porpoises. Nearly all of it was local produce. England had a well-stocked larder.

No wonder John Barton, a wool stapler from Newark, etched the following couplet into the expensive stained-glass window of his new home:

> *I praise God and ever shall.*
> *It is the sheepe hath paid for all.*

If Chipping Campden represents the first stage of the wool trade in the Cotswolds (the harvesting of raw fleece), and Castle Combe represents the next (the weaving village), then

11 They accommodated 150 rowers, who required twenty tons of biscuits to keep them going during the voyage from Italy.

Bradford on Avon symbolises the third – production on an industrial scale.

Nestled in a steep valley eight miles upstream from Bath, it is a sumptuous pile of pale stone buildings above the river crossing that gave the place its name: this was once a 'broad ford', and the picturesque setting gives Bradford on Avon its fame today. But it is not just a pretty space. People lived here in the Iron Age, long before the Romans arrived. Indeed, the rolling chalk hills of Wiltshire had been busy since Neolithic times, when Stonehenge, Avebury and Silbury Hill (the largest hand-built tumulus in Europe) took up their dominant positions in the landscape.

Bradford was less than a day's march from Aquae Sulis, so there are strong echoes of Roman occupation. A mosaic was discovered beneath the playing fields of a local school, and Roman coins are routinely found in the surrounding meadows. There was a monastery here as early as the eighth century (it is mentioned by William of Malmesbury), and the Normans constructed a fine bridge across the river, with a stone chapel at the halfway point.

If the village was already busy in medieval times, it was the second wave of Cotswolds cloth production that made it a centre of enterprise. In the seventeenth century the small looms became thumping factories, powered by water, when a seam of fuller's earth was discovered in nearby Limpley Stoke. And when the Kennet and Avon canal was dug in the nine-teenth century, linking the Avon to the Thames, and Bristol to London, the cottage mills became textile works. Soon there were thirty along this stretch of water.

It gave Bradford the prosperity to become a miniature city, with an extraordinary range of buildings – halls, mills, villas, cottages and garrets – all dressed in the same biscuit-coloured stone and huddled together on the steep hill north of the river. It is spectacular and knows it: one of the olde-worlde shops in Market Street houses a salon called The Beauty Spot.

All of this happened in a town that was already old – old enough to forget its own past. In 1856 the vicar of the church of the Holy Trinity, a keen local historian, was enjoying the view from his roof when he noticed an odd-looking cross he could not recall seeing before. Closer archaeological inspection revealed the ancient chapel of an Anglo-Saxon church.

The building was being used as a school hall at the time, but in due course it was restored and became St Laurence's. It is now recognised as an extremely rare monument dating back to the tenth/eleventh-century. There isn't a great deal to see inside – no frescoes, no altar pieces, no stained-glass miracles – but that is the point. It is an unassuming stone barn dedicated to the Anglo-Saxons' God – a plain and holy whisper from another time. Only a pair of carved angels suggest any sort of decorative urge; the rest is quiet simplicity.

On the south of Bradford's bridge stands a scarcely less venerable monument – the great tithe barn at Barton Farm. It too has the lordly dimensions of a place of worship: its cavernous nave is fifty-six yards long – equivalent to two tennis courts – and built from the same creamy Bath stone as the religious buildings in these parts. But everyone who ventures inside immediately notices the resemblance to something else – the upturned hull of a ship. Gigantic oak beams form a cruck roof of high, spacious arches that support the vault. Flip the thing over, and you could sail it across the Atlantic.[12]

The important point about Bradford on Avon, though, isn't so much its sheer antiquity as the coexistence of so many different, historic layers, which fill the town like petals pressed in a book. There's a Tudor inn, a fifteenth-century priory, a seventeenth-century bank, Georgian houses with tiny

12 This barn was once full of wool. The sheep in these parts were owned by the Abbess of Shaftesbury, whose nunnery was one of the richest in the land. If she had married the Abbot of Glastonbury, they would have had more land than the King himself. As abbess, she was entitled to one-tenth of the wool that the nunnery produced, and she piled it up in barns like the one at Barton Farm. She owned an even bigger wool store at Tisbury.

windows designed to evade the tax on glass, a towpath, cloth mills, a workhouse and a viaduct that Brunel built for the Great Western Railway. The Norman bridge was the scene of skirmishes between Royalists and Roundheads in the Civil War, while a copse of trees hides the house of John Methuen, son of a clothier who became Lord Chancellor of Ireland and brought Flemish weavers to revive Bradford in the seventeenth century. (In the early 1600s James I had ruled that all cloth-dyeing must be done in London ... by one of his friends.)

Time clings here like dew. The B&B was once a windmill.

This is not just an aesthetic matter. Bradford on Avon's history made it well placed to capitalise on fresh opportunities when steam power started to spread across England at the end of the eighteenth century. It already had all the mills, looms and technical know-how it needed. Sadly, the local worthies turned their noses up at the spike in demand for 'shoddy' – the cheap, recycled cloth aimed at the man in the street – dismissing it as a rather plebeian segment of the market, beneath their fine-textile dignity. That was a serious mistake: as so often, a market leader was slow to adapt to the latest development. The slack was taken up by mills on the River Aire in Yorkshire, and a village near Leeds (also on a broad ford) became a textile powerhouse in its own right.

The last mill at Bradford on Avon closed in 1905. But by then its beauty guaranteed its future as a tourist attraction – not to mention a fine place to live for the business leaders of Bristol and Bath. Meanwhile, it stood as a dramatic reminder of how much English life had changed. The fact that it had been a wool town for six centuries showed how grand England's sheep empire had been; even the Roman occupation had endured for only four. Yet Bradford on Avon's prosperity was also a sign that it was possible to thrive *without* land. It was no longer necessary to inherit an estate: an individual could grow rich by renting a studio, setting up a loom and producing fabric for sale. In short, a person could prevail through *work*.

This was an idea guaranteed to play well in Protestant England, where self-reliance was a sacred duty. And if everything went well, the sky was the limit. As long ago as 1727 Daniel Defoe noted that it was 'no extraordinary thing' to find clothiers worth up to £40,000 (making them, in today's terms, multimillionaires).

The great English link between wealth and land was already beginning to fray.

Eleven

Immortal Longings

As we have seen, the eastern shires lacked fast-running water, so they were not well suited to producing the plain broadcloths and fine serges of the Cotswolds and West Yorkshire. But they were not done yet, because the flat lands of the North Sea shore had a limitless supply of something that was almost as useful as water: wind. The gales that blew along the east coast could be harnessed to turn stones and pumps, so from the end of the thirteenth century onwards hundreds of new buildings started to appear on the region's broad horizons.

The earliest windmills were built at Beeford, Friskney and Ravensrodd, a Viking settlement on a sandbank in the Humber estuary which was drowned by a storm in 1362 and became an underwater ruin off Spurn Head.[1]

Holderness soon became the windmill capital of England. Sails and turrets appeared at Burton Pidsea, Out Newton, Burton Constable, Halsham, Barmby on the Marsh, Grindale, Great Cowden, Drewton, Fraisthorpe and Ellerby. They added an upright note to a horizontal landscape, like herons on mudflats, and by the middle of the fourteenth century were a common sight; they even started to appear in illuminated manuscripts. At first the property of manorial estates, which claimed rights over everything, including the air, windmills soon became independent businesses.

---

1 This is still a good place to catch the breeze – it is now the site of a major wind farm.

Milling by wind was an apt occupation for a people who lived on the coast, because millers had to think like mariners. With one eye always on the sky, they had to trim their sails when the wind shifted, and lighten the load when it strengthened. Moreover, as they moved inland, they introduced a nautical way of thinking even to people who had never seen the sea.

Windmills grew out of the landscape in another way. The moving parts – the hearty basis of the mechanical revolutions to come – were usually made of good old English oak. More to the point, they helped to ensure that the eastern zone of England continued to be a powerful sheep realm throughout the Middle Ages. The Cistercians of Meaux kept a flock of eleven thousand on the marshes of Holderness, while the diocese of Ely had thirteen thousand. Now, thanks to wind power, East Anglia had the means to turn all those fleeces into cloth.

The flow of migrants from the Low Countries acted as a spur, too. As the Hundred Years War took hold in the middle of the fourteenth century, more craftsmen fled to East Anglia to plant Flemish weaving in England. Although the pioneer John Kempe headed further north to make 'Kendal Green' in the Lake District, his compatriots soon turned the eastern region into a booming cloth manufactory: fustian in Norwich, serge in Colchester, baize in Sudbury.

This was an important migration, since the weavers also brought Protestant ideas and 'hoppynge beer'. As one medieval rhyme put it:

Hops, Reformation, Bays [i.e. baize] and beer
Come in England all in a year.

With its herring and cheese diet, open landscape, windmills, ditches, flooded meadows and enormous skies, East Anglia started to resemble a Dutch province.

*

The village of Worstead, a day's walk north of the Norfolk Broads, is one of the best places to hear echoes of this world. After Flemish clothworkers arrived here (and in neighbouring North Walsham) during the reign of Edward I, the fabric they made was soon associated with the village name. In time, 'worsted' wool would be the stuff not just of English suits, but of English legend.

In 1309 Norwich Priory ordered 'cloth of Worstead' for its monastic habits, and more than a century later William Paston – in one of the famous 'Paston Letters' – ordered a consignment of the same material, adding that it was 'almost like silk' and declaring: 'I shall make my doublet all Worsted for the glory of Norfolk.' Chaucer's Friar sports an impressive 'semicope' of 'double worstede' as he rides to Canterbury in the company of his fellow pilgrims (who include by the way, a number of people associated with wool – a 'webbe', a 'haberdasherre', a 'dyere' and a 'tapicer'[2]). This highly desirable cloth was made from yarn that was intensively twisted to make it strong, and intensively brushed (with hot combs) to make it smooth. This was then oiled, spun and woven into the finished product. Smooth yet strong, light yet hard-wearing, it was a clear leap forward from the heavy broadcloth that England had previously produced. Best of all, it did not require much fulling – the process of pounding with feet or hammers to thicken and strengthen the fabric – so it did not need a gushing river.

Worstead (the village clung on to the 'a') became a hive of weavers' homes, each spacious enough to house a large Dutch loom. One of them – Geoffrey the Dyer's cottage – is now a heritage attraction, with twelve-foot-high ceilings and exposed beams from which the cloth was hung to dry. Forty-five 'websters' were living in the village by 1379, and over the century to come they turned a little row of cottages into a cash cow. The sign that welcomes today's visitors (who may be following

2 A webbe was a weaver, while tapicers specialised in making tapestries – or, perhaps, carpets.

the 'Weaver's Way' – a walking trail from Great Yarmouth to Cromer) features a horned black-faced sheep.

But the chief glory of Worstead, as in so many wool centres, is its church. It towers over the rooftops like a forbidding parent. And it is not alone. Norfolk has by far the highest concentration of medieval churches in England – of the 921 that were built, 699 survive – and if the absence of a ready stone supply[3] meant that they tended to be built of rubble and flint, and so are not quite as drop-dead gorgeous as the limestone churches of the Cotswolds, they remain magnificent. Indeed, they have a rough, braced-against-the-wind, tugboat quality that sits well with the land they overlook. Moreover, since the building materials made it hard to create square corners, many have round towers – of the 120 circular turrets in England, 118 are in East Anglia.

And nearly all of them owe their existence to the same trade. They appear in the tourist literature as 'wool churches'.

The list of such churches is long: Aylsham, Blofield, Cawston,[4] East Dereham, Salle, Wymondham and many others are monuments to the riches clipped from the surrounding fields.[5] So while we have said that East Anglia was medieval Europe's Wild West – a rugged world of pioneers and adventurers – the scale of its ecclesiastical buildings meant that it was also a kind of Holy Land. In addition to the impressive churches and monastic houses (Bury St Edmunds, Castle Acre, Thetford, Walsingham), the region boasted two enormous cathedrals (Norwich and Ely).

*

3 Norwich Cathedral used stone that was shipped from Caen in Normandy: low barges heavy with building blocks sailed up the Wensum and the Yare, right into the city centre. The monks excavated a canal so they could sail all the way to the building site.

4 The church of St Agnes, in Cawston, may have been named after the Latin for lamb (*agnus*).

5 Many still let sheep graze in their churchyards. It's easier than mowing, and far prettier.

But there was an even greater power inland – in Lincoln. The diocese stretched all the way from the Humber to the Thames, and the capital of this capital, high on a hill overlooking medieval England's third-largest city,[6] was the cathedral.

The superficial facts are simple: the Normans placed a church on this spot soon after the Conquest, but it was laid low by fire and even the occasional earthquake until, in 1186, a Carthusian monk from Switzerland named Hugh of Avalon became bishop. Not content with repairing the existing fabric, he ordered the creation of a stunning new structure, with superb transepts and towers, a new choir, a chapter house, extra cloisters, and a central turret which was – at 525 feet – the tallest in Europe. It was taller than the Egyptian pyramids, if you really wanted to know. It was a work in progress for over a century. Edward I held three parliaments in the chapter house, making it a seat of temporal as well as spiritual power.

However, this only hints at what Lincoln Cathedral meant to the Middle Ages. If we imagine our medieval stonemason once more, returning to the city after his trip to Rievaulx, we can hardly guess at the sights and sounds that must have greeted him. To start with, the structure would have been visible for three or four hours as he walked towards it. Built on a mound above the river, it soared over the surrounding plain like a fairyland castle, floating on a bed of sheep. And the noise: a cacophony of hammering, chiselling, scraping, pounding and clanging that seemed to come from the heart of a cloud of dust. And just think of the swarms of men – buzzing, hauling, climbing and pulling on cranes, levers and winches – in a cloud of dust and mud. There might be cries of warning as a rope whipped free or a basket fell to the ground. And all around would be the relentless harsh ring of iron on stone.

Striding on through the cluttered roads, the mason would see the great towers, looming up like a cliff. The volume would

6 The two cities with larger populations were London and the great wool capital, Norwich.

swell as he approached the site itself, where tents full of men were blowing glass, making tools (saws, nails, mallets and drills), heating lead in crucibles, carving wood or chiselling stone.

No one could say how many men were involved in the project, but it must have been thousands. And it had been going on for decades. Our stonemason knew a man who had been working on the cathedral since he was a boy; now an old fellow of forty-three, it had been his one and only occupation. But he had never complained, because this was the centre of the world. The cathedral precinct was a veritable Babel of foreigners: Dutch, French, German, Tuscan, Welsh and Irish craftsmen. There were even a few Moors perched on the scaffolding up there.

When he finally reached the cathedral wall, the mason ran his hand along the stone as if stroking the flank of a favourite horse. He loved the texture of this Lincolnshire limestone – it was cool and strong, yet soft enough to be worked. He had done some time in the quarries, where labourers chopped blocks according to templates drawn by master masons with fine instruments. But even after all their craft and guile, and the skill of the journeymen, the church still looked like a natural outcrop of the rocks on which it sat.

The mason craned his neck and smiled. He had worked on those flying buttresses himself, a few years back, and they looked magnificent. At first he had scoffed at the idea – surely a massive waste of time, stone and labour. But once he understood the science of the scheme – the way the buttresses spread some of the weight of the high vault away from the curtain walls, allowing the latter to be thinner and lighter – he fell in love with them. They stuck out like a spider's legs, making the monstrous edifice look nimble. And they allowed the cathedral's walls to accommodate huge windows, which was why so many foreign glaziers were here.

The master builders had borrowed this trick from the cathedrals in Paris, it was said. But the mason had never journeyed outside of England, so he did not know if that was true. However, he did know all about the vault over the nave. He had spent several summers with his chisels in Durham, so he understood the thinking behind the fine stone ribs up there.[7] Indeed, he had often thought, as he lay on his back, carving oak clusters into stone, that the fanned ceiling resembled the spreading canopy of an oak forest. Entering the cathedral was like tiptoeing into a wood: it was cool, dark, silent ... and tense with expectation.

The gritty dust made the mason cough. He had been spoiled up in Ryedale, where a summer breeze swept along the valley and kept the air fresh. He winced at the prospect of the toil that lay ahead: the working day that would run from sunrise to sunset. But his mood lifted when he saw the lump of Purbeck marble that had been ferried all the way from Dorset. It would be his job to sculpt it into pillars for the choir.

Did he think that the modern, urban world was drifting far from its primitive, rural ways? Maybe. But of course it was those rural ways – in particular the transformation of grass, through sheep, into wool – that was paying for all of this.

It is hard for a modern imagination to contemplate a building project whose patrons, architects, craftsmen and labourers were well aware that they would never live to see it completed. We can only marvel at the range and depth of skills that were needed for such a monumental task: carpenters, glaziers, masons, carvers, roofers, joiners, painters. Few of them were well rewarded, but in medieval England not one of them was quite a slave.

But the scale of it all ... The foundation stones of Salisbury Cathedral were laid in 1220, and the first draft was finished forty-six years later (making it one of the quicker cathedral projects in the Middle Ages). In total, 60,000 tons of stone were transported from a quarry twelve miles away, on carts

7 The stone vault at Durham was an English innovation that resolved an age-old problem. The cathedrals at Caen and Jumièges, built at the same time, both had magnificent wooden ceilings, but these had a nasty habit of catching fire.

which rattled into the town at a rate of ten per day. In addition, 12,000 tons of marble, 28,000 tons of timber, 400 tons of lead and almost an acre of glass went into the building. But the final flourishes were not applied until 1280, and the graceful spire was added a full century later.

Lincoln Cathedral. It is hard for a modern imagination to contemplate a construction project, and a leap of faith, destined to take a hundred years or more.

The time frame alone would make a modern construction company sigh.

Then there is the religious imagination that was required even to conceive of such a scheme.[8] The worldly impulse in such conceptions is plain enough, but so is the otherworldly

8 On the BBC radio show *I'm Sorry I Haven't a Clue*, Humphrey Lyttelton once joked – when recording in a cathedral – that it was hard to comprehend a building project that took a hundred years ... but we had to remember that people did work much faster back then.

one. The soaring towers were projections of secular power, of course, but they also sought to communicate sacred truths. The patrons, architects and builders were attempting to write the Bible in stone.[9]

These were not churches in the modern sense of the word. They were not designed to encourage the public to dress up in their Sunday best and enjoy a communal sing-song followed by a post-Mass sherry. Rather, they addressed Heaven itself. They were shrines. Walk through Westminster Abbey and the first thing you notice – apart from the splendour of all that stone – is how *inconvenient* it is. The enclosed choir in the centre excludes the congregation, while the shaping relic – the tomb of Edward the Confessor – is hidden at the back. This was not a civic centre; it was an offering to God.

Its lavishness owes something to the fact that there was what we might call an international 'alms race' in the Middle Ages – an urge to raise the highest nave, the most spectacular vaulting, the brightest and most colourful stained glass. As a result, thousands of labourers were set to work on Westminster Abbey for scores of years. Many, no doubt, worked in York and Oxford, too. Some were itinerant foreigners; others were Londoners. The investment of time and treasure was staggering: in one way or another, the project swept almost every able-bodied working-age soul in the area on to its teetering scaffolds.

Yet it was just one of dozens of colossal building projects at that time. Beaumaris Castle in Wales employed four hundred masons to cut, grade and lay stones, along with a thousand labourers, quarrymen, carpenters, hauliers, glaziers, blacksmiths, sculptors, cooks, ropemakers, bakers, toolmakers and so on. Given that Lincoln was engaged in two projects of a similar scale (construction of its castle coincided with work on the cathedral), several thousand men were probably beavering

9 As William Golding said, thinking of Salisbury Cathedral, in *The Spire*.

away in the city at the end of the thirteenth century. That is well over half the available working population of Lincoln.

Not all of them were natives, of course. These construction projects depended on a cosmopolitan workforce. Lincoln, along with Exeter, Salisbury, Ely, Durham, Hereford, Gloucester and Worcester, attracted a large cohort of skilled, itinerant artisans who walked from job to job and city to city. These days we would call them migrant labour, and if any of them had known what a bike was, they would have been getting on to it.

Their supervisors were migrants, too – master masons who travelled the world to oversee the building of these fabulous monuments. Henry Yvele grew up in Derbyshire but became a freeman in London in 1353 after working on St Albans Abbey. Seven years later he won royal approval and directed numerous A-list projects, including Westminster Abbey, the Tower of London, New College, Oxford, the high nave at Canterbury Cathedral and London Bridge. Meanwhile, William Wynford, who hailed from the West Country, made his name working alongside William of Wykeham at Windsor and Winchester, where he is depicted in the stained glass. He added a tower to Wells Cathedral and worked on Queen's College, Oxford.

The quality of such work gave rise, indirectly, to a term that still serves as a byword for artistic excellence: the masterpiece.

With wool as its paymaster-general, medieval England gained twenty-six cathedrals, several hundred religious houses, and thousands of stone churches (two hundred in Lincolnshire alone). By 1300, it had ten of the fourteen largest cathedrals in Europe[10] – not bad for an isolated kingdom on the edge of the civilised world. It was certainly motivated by a deep sense of piety: in the middle of the thirteenth century there were

---

10 The four continental buildings were St Peter's and San Paolo in Rome, Cluny in France, and Speyer in Germany.

twenty thousand monks and nuns in England.[11] But it could not have been achieved without the wealth that flowed from the nation's unrivalled sheep conglomerates.

It was an extraordinary creative and material eruption of cultural energy, and the social consequences were equally colossal. We can only guess how many people were needed to cut, transport, hoist and position so much stone, timber and glass, but as many as 100,000 labourers may have been involved – some 5 per cent of the total labour force. We have to imagine roughly 1.5 million people working for a single employer to find a modern equivalent of the medieval Church.

As it happens, that is almost exactly the size of the National Health Service.

And it wasn't only churches. There were castles, guild halls, manor houses, bridges, gatehouses, villas and colleges to build too. Each and every one demanded not just large numbers of skilled craftsmen but a well-oiled transport system. England had both. Consider the two-month-long siege of Bedford in 1224, when King Henry III tried to bring a disloyal baron to heel. Siege engines were dragged to the town from as far afield as Lincoln and Oxford. Ladders, carts, catapults and battering rams were lashed together on site using wood from nearby Northamptonshire and rope from distant Southampton. Some 15,000 crossbow bolts were sent from Corfe. Miners travelled from Hereford and the Forest of Dean. Victuals were purchased in the London market, but may have originated anywhere in England or even overseas.

We have already noted that many common English surnames have roots in the wool trade, but the great burst of medieval construction generated many more: Carpenter, Carter, Carver, Driver, Mason, Sadler, Skinner, Stone, Tanner, Tyler and plenty of others. These artisans, tradesmen and craftsmen had to be mobile because medieval life was feast or

11 Given that the population is now twenty times larger, that is equivalent to 400,000 people living in religious orders today.

famine – if there was destitution in one part of the country, there might well be surplus in another. So, although they were not free in the footloose modern sense of the term, nor did they labour only under feudal obligations of tenure. Rather, they were members of a wage economy; they expected pennies for their pains. Under Edward I, an unskilled labourer could earn a penny a day, while a mason, a thatcher or a carpenter could make three or four. A husband and wife team might earn five pence between them for reaping and binding an acre of wheat – not much, but enough to buy a couple of chickens, several dozen eggs and a lump of cheese.[12]

It means that we can sense, at this time, a tremendous coming together, like a great army assembling. It may be premature to call this period the beginning of the Industrial Revolution, but the rural population was certainly starting to equip itself for the transformations that lay ahead.

Christian observance is almost vestigial in England now. In 2014 churchgoers dipped below a million for the first time – a serious decline from the peak of ten million in 1930. But the cultural legacy of the medieval church-building programme, especially in the wool-rich West Country and East Anglia, lingers on. Although much of it is draughty, some of it is rotting, and parts of it are falling down, it remains a resonant cultural fact of English life.

Whenever the sound of church bells rings across an English field, we are hearing an echo of this candlelit world.

This spirit continues to hang in the cloisters and quadrangles of historic England. From Tewkesbury to Wells, from Lichfield to Beverley, from Canterbury to Ripon, the bare bones of the

---

12 We usually imagine the Middle Ages as a time of privation and need, but it was easy enough to put on weight. There is not much English art to guide us, but the peasants in the paintings of Pieter Bruegel are undeniably *chubby*. Medieval life was violent in many ways, but there was usually plenty to eat. Even the homeless outlaws in Sherwood Forest sat around the fire with a hearty roast.

English sensibility were laid down in stone on the proceeds of sheep. The memory of wool lurks in England's crooked lanes, cobbled squares, stone-clad troughs, packhorse bridges and drovers' trails.

Pevsner insisted that 'the architecture of England between 1250 and 1350 was, although the English did not know it, the most forward, the most important and the most inspired in Europe'. It is difficult to dispute. The cathedrals and churches from that century of extraordinary vision and effort remain icons of the landscape. In his introduction to *England's Thousand Best Churches*, Simon Jenkins suggested that we should see them, collectively, as England's grandest achievement: 'a dispersed gallery of vernacular art ... without equal anywhere in the world'.

And this art was not aristocratic; quite the contrary. Even the greatest cathedrals are graced by demotic touches – gargoyles, fonts, lecterns, screens, pews, emblems and other devices that are imbued with the inventive wit of the common craftsman. John Ruskin revelled in this aspect of the medieval aesthetic: it found a place for the creative energy of the humble artisan.

But just as England reached this civilised peak, something terrible happened.

Twelve

Black Days

No narration of England's growth can ignore the lethal cataclysm that was the Black Death. It can hardly be counted a natural English ingredient, but it did have enormous consequences for the landscape – beyond even the unimaginable number of people it slaughtered.

It began in England in the summer of 1348, when a flea-bitten rat crept off a ship at Melcombe Regis, near Weymouth. The cargo may have been wine from Gascony, spices from Genoa, soldiers returning from the Hundred Years War, fish from the Channel Islands, or stone from Normandy. We do not know. But within weeks the 'terrible pestilence' was rampaging across the country like a bush fire. That, at least, is the traditional start of the story. In truth, other rats probably slipped ashore in other ports – Falmouth, Rye, Rochester – around the same time. However it arrived, though, bubonic plague soon found England to be the perfect host: lots of people, lots of dirt.

The consensus view is that roughly a third of the population died from the disease over the next few years, although some recent studies put the figure at closer to a half. A plaque in Weymouth hedges its bets by suggesting that '30–50%' of the population fell. For comparison, only a thirtieth of the British population – the vast majority of them men – perished in the carnage of the First World War. The plague claimed men, women and children indiscriminately.

This is not the place to rehearse the horrifying miseries of the Black Death. And it is hard, in the face of such a catastrophe, to suggest that there may have been anything resembling a bright side. But the plague did have far-reaching, long-term consequences. Cold-eyed geneticists have suggested that it may have strengthened the gene pool by wiping out the most vulnerable members of medieval society. And the sudden, massive contraction in manpower certainly created an immediate labour shortage, which for the first time put the boot on the working man's foot: he was now a scarce resource able to demand higher wages (regardless of what Thomas Aquinas might say). Ploughmen who had earned two shillings a week for decades started to demand three. A landlord who had paid workers threepence an acre during the harvest now had to fork out twice as much ... or see his crops rot in the fields.

The result was a burst of inflation and a jolt to the status quo that the ruling class sought to control by outlawing pay increases and raising legal obstacles to stop workers moving around in search of better deals – the 'Ordinance of Labours' of 1349 and 'Statute of Labourers' of 1351. A generation later, ongoing conflicts over workers' pay and the right to move freely led to a storm of public disobedience. The so-called Peasants' Revolt may not have been altogether an uprising of the dispossessed – it was led by the semi-independent yeoman class in response to the imposition of tough new taxes[1] and was no sudden eruption of rural ill-feeling. If anything, it was the culmination of a political stand-off that had begun during the labour shortage created by the Black Death. After three decades of frustration and resentment, the plague finally inspired England's first howl of collective disorder – its first general strike.

[1] Many of those who joined the revolt were not humble labourers but farmers or craftsmen who were bridling at the restrictions that had been placed on their right to trade. Wat Tyler may have been (as his name implies) a tiler. But John Ball was no son of the soil, but a Latin-speaking priest, and Jack Straw seems to have been a churchman too. And though they were demanding equality from the King, they were also targeting foreign (i.e. Flemish) workers.

What was worse – from the landlords' point of view – was the fact that the price of agricultural commodities crashed as the contracting population found itself over-supplied. In some accounts, England's landowners may have suffered a 20 per cent fall in income between 1347 and 1353. They responded by 'farming out' estates to labourers, leasing their land instead of working it themselves, and simply living on the rent. This was a new and lazy form of landholding, but it did create not just a new aristocracy of absentee rent collectors (fat-cat property magnates) but a new class of self-sufficient smallholders who could, for the first time, own their own small piece of the agricultural action.

The shrinking workforce had other unexpected side-effects, too. For instance, it created a financial incentive for England's merchant class to mechanise by coming up with new labour-saving devices. If one clever engine could do the work of a dozen poor souls who had died, then so much the better. A thousand inventions later – in milling, shipping, weaving, pumping and sowing – England was an industrial superpower.

Surprisingly, given the deadly way it touched the entire country, the plague did not inspire much English literature. In Italy, Boccaccio began his *Decameron* by dilating on its terrors (tumours as big as apples), as an introduction to his escapist tales of princes, grail quests, lusty monks, jealous lovers, pompous clerics, Jews and Mohammedans, parables of avarice and virtue, and shipwrecks. The pilgrims who made their way to Chaucer's Canterbury, on the other hand, seemed oblivious to it.

The Black Death had other repercussions. To some extent, its horrors gave religious authority a black eye by bruising the common faith in divine justice. What sort of God would inflict such a calamity on a pious nation? This also boosted the advance of English as the *lingua franca* by injuring the prestige of Latin – the language of priests. And it set in motion a ripple of social change by encouraging people to flee to safe havens. Some villages died as a result; others received new leases of life.

This was not a complete novelty – as we have seen, medieval people were more mobile than we often imagine – but the dread of plague dug a spur into the natural English desire to up sticks and seek pastures new.

It may even, in a contradictory way, have boosted the church-building programme. The wealthier survivors felt a need to donate more of their money in public displays of atonement, and there was, of course, something of a boom in the gravestone and mausoleum business. As many as half of the parish churches in England today were built between 1380 and 1530. There were many reasons for this, but the penitential dimension should not be overlooked.

Finally – though this is indirect, and looking far ahead – the labour shortage may have allowed a particularly wicked germ to burrow its way into the national mindset. With English workers demanding pay rises, some landowners and merchants started to notice that foreigners might work for less, or even nothing at all. There was little they could do with this idea in the Middle Ages, but a cruel solution to the labour crisis began to swim into focus when English ships started sailing around the world: labour could be rounded up in one country, shipped to another, and worked into the ground.

England was not alone in suffering from plague, but in combination with the factors already in place – the marine location, moist climate, fertile fields, construction and engineering expertise and extraordinary wealth – the Black Death did operate a bit like a performance-enhancing drug. It may even have launched a new era of landownership, and thus a new phase of wool wealth. As we have seen, large estate holders, such as the Cistercian monks, already knew that sheep-rearing was less labour-intensive than arable farming. Plague only underlined the fact. With ruthless skill, evolution did its cruel work by ridding England of its least fit farms – those with thin soil, weak water, poor woodland. In the process, it created thousands of acres of vacant land that could be given over to pasture. The move 'from corn to horn' gathered pace; and the towns that thrived were based on trade, not farming.

A sheep-rich land became even woollier. The Bishop of Winchester had 22,500 sheep in 1348; twenty-one years later he had 35,000. Romney Marsh, with hardly anyone left to work the land, was repopulated with 160,000 animals. By the beginning of the sixteenth century, when Henry VII was counting his money and European ships were beginning to tiptoe across the Atlantic, England's sheep outnumbered human beings by more than three to one (8 million against 2.5 million).

Finally, since sheep husbandry generated cash rather than food, it encouraged the further development of an economy based on finance and trade, rather than subsistence agriculture.

This may have been a disaster for the rural people who survived the plague only to be turfed off their land in favour of sheep. But with the benefit of six hundred years of hindsight, we can see that the villages which survived the cut prospered as never before. And their inhabitants started to embrace new crafts. The Tudor period was a good time to be a builder or an architect. In addition to the churches, manor houses and palaces, England became a land of everyday cottages and farms. The philanthropic impulse (or guilty conscience) that paid for the raising of cathedrals also financed schools (such as the colonnaded studio that still straddles the High Street in Market Harborough) and almshouses. Taken together, these developments gave England a *raison d'être* that would make its pulse race for centuries to come.

By the seventeenth century, the country could look back on the Great Plague (with a shiver of horror) as the time when it had all begun.

It came at a hefty price, however. In 1925 a pilot named Osbert Crawford was flying over the windswept fields south of the Humber when he noticed an unusual formation on the ground below. At eye level it would have been tricky to decipher the dips and bumps: they looked like the contours of an abandoned golf course that had blown inland. But from the air it was a tidy grid of rectangles and squares.

Crawford smiled. It was what he was searching for.

An observer for the Royal Flying Corps in the First World War and a geography graduate from Oxford University, he was now Archaeological Officer for the Ordnance Survey. He had already used aerial reconnaissance to help locate Woodhenge – the neighbouring sister of Stonehenge – and was on the lookout for similar sunken layouts.[2] Some 1300 of the villages mentioned in the Domesday Book had vanished, almost without trace – 150 in Lincolnshire alone. They were dotted all over the countryside: ruined churches, a tree pushing through the roof; aristocratic parks with faint imprints of earlier buildings visible in the meadows; incongruous banks in the middle of fields; odd lumps of wall and surprising platforms cut into slopes where huts had once stood. This seemed to be one of those places.

He took a careful set of photographs and headed for home.

It turned out that the outline he had seen from his cockpit was indeed the shadow of an ancient village – Gainsthorpe. The settlement had a neat manorial shape: barns, crofts, fish ponds, dovecotes, a chapel, a windmill and two hundred smaller cottages and buildings.

It was an exhilarating moment. Gainsthorpe had been famous since a seventeenth-century antiquarian noted that it was 'eaten up with time, poverty and pasturage', but the world had lost track of it. It may well have been ravaged into oblivion by the Black Death – and by the eruptions of plague that reverberated in its wake for centuries after – but it was beginning to dawn on medieval archaeologists (a new field in the 1920s) that

2 Crawford generously credited a fellow pilot, Squadron Leader Gilbert Insall, with the discovery. The site contained rings of wooden posts (168 in all) which have since been replaced by concrete pillars.

the disease might not have been the worst thing to befall a village. Sheep-rearing to supply the insatiable appetite of the wool trade might have been an even more lethal enemy.

Gainsthorpe may have been shut down for sheep.

That is what happened to a village on the other side of the Humber, just off the road from York to Scarborough. Wharram Percy is the most famous of all the habitations grazed to death by sheep. Lying in a dip of soft slopes, its fields have the same rumpled texture as at Gainsthorpe. But for a deserted medieval village (DMV), it is rather well kept: there's a ruined church, a graveyard, a mill pool and a farmhouse.

Eaten up with time . . . The ghostly outlines at Wharram Percy are a permanent reminder that nothing is timeless.

In the thirteenth century the Percy family built a manor house at Wharram Percy, and rows of cottages for two or three hundred people. But the following century the estate failed, partly because the family had no male heir, partly because Scottish raiders came this way, and partly because the Black Death came calling. The village survived all of these disasters, but the rise of sheep did for it in the end. The new owners, a

Sunderland family named Hilton, closed it down. From their angle, it was the only sensible thing to do. Tending sheep was so much easier than raising crops; a couple of shepherds could watch over a sizeable flock. The remaining tenants had to be evicted, but who said life was fair? The sheep moved in; the villagers moved on.

It was callous, but inevitable. The fourteenth-century aristocrat, fat and smiling on the proceeds of his acreage, watched the price of wool rising during the Forty Years War (who knew that it still had more than sixty years to run?) and did some quick sums. When he looked at the villeins on his estate, with their scrawny cows and pigs, as well as the sheep on the common pasture, he could not help stroking his perfumed chin and asking: 'Is this green land not mine? Am I not descended from the Conqueror? Have I not done enough for these people already? And, given that they toil all year to produce my grain, would they not be happier elsewhere anyway?

Finally: would it not be better to grow a hedge round the field and keep naught but sheep? The abbot has been doing that for years, and no one serves better wine than him. It must be God's will.'

Without further ado, the landowner magnanimously released the villagers from their feudal obligations. They were free! They could do whatever they pleased, answer to no one but themselves and go wherever they chose. There was only one caveat: they could not stay here.

Forty families lived in Wharram Percy in 1280. By 1500, there were only four. The faint relic that survives is suggestive of the way civilisations rise and fall, but also bears witness to the transforming effect of the wool economy on individual communities. When the last humans were evicted in 1517, the process of enclosure was still gathering pace. By the end of the sixteenth century, a third of England's once-fertile land had been cordoned off to create a single immense sheep run. It amounted to a bold and far-reaching seizure by the landholding elite.

Wharram Percy did not re-emerge until Maurice Beresford began to excavate the site in 1950, having been tipped off by the Ordnance Survey's aerial photographs. What followed was a lengthy process – his report ran to thirteen volumes – and a whole new discipline of rural history was launched. But the underlying message was simple: a buried world had come to light, and it was one of hundreds whose vague outlines were still imprinted in the landscape.

In 1516, in *Utopia*, Thomas More accused sheep of 'eating up people'. He included his own cherished Roman faith as a guilty collaborator in their destruction: 'Abbots leave no ground for tillage, they enclose all into pastures . . . they pluck down towns, and leave nothing standing but only the Church, to be made a sheephouse.' As for the humble people of the parish, 'By one means or another, by hook or crook, they must needs depart away, poor, silly, wretched souls, men, women, husbands, wives, woeful mothers with their young babes, and their whole household.' It was satire, but this was a serious complaint. And it was places like Wharram Percy that he had in mind. Sheep really were taking over the realm, enriching landowners, impoverishing the landless, and reshaping entire regions as they went.

The simple fact was that sheep pasture was more productive, and thus more valuable, than arable land. It yielded sixpence an acre instead of four. The effect on the rural scene was more than physical (all those drystone walls criss-crossing the hillsides). Out of sight, the biggest fault line in English history – the divide between public and private property, and the uneven distribution of English wealth – became ever more set in stone.

Another fissure opened up at the same time. In the early Middle Ages, people were power: the greater the number of hands, the lighter the burden of work. Sheep farming upended this equation by introducing the idea that people were a *drain* on resources. Inevitably, as enclosure and eviction spread across the shires, a second Peasants' Revolt flared into life. Like the first, it was not quite the outcry of a stricken peasantry. Led by Jack Cade in 1450, it was supported by church leaders and men of property who objected to the impositions of royal governance. And, as before, it failed: Cade was hung, drawn and quartered, then his head was displayed on a pole at London Bridge. But it was further evidence that the husbandry of sheep could have weighty political consequences.

History remained blind to this inglorious chapter in England's story for a long time, because it was only aerial reconnaissance that rendered the facts visible. Every now and then, ramblers would stumble across a few tell-tale signs – a sunken road, the outline of a pond, a pile of stones that suggested a wall – but it wasn't until photographers started taking to the skies that the dimpled evidence shone out. All at once, the past sprang to life: those combed lines that caught the shadows on frosty mornings were the patterns of ridge and furrow farming; that unnaturally straight line in the grass could only be a buried village lane. These ghostly outlines of abandoned villages are useful reminders that nothing is as timeless as the heritage industry likes to suggest. They also undermine the rosy view of Tudor England as a golden age. Until recently, historians were mostly content to go along with the line that enclosures were a harsh but necessary process of economic readjustment. Trevelyan dismissed them as 'sporadic and local', while Sir Arthur Clapham claimed the death of a village was 'singularly rare'. Cameras in planes soon put paid to that argument.

Then along came Beresford and Hoskins, and other historians were obliged to put down the rare manuscripts in cathedral libraries and head out into the fields with tape measures.

Not everyone hates a disaster. Financiers try not to waste a good crash, while shares in construction companies leap when an earthquake strikes. So we should not be surprised that the Black Death had the paradoxical effect of fostering a boom. Or, if not a boom, then at least an alteration. And there was a

bright side: the shift of power in the workplace – the countryside – meant that the peasant–squire model of feudal England
faded faster than it might otherwise have done.

Frederic Maitland, one of the grand figures of Victorian
history, understood this, arguing that England had 'practically
completed' the move from a feudal to a rent society by 1485.
Similarly, William Warburton, in his 1865 life of Edward III,
observed: 'Within fifty years of the visitation of the Black
Death, serfdom and villeinage were practically abolished in
England.' Lord Ernle (Barrister, Fellow of All Souls, MP,
cricketer and agricultural historian) agreed that England was by
then a land of 'freeholders, leaseholders, copy holders and hired
hands' bound to no man.

Several decades later, in his 1966 *Economic History of Britain*,
Sir John Clapham suggested that the English labourer was at
least partially free when Henry VII came to the throne, and
'by 1500 only a small minority were in any real sense ser-
vile'. Eileen Power looked at wills and marriage records and
concluded that medieval England had 'a large and prosperous
middle class, whose wealth was based not on landed property
but on industry and trade'. Michael Postan agreed that the
Black Death accelerated the decline of serfdom and felt that
'the medieval countryside was not uniformly the land of the
unfree'. Philip Ziegler noted that 'the hedged fields of England
can plausibly be argued to have had their genesis in the aftermath of the Black Death'. Anthony Bridbury agreed: 'It is
impossible to exaggerate the importance of the Black Death as
an agent of emancipation.' And Robert Gottfried wrote that
the depopulation it engendered 'virtually ended serfdom'.

None of these historians tried to argue that the Black Death
was a blessing in disguise. But they all conceded that it delivered the kind of jolt from which economic and social progress
often springs. Places like Wharram Percy remind us that this
sort of progress leaves a bitter list of casualties in its wake.

Thirteen

Trading Places

What was bad for the countryside was good for towns. The enclosure of land for sheep turned England's urban centres into vibrant (if evil-smelling) focal points where people could mingle and do business. Yorkshire's wool growers and merchants met in Leeds; Winchester and Norwich performed the same function in the south and east. Many smaller towns – Market Rasen, Market Harborough, Chipping Norton, Chipping Sodbury – bear names that betray similar origins. The places where roads met rivers became regional capitals.

This was a major change, because it gave all parts of England, even the more secluded rural regions, an outward-looking mindset. Once again, it helped that England was small. No one was too far from other people.

A typical town would hold four markets a year – one for each season – but the most spectacular were the great fairs. The Church sponsored these as adjuncts to its calendar of holy feasts, but they were not very religious. London's Bartholomew Fair was one of the most unruly, but towns like Boston, Northampton and York all became famous for boisterous gatherings.

The Gazetteer at the National Archives lists 2400 towns that were entitled to hold fairs – from Abbots Bromley in Staffordshire to Zoyland in Somerset. But the daddy of them all took place at Stourbridge, on the banks of the Cam, and reachable by barge from the Wash. These days the fairground forms part of a tranquil suburban park on the outskirts of Cambridge; from time to time a university eight skims by, scattering the mallards. But in Tudor times it hosted an annual jamboree that lasted a month or more. In a way it was a festival of England: merchants congregated here to buy and sell wool, grain, cheese and vegetables from East Anglia, lead from the Pennines, tin from Cornwall, salt from Cheshire, and livestock from throughout the land, all bustling together in a heaving mass of stalls and tents. There would have been a swirl of foreign accents too, as traders from Venice and Genoa brought their silks, gems and spices from the exotic East, while merchants from Liège, Bruges and Ghent poked around for high-quality cloth. French and Spanish sea captains would unload wine, while Norwegians brought tar, pitch, fur and amber from the Baltic.

England was trading with the rest of the world like never before, and the fairground became a test bed for English products, English vices, English amusements and English games. When Queen Elizabeth put the university in charge of Stourbridge Fair, it became an arts festival as well as a continental hypermarket. A century later, Isaac Newton picked up a copy of Euclid in one of the bookstalls, along with various intriguing new optical instruments.

But the licentious side tended to dominate. There were freak shows, circus acts and more than a bit to drink. In *The Pilgrim's Progress* (1678), John Bunyan held it up as a model of entertaining misrule: 'there is at all times to be seen juggling, cheats, games, plays, fools, apes, knaves and rogues, and that of every kind'. He dubbed it 'Vanity Fair' and made a point of mentioning its cosmopolitan nature: in addition to English products there was 'the French Row, the Italian Row, the Spanish Row, the German Row'. A generation later, Defoe marvelled at the range of goods on offer: 'Scarce any trades are omitted – goldsmiths, toyshops, brasiers, turners, milliners, haberdashers, hatters, mercers, drapers, pewterers, china-warehouses, and in a word all trades that can be named in London; with coffee houses, taverns, brandy shops and eating houses, innumerable, in tents and booths.'

By then, Stourbridge was a major annual event – the Stock Exchange meets Glastonbury. It was a showcase for two great English pastimes, shopping and drinking.

Fairs were so popular that even small villages wanted to have one of their own. It had long been a custom to keep a grassy field in the heart of the village for grazing sheep and geese, and these greens now became ideal places for fêtes and fireworks. They came in all shapes and sizes – Chipping Campden's was long and thin; Great Dunmow's was triangular; Lavenham's was paved – but all of them transmitted a powerful sense of communal togetherness. They were the centre of village life, the ideal place for an inn, a pond or a well. They were perfect for community meetings and ceremonies, and also served as recruiting office and penal theatre (stocks,[1] whipping posts and ducking stools were all set up there), cricket pitch, archery lawn and playground. This was where the maypole, the war memorial, the marquee, the statue and the bandstand stood. And the itinerant workforce that moved around the country building outsized churches would camp in the open space.

Once again, a small architectural innovation – the requirement for a plot of land where sheep could safely graze, or be sold – begat another, and another, and another, until a recognisable slice of English life emerged out of the mist.

The individual shapes of village greens tend to reflect their origins. Chipping Campden – like its Cotswold neighbours Broadway and Moreton-in-the-Marsh – has a ribbon of open space stitched into a wide High Street because it developed along the road that ran at the base of the hill. Great Dunmow and Lavenham, on the other hand, occupied the meeting

---

1 In 1376 Edward III ordered that every village must have a set of stocks, and they were busy for centuries: one set was still in use as late as 1865. A few of them survive to this day, including on the village greens at Bainbridge in Yorkshire and King's Sutton in Northamptonshire.

point of three routes and therefore grew around a triangular space. (Other villages had triangular greens so three open fields could lie on their flanks.) Settlements on major routes, at river crossings or at the end of a cul-de-sac took another shape again – they were likely to have a square green or a round circus rather than an elongated verge. But they have something in common – they all derive from a specific historical time and place: medieval England. The particular elements of medieval life (sheep, manors, churches) were what created this heart-shaped green space in the centre of the English townscape.

Many a thesis could be written on the significance of village greens in English national life. They are symbols of royal power and popular dissent, of lively commerce and light-hearted amusement, of faith and charity. Echoes of them linger on in our city centres: London alone boasts Bethnal Green, Clerkenwell Green, Islington Green, Paddington Green and Parson's Green. And some later town planners included them not because they needed somewhere for sheep and a maypole, but because the green had become an indispensable part of the English scene. Old greens had ponds because the horses needed a drink and the geese needed somewhere to feed; the new ones had them because they looked pretty.

When settlers from England crossed the Atlantic and established a home from home in New Haven, one of the first things they built was a village green. It is now a sixteen-acre park in the city centre – a little plot of old England in Connecticut.

Civic life gave a boost to a new class of traders whose wealth came not from land granted by the King, but from their own sweat and energy. Some were farmers; some were manufacturers; some were brokers; some were retailers; some were agents or middlemen. They were a potent new force in the body politic.

But the biggest game in town – by a country mile – was still wool. And it was responsible for England's first cluster of independently wealthy men. One, John Cely, bought fleeces at Northleach in the Cotswolds, sold them in Flanders, and through his sons Richard and George created a dynasty. The family even had a ship, the *Margaret*, named after John's wife.

The English Channel at that time was full of pirates, so wool ships of this sort had to be fitted with cannon and shot, while a lookout scanned the horizon for sails. Like Antonio, Shakespeare's Venetian merchant, Cely was in a perpetual fret over his precious 'argosies': 'This day the 16th August,' he wrote in one letter, 'the wool fleet came to Calais both of Ipswich and of London in safety, thanked be God.'

Thomas Cole, a 'rich clothier of Reading' at the end of the thirteenth century, was said to command three hundred men – pickers, sorters, carders, spinners, weavers, dyers and teasers. His carts filled the road from his home town to London. John Winchcomb (alias 'Jack of Newbury') had a hundred looms, was famous for his kerseys, and sent soldiers to Flodden.

But few could rival London's Sir John Pulteney. He owned a fulling mill in Stepney, was mayor three times, and was knighted in 1337. Pulteney was unusual in that he started life as an aristocrat, then became rich by sliding *down* the social scale. He was apprenticed to a draper, like many younger sons of the gentry, but by 1341 was so wealthy that he was able to build a lavish country house in Kent – Penshurst Place.

John de la Pole was a wool and wine merchant in the reign of Edward I, and was rewarded for his loyalty to the King with manorial rights over the village of Kingston-upon-Hull. He opened a brick kiln there and the place soon became the first (and for a long time the only) brick town in England. His son William inherited the family business and became a leading banker to Edward III, advancing £110,000 to the royal war coffers. In return, he became the first merchant to take up a seat in the House of Lords, and his son Michael became the Earl of Suffolk.

There were many such success stories. Some are remembered as great men of the age: Thomas Betson, William Stonor, Roger Norman. Others survive only as evocative sobriquets, like characters in a play: Cuthbert of Kendal, Hodgkins of Halifax, Brian of Manchester.

Some of them, perhaps surprisingly, were women. Although society usually assigned them subservient roles, a few became dominant not only in the home but in trade. This was partly because one form of medieval womanhood enjoyed something like independence: the widow. If a widowed woman did not remarry, she could command an empire. The founder of Clare College, Cambridge, was a one-time 'Lady of Clare' who became Elizabeth Burgh of Suffolk. Abbesses enjoyed a similarly high status, at least until Henry VIII dissolved their abbeys.

Not all widows were elderly: early death was not rare in the Middle Ages, and nor was early marriage. Grace de Selby wed her first nobleman when she was four, and another when she was eleven. When the second died she became a teenager of substance. Other ladies, left fortunes by husbands lost to war or disease, became dowager-empresses of all they surveyed. Margery Kempe was the richest citizen of King's Lynn when, at her father's death, she inherited his brewery and mill. It drove her mad, but you can't have everything.

Chaucer's Wife of Bath is the most celebrated portrait of this type. She honed her sharp tongue not in the kitchen, but by being an established clothier: 'Of cloth-making she hadde swiche an haunt / She passed hem of Ypres and of Gaunt.' She was the equal of any Dutchman, in other words.

Historical periods have fuzzy edges. No one can say precisely when the Bronze Age gave way to the Iron Age, or when the Middle Ages ended. But for the sake of argument we can say that the Great Age of Wool ran for roughly three centuries – from the reign of Edward I to the fall of Calais in 1558.

It is well known that Mary I reacted to the shocking loss of England's last possession in France by saying that the name would be engraved on her heart when she died. But few who are not scholars of the period can remember exactly what she was driving at, beyond the fact that it was a bad reverse.

As it happened, the day Calais fell was already a sad one for Mary – it was the anniversary of the death of her mother, Catherine of Aragon. But there was more to Mary's distraught reaction than wounded pride or grief . . . and nearly all of it had to do with England's wool.

As we have seen, the English Crown had long counted on the wool trade for its revenue. Sheep had ransomed Richard I out of captivity, funded Edward I's excursions into Wales and Scotland, and paid for the castles, cathedrals and churches that were the nation's cultural glory. But in the early part of the fourteenth century it became a hot-tempered *casus belli* between the old relatives – England and France.

There was no one spark; on the contrary, the conflict had been brewing for years. The tax on wool was all very well, but the disappearance of his principal money-lenders and their 'loans' (they were not quite voluntary, and unlikely to be repaid) left a significant hole in the royal budget. Italian merchant bankers offered to help, but the King needed more.

The gap was filled by men such as Laurence of Ludlow, a Shropshire wool merchant. He had just built a castle at Stokesay, near Shrewsbury, and was a senior player in the cross-Channel trade with Flanders. In this capacity he became one of Edward I's chief paymasters, and in 1294 he encouraged the King to triple the tax on wool exports. It was a self-serving ploy in that it hit wool farmers harder than intermediaries like Laurence himself. But the farmers were powerless to object.

Nature exacted a nice revenge on their behalf. In the winter of 1294 Laurence was sailing to Flanders when his ship sank off Suffolk and he drowned. But his tax survived and was warmly welcomed in royal circles, since war was not cheap especially when it went on for a hundred years or more. It was hard to administer, however, so in 1313 Edward II decreed that all of the wool that was destined for export should be taxed in one place – a central mercantile exchange that became known as the Staple. At first this moved around the country to towns like Lincoln, Boston, Bury St Edmunds and London (where its ghosts still haunt the half-timbered chambers of Staple Inn, Holborn). But in due course it pitched its tents overseas, close to the wool markets of the Low Countries. The important point was that all of England's exported wool could be weighed and taxed in one place. Ghent, St Omer, Brussels, Dordrecht and Antwerp were all Staple towns.

The fortunes of England and Flanders became tied together, in an ever closer union.

The relationship was not always harmonious: tempers frayed; cargoes were confiscated; debts were repudiated. But business thrived: England produced the wool, and Flanders wove it into cloth. As Thomas Walsingham wrote, there was hardly a lady in England who did not wear the fruits of this partnership. The Crown and the merchants did particularly well out of the system, since the Staple was, in effect, a cartel that kept wool prices high – an arrangement that suited both parties.

Inevitably, its success soon attracted the attention of King Philip VI of France, and since the main Flemish ports were also a key element in England's wine trade with Bordeaux and Gascony, he began to agitate against England in the Low Countries. Riled, the new English King, Edward III, sent a force of fifty ships across the Channel to make a martial statement. They were made from stout English oak – a reminder that the nation's shipping, like its sheep industry, was in one sense a natural resource.

Edward may not have been seeking a fight, but when his army ran into a French force near Crécy in 1346, he had no option but to unleash his archers, with their fearful longbows crafted from English (and Welsh) yew. Chroniclers presented this as a heroic David-against-Goliath victory – given that the French outnumbered the English – but in truth the English were roving plunderers. Edward followed up this triumph by laying siege to Calais.

After resisting for almost a year, six brave and half-starved citizens offered themselves in sacrifice to prevent a massacre.[2] The men were reprieved after the intervention of the King's Flanders-born wife, Philippa of Hainault, but Calais duly fell.

Rodin's Burghers of Calais *immortalised the town's surrender to Edward III in 1347, after Crécy. Calais would be a prominent English metropolis for nearly two centuries.*

The town's new nationality became official in 1360, and France surrendered not just Calais but a parcel of land around it – known as the 'Pale'. The inhabitants were evicted and the town was restocked with English and Dutch settlers. It was defended by a military garrison (England's first standing army), the captaincy of which became a prestigious post. To counter wool smugglers – stealthy ships would try to load fleeces at night to

2 Rodin commemorated the episode in *The Burghers of Calais* (1885) which captured the anguish so successfully that bronze casts of it now stand in Paris, London, Copenhagen, Basel, New York, Pasadena, Philadelphia, Washington and Tokyo.

evade the tax – two royal agents were given the power to inspect any suspicious cargoes, and the world had another new thing: customs inspectors. Before long, Calais was sending its own representatives to Westminster, like any other English town, and a towering church (Notre Dame) was built in the English Gothic style.[3] A famous inscription on the city gate swore that Calais would remain English until iron and lead floated like cork.

The town was war booty, but ideally placed to become the new, permanent Staple. It was closer to London than many of the English Staple towns; on a clear day you could see Calais from Dover. It was handy for the Flemish cloth market, and was easy to supply. Not that the Channel was safe for shipping: it was still full of buccaneers, so the wool fleets had to be shepherded across in armed convoys. Twice a year, English ships would slip out of eastern harbours, form a great wool armada, then set sail for Calais.

Soon, almost half the population of England's French territory was involved in the wool trade, and the Pale was generating a third of the Crown's income. Wool was not the only export to pass through the new trading post – leather, tin, lead and even coal all added grist to the royal mill – but it was by far the most important. Edward III invited a group of wool merchants to establish a mercantile colony over there. John Cely of Northleach was one of its first leaders – the canopy in his church at Northleach bears the arms of the Staple of Calais – and he was soon joined by a remarkable gang of notables, including William de la Pole of Hull, John Pulteney of London, Sir William Browne of Stamford and William Canynges of Bristol. They were the Merchants of the Staple, an association of twenty-six wool and cloth traders, and they guaranteed an income to the King in return for a monopoly over the business. Incorporated by royal charter in 1319, but operating long before then, they had but one aim: to keep the price of wool as high as possible.

3 Charles de Gaulle was married in this church in 1921.

That is why Calais mattered. It was a Cotswolds wool town that had drifted south-east. It had a mayor, a castle, an inn, stables, shops, even a mint (which stamped legal coins out of the merchants' gold). But this little corner of England in France also opened a doorway to the international realm, and all its ingenious novelties. William Caxton first travelled to the Low Countries on wool business, during his apprenticeship to a mercer. From there he made his way to Cologne, where he saw Herr Gutenberg's wonderful machine.

The Merchants of the Staple were a new wool aristocracy. Their crest featured a pair of sheep, hooves resting on a shield and helm, above the motto: 'God Be Our Friend'. In the coming centuries, many members of the brotherhood would recycle their wealth into monuments: William Dauntesey of Wiltshire and Andrew Judde of Tonbridge endowed schools; Thomas Kitson built Hengrave Hall in Suffolk. Many years later, Thomas Leigh of Shropshire, a leading merchant and lord mayor, bought a dissolved monastery in Warwickshire and turned it into a stately home, Stoneleigh Court.

Every now and again, a non-merchant with the right connections was able to gain entry to this magic circle. William Somers had nothing to do with the wool business – he was Henry VIII's court jester – but he became a Merchant of the Staple because he knew how to tickle the King's funny bone.

They were soon rich enough to rival the power of the Crown itself: Eileen Power called them 'a constitutional menace'. In time, they became the Company of the Staple in Calais and enjoyed a monopoly on all of England's wool exports. They conducted their trade in Italian florins, Dutch guilders, English crowns, Burgundian groats, French Louis d'or and several other currencies, so, inevitably, they also became a significant force in international banking. As the Company diversified into new activities, it needed lawyers, brokers, clerks, doctors and other middlemen. In effect, as a foreign town under English governance, Calais served as an early experiment in colonial rule. In time, the Company of the Staple would morph into the Company of Merchant Adventurers and start to cast its nets across half the world.

This is all a way of saying that England went to war with France largely to protect – and further – its wool interests (just as, centuries later, British ships sailed to defend sheep farmers in the Falkland Islands). The task force that went to Crécy was the spearhead of a commercial invasion. This was why the surrender of Calais in 1558 was such a calamity. For 200 years it had been the Crown's most important cash machine. When Dick Whittington rose through the wool trade to become Lord Mayor of London, he, like his predecessors, became Mayor of Calais too. It was the capital of English wool, and its most precious possession.

No wonder Mary's heart ached.

Fourteen

Down on the Farm

E ngland may have stumbled when Calais was lost, but it
did not fall. On the contrary, it was by then embarked on
a forward march that would drive it to master new trades and
new swathes of the world. As the age of wool drew to a close,
a new chapter began.

Five men play the leading roles in the standard version
of what happened next. The first, Jethro Tull, was born in
1674 in Bradfield (according to the *Dictionary of National
Biography*), Hungerford (the *Encyclopedia Britannica*) or Basildon
(Wikipedia). The documentary evidence on his early life is not
exactly copper-bottomed.

It is agreed, however, that he was the child of landed gentry,
studied at Oxford University and trained as a barrister in London's
Gray's Inn. He was a scholar, a musician and a Grand Tourist –
by no means a son of the soil. But when he became a gentleman
farmer, on a none-too-promising strip of land near Crowmarsh,
not far from Reading, he turned himself into an ingenious home
improver. On his European travels he had been much taken by
the organ pipes of continental churches, and in 1700, after much
determined trial and error, he invented a pipe-shaped device that
could be dragged behind a horse. It scored a groove in the soil
and dribbled seed into the earth at just the right depth to keep it
safe from birds and other pests. It also sowed in arrow-straight
lines, allowing farmers to hoe the weeds from the gaps.

Tull called it a seed drill, and when it was combined with lighter, stronger ploughshares it increased crop yields fivefold.

As so often with new technologies, it was not greeted warmly by the existing workforce. Labour-saving gadgets were all very well, but this one imperilled the farm hands' livelihoods. Tull's seed drill could not be wished away, however: its spectacular effect on productivity made it irresistible to landowners, and ushered in a period of abrupt change in English rural life.

The second great figure – 'Turnip' Townshend – has a name that suggests humble origins. In fact, he was of even nobler birth than Tull. Better known as Charles, the 2nd Viscount Townshend, he was a notable aristocrat who inherited a grand Norfolk estate at the age of just thirteen. After attending Eton, he enjoyed a political career as, variously, Lord Privy Seal, Ambassador to The Hague (from where, along with the Duke of Marlborough, he led an army against France) and Secretary of State. In 1730 he retired to Raynham and, like Tull, became a gentleman farmer. He was similarly keen to improve productivity by harnessing the latest scientific discoveries, but his great innovation was not technical. Rather, he hit upon a new way of managing the land. As we have seen, in the medieval open field system, a third of the land was left fallow to regenerate each year. Townshend gave this time-honoured routine a twist by planting turnips in the fallow field, which produced winter fodder for livestock while replenishing the soil with nutrients. This four-course – or Norfolk – crop cycle, alternating barley, wheat, clover and turnips, proved highly effective and established the county as the fertile heart of English arable farming.

The third member of the quintet was Robert Bakewell of Leicestershire. Another Grand Tourist, he too inherited an estate (440 acres near Loughborough), and though his primary interest was livestock rather than crops, he was just as eager to maximise his returns.

His first and most significant innovation was the introduction of a methodical approach to breeding. Not content simply to release prize rams and bulls into flocks of ewes and herds of cows, and trust to luck, he kept the breeds apart and mated them selectively. Before long, he was able to unveil the new Leicester sheep, and a brand of new cow: the Leicestershire Longhorn. These high-yield animals made him rich – he collected some £3000 a year merely by hiring out his rams – and set the template for pastoral progress elsewhere. Other farmers followed Bakewell's lead and bred animals that were richer in meat, wool and milk than their ancestors. And all a century before Charles Darwin was even born.

Nor was this the end of Bakewell's inventiveness. He found fresh ways to exploit water, both as a transport system and for irrigation, by digging canals and channels on his land. And he discovered that animals could be rendered more productive by the simplest method of all: they responded well to kindness, to a gentle touch.

The fourth man, Thomas Coke, is perhaps the most controversial, if only because he was an eager self-publicist whose boastful claims have been much contested. Like Townshend he went to Eton, where he won renown by hanging seventy snipe in his college room, and embarked on the Grand Tour. Then, in 1776, he inherited an enviable manor at Holkham in Norfolk. The pattern is obvious: inventiveness, in eighteenth-century England, was a by-product of inherited wealth. Good ideas were ten a penny, but investment capital, the store of finance built up by wool . . . that was the hard part.

Coke was Earl of Leicester and MP for Derby for some fifty years, but it was at Holkham that he really made his mark. Over the course of four decades he expanded the estate to some 3500 acres and made it a show ground for Tull's seed drills, Townshend's rotation system *and* Bakewell's breeding methods. All three innovations were tested here like nowhere else. In so doing, Coke tripled his sheep population to over two thousand, and celebrated the fact by holding a public shearing festival every year. A monument to him still stands at Holkham. At a time when most grandees were commemorated in mythological terms, the redoubtable column to 'Farmer Tom' was crowned with a wheatsheaf and decorated with a bull, a flock of sheep, a plough, a seed drill and – last but not least – some of the labourers who made his success possible.

The fifth and final member of the team, Arthur Young, was the only non-aristocrat, but he *was* a child of East Anglia's historic wool heritage. The son of a clergyman, he went to school in Lavenham and then joined a mercantile house in King's Lynn, but he soon realised that the merchant's life was not for him. He tried his hand at publishing a journal in London, did a little travelling and pondered a commission as a cavalry officer before finally settling down as a farmer when his mother gave him eighty acres in Essex. Young studied the principles of Norfolk husbandry and became a revered economist, editing a publication titled *Annals of Agriculture* under the pseudonym Robert Andrews.[1] In 1793, having both witnessed and been shocked by the violence in France, he became Secretary of the Board of Agriculture. England was having a very different sort of revolution.

Historians no longer like to cast this quintet of well-born men – a proper squirearchy – as the leaders of an agricultural upheaval. If anything, they suggest that they were its beneficiaries, rather than its visionaries. Modern scholars suggest that Coke, in particular, exaggerated the success of his initiatives, claiming much more credit than was his due. This is plausible: change is often more muddled in real life than in the thumbnail sketch. England's arable culture had been evolving for centuries – a step forward here, a step back there – and it would have taken more than five men to alter the way the nation farmed. Who knows how many forgotten souls experimented with contraptions similar to Tull's seed drill? Hundreds of men and women may have sung the praises of turnips without having access to the official

1 The name was not an invention: Young was a great admirer of the real Robert Andrews, whose estate in nearby Sudbury would soon be the subject of a famous painting.

record. And many shepherds must have known the benefits of breeding the fittest ram with the fittest ewe.

But even if their place in history is somewhat symbolic, the fact remains that the fields of eighteenth-century England were overhauled by men of this sort. Even if the Famous Five should be seen as no more than figureheads of a larger movement, their innovations *were* radical. And there is no denying that Holkham was the first Norfolk estate to grow wheat rather than rye (in 1787),[2] setting in motion a train of events and an attitude to bread that would one day make the county the wheat capital of England. Nor should we overlook the awkward truth that scientific advance often depends on resources (in terms of money and time) that are available only

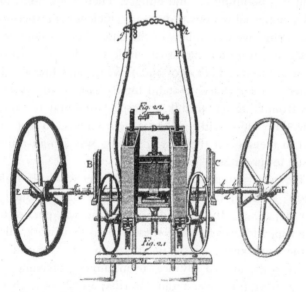

Jethro Tull seed drill: a head-turning innovation that turned farmers into profiteers.

© Mary Evans Picture Library

2 Wheat and rye are related, but the former produces fine flour for soft white bread and cakes, while the latter has a stronger, slightly sour flavour which is better suited for whiskey and darker bread.

to the well heeled. Progress is often built on existing assets: fortune favours the already fortunate. As Jethro Tull declared: 'I owe my principles and my practice originally to my travels, as I owe my drill to the organ.' It is almost certain, given the clamour for higher yields, that something similar would have emerged elsewhere in due course. But Tull's achievement grew out of his well-favoured early life.

There is another element here. The blizzard of mechanical innovation that gave rise to the Industrial Revolution was prompted in significant ways by *rural* breakthroughs. The search for stronger ploughs, keener scythes, better seed spreaders, more powerful threshing devices and faster mills was spurred by the desire to produce more food. The population was booming ... and hungry. There were political as well as financial reasons to increase efficiency. Furthermore, though they were members of the elite, these groundbreaking farmers were not the usual ruthless landlords. Coke and Townshend were both prominent Whigs and liberals. The former was persuaded to stand for Parliament to prevent a Tory from winning Norfolk, a prospect he found unconscionable – 'my blood chilled all over me from head to foot'. The latter, a member of the Royal Society, was a high-minded apostle for progress.

They were untypical aristocrats, in other words: England's huntin', shootin', fishin' landowners were hardly famed for their dynamism. In Alexander Pope's satirical phrase, they were happy to wait for interest rates to do their work, allowing them to luxuriate in 'the silent growth of ten per cent'. But thanks to the myriad advances in machinery, breeding, land management, finance and transport, that was about to change. Whether it was led by five, five hundred or five thousand men (not to mention the women who toiled by their sides), a revolution in agriculture really did begin to stir at this time.

Technical advance may have changed the way the English earth was used, but it was the inherent potential of the land itself that made it possible. A sandy waste land would not have inspired anyone to brood on the best way to sow seed; a rocky wilderness would not have led anyone to experiment with turnips. Rich, well-watered soil was the basis of English farming, as it always had been.

The value of that soil was about to stimulate another great shift in the way it was owned and managed.

In medieval and Tudor times, as we have seen, a huge amount of rural land was turned over to sheep-rearing. Now, boosted by the new methods, it happened again. A second wave of enclosures swept the country, this time backed by parliamentary muscle. The government was dominated by landowners, and the interests of the landed gentry were always to the fore in its deliberations. So when England spoke of the strong arm of the law, it really meant the strong arm of the law*makers*.

The first piece of land to be enclosed by a formal Act of Parliament was the village of Radipole, near the spot on the south coast where the Black Death had crawled ashore more than 250 years earlier. In 1604, as Shakespeare was writing *King Lear*, the residents were swept aside, and the village was hedged. The only trace that remains today is a hummocky patch of grass known as Humpty-Dumpty Field.

The end of Radipole was the start of a much bigger story. The first phase of enclosures – which ran up to 1700 – created safe pastures for sheep, and accounted for roughly a third of the available land in England: over four million acres. But in the eighteenth century the process found an extra gear. Between 1750 and 1870 some four thousand Acts of Parliament delivered another six or seven million acres into the hands of the enclosure commissioners. A tremendous swathe of shared terrain, perhaps half the country, was privatised. This was not why one of Parliament's chambers came to be known as the House of Commons, but it might well have been. The land seizure was especially determined in the central clay belt of the Midlands.

And this was about more than wool. It was thought, and taught, that animals *and crops* could be better managed on smaller plots using a system of rotation. As Winston Churchill put it, the 'dismal dukes' who led the movement believed that England's fields were 'nurseries of idleness and indolence'. Even cows did better in small fields rather than on wide ranges, since moving from one to the next gave them fresh grass throughout the year. It was a hazy and complicated subject, but the estates with hedged-in fields became arable powerhouses. Sheep were happy on the less fertile, harsher hillsides, while crops thrived in the vales. The rural population was shunted to ... well, who cared?

Technically, the ownership of England's earth was still concentrated in a few feudal hands, but centuries of custom had encouraged the idea that the land 'belonged' to the people, especially the marginal or 'waste' areas (heaths, moors and commons). But the new farming methods were making even those areas more fertile, so it became increasingly cost-effective to claim them for crop-growing (particularly as the price of prime terrain continued to rise). One way or another, the enclosure system trampled over established rural tradition.

Plenty of people were outraged. In 1732 the farmer and pamphleteer John Cowper wrote:

> I myself, within these 30 years past, have seen about 20 Lordships or Parishes inclosed, and every one of them has thereby been in a manner depopulated ... In some Parishes, 120 families of Farmers and Cottagers have in a few years been reduced to Four, to Two, nay, and sometimes to but one ... If anyone can shew me where an Inclosure has been made, and not at least half the inhabitants gone, I will throw up the argument.

This was a familiar cry, and it resonated down the generations thanks chiefly to Oliver Goldsmith, who captured its forlorn essence in 'The Deserted Village':

> *Sweet smiling village, loveliest of the lawn*
> *Thy sports are fled, and all thy charms withdrawn;*
> *Amidst thy bowers the tyrant's hand is seen*
> *And desolation saddens all thy green.*
> *One only master grasps the whole domain*
> *And half a tillage stints thy smiling plain.*

John Clare was similarly contemptuous: 'Inclosure, thou'rt a curse upon the land / And tasteless was the wretch who thy existence planned.'

Historians, for the most part, have agreed with the poets. For a while they were content to go along with the idea that enclosure was a painful necessity, but it was hard to be sanguine about what had happened when a government survey of 1872 found that a quarter of Britain's land was owned by just seven hundred people. This was little more than the theft of England's heritage – an outrage. Under the radiant banner of 'progress' it was national policy to shove people off land that had supported them for generations.

Enclosure proposals were generally posted on church boards, and although there was a theoretical right to object, not many could even read the warnings, let alone heed them.

Opposition to the enclosure movement soon expressed itself in more than rhyme. The English had always been quick to take up arms, and now they did so again. Bows and arrows, pikes and bills, most of them hand-crafted in the woodlands threatened by the new laws, were waved in angry protest.

In May 1607, only three years after the death of Radipole, there was a flurry of unrest in Haselbech, in Northamptonshire, when the Tresham family started enclosing fields to create sheep meadows in the rolling countryside west of Kettering. They fenced off four hundred acres that had been supporting nine families (sixty people) for half a millennium. And this was no isolated manoeuvre: according to a 1607

Royal Commission, some 27,000 acres were enclosed in this way, involving the eviction of 1500 people, in this part of Northamptonshire alone.

For one local man, a travelling tinker named John Reynolds, it was too much. He assembled a gang of aggrieved farmers near the village of Newton and they started ripping down barriers put up by the Tresham family in Rockingham Forest. Reynolds was inspired by a talisman he kept in a pouch, which offered – so he claimed – divine protection.

Thanks to this accessory, he was known as 'Captain Pouch'. The torch he lit was taken up across Leicestershire and Warwickshire, where protesters tore down hedges and blocked ditches. It was a major revolt. The rebels may have thought that the Crown would not stand by the landowners, especially as Francis Tresham had been implicated in the recent Gunpowder Plot,[3] but their hopes were misplaced. With royal backing, and the help of Sir Edward Montagu from nearby Boughton House,[4] the Treshams were able to send militia into battle against Pouch's men.

Some fifty rebels died in the struggle, and the ringleaders were executed with due ceremony and display.

Royal support for Tresham extended only so far – they were a noted Catholic family, and Sir Thomas was dubbed 'the most odious man in the country'. But it was too late to save the unhappy farmers. And Captain Pouch's precious talisman turned out to be a lump of mouldy cheese ... so the authorities claimed, before they hanged him.

There is not much in modern Haselbech (population: eighty-seven) to suggest that anything of moment ever happened here. It is a peaceful hamlet on a patch of high ground amid rolling fields. There is a quiet medieval church, a fine

---

3 He died in 1605, before he could face trial, but the authorities had little doubt about his guilt: they decapitated his corpse and displayed the head in Northampton.

4 A graceful mansion noted for its 365 windows, one for each day of the year.

Georgian rectory and a grand country house, Haselbech Hall, in which Lord Ismay (head of the White Star Line) retired to hang his head in shame after climbing into one of the *Titanic*'s last lifeboats in 1912.

Yet Captain Pouch's rebellion was an early tremor of the later, much more widespread uprisings of the Levellers and Diggers – two groups who also objected to restrictions imposed on land they had traditionally been entitled to use.[5] Once again, we can note that geography was the parent of politics – it was the productive richness of English land that ignited these bonfires of protest. But it was in the animosity surrounding enclosures that the long, defining tug-of-war between the haves and the have-nots, the landed and the landless, was kindled. The enduring fault lines of modern English politics were laid down right here.

In truth, England has always been two nations, if not more. At different times the land has been divided between Saxon and Dane, Angle and Norman, West and East, North and South, rich and poor. One reason why Victorian sportsmen liked the myth of the level playing field – a metaphor for meritocratic justice – was the fact that the actual fields, in the actual countryside, were anything but level. One of the supposed virtues of golf, in this context, was that it exposed players to the fickle 'rub of the green'.

The history of enclosure, and its effect on English society, is one of the thorniest in the syllabus. As E. P. Thompson pointed out: 'A novice in agricultural history caught loitering in these areas would quickly be dispatched.' We will not, therefore, trespass in them for long.

---

5 The latter created a significant tableau in 1649 when they planted vegetables on an enclosed area of St George's Hill, Weybridge. This stunt is often hailed as one of the first blows of modern political struggle. Yet the vegetable patch now forms part of one of England's most refined golf estates, a velvet swirl of palatial fairways and mansions hidden behind the pines.

For a long time, commentators accepted the received wisdom that the old way of farming really was sluggish and in need of a shot in the arm. Promising new techniques were available in the early seventeenth century, but it was impossible to experiment with them in the open field system, where conformity and neighbourliness ruled the roost. Lord Ernle was one of many leading historians who felt (in 1912) that the old way was 'impervious to change' and concluded: 'Small yeomen, open field farmers and commons could never have fed a manufacturing population. They could not have initiated and would not have adopted agricultural improvements.'

He was not alone. Agronomist after agronomist – and landowner after landowner – agreed that the open field system was 'a drag on productivity'. Even Arnold Toynbee conceded that enclosure, however cruel and clumsy, was 'a distinct improvement from an agricultural point of view'.

Much later, in a famous 1968 essay, 'The Tragedy of the Commons', Garrett Hardin argued that the medieval approach amounted to rural neglect. The tenants who worked a new strip of open field each year had no stake in the land's future health. Someone else would be farming it next summer, so why not milk it for all it was worth? In the same way, common pasture was overgrazed because why tread lightly when others were exploiting every last inch? The system incentivised overuse. Too many animals were on the land for too much of the time, and it was worn out.

But not everyone shared this view. Some denounced it. Hardin hit a nerve by telling the story of enclosures as if it were an allegory for the larger private versus public sector debate – a lively political topic. Both right- and left-wing theorists accepted that efficient agriculture was a worthwhile goal, and that the land needed better management, but the question remained: better for whom? Enclosure enriched landowners, not labourers. In fact, the latter were pauperised. Some were sucked into the greedy factories of industrial England. Others went further afield – to the colonies. In both cases, the consequences of a shift in English land use were momentous.

It is easy, in retrospect, to see the whole upheaval as a painful but 'inevitable' corollary of 'progress'. But that should not blind us to the wrenching disparities that whipped it along. Writing about the way in which the impoverished rural population flocked into urban factories in the late nineteenth century, Thomas Hardy sarcastically pointed out that the movement should be seen not as progress, but merely as 'the tendency of water to flow uphill when forced'. The depopulation of the countryside tore apart not just individual lives and livelihoods but social ecosystems (villages) that had been hundreds of years in the making.

It is probably best to resist generalisation in this area. It may be true that some of the enclosing (especially in the first wave, when the Black Death shrank the population by at least a third) was a force for economic good over the long term, despite the hardship it caused. It may also be true that some of it was the work not of feudal landlords but of smallholders, who also saw that sheep-rearing was more profitable than subsistence farming and wanted to carve out their own little realms. But in the second phase, the enclosure of land was a form of privatisation, enhancing the wealth of the wealthy and throwing the dispossessed on to the mercy of the parish. So it was good in one way, but bad in another: a typical English mixture.

It was a short step from here to the unequal whirl of Victorian times – the grim culture of destitution, workhouses and asylums that marked England's social structure so deeply. In 1833, a French visitor, Alexis de Tocqueville, found the contrast between rich and poor one of England's most striking features. The English, he wrote, were 'still convinced that extreme inequality of wealth is the natural order of things'. It was a philosophical observation, but one raised by an argument about the value of English land.

This is one of those unanswerable questions. Did the ideology of unequal spoils drive agricultural change; or did the requirements of sheep and soil give birth to the aristocratic shape of country life? It is certainly ironic that this greedy land seizure gave rise to the 'champion' landscape – rolling fields, hawthorn hedges, cosy villages, rambling manor houses, quaint churches, oak-fringed cricket pitches – that makes patriotic English hearts beat faster to this day. It was by no means the natural order of things – those hedges did not plant themselves – but it felt eternal. Its subtle tones – pink in spring, green in summer, chestnut in autumn, dun in winter – had become almost the colours of the English sensibility.

Either way, the long process of enclosure encouraged England's agriculture to become a large-scale capitalist venture long before the rest of Europe followed suit. While other nations maintained their ancient patterns of rural smallholdings (supporting the thousands of well-stocked little food markets so loved by holidaymakers), England became a realm of massive conglomerates. This was a major fork in the road, because once the big farms were up and running, buttressed by investment capital, scientific know-how and economies of scale, it was hard for smaller rivals to compete or even survive. The shift consolidated into a permanent change.

There were other costs. Strip-farming may have been rigid, but it did allow the new class of yeoman farmers to increase their holdings either through marriage or by making the most of a bumper harvest to lease a new furrow. In the space of a few generations they might, if the sun shone, become modest landowners in their own right. Enclosure ushered in something new by creating room for the independent smallholder, even as it threw such social advances into reverse by restoring the feudal model: big estates run by tight platoons of hired hands. It was double-edged from the beginning.

In these and other ways the nature of the land conditioned the political culture of the people who lived on it. It spawned both the lordly desire to possess land as far as the eye could see, and the dissident urge to fight for one's corner, however small. The great gulf in English politics – between the impulse to own property and the urge to resist exploitation – yawned in these historic disputes over farmland long ago.

One last thing. Those now-deserted villages had once supported a diverse society of potters, bakers, glovemakers, cobblers, basket-weavers, coopers, tanners, beekeepers, brewers, carpenters and many other craft workers. The enclosing of the land left this rural workforce with no choice other than to migrate to factory towns (or overseas). As a direct consequence, England's cottage industries started to wind down. For hundreds of years, households had grown extra crops, kept extra sheep, made a few jars of honey and spun a little wool at home. And women had worked alongside men in the fields. The new world of mills and factories would introduce them to production lines and a more severe division of labour. It really was farewell to a familiar strand of English life.

Farming was uphill work, God knew, but these factories were something else.

Many of the enclosed commons have been swallowed up by modern England's urban sprawl, although a few survive: Clapham Common, Mitcham Common, Wimbledon Common. It takes considerable effort to imagine a time when Croydon, say, was just a cluster of huts in wooded hills inhabited by charcoal burners and wood-bodgers, but it was precisely that way for centuries, turning out home-made implements on rough-and-ready lathes: broom handles, chairs, paddles, boards, bowls and pipes.

That world is long gone. But every now and then, waiting at a bus stop in the drizzle, we might notice a suggestive street name or signpost – Field End Road, Brook Farm, Old Green Lane, Meadow Ridge, The Commons, Elm Close, Heath Avenue – and feel a sudden chill as a ghost from the past grazes our shoulder. A sunken lane through the woods, a narrow alley in the old part of a city, an ancient bridge, a cracked square – the old shapes remain even when all else has faded.

We can sense this in the oldest place names, that come from the world before the enclosure movement. The suffix '-ton' – as in Bolton, Islington, Kingston, Leamington, Preston, Heston, Beeston, Manton, Donington, Alton, Southampton and countless other places – means 'enclosure'. But anyone who lives in a close might shudder at the implication.

The enclosure of England's commons may seem like a digression from our theme, since it was driven by England's class-conditioned political system rather than geographical facts. But the movement was all about the land – its ability to produce not just wool or food, but cash – so it lies close to the heart of the English story. The urge to possess one's own plot of earth, a place in the country, has long been a powerful English fantasy, and it began with a process whose ramifications are too broad to be compressed into a simple morality play. After all, those hated hedgerows soon turned into much-loved friends, full of hazel and catkin, bramble and elderflower, wrens, butterflies, rabbits and foxes. Before long they seemed like a timeless English habitat, a classic emblem of old rural ways.

Indeed, when modern machines started to pull them up to make room for combine harvesters, nostalgic souls cried out in anguish. John Betjeman grieved for England's lost hedgerows and 'grassy edges', and thousands mourned with him.

The often iniquitous history of enclosure had created a landscape which people saw not just as natural but as primordial. It was, they thought, the way England had always been: green, pleasant and all the rest of it. They had lost sight of the extent to which those evocative features were man-made.

This was the countryside over which (and *for* which) Spitfire pilots fought in the Battle of Britain – the closely woven Betjemanesque tapestry of bonfires and country lanes, pillar boxes and log-fired pubs, twisted gates and hawthorn copses. But none of this was 'natural'. It was the outcome of a centuries-long wrangle over the land that lay beneath.

The new, enclosed countryside played a major role in the development of another English tradition by creating ideal terrain for fox-hunting. It was not a coincidence that this thrived in the region where Captain Pouch had fought. The fields around Melton Mowbray, in Leicestershire, became home to three famous hunts (Belvoir, Cottesmore and Quorn). The land was open enough to carry a clear scent and allow for a high-speed pursuit, while the criss-cross pattern of hedges made it a steeplechase.[6] Riders loved to gallop across the farmland, and leap over the obstacles, in part because it allowed them to feel as if they were exercising some ancient seigneurial right – 'We'll ride where we please, and devil take the hindmost!'

6 The word itself – 'steeplechase' – carries reminders of these days when it was literally that: a race between two church spires. A less grand race was merely between two less distinctive markers, a 'point to point'. Even now, on a racetrack or in an athletics stadium, a steeplechase includes fences, hurdles and water jumps that echo these cross-country origins.

Fifteen

Middle England

I s it possible to name the most English place in the country? Probably not: there are too many contenders, all with excellent claims. Some might nominate a garden in the Cotswolds, but equally strong cases could be made for any of a dozen cathedral closes, steelworks, bowling greens, stately homes, shipyards, fields of wheat, riverside pubs, moorland ridges, Georgian terraces, railway stations, red pillar boxes ... or, if this is too genteel a collection, a car-boot sale, a plastic bag stuck up a tree, a supermarket car park, a bus stop in the rain.

If you draw a cross with York and Portsmouth on the vertical axis, however, and Ludlow and Lowestoft on the horizontal, the lines meet near Kettering, in the northern part of Northamptonshire. Draw a diagonal cross, with lines from Lancaster to Dover in one direction, and Gloucester to Lincoln in the other, and you find yourself in almost the same place.[1] The nearby village of Meriden, between Coventry and Birmingham, claims to be England's topographical centre, although modern surveyors place the spot a few miles to the north, closer to Nuneaton in Warwickshire. Either way, one could balance a cardboard cut-out of the country on approximately this point.

1 This is why cricket writers often base themselves in Northamptonshire. It is the most convenient location from which to access all the classic Test match grounds – in London, Birmingham, Leeds and Manchester.

Topography is not everything, but there are more than enough historical echoes in Northamptonshire to make it a serious contender for the crown. The fertile land between the rivers Nene and Welland, now a rolling expanse of woods and open fields where Captain Pouch resisted the Tresham family, was once Rockingham Forest, an ancient hunting ground. William the Conqueror co-opted it as a royal park (wild boar and deer, mostly), and the castle he built was visited by many of his successors: William II, Richard I, John, Henry III and Edward I all hunted and held councils there. As we have seen, the funeral cortège of Edward's queen, Eleanor of Castile, paused on its way to London at the village of Geddington, an arrow's flight north of Kettering. Indeed, it boasts the best pre-served of the three surviving Eleanor crosses, those grey gothic spires which mark the places where the dead queen rested.

Rockingham Forest also lies in the middle of a triangle formed by the three market towns of Stamford, Leicester and Northampton, with their wool-trading cultures and royal connections. Indeed, the county was thriving at exactly the

Eleanor Cross, Geddington. A nation mourned, in Gothic stones.

moment when our story began: in 1290 there were regular fairs across the shire, in Bulwick, Corby, Geddington, Kettering, Oundle, Rockingham and many other towns and villages. Upper-class sportsmen could bag their deer in peace in the wolf-free forest, and monasteries like the Cistercian house at Pipewell were growing rich on the proceeds of their ever-expanding flocks of sheep.[2] The area was both a wool and a religious capital. Thomas Becket was tried (for contempt of royal authority) at Northampton Castle in 1164, and the town was an important centre of scholarship. When Charles II built a new church there in 1680 (a remarkable act of conciliation, given Northampton's support for Parliament in the Civil War), it was emblematically English, using stone from Portland and oak from the New Forest.

And the church of All Saints is far from unique: the surrounding countryside is a treasure trove of important buildings. It is said that you are never more than a fifteen-minute drive from a stately home or a site of historic interest in England, but even by this standard Northamptonshire is thick with monuments. Not for nothing is it known as the land of squires and spires. The ruins of Fotheringhay Castle, where Mary Queen of Scots was executed, stand near Althorp, Burghley, Boughton ('the English Versailles') and Holdenby, in its day the largest house in England.[3] Not far off is Deene Park, home of the Earls of Cardigan, one of whom led the Light Brigade in its blundering charge up the wrong valley, and Rockingham Castle, where Charles Dickens was a frequent visitor. He borrowed some of its moods for Chesney Wold, home of the Dedlocks in *Bleak House*, where

2 Climb a tree at Pipewell today and you might see, across the fields, the roofs of the British American Tobacco plant. The days of locally sourced produce are long gone.

3 Pronounced 'Holmby', in its Elizabethan heyday, Holdenby's footprint was reputed to be roughly 18,000 square feet – larger than a rugby pitch. Now only two stone arches and a fragment of kitchen wall, resting like gravestones on a lawn, survive. Nothing beside remains . . .

rain fell – 'drip drip drip' – on the sodden terrace. He may have written part of *David Copperfield* there as well, while the old coaching inn at Towcester (yet another Saracen's Head) is proud of the fact that Mr Pickwick stayed there on his gloomy, rain-soaked journey to Birmingham.

There is much more. A cutting clipped from the mulberry bush in Shakespeare's garden at Stratford-on-Avon still grows in Abington Park; there are stone crosses, medieval market squares, village greens, packhorse bridges and monuments to dignitaries who died while fox-hunting; there is England's largest Anglo-Saxon church as well as its largest dovecote; and a conker festival is held at Ashton every autumn. Some eighty deserted medieval villages are dotted throughout the county, a reminder that its seemingly timeless folds have been contested and fought over for centuries.

Weldon in the Woods boasts a church capped by a light-house to guide lost travellers on dark nights (it is lit every New Year's Eve), and in the fields close to Barnack is an expanse of hollows that look like Somme shell craters, but in fact are the remains of medieval quarries. Within hailing distance is a quartet of historic public schools: Rugby, Oakham, Oundle and Uppingham. Various ancient ceremonies live on, too. Geddington plays host to a 'bread and bun dole', in which the church hands out fresh white bread as a charitable gesture. These days the bread is provided by the local supermarket, so the medieval flame may well have been kept alive with a little touch of Chorleywood in the night.

The last sliver of Rockingham Forest boasts a wide range of English wildlife (adders, newts, nightingales, warblers), and it is not far from Melton Mowbray, home of both the pork pie and English fox-hunting. And early ironworkers were drawn by rust-coloured deposits in the woodland soil.

As we have seen, Northamptonshire was an epicentre of the enclosure movement, and it all began long before Captain Pouch. Two villages at Fawsley, a manor bought by a lawyer named Richard Knightley in 1415, were turned into a park for 2500 sheep. At Thrupp, in 1489, eighteen houses were swept away to make room for a priory. Fifteen years later the entire village of Glendon was enclosed (i.e. flattened) and turned into grazing land.[4] And the same thing happened at Althorp, where John Spencer emptied a village and installed 1200 sheep, enabling his lucky descendants to enjoy one of the finest stately homes in the land. An ancient church still stands, in refined isolation, on the estate, one of many such churches retained when villages were cleared: they looked so lovely in the morning sun.

Nor is it only medieval memories that glimmer in these parts. The Grand Union Canal, which linked London to Birmingham, cut straight through the shire – the underground stretch at Blisworth was England's longest navigable tunnel – and tall viaducts bore a Victorian railway line across the meadows. Later, the huge steelworks at Corby towered over the traditional wool scenery for most of the twentieth century, giving this corner of the English Midlands a peculiarly Scottish accent, as workers from Glasgow brought their skills south.

Northamptonshire played a major part in the Second World War, too. Both the first and the last US bombs to fall on Germany were carried by planes from the air-force base at Grafton Underwood. But the resonance from a much earlier conflict is even stronger. A few miles west of Kettering, on the road to Rugby, lies the battlefield of Naseby. It was on these dun-brown acres in June 1645 that the English Civil War was decided. The King's troops, camped in Market Harborough, were surprised to run into Fairfax's Parliamentarians, and had little option but to step up and fight. Fairfax spread his evangelical soldiers – known as the New Model Army – along a low ridge south of Clipstone as Prince Rupert of the Rhine

4 In recent times it has been enclosed again. It is now a commercial zone on the ring road: the North Kettering Business Area.

marched the royal squadrons straight towards him. The Roundheads, in particular Cromwell's determined Ironsides, proved too tough for the hot-headed Cavaliers. Three years of inconclusive engagements came to an abrupt end. The King's army was shattered (1000 of its 7500 men were killed, and 5000 were taken prisoner). Artillery, baggage train, weapons and horses . . . all were lost.

Charles I was finished. His head was almost literally on the executioner's block.

The visitor heading out of Clipstone today passes a roadside memorial that marks the spot where Prince Rupert planted his standard. It is a rudimentary affair: a car park with grass in the cobbles, a raised wooden platform, a map of the battle and a flag of St George. It is the same story at the other end of the battlefield: car park, viewing step, lonely fluttering flag.

It is routinely said that the English cherish history to the point of fetishising it, but that is not the case at Naseby. There is no museum, no study centre, no 'Civil War Experience' in which schoolchildren can relive the day Parliament put the Crown to the sword and ended the divine right of kings. There aren't even many visitors. On the day I drove between the two placid memorials, I formed an attentive throng of one. And it is no easy task even to locate the southern memorial. The hand-painted sign in Naseby announces that it stands four hundred yards up the road, so I drove that way for half a mile, realised I must have missed it, turned round, missed it again, and found myself back at the sign.

Oh well. If at first you don't succeed. I turned the car round yet again.

This time I spotted a small lay-by with space for a couple of cars and a wooden gate cut into the opposite verge. It did not look promising, but I pushed through the nettles and brambles, and finally reached a grove of oak trees. In the middle was an obelisk on a mound, looking for all the world like one of Cleopatra's needles.

The Naseby memorial. The absence of hedges in this part of Northamptonshire made it the ideal spot for a battle.

An odd thing to find in this blood-soaked shire. I climbed the steps and, standing on tiptoe, could see the land on the other side of the road: the characteristic English chequerboard of fields and hedges where the two armies had fought that day. It had been a misty morning, by all accounts: the melée must have been utterly confusing to everyone. According to the map on the board, this was where the Parliamentary army had lined up to rebuff the royal thrust. Rupert's cavalry had charged towards them with their usual reckless haste, and that copse over there was where Cromwell's iron-willed squadron of horse had sallied forth to cut them down.

So far, so familiar. But one stray detail scratched at my attention, like a thorn snagging a tuft of wool.

It said on the board that the farmland around Naseby was not fully enclosed until 1820. But the battle had taken place in 1645, nearly two centuries earlier.

The significance eluded me. But then I saw the light. These oh-so-English hedges had not even been here when the sun rose on those fog-bound Civil War regiments. On the day of the battle, this was all open land. In an age when a simple hedge was enough to stop an army in its tracks, this was one of the few places left in central England where it was still possible to stage a full-fledged pitched encounter on a roomy field. The armies did not meet at Naseby by chance. Nature and the condition of England's landscape drew them there.

We shape our fields, and then they shape us.

This wasn't the only time that the scenery in this part of England had helped decide historic events. Only a few miles up the road lay Bosworth, where Henry VII had seized Richard III's ill-gotten throne in 1485. In both cases it was not chance that placed the battles close to the geographical heart of the nation, and in this specific terrain.[5] Even the most foolhardy general (and Prince Rupert was more renowned for courage than wisdom) would not attack an enemy across ground divided by hedges, any of which could conceal musketeers.

Northamptonshire has neither coal nor a coast, so the county is lacking two signature components of the national character. But its rivers link it to the Wash, and in the environs of Northampton itself the River Nene provided the inspiration for the first water-powered cotton mill. Known as Marvell's Mill, it was the speculative brainchild of Edward Cave, founder and owner of the respectable *Gentleman's Magazine*. In 1742 he bought a corn mill on the Nene, demolished it, and installed a brand-new roller-spinning engine made by Lewis Paul, a Huguenot engineer based in Birmingham. Cave's aim was to mechanise the carding process – in which raw cotton is untangled into threads – and his innovation was an early sign that wool's days might be numbered.

By 1746 the mill had a workforce of a hundred, but it was

5 There were two battles at Northampton in the Wars of the Roses. The second, in 1460, saw the capture of King Henry VI. The Archbishop of Canterbury, who was camped by an Eleanor cross in the grounds of Hardingstone Abbey, watched the battle unfold.

plagued by teething troubles – mess, noise and unreliable machinery – and never established itself as a successful concern. But the principles on which it was based were solid, and thirty years later, when Richard Arkwright perfected his own water frame at Cromford, in Derbyshire, he founded a giant mill on the River Derwent that really would change everything.

Arkwright became the wealthiest non-titled man in the kingdom. But he was following a script that was written in Northamptonshire.

Taken all in all, this is as rich a cross-section of English textures as can easily be imagined in one small space. And we haven't even mentioned the trades for which Northamptonshire is most famous: leather tanning and shoemaking. Using hides from local livestock and bark from local oaks (for the tanning process), leather-working was already a significant trade when cavalry reached Naseby. Thereafter, it grew – helped by the county's strategic location at the centre of England's transport system – into an international business.

Northampton made boots for King John in 1213 – perhaps he wore them when signing the Magna Carta two years later – and didn't look back. By the seventeenth century, it was said that the town's prosperity stood on other men's feet. In 1841 there were eighteen hundred shoemakers in the town, some large, some small, but all using the latest machines. Two-thirds of the boots used by the British army in the First World War were made in this one shire.

Few of the county's towns were not involved in the business. Wollaston supplied Fairfax's army before going on to make steel-capped boots for coal miners, then became famous for Doc Martens – originally designed as tough footwear for farm workers. Bozeat made the football boots worn by Bobby Moore and Bobby Charlton on that sunny Wembley day in 1966. Kettering was home to both Dolcis and Freeman, Hardy & Willis. Long Buckby specialised in equestrian and surgical footwear, and built a reputation for bespoke shoemaking. Size 18, sir? Come this way.

Almost all of the magnificent riding boots that feature so prominently in the portraits of England's gentry on horseback were the work of Northamptonshire's cobblers.

And speaking of painting ...

Sixteen

Painting with Rakes

By the seventeenth century, England's landscape was natural only to the extent that its basic shapes and colours had been planted by ancient geographical forces. Now, England's artists began to give it a civilised polish and turn it into something else: a landscape of the mind.

In the middle of Sudbury, Suffolk, stands a two-storey townhouse. Though it dates from Tudor times, its calm proportions, elegant brickwork, large windows and classical front porch seem Georgian. Roses clamber through the quince, rosemary and medlar in the formal walled garden. It is so thoroughly English that it's impossible to imagine it anywhere else.

It was once the home of the painter Thomas Gainsborough (a statue of him dominates the centre of the town). He was born in this 'most excellent Brick't Mansion' in 1727. His father, a successful purveyor of woollen goods, packed young Tom off to London to train as an artist when he was just thirteen years old. But the silvery fields of his boyhood, where cows stood knee-deep in water meadows, had already left their mark. At a time when professional painting meant portraiture, Gainsborough only ever wanted to produce 'landskips'.

A twenty-minute stroll south of Sudbury lies a clump of trees which is all that remains of the sweeping woodland that once coated this terrain. To the right, through a gate marked 'Private', between a pair of stone columns, lie a tree-lined drive and, on the crown of the hill, a statuesque English oak. The tree commands a panoramic view across the broad vale and river below. It is a classic vista, and if you had your water-colours you might feel some sort of painting coming on.

Gainsborough stood on this same spot in 1750, and asked his subjects to hold their poses at the foot of this very tree. They were two newlyweds: Robert Andrews (the landowner from whom Arthur Young would later borrow his nom de plume), and his wife Frances, née Carter, the daughter of a local draper. The extensive park was their marital estate, and they were cel-ebrating the fact by commissioning a painting.

Mr Andrews may have remembered him – they had been at school together. But Andrews had gone up in the world since their days at Sudbury Grammar. In addition to this enviable 3000-acre estate, he owned a fleet of ships, a town house in Grosvenor Square, London, and a substantial stake in an impe-rial trading company. In Gainsborough's painting he is shown lounging, legs crossed, indolent with self-regard – the prince of all he surveys.

His wife fares little better. Some have found her demure, even flirtatious, but to most observers she looks shy. Her own family farm is visible in the far distance, and with the uncocked shotgun on his hip, and his faithful retriever gazing up at him, her husband has the look of a hunter who has just bagged a pliant young trophy. Indeed, Frances was only sixteen when they married, and her slightly awkward air is highlighted by the fact that Gainsborough left her unfinished: her hands rest on a square of unpainted canvas where her lap should be.

That empty space has been an art-history puzzle for years. Some have suggested that Gainsborough intended a lap dog (perhaps a feisty blighter that refused to sit still); the National Gallery argues that he may have been leaving room for a game bird or an as-yet-unborn child; Freudians drool over the sexual implications of the untouched lap. My own theory – pure speculation – is that he was planning to accessorise Mrs Andrews with a sketchbook and *porte-crayon* when he fell out with her husband, who felt that the portrait was insufficiently flattering.[1]

Mr and Mrs Robert Andrews, by Thomas Gainsborough. Suffolk scenery as civilisation – English civilisation.

It hardly matters. The painting is famous not because it hides a riddle, but because it illustrates the social fabric that ruled the English landscape in the eighteenth century. For a long time, it was seen as a straightforward depiction of the countryside at its most alluring. Today, it is viewed as a portrait of upper-class vanity, ownership and entitlement. The couple's gracious half-smiles now look like smirks,[2] and Gainsborough seems to have turned nature itself into a knowing pundit: ominous dark

1 One of his earlier works, *A Couple in a Landscape*, shows another married couple in an almost identical pose, with the drawing materials in the lady's hands.

2 Some art critics winced when John Berger famously emphasised the proprietorial reflexes behind this painting in *Ways of Seeing* (a 1972 BBC book and documentary series). But what they saw as doctrinaire Marxism despoiling an innocent depiction of beauty now seems a bland statement of the obvious.

clouds stack up over the happy couple, whose silk clothes seem too dainty for the outdoors, while the fields of cows and sheep invite the notion that this is a land in which brides too can be traded. In this light, Mrs Andrews is a best of breed, fresh from the local cattle auction.[3]

No wonder she looks nervous.

It is as if the land itself, sculpted by centuries of enclosure, sheep husbandry and science, has been invited to pose. Elegant sheaves of corn suggest an estate in tune with the latest arable know-how (Robert Andrews may well have invested in one of Jethro Tull's seed drills). But the painting is also remarkable for what it does not show: the army of labourers who made it unnecessary for the owners to get their hands dirty. The partitioned fields, the tidy hurdles keeping the sheep corralled, the well-pollarded trees, the fresh white gate and the neat lines of corn are all man-made (by hired hands).

The green slopes and coppiced woods, the hovering birds and grazing animals, even the rococo bench at the base of the tree also make the point that the country setting is a display case – very like the frame of the canvas itself. Mr and Mrs Andrews are not admiring nature; they are inspecting their property. The matching churches suggest not only the conjugal union of a happy couple, but the twinning of two parishes. On the left is the wool church of Long Melford (this was sheep country, after all); on the right is All Saints, Sudbury, where the wedding was held.

In portraying ownership, Gainsborough was also sketching the latest expression of an archetypal English trait: the property bug. Robert Andrews wanted to possess not just the land but a painting of the land. He wanted it in his drawing room, where visitors could admire it without getting their feet wet. The church towers in the distance are another deliberate touch. This is scenery as civilisation ... *English* civilisation. Even the gap in

3 Years later, Gainsborough painted Frances's mother in the same sky-blue silk dress and stiff pose as her daughter. Both women are depicted as dolls.

the trees which affords a good view of one of the steeples was
put there not by providence, but by design.

Landscape, in Gainsborough's hands, is also history. And it
is an open book.

This is what prompted W. G. Hoskins to write *The Making
of the English Landscape*. He understood that since the modern
countryside was man-made, it could serve as a lucid guide to its
own past. Its winding lanes and bosky hollows were clues (ele-
mentary, to the trained observer) to long-forgotten adventures.
The importance of Gainsborough's painting, in this light, lies
not in its unsurprising social commentary (*of course* the rich
inherit the earth), but in the way it shepherds scenery from
nature into the aesthetic domain. In the eighteenth century,
moulded by human ingenuity, landscape became 'landscape' –
a pictorial genre.

It was not just a way of looking. It was a way of thinking.

This was only the start of Gainsborough's career as a landscape artist. Society portraiture may have put bread on the
table, but he never lost his desire to capture the countryside –
be it on canvas, paper or glass. And, as *Mr and Mrs Andrews*
showed, he was always alert to its social significance as well as
its colours and forms. He referred to his art as the conjurings of
his 'own Brain', and often worked at night: the radiant glimmer
in those rural images came not from sunshine but from candles.
He was no photorealist; he painted more than he could see.

Gainsborough's style of landscape art soon became much-
copied. Aristocrats posed in front of their parks, sometimes
with their wives and children, often with horses or dogs.
Hogarth, as ever, was quick to take a sardonic line, depicting the Fountaine family inspecting a pastoral painting ... of
a fountain! It was clear even then that such scenes were not
intended to display the 'natural' world but to show the way in
which the countryside had been seized, arranged and cultivated
by its owners.

*

Ten miles downstream from Mr and Mrs Andrews' exquisite hilltop, the river reaches countryside that is even more familiar. A stream of water, a white cottage, a barge drifting by, tall trees, an old mill, a cow, a horse, a boy with his dog ... Again, it looks like a picture.

This is Constable Country.

John Constable was born in East Bergholt in June 1776. His father was a corn merchant with mills here and in Dedham, where young John went to school.[4] This part of the Stour valley infused his boyhood and became his artistic home. He studied Gainsborough, but left well-upholstered landowners out of his own landscapes, because he wanted the land to do all the talking. Sometimes he painted nothing but clouds – illuminated by the sun or grim with impending rain. It was 'difficult', he explained, 'to name a class of landscape in which the sky is not the key note ... the chief organ of sentiment'.

Even his gentlest work has a stunned, heat-struck quality. Although he liked to paint dramatic weather events – thumping squalls and showers – in Dedham Vale he sought to capture the hot dazzle of a midsummer's day. The painting we know as *The Hay Wain* was originally titled 'Landscape: Noon'. This was the land that Constable loved and made immortal. Mountains did little for him. So far as he was concerned, no scene was complete without a pretty roof, a mill, a steeple, a brick wall and wet wood. The stubby church at Dedham is depicted in no fewer than twenty-six of his works, and not always in the right place – he often moved it to create a wistful focal point.[5]

He was making art, not recording nature.

4 Later, he was a boarder in the capital of the region's wool trade, Lavenham.

5 Similarly, the mountainous backdrop in J. M. W. Turner's *Snow Storm: Hannibal's Army Crossing the Alps* certainly seems to be Swiss – an elemental uproar splashed across an eight-foot-wide canvas. Yet it was sketched in Wharfedale, Yorkshire, two years earlier, with something very different in mind. Turner painted not only what he saw, but what he thought and felt.

Along with Turner and Gainsborough, Constable is one of the great triumvirate of English painters. And while all three were inspired by other artists – Gainsborough, in particular, adored the classical images of Claude Lorrain and the Dutch school – it was their raw feeling for English scenery that led them to create a new kind of landscape painting. In so doing, they made a distinctive English contribution to European culture.

The ingredients are as familiar as the characters in a soap opera: sheep, mill, church, trees, river and swirling sky. They seem like timeless aspects of the national scene, and as you wander around Constable's Flatford Mill, you would swear that it has not changed in the two centuries since he painted it. When I stood by the water's edge, trying to locate the exact spot where he set up his easel for *The Hay Wain*, I was joined by two men with cameras who had travelled all the way from India to see it.

'I first saw this on a biscuit box when I was ten,' said one. 'Now I'm fifty-six, and this is the first time I've seen the real thing.'

As at Naseby, time slipped a cog.

'Is this how you imagined England, then?' I asked.

'Yes. And it's still here.'

'It's not all like this, of course.'

This is what English people say to tourists to demonstrate their world-weary superiority to the rose-tinted National Trust image of their country. But I was soon put in my place.

'Well, of course not,' he said. 'But *this* is still here.'

He was right. The air was ripe with the smell of nettles and cowslips, and overhead was a classic Constable sky – a pile of white clouds formed by the collision of warm Suffolk air and the cooler North Sea breeze.

I wanted to say that such typical English visions are not innate, but the product of specific histories – in this case, the long reigns of wheat, cows, sheep and water. I even wanted to suggest that the archetypal style of English landscape art was invented right here, in a single placid vale where a soft river

The unchanging view of Flatford Mill. In Constable country, where landscape became 'landscape'.

trickled through Essex and two boys, Tom and John, grew up watching barges drifting through the locks.

But I said nothing. The fact was, this one corner of England, where landscape had become 'landscape', had left a powerful imprint on the whole world. It had even touched India.

There are not many places where a small patch of the rural scene has come to symbolise the whole. Germany has Wagnerian forests, but also Baltic beaches; France has ancient villages, snow-capped Alps and sun-kissed coves; Italy and Spain have mountainous norths and balmy, Mediterranean souths. England's countryside, though varied, falls within more moderate boundaries: it has hills rather than mountains, woods rather than forests, gentle, meandering rivers rather than the mighty Rhine or Loire. And every inch has been lived in, cultivated or rambled over: it is all well-thumbed.

A little too well-thumbed, perhaps. Gainsborough and

Constable have appeared on so many cake tins and calendars that theirs can seem a hackneyed vision. The souvenir industry plasters their work on aprons, cushions, jigsaw puzzles, caps, cards, pots of jam, mugs and pencils. It was no coincidence that William Gilpin coined the term 'picturesque' just eighteen years after Gainsborough had painted *Mr and Mrs Andrews*. He defined it as 'that kind of beauty which is agreeable in a picture', and it is clear what he meant. Gainsborough had laid down a template; from now on, rural scenery would be judged by the extent to which it resembled art.

This meant that some scenery simply would not do. The term 'picturesque' was highly specific. It suggested nature – it was never used to describe a person – but did not hold with wild or rugged landscapes, which belonged to a more sublime or romantic category. To be truly picturesque, the countryside had to include elements of human charm – an ivy-clad wall, a cart, a chimney. These grace notes gave the hills and streams a lived-in character; indeed, are why 'picturesque' is now often used as a put-down ('*merely* picturesque'). Thatched cottages draped in wisteria; cathedral spires at dawn; misty deer parks; sheep standing beneath a rainbow; moss-covered barns. These pastoral clichés all had a common origin in the same period. No rural view could be deemed idyllic unless it had a crumbling cottage or a ruined abbey, along with a pool of still water to reflect the racing clouds.

Something similar holds true today: we are still addicted to imagery rooted in the past. The Middle Ages cast the longest shadow, but other eras catch our eyes, too. Mere age has transformed England's abandoned mines and mills, which Blake decried as evil abominations against nature, into endearing relics. We cherish chimneys, wharves and rusty wheels as if they were Renaissance arches, while chafing at the pylons and grain silos that have 'ruined' the view.

Does art imitate life, or is it the other way round? Gainsborough and Constable both painted what the landscape offered them, but the ideas and emotions they brushed into their views rendered them evocative in a new way. Their England was an England transformed by the mind's eye.

We are jumping ahead of ourselves, however. Long before Turner ever put sable to canvas, an earlier generation of artists was rendering England's rural scenery in a way that actively encouraged the native landscape to be remade by human hand. England's aristocrats came to believe that their land looked almost *too* natural. How much better life would be if their estates resembled paintings instead.

This odd, circular process happened fast: no sooner had artists started to depict English estates on canvas than the opposite began to happen too: life began to imitate art. By developing 'landskip' as a national genre, Gainsborough and his contemporaries inspired a new band of horticultural heroes to create art by reshaping the land itself. With picks and hoes, rakes and rollers, they began to turn the pleasure grounds of England's great houses into pictures that people could both admire and walk in.

It was not a paradox that the great age of landscape gardening coincided with a drift *away* from the countryside and into towns and cities. Urbanisation generated a tenderness for rural imagery. It was rose-tinted: people started to forget the grinding reality of agricultural life. Nature – until then an arena of danger and struggle ruled by elemental forces indifferent to human comfort – became a tame and lovely version of its raw and stormy self. England's new gardens were not designed as fragrant sanctuaries from the threatening wilderness outside, but as sedate renderings of the great outdoors, carefully contrived to appeal to an urban audience.

Continental gardens, lacking the hosepipe sprinkling in the English sky, tended to be formal: geometric lines, crisp, sculpted topiary, knots, parterres, fountains, and very little grass. Georgian England (the dominant party in the British union) preferred sweeping lawns, serpentine lakes and copses of trees arranged to create the illusion of distance. Grazing animals were installed to complete the pastoral picture ... and to nibble the acres of grass into a well-brushed sward.

This was landscape gardening, and it was an art form: painting with scythes, sculpting with shovels, etching with rakes. The noun became a verb – you could landscape any piece of ground into a garden, a park, even a golf course. The only rule was that the end result had to seem 'natural'.

The leader of this fashion – for that was what it became – was William Kent. Originally from Bridlington, in Yorkshire, he travelled widely and studied architecture in Rome. Back in London in the 1720s, he won a commission from Lord Burlington, who asked him to create a garden for his country seat in Chiswick that would marry the polished aesthetic of an oil painting with the classical pedigree of Palladian Italy (his house was modelled on a villa in Vicenza). But Kent strayed from his brief and gave the polite symmetries of the Veneto an English makeover: rolling expanses of grass were arranged to resemble country glades, with trees, winding paths, views across water, and stone arches.

It was a marvellous new style. And a few years later, he gave even fuller rein to the same impulse at Stowe. One of his apprentices there – Lancelot 'Capability' Brown – became a maestro in his own right. Indeed, he is now synonymous with the concept of creating naturalistic parks busy with allegorical overtones – temples, crypts and pagodas. He enjoyed the support of a significant new publication, the *Spectator*, which argued that old-fashioned, formal gardens, such as those at Versailles, were intrinsically despotic. Brown took such views to heart, adding that he approached his work with a literary mind: 'Here I put a comma; there, when it is necessary to cut the view, I put a parenthesis.' When the banker Henry Hoare created a garden at Stourhead, he too sought to reproduce both art (Claude's paintings) and literature (Virgil's *Aeneid*) in water, grass and trees.

It was Capability Brown, however, who first realised the necessity of keeping everything in careful proportion. He understood that it would be impossible to 'see the wood for the trees' if the design was careless. This simple observation became a profound English mantra: don't worry about the details, but always keep an eye fixed on the main prize (or the big picture). It is hard to overstate the importance of this precept in subsequent English culture. It gave rise to an impatience with fussy side-issues and pettifogging digressions. It promoted an intellectual value-system in which nothing was prized more than the ability to 'cut through' to the nub of an argument or march through a 'minefield' of contending claims. It lies close to the heart of English academic life and English law. Yet, originally, it was nothing more than an aesthetic observation arising from landscape gardening.

Finally, there was Humphrey Repton, the man who literally wrote the book on this subject – *Observations on the Theory and Practice of Landscape Gardening* (1805) – and indeed coined the phrase itself. He too grew up in East Anglia (Bury St Edmunds), not far from Gainsborough and Constable, and was similarly influenced by the drowsy spirit of the scenery. Through his work at Castle Howard and elsewhere, he established the principle that such parks should be 'appropriated to the use and pleasure of man', 'cultivated and enriched by art' in order to resemble 'the landscape of nature'.

In a nice twist, these wonderful new landscapes, inspired by lofty considerations of artistic composition, often made poor subjects for painters. Hard to say why, exactly. But the uneventful expanses of grass and studied arrangements of trees and lakes made them seem ... unnatural.

The pioneers promoted a vision of cultivated nature that has gripped England for three centuries. Horace Walpole, the first notable historian of such topics, declared that 'the science of landscape' should be placed alongside poetry and painting as one of the 'three new graces' of English culture, while the

Dictionary of National Biography lauded Capability Brown for producing images 'as deeply embedded in the English character as the paintings of Turner and the poetry of Wordsworth'.

In a 1944 essay, 'The Genesis of the Picturesque', Nikolaus Pevsner hailed this type of landscape gardening as 'one of the greatest aesthetic achievements of England'.

It was certainly widely imitated abroad. The Englischer Garten in Munich and the Rose Garden at Cintra (created by William Cook, son of Thomas Cook the travel agent) are both tributes, and there are *jardins anglais* in Boulogne, Chantilly, Compiègne, Dinan, Fontainebleau and Geneva. Much the same aesthetic informs the landscaped garden at Thomas Jefferson's house – Monticello – in North Carolina. Ignore, if you will, the blinding sunshine and lush greenery – hot grasses and ferns, magnolias the size of oaks – and you could fancy yourself on the banks of the Thames in Chiswick. It is as English as a country churchyard.

Like many English archetypes, though, it is more cosmopolitan than we like to admit. The poet–courtier Andrew Marvell sought to emphasise the native glory achieved by Sir Thomas Fairfax's Appleton House in Yorkshire when he declared: 'Within this sober frame expect / Work of no foreign architect'. But while the inspiration behind the landscaped garden may have been English, it rested on imagery borrowed from abroad. Kent, Jones and others were all devout disciples of Palladio, while Gainsborough's brush was guided by Rubens, Claude and the Dutch masters. Just as the gilded interiors of Chiswick House were filled with works by Leonardo, Veronese, Titian, Rembrandt and Bruegel, the classical touches in the garden – the temples to virtue, the statues of Venus, the grottoes – alluded to fragments glimpsed in Rome.

Even Gilpin's nationalistic concept of the picturesque crystallised not in England but in Wales, in the meandering Wye valley, in 1770.

But if the stems and flowers of this new plant were varied, the stock was indeed English. Something in the soil, the air and even the human touches that nursed it to life gave it a singular quality that was found nowhere else. A river winding through trees, a hint of grey stone from a ruined monastery, a delectable bridge, a cow licking a puddle, a milkmaid with a dog ... these were all references to a very *English* past. It was *our* landscape, *our* history.

Art critics have enjoyed dismissing the picturesque strand in English art as 'chocolate box': it is so quaint. But there is no disputing the chord it has struck with the general public: it was hugely popular in the eighteenth century and it remains so now. There is a paradox here, though, because landscaped gardens have always been symbols of aristocratic hauteur. A list of them – and it soon runs into the hundreds – reads like a Betjemanesque fantasy of a perfect English railway line:

> *Badminton and Castle Howard,*
> *Cirencester, Charlecote Park,*
> *Ditchley, Holkham, Wilton, Burghley,*
> *Chatsworth, Tew and Houghton Hall.*
> *Ickworth, Longleat, Harewood, Petworth,*
> *Compton Wynates, Luton Hoo ...*
> *Passengers for Milton Abbey,*
> *Please alight at platform two.*

Even today, within strolling distance of William Kent's Chiswick Park, one can wander through the haughty grounds of Kew, Ham House, Gunnersbury, Osterley, Sion House, Marble Hill, Orleans, Strawberry Hill and Hampton Court. These extravagant villas were built on the banks of the Thames (the main route out of London), and were shaped by English geography in another way: they were all planned as summer houses. In winter, their affluent owners occupied grand apartments in Whitehall or Piccadilly; only when the sun came out would they decamp to their place in the country.[6]

6 Lord Burlington's central London pad is now the Royal Academy.

The scale of these projects – the sheer acreage of prime real estate they occupied – is breathtaking. And when we consider that the enclosing of agricultural land was taking place at precisely the same time, there is no hiding the fact that all of this beauty came at a price. A handful of labourers with time-honoured stakes in the land (but no legal right to remain on it) might be retained as park keepers – those gravel paths didn't rake themselves – but the vast majority were redundant. England was starting to rely on faraway dominions for its grain, wool and other commodities. Its own land was being turned into a work of art – there to be looked at, not cultivated.

It was a new twist in an old tale. The enclosing of open country – first for sheep, then for crops, and finally for the sheer pleasure of it – continued to feed the cult of private property in England. Those majestic landscape gardens have a bitter edge: on the one hand, they are pinnacles of English civilisation; on the other, they are crime scenes. Intended as emblems of impeccable taste, they are also symbols of unholy wealth, with no small amount of blood on their hands. Perhaps this is why they are so eclectic: for every Doric column there is a medieval cross; for every wilderness a neatly trimmed hedge. For every rolling vista, with lakes and spreading oaks, there is a dense and claustrophobic maze. They seem tranquil, but there is violence in their foundations.

Is there a telling hint of Englishness in this contradiction, further evidence of England's split personality: elegant manners alongside shocking cruelty? This was the nation that made perfect gardens while branding slaves (at more or less the same time). It filled cathedrals with soaring music, yet worked small children to an early grave. Goldsmith's 'tyrant's hand' is still visible even in the national treasures we hold most dear.

The deserted village that so inflamed him is now thought to be the medieval settlement of Nuneham Courtenay, near Oxford. The cottages and their inhabitants were shunted aside to create space for an ornamental makeover, and the ancient tie with the land was severed for ever. The lane became a footpath; the church became a temple; cows went from field to field via underground passages. And it was all done in the best possible taste, of course.

This sort of thing went on everywhere. The great abbeys, such as those at Fountains and Rievaulx, planted themselves in desolate valleys, but after their dissolution they were 'emparked' for aesthetic rather than practical reasons. A village was flattened so that Harewood House's already vast park could be enlarged. And Robert Walpole (the first Prime Minister) swatted aside another in Norfolk (a replacement was built a mile away) to make room for Houghton Hall, an enormous mansion set in a thousand-acre estate famous for its ha-has, discreet walls artfully designed to create the illusion of a con-tinuous – *unenclosed* – landscape. Sheep and cows can saunter where they please without encroaching on the guests enjoying the view from the terrace.

England is rich in such places. At Kedleston Hall, in Derbyshire, an ancient village was swept aside to make room for Sir Nathaniel Curzon's superb arrangement of temples, walks, lakes, lodges (designed by Robert Adam), gardens and bridges. The grounds of Hardwick Hall (the name means 'sheep farm') are punctuated by a series of ridges and furrows, suggesting that the land was once farmed in a very different, older way. The ageless oak avenues and refined beech drives at Kingston Lacy, in Dorset, stand on manorial land that was once as heavily populated as the neighbouring village of Wimborne.

Famous gardens of this sort – poster children for the English way of life – epitomise refinement, yet in their groves and lakes we can always detect the ghost of a guilty conscience. An important strand of England's culture can be found right here, in the groan of violence that stirs beneath the courtly manners of these Georgian pleasure grounds. But it may be too easy to denounce the past from our 'enlightened' vantage point in modern times. There are heritage complications in condemning too blithely the crimes of an earlier age. After all, the families who owed their wealth to slavery and land seizure spent a large portion of their ill-gotten gains on buildings whose absence would now be seen as a disaster. The past is never simple. We need to pack at least two minds when we travel into England's history, and prepare to contemplate it with mixed feelings.

That is certainly the case with the medieval spirit that lingers on in the nation's cathedrals, castles, wool churches and ruined monasteries. These are now England's top visitor attractions, but we cannot forget that those knights in shining armour carried cruel swords, and were not afraid to use them.

Just as sheep-rearing prodded England's literary reflexes in earlier times, so the vogue for landscape gardening and the artful cultivation of 'nature' influenced the literature of this later age. The 'emparking' of all those fields led to a new tone, even in poetry. The arching enormities of Chaucer, Malory, Shakespeare and Milton seemed to belong to another time. Poetry now came neatly clipped, like a hedge.

This was most obvious in the continuing prominence of pastoral works. For Spenser and Raleigh (whose world danced with classical nymphs and shepherd boys), then Marvell and Herrick, and finally Pope, Crabbe, Thomson, Gray and Collins, it simply wasn't English verse if it didn't have a meadow, a maiden, a flock of sheep, a bubbling stream, a shady hollow, a lazy cow and a daisy or two. There was an ambiguity here. As William Empson pointed out, the image of the happy shepherd, gambolling in his bower like a milk-fed lamb, was built on a myth. In fact, the contented peasant was being sentimentalised at exactly the moment when he (and she, and their children) was coming under determined and organised assault.

The creation of civilised parks influenced more than poets' choice of subject-matter; it also gave them trim new manners. Dryden and Pope favoured tidy couplets that evoked the well-ordered lines of a gravel path. It was as if the overgrown tracks of an earlier literature had been raked into strict alleys. The 'Augustan' age had Roman qualities, to be sure, but also brought to mind a lovingly tended English garden.

The wilder aspects of nature were kept at arm's length by laying them out in symmetrical patterns. As Pope wrote, in his tribute to Kent's garden in Chiswick, the important thing was stately balance:

> Grove nods at grove, each alley has a brother
> And half the platform just reflects the other.
> The suff'ring eye inverted nature sees
> Trees cut to statues, statues thick as trees,
> With here a fountain, never to be played
> And there a summer house that knows no shade.

Pope followed this principle at the garden of his own riverside villa at Twickenham. It was a cultivated arrangement of neo-classical features: grotto, mounds, orangery, vineyard, bowling green and vistas studded with urns and obelisks.

Thousands followed suit. England became a land of walls and borders.

The enclosing of England into parks and gardens is an ambiguous hallmark of the national temperament. On the one hand, it planted the seeds of a superb architectural legacy – the much-loved world of Blenheim, Longleat, Montacute and Hampton Court. It inspired the fictional realms of *Brideshead Revisited* and *Downton Abbey*. But it also called forth a vibrant tradition of egalitarian protest. The headline acts of the dissident movement are well known – Cobbett, Dickens, Engels, Orwell and so on – but there is a broad sweep of less famous tracts and pamphlets, some written by zealots, many more by decent-minded citizens baffled by the eternal English conundrum: how could a country that was among the most civilised in the history of the world also be, at times, the most sordid?

There is no answer to this question. But England was becoming rather good at containing contradictory forces within a single harmonious design.

The role of landscape in English culture, moreover, found its most avid expression not only in the pantheon of noted painters (and many poets) but in the profound amateur fondness for watercolouring. A hobby as well as an art form, it straddled the class divide: princes, explorers, teachers, postmen and factory workers all set up easels, brushes and jars of cloudy water in front of a view. Watercolouring also crossed the talent divide: great artists have achieved miracles with it, but prime ministers and shipbuilders could also console themselves with its gentle procedures. Millions of clumsy beginners could splash around with the same soft ingredients.

How could it be otherwise in a land so persistently wet?

It may be that the urge to sit beside a river and create a pastel picture is a product of industrial, not rural, surroundings. Watercolour pigment in tubes was machine-ground in 1846 by companies such as Winsor and Newton, and the 'shilling paintbox' was a Victorian bestseller – eleven million were purchased between 1853 and 1870. In other words, it was put within reach of the masses at a time when oils and canvas were prohibitively expensive. Any Tom, Dick or Harriet could dig out the watercolours on a Sunday afternoon and sell the resulting work for a few bob at the church fête.

Watercolour is not an exclusively English art form, of course, but it has played a noteworthy role in the humdrum culture of the nation. It is part of a weave that also includes choirs, teams of bell-ringers, flower shows, allotments, baking contests, sheepdog trials and cricket clubs – a long and living thread in the national tradition.

The landscape artists of the past were not journalists. Gainsborough did not paint the Suffolk countryside so much as capture its aristocracy; Constable was not an expressionist, but he did see his own sensibility reflected in the 'scenes of my boyhood'. Though not concerned with Englishness as such, these and other artists were gripped not only by the appearance of England – the fruitfulness of the land, the patience of the beasts of burden, the farmyard fixtures and fittings, the shade and flutter of passing clouds – but also by its historic resonances. The land they painted had been composted by the ancestral generations who left their mark on every inch of English soil.

This reverent attitude to England's past, along with the transformation of landscape into 'landscape', opened the way for another powerful national habit. Many have mocked England's nostalgic preoccupation with heritage as fusty and backward-looking. But even those who are inclined to satirise it cannot deny its strength. Whatever we feel about the embedded fondness for stately ruins, it is an undeniable fact of English life.

The best example of this is the National Trust, the charity that has dedicated itself to the relics of bygone times for more than a century. From very small beginnings – a couple of hundred members paying ten shillings a year to clear a few footpaths – it is now a major force for conservation, holding 618,000 acres of England's (and Britain's) landscape in its embrace, including 775 miles of coastline, 200 historic buildings, 160 gardens, 59 villages and one-tenth of the country's museums.

It has four million members (five times the number that attends Anglican churches, six times the membership of all the political parties combined), and some 60,000 volunteers. Its most popular sites (Stourhead, Cliveden, Fountains Abbey) each host in the region of 400,000 visitors per year. Indeed, on an average Saturday, more people visit National Trust properties than attend football matches (although few newspapers devote sections to historic monuments, and no one rushes home from the pub to catch *Maze of the Day*). The landmarks it owns range from the modest to the gigantic. On the one hand, there is the apple tree outside Isaac Newton's house in

Lincolnshire, whose falling fruit led him to grasp the power of gravity. On the other, the Trust owns a quarter of the Lake District, and much of the Cornish coast.

The meeting that launched the Trust in 1895 was held in the Westminster offices of the Commons Preservation Society, an agency set up by well-born nature lovers to protect beauty spots from the ravages of Victorian life. It was not, initially, much concerned with stately homes. The driving force, Octavia Hill, had seen her rural village of Finchley slowly subsumed into the metropolis, and this inspired her to pioneer the development of what we would now call 'affordable housing' in London's humbler neighbourhoods (such as Notting Hill – how things change). It also made her an energetic protector of green spaces, where people could 'rise above the smoke ... feel the refreshing air for a time and see the sun setting in coloured glory'.

There is an irony here. Few supporters of the historic conservation project would have consented to the nationalising of England's treasures by the government, yet they were quite happy to see them adopted by the National Trust. Perhaps the contradiction is explained by the fact that the Trust was and remains a voluntary club – like the scout movement or the Women's Institute – rather than a Whitehall department. It seemed harmless, charming ... and frightfully English.

It is no paradox, as we have seen, that England's love of rural scenery deepened as people moved to towns and cities in the nineteenth and twentieth centuries. Indeed, it was a logical, equal-and-opposite reaction to urbanisation. The faster the sky disappeared above a blanket of smog, the greater the hankering for fresh air and open space. This was certainly one of the impulses that gave rise to the National Trust. Drawing strength from William Morris and his love of traditional country ways, the new organisation rushed to defend places of 'historic interest and natural beauty' that were threatened by so-called 'progress'. Its schemes were modest at first – a workhouse in Deptford, a clergyman's house in Sussex, rambling rights in the Lake

District, a cliff in Wales, a poet's cottage in Grasmere, a butterfly haunt in Cambridge, a post office at Tintagel – but before long it became a care home for all the nation's unaffordable heirlooms.

In other countries the maintenance of such monuments is handled by government agencies, and indeed England has one of its own, English Heritage, which began life as the Office of Works in 1378. It now oversees nearly a thousand historic buildings and ruins, including Hadrian's Wall, Stonehenge and Rievaulx. But the immense charitable effort behind the National Trust makes it a rare and special beast. And its continuing success is strong evidence that the impulse behind its foundation – the desire to protect England's precious past, the same urge that led the people of Tewkesbury to rally to the defence of their abbey in the fifteenth century – is still a national trait. It is not wholly English: it was born in the capital of Britain, and it drew strength from all corners of the United Kingdom. But much of the aesthetic impetus behind it – as well as most of the funding – has come from England.

It is fair to say that there is more to the National Trust than dreamy nostalgia. In an interesting fusion of two distinctly different fields, it cherishes architectural *and* natural history as if they were one and the same thing. It loves Norman dovecotes but also maintains coastal footpaths. A waterfall, a cabinet, a mountain, a library, a lake, a blast furnace – all are folded in the same genteel embrace. Most of the world's national parks focus on the wilderness (the Bavarian Forest, Yosemite, the Cevennes, Parco Nazionale dell'Abruzzo) and very fine they are too. But in England the National Trust makes an unusual virtue of the fact that nature and history are closely entwined. As John Constable said, when he was told that history was a more serious subject than mere landscape: 'landscape is the child of history'.

He might have answered, landscape *is* history.

And not just any history. As the novelist John Buchan once observed, the English landscape is redolent of one period above all, the Age of Wool: 'In such a landscape you can cheat the centuries, for all that is presented to your ear and eye is what medieval England heard and saw.' Even its novelties bear the fingerprints of that old realm: 'New' College, Oxford, was built in 1379, 'New' castle was so named in 1080. The English have been sighing over vanished glories since the time of Camelot, and before.

Stourhead, Wiltshire. Art and literature expressed in water, grass and trees.

The National Trust has been able to harness this bond between landscape and history to a vigorous charitable effort. If it is a dream, it is a powerful one: a recent *Country Life* survey found that 80 per cent of respondents wanted to live in the country-side, while only 20 per cent actually did. Here is another marked English characteristic: the heightened affection for refined country living at a time when it barely exists. Few of us live in houses with a dozen chimneys, a choice of stable blocks, a chapel and a lake, but we love the idea of doing so. Even a cottage with a view over the cedars and a footpath through a bluebell wood down to the village pond would do quite nicely, thank you.

The National Trust also reflects the deep English love of the great outdoors. And of all its monuments, none stands taller or expresses this emotion more resonantly than the bronze plaque that was placed on the summit of Great Gable in 1924. A gift from the war-weary, nature-loving members of the Fell and Rock Climbing Club (which somehow raised enough money to buy three thousand acres of this high ground), the Trust decided to turn the entire hill into a war memorial, a fell for the fallen: 'our comrades on these cliffs'. It enjoys one of the best views in Lakeland.

The significance of the National Trust swims into focus most readily when we stand in scenery that it has not protected. The vantage point from which Constable painted Dedham Vale, for instance, no longer offers the prospect he loved. It is a bit too close to the cars and trucks zooming from Colchester to Ipswich on the A12.

By contrast, the bee-hum vista across the mill pond at nearby Flatford is unchanged. The trees behind Willy Lott's cottage have grown, and there used to be more elms interrupting the view of the fields. But the sun-struck mood remains more or less as it was in 1821, when Constable painted *The Hay Wain* here. The Trust acquired Flatford in 1943, and made it an abiding symbol of the land that inspired so much affection ... and so much art.

Seventeen

Black Beauty

We tend to think of the Industrial Revolution as occu-
pying a smoke-filled landscape of belching fumes and
roaring engines. Indeed, it has so often been presented as a
polluting enemy of nature, poisoning the ground on which
it squats, that we forget the extent to which it had roots deep
in England's mild and pleasing countryside. Industrial development was the product of a remarkable marriage between
coal and water; and as geographical good luck would have it,
England was rich in both. The child of their union was a force
of unprecedented power: steam.

Three different spots in the English countryside illustrate
the point.

The first is in the Severn valley, a few miles east of Shrewsbury. And as before, the tale begins with a geological twist.
Before arriving here, the Severn trickles to the surface in
the 500-million-year-old Cambrian mountains of Wales, as
it always has. But until the last Ice Age (a mere 20,000 years
ago – just the other day, in geological terms) it then ran
north – to the Mersey estuary. Only when that route was
blocked by a wall of ice was it diverted south, to its present
course, wriggling through drowsy countryside on its way to
the Bristol Channel.

Not far from the ruined Cistercian abbey at Buildwas, the

land rears up on either side. To the right, above the brick-coloured turrets of the power station, you can see Wenlock Edge, a limestone spine that runs all the way to Malvern. And then, in an awe-inspiring demonstration of water's power to cut through solid rock, the river bores through a line of hills and cuts into the wooded valley that is now known as Ironbridge Gorge.

It happens with surprising speed. One minute the Severn is curving across a broad plain; the next it is surging through a tree-filled glen. In the hush you can hear the hum of bees and the cries of predatory birds; dragonflies skitter across the bright water, and wagtails flit through shafts of sunlight. It is very quiet. There is a faint whisper of breeze through the treetops and you might catch the splash of an occasional otter or the cough of a distant sheep.

That's how it is on a good day. When I visited, the only bird I could hear was a raucous cockerel in a caravan park; and in place of otters and dragonflies there were nettles, wasps and the groan of lorries grinding along the main road to Telford. But this is still a beguiling spot. Forest trees cling to even the steepest parts of the cliff, throwing cool shadows over the water. And it is ripe with history. The abbey dates back to 1135, when it was established as part of the nearby Much Wenlock foundation. The monks scratched a living not from sheep but from water. The river is only thirty yards wide at this point, so the priory was able to build a toll bridge out of local sandstone, throw out nets for fish, and charge travellers fees to make the crossing. When the monastery was dissolved in 1536 it mouldered into yet another English ruin that stands quietly in the field to this day.

It is one of the high points of English scenery. Yet this is where the Industrial Revolution was born. The abrupt banks alongside this quiet stretch of river were the setting in which burning coal first met hissing water to produce the steam that powered the new world of furnaces and foundries. It is called

Coalbrookdale[1] and it was where Abraham Darby and his engineers hit on a new way to smelt iron from rock.

Darby was an experienced metalworker who had made iron and copper tools in Bristol before coming to Coalbrookdale in 1709. He instantly saw that the valley was a geological miracle: the folding of the earth and the erosive power of the river had exposed, in the same convenient strata, all of the raw materials an ironworker could possibly need – coal, iron, limestone and clay. Better still, it had a wonderful highway – the Severn – running right through the middle of it. If Darby had sketched the ideal

© Design Pics Inc/Alamy Stock Photo

Coalbrookdale, Shropshire. This secluded stretch of the River Severn is where the Industrial Revolution was born.

---

1 The name is a mineralogical fluke: it began life as Caldebrok – 'Cold Brook'. Other English place names betray their true origins more readily: Bournemouth is where a stream meets the sea; Chester-le-Street was on a Roman road; Chiswick and Keswick were both cheese farms; Woolwich was a textile port; Whitchurch was famous for its white church ... and so on.

place to set up an ironworks, he would scarcely have dared come up with something so perfect. Jan Morris once wrote that Britain's pre-eminence in the age of steam was thanks to 'the chance of history', but on this stretch of the Severn it is hard not to edit this into the 'chance of geography'. A few decades later, in large part because of its amazing geology, this delightful wooded valley in the wilds of Shropshire (not far from where Peter Corbet had set his dogs on the last wolf) was the boiling, smoking, sparking centre of the world's first iron industry.

For centuries, iron had been made by heating ore, coal and limestone (for carbon) together until the molten metal dripped into waiting moulds, but the gaseous impurities released by the coal made for a brittle end product. So Darby's first task was to find a way of purifying coal into a new substance: coke. He bought a disused mill and started to experiment. The solution proved to be surprisingly straightforward: just as charcoal was made by burning wood, so coke could be made by burning (and then cooling) coal. Darby was soon producing excellent iron, which he hammered, wrought and cast into a variety of shapes. He started by turning out iron pans and kettles, and it was quite a while before anyone grasped the full potential of this innovation. Coalbrookdale began producing railway wheels in 1729, though there were hardly any iron rails on which they might run. But time eventually caught up, and Darby was soon making the world's first generation of cylinders for steam engines. In 1779, under the stewardship of Darby's grandson, the ironworks at Coalbrookdale constructed the famous bridge across the gorge that now bears its name: Ironbridge.

That bridge, now a UNESCO World Heritage Site, quickly became the emblem of the brave new world of iron and smoke. In 1787 a fellow ironmaster named John Wilkinson launched the world's first iron boat – an eight-ton monster fittingly named the *Trial* — on this stretch of the Severn.[2] The vessel astounded a curious crowd of onlookers by not sinking and thus heralded a new era of shipbuilding know-how that would carry Englishness around the world at a time when the Severn's fishermen were still bobbing along in coracles.

The rails that would soon pave England were first forged in this green dale; the first iron-framed building went up in nearby Shrewsbury in 1797 (an advance that ushered in the prospect of skyscrapers); and the foundries rapidly became famous for their decorative railings and grilles. The imposing gates for the Great Exhibition of 1851 — the celebration of industrial manufacturing that formed the basis of South Kensington's museums — still stand in London's Hyde Park as monuments to early iron. It was the Silicon Valley of its day. Embryonic tram lines were built to drag coal and lime up and down the steep hills to fire the foundries, and large brick kilns sprang up downriver, in Coalport, to make the tiles for thousands of new churches, town halls, schools and regimental buildings springing up in England and beyond.

Ironbridge Gorge seems a world away from the dark satanic mills of Lancashire and Yorkshire, the ash pits of Nottingham and Durham, and the smokestacks of the Black Country — the zones of smog, slum and unremitting labour. Yet all these tremendous horrors had their origins in this peaceful valley, with its willows, swallows and darting kingfishers. The Industrial Revolution was intimately attached to the nature of this area. Now a heritage centre, with a dozen museums devoted to its ironworks, it is world-renowned as the 'Birthplace of the Industrial Revolution'. But it is also one of the places where English industry first died. The

---

2 This, at least, is the standard history, but the details of the launch are cloudy. Some accounts claim that the boat was thirty-two tons (which seems unlikely for a prototype); others insist that the launch took place on the Birmingham Canal in the Black Country. But Wilkinson certainly lived in Coalbrookdale. For a man of his interests, it was the only place to be.

great chimneys of the power station – dyed an autumnal shade so as not to clash with the landscape – have long since been decommissioned.

One day, perhaps, its elephantine turrets will be an atmospheric ruin, just like the medieval abbey that lies at their feet. A passing poet might even be moved to compose an ode, with a nod to Shelley, on the vast and trunkless legs that rise above the ancient trees.[3]

Revolutions have many parents, and if Coalbrookdale can claim to be the mother ship, than England's rocky south-west coast should be granted at least some paternal rights. Sailing up the Dart estuary today, it is hard to believe that this area was ever home to anything other than weatherbeaten fishermen, smugglers and pirates. And yet, in the sun-kissed harbour town of Dartmouth, next to the Tourist Information Office, and the sunburned holidaymakers queuing for orange crabbing lines, stands the Newcomen Engine House. Inside is one of the first steam engines ever built in England (in 1720), and it is here because its inventor was a native of the town.

Even those who revere Thomas Newcomen as an engineer do not always associate him with a seaside resort.[4] Dartmouth, like Coalbrookdale, is a beauty spot. Yet it was here that Newcomen, a toolmaker and blacksmith, poorly educated but with a flair for practical challenges, developed the machine that would revolutionise England, Britain and the world. Building on scientific principles established by a French refugee, Denis Papin,[5] Newcomen constructed a larger – and more useful –

3 If so, he would be in esteemed company: J. M. W. Turner and John Sell Cotman both visited Coalbrookdale and found it inspiring. Turner's tender image of a lime kiln is reminiscent of the manger at Bethlehem.

4 Dartmouth is better known as the home of Sir Walter Raleigh and the Royal Naval College.

5 Papin's pressure cooker – or 'steam digester' – was unveiled at London's Royal Society in 1679. Savery was another Devon man, born in Shilstone, near Modbury.

version of Thomas Savery's steam pump, with an oak beam to generate the vacuum that drove the device.

But why did this experiment take place in Dartmouth? Once again, the explanation is geographical. When Newcomen grew up, the great local issue of the day was the lethal flooding of nearby tin mines, especially on the Cornish coast. The traditional method of evacuating water from the mines – using a circling horse or a mule to haul up a rope laden with buckets – was painfully slow, and there were many mishaps and accidents.

Dartmouth, Devon. We do not always associate pretty south-coast harbours with industrial innovation. But this is where Thomas Newcomen pioneered the steam engine.

It was also expensive. There had to be a better way.

Along with his assistant, an unjustly forgotten plumber by the name of John Calley, Newcomen set to work. It took years of patient trial and error before he built his engine. The breakthrough came when he hit upon the idea of using steam to create a vacuum inside a cylinder, which in turn could power a pump. The first documented Newcomen engine was operating at Dudley, in Staffordshire, in 1712, but similar pumps were probably deployed in Cornish mines two years earlier, and there was certainly one at Wheal Vor, near Penzance, in 1713.[6] By the time of Newcomen's death, more than a hundred of his machines were clanking and grinding across England; by the end of the eighteenth century, the number was closer to a thousand.

There was a pleasing symmetry to it. Water was being used to shift . . . water.

Of all Newcomen's engines, none was more important than the one Abraham Darby II installed to drive the great bellows in his father's forge at Coalbrookdale in 1742. It lit a bright spark that could not be dimmed. A few decades later, the whole country was ablaze with hot industrial endeavour.

Not that Newcomen's products were perfect; far from it. In the 1770s James Watt, a Scot who moved south to Birmingham to consummate a happy British marriage of Scottish ingenuity and English muscle, improved the design by adding a condenser, so the cylinder no longer wasted energy being cooled by fresh water. This terrific innovation meant that Newcomen's barn-sized contraptions could be replaced with more powerful but much smaller machines (just as a smartphone has more zip than the room-sized mainframes of the 1970s).

Even here we are obliged to notice the crucial part played by nature, because it was England's compact size and efficient, water-borne transport system that allowed novel ideas and practices to race across the country – from colliery to mill to city to foundry to port. That is what allowed a harbour in Devon and a valley in the Upper Severn to be the delivery rooms for the age of iron, coal and steel – and in time the railways and ships that carried Englishness around the world (under the British flag).

*

6 But when you solve one problem, you often create another. Because Cornwall had no coal, the fuel for Newcomen's engines had to be shipped from elsewhere, then lugged up roads or primitive tramways. It was said that eighty mules delivered the coal that drove the engine at Wheal Vor.

Cornwall's Atlantic coast is perhaps the most spectacular in England, with a footpath that is a national treasure. It is also central to England's imaginative ancestry, since it is the home of Arthurian myth: the great King was magically conceived at Tintagel; and it was to this wild and rocky shore that Isolde sailed to be dazzled first by a love potion and then by Tristan.

A remote granite peninsula, it is thrashed by the sea and moulded by many rivers, powerful natural forces that handed Cornwall an important role in the mechanical development of England. It was never touched by the ice sheet, which meant that its alluring veins of tin and copper were not buried beneath glacial debris. And millennia of Atlantic storms carved out a gritty landscape of hills and gullies. The region's first miners were not even human: fast-flowing streams washed precious metals straight from the earth.

We are going back a long time here. Copper and tin combined to make bronze, so Cornwall and Devon were already significant in the ancient world. Indeed, the Greek historian Herodotus might have been thinking of Cornwall when he referred to the 'tin islands' of the west. The area was certainly well known to the Romans, who used Cornish metal to make their coins. A thousand years later, in the twelfth century, the region was producing almost all of Europe's tin; and by 1400 eight hundred tons of ore was being mined on the peninsula every year. Later, when Tudor kings talked about taxing Cornwall, as they often did, it was the county's tin wealth they had in mind.[7]

The mines started to close in the nineteenth century, when it became cheaper to import tin from Africa and Asia. Ruins of the old mines are now tourist attractions. There are tin-themed museums and heritage events, but the poster boy for this slice of Cornish history is the engine house and chimney stack at St Agnes, which stands in a sea of purple heather

---

7 The Cornish Rebellion of 1497 was primarily a protest against Henry VII's attempt to impose a tin tax (to pay for a war against Scotland).

overlooking the kind of view a five-star hotel would kill for – crashing waves, perfect sandy cove and a blue horizon which carries an alluring hint that Isolde may be on her way.

Its long experience with tin meant that Cornwall possessed not only the raw material but also the technical know-how to meet the rising demand for copper in the eighteenth century. There was plenty of copper in the county, and it was needed not only as a worm-proof lining for ships' hulls (copper-bottomed), but to make brass cogs, machine parts and scientific instruments. (All of this was long before it became a crucial component in the electronics industry.)

By 1720, Cornwall was producing six thousand tons of copper a year; fifty years later it was up to thirty thousand; and by 1850 this isolated, sea-washed promontory on the edge of England was generating two-thirds of the world's total supply. The 350 copper pits in the growing conurbation of Redruth–Camborne employed some fifty thousand workers.

This leads to another quiz: where was the first house in England – or indeed the world – to be illuminated by gaslight?

Stockton? Manchester? The Potteries? These are the places we usually associate with industrial-era breakthroughs. In fact, the answer is: Redruth.

The house belonged to William Murdoch, a Scot who had once walked three hundred miles from Glasgow to Birmingham to make contact with his hero, James Watt. By this time the joint venture that was Great Britain was making it hard to disentangle England from Scotland, Wales and Ireland, so Murdoch was hardly exploring foreign parts. After signing up with Boulton & Watt[8] he had continued on to the south-west coast, lured by the bright flame of the new industries on England's Atlantic rim.

His house in Redruth soon became an R&D laboratory, home to the world's first working model of a steam

8 Matthew Boulton, a native of Birmingham, had entered into partnership with Watt in 1775.

locomotive – a toy train that chuffed around the sitting room – and some early experiments with gas piping. Inspired by the difficulty of groping for his front-door key in the Cornish darkness, in 1794 he built a contraption involving a bladder and a tobacco pipe, and created a lamp that burned with a bright flare. A plaque on the house commemorates his achievement, but perhaps not quite as glowingly as it should.

Redruth and its twin Camborne grew fast, soon becoming a single gold-rush conurbation. Today, they are perhaps the only area of Cornwall that tourists deliberately skip, but in those days they were a copper metropolis. The high mound of Carn Brea above the two towns dominated a terrain that was richly furnished with the precious metal, and some of the mine shafts ran far out beneath the sea bed.

There was a high risk of flooding. And that is what Thomas Newcomen was working on down in Dartmouth.

One of Murdoch's neighbours was a fellow by the name of Richard Trevithick. The son of a Cornish mine manager, he was also the grandson (on his mother's side) of a blacksmith and foundry maker who manufactured both Newcomen and Boulton & Watt engines. Partly to avoid paying royalties to Boulton, he gave the Boulton & Watt engine a tweak, using high-pressure steam to generate even more pumping power. The result was the Cornish beam engine, a device that not only propelled much further industrial development but left a lasting mark on the county's landscape through the upright stone sheds in which it was housed. The surfers and campers who visit Cornwall today are never far from a disused chimney – a gaunt and stony finger poking up to the sky.

Trevithick did not stop there. In 1801 he mounted an engine on wheels and came up with England's first steam-driven road carriage – in effect, the world's first car. But it was cumbersome, so the following year he adapted it to run on rails. Before long, one of Trevithick's rail-mounted engines was dragging coal and iron along the tramways of Coalbrookdale.

It was the Puffing Devil. The age of the railway had arrived.

Like Newcomen, Trevithick was not some madcap boffin, but a dogged mechanic. His schoolteacher at Camborne had called him 'disobedient, slow, obstinate ... very inattentive', and no one had predicted any sort of a future for him. But, again like Newcomen, he had an inquiring mind, a determined approach to problem-solving and an instinctive feeling for machines that amounted to genius.

This was starting to be a theme in English life: centuries of rural craft had fostered an immense number of small mechanical innovations which now, driven by a new source of power – steam – joined forces to foster an industrial leap forward. Newcomen, Trevithick, Watt and others achieved fame by attaching their names to key advances, but the secret of the revolution's success was that it was broadly based, supported by a social movement of largely forgotten figures who did innumerable clever things with screws, grilles, drills, valves, cylinders, gauges, filters, tubes, rods, gears, whistles, brakes, lamps, boilers and pistons. Whole new trades and industries emerged to service and supply the headline acts.

The new machines of Dartmouth and Coalbrookdale were a beginning, certainly, but also a culmination: only the latest stride of a marathon engineering tradition. Generations of farmers, millers, smiths, farriers, carpenters, metalworkers and weavers – most of them nameless – had long been laying the groundwork for this momentous step. There had been ironworks in the shires for centuries – in the Weald of Kent, the Forest of Dean and Northumbria. The Cistercian monasteries of Yorkshire smelted red ore to make bells, ploughs, locks, keys, grates, roasting spits and other fittings for their great buildings; and it was a rare village that did not have a blacksmith pounding away in a shower of sparks.

But this rustic tradition had always relied on a marvellous natural resource which was, by the eighteenth century, starting to wear thin. It was hard to believe, but England was running out of trees. The great native forest started disappearing many years before it became urgent to bandy around modern notions of 'sustainability'. Wood had been vanishing since ancient times, providing building material, fuel for fires and charcoal for blacksmiths. A single tree feller might topple as many as 30,000 oaks in his lifetime. Modern estimates suggest that only 10 per cent of the country's natural woodland was still intact by the 1350s, but the demand for wood continued to rise. The medieval building boom – all those manor houses, cathedrals, churches and village halls – meant that ever more trees were chopped down each year. The growing population added fuel to the fire; and the Tudor naval expansion lit a whole new flame. A typical man-of-war required four hundred oaks, and though most vessels were smaller, something in the region of a hundred thousand trees must have been harvested to create the fleet that saw off the Armada.[9] There was the growing cargo trade too – fifteen hundred ships ferried coal from Newcastle to London alone – along with fishing boats, barges and other small craft.

Inevitably, the price of timber began to rise. And as one resource fell (or was felled) it became cost-effective to look for another. It was time to start digging for coal.

Some historians have traced a bubble-like price hike for timber during Tudor times; others dispute such claims. But even if the market was uneven – the price seems to have risen faster in London than elsewhere, for instance, due to transportation costs – there did come a point when coal became more cost-effective than wood.

As so often in England, the first beneficiaries of this boom were not entrepreneurs but landowners. A coal seam was just as natural an earthly inheritance as an oak tree, was it not? Many great estates profited simply by 'granting' (i.e. selling)

9 When Elizabeth became Queen in 1558, England had only 39 warships; by 1805, the year of Trafalgar, Britain boasted 950. At a conservative estimate, roughly a quarter of a million oaks must have been vanquished to build such a fleet.

the right to dig a pit on their land.[10] But the common people benefited too, since coal could warm a room and heat water much more efficiently than wood. Domestic life changed, and so did working practices. Coal conquered the English winter, and by loosening their dependence on the sun, allowed people to move to areas where only ascetic monks felt at home. They could also continue to work even when snow lay deep, crisp and even across the land. In short, England became more *industrious*. People could work indoors all day – and all night, if they wished. Coal, as Ralph Waldo Emerson once remarked, was 'portable climate'. When we talk about England's 'Protestant work ethic', we usually think of it as a spiritual quality, but perhaps we should see it as carboniferous. It was kindled, to a large extent, by coal.

This is all well known. The surprise, however, is the extent to which the hot spots of this convulsion lay not in what we now consider the industrial heartlands of England, but in remote, scenic pockets of countryside. Industry was born in beauty spots. It was in our nature.

Coniston, in Cumbria, is one of the loveliest parts of the Lake District. It has inspired legions of writers, from Wordsworth and Ruskin to Beatrix Potter, who dreamed of naughty rabbits and hedgehogs on these beguiling slopes. But in Victorian times Coniston, like Cornwall, was a copper mine. The streams that tumbled down these fells provided the power that was needed to haul ore to the surface. Once again, English rock and English water combined to make English industry.

The story follows the same trajectory as metal-working in the south-west: ancient traces, Roman scratchings and centuries of manual digging using animal-fat candles to locate metallic glints. Even with this basic toolkit some of the early mines went deep – two thousand feet – and they were prone

10 Many of these coal tycoons were bishops. As a major landowner, the Church did well out of coal. It then recycled the proceeds into a church building programme.

to flooding. There was lead here too, and German miners were lured to Keswick in Tudor times to dig for both metals. In the middle of the nineteenth century, a railway was built to carry the growing tonnage of copper ore to the new port of Barrow-in-Furness, which was built (on the site of what was still no more than a hamlet as late as the 1840s) to service a sizeable local industry. A few decades later, it was all over, as Cumbrian producers struggled to compete against copper mines overseas.

Hill farmers gradually reclaimed the landscape. As in Cornwall, a few relics – broken walls, wheelhouses, chimneys, shaft entrances and abandoned quarries – still give the place a sombre undertone: the air of an abandoned ship. They are faint reminders that England could not have become England without the raw materials that lay in its native rocks.

The same forces operated in other parts of the country. The chemicals industry settled in the village of Widnes – from the Viking for 'wide nose', a reference to the bulge of land on which it stands – because it was close to an indispensable ingredient: salt. Staffordshire was home to thousands of ceramics kilns thanks to an almost infinite supply of clay.

But nothing influenced the shape of industrial England as decisively as coal. As we have seen, it was being shipped from Newcastle as early as the 1290s, but the pace accelerated in Tudor times, when 200,000 tons sailed down the Tyne every year. In 1555 the Venetian ambassador wrote that England was lucky to be warmed by 'a certain sort of earth, well nigh mineral', which 'gives great heat and costs little'. Production jumped fivefold in fifty years, and by 1650 England was burning a million tons – effectively of itself – each year.

We speak easily of the Bronze Age and the Iron Age, and England at least can be said to have enjoyed a Wool Age. But we rarely give the same weight to the notion of a Coal Age. Indeed, the place of coal in the national consciousness is fading much faster than it should. And this is not just due to popular forgetfulness, exacerbated by the fact that there are no working mines left. Much scholarly energy has been devoted to the argument that coal's part in the so-called Industrial 'Revolution' has been exaggerated.

In keeping with modern practice, this thesis has been given a dreary, pseudo-scientific name – 'cliometrics' – designed to deter the passer-by. Applying avant-garde mathematical modelling to historical statistics, cliometricians reject the traditional view that coal was central to England's rise, suggesting instead that the decisive factor was the availability of capital. In this analysis, England dug up its coal because it was rich. And if it hadn't found any at home, it would have bought it elsewhere.

Only a fool would dispute the importance of the capital generated by all those centuries of wool trading and grain farming. But to leap from there to the claim that coal was a minor factor seems, as the historian David Landes put it, rather 'cart before horse'.[11] As we have seen, France had only a tenth of Britain's coal reserves, which left it much less able to develop the machinery needed to boost agriculture, let alone industry. At the beginning of the nineteenth century, Britain was producing three million tons of coal a year – more than the rest of the world combined. In 1861, when France produced seven million tons (and Prussia/Austria a mere four), Britain dug out sixty-six million tons. One has to concentrate quite hard to see this as a matter of secondary importance.

Eighteenth-century England was of course a capitalist (and class-ridden) society: huge sums of money were indeed being ploughed into new industrial ventures. But the ready supply of coal – and the ease with which it could be ferried around the country – was not marginal. This remarkable resource generated the steam that drove the engines that powered the mills, trains and ships. It warmed English homes and produced the gas that lit the streets. Money alone could not buy that.

---

11 Milan Kundera once referred to gaffes of this sort as 'sophisticated stupidities'.

Natural resources matter. One only has to consider oil, or look at the states fortunate enough to sit on iron. Britain, China, France, Germany, India, Russia, Spain and the United States: that is more or less a list of the world's major powers.

In England's case, abundant coal and iron helped drive not just new industries at home but the nation's restless expansion across the world. Hundreds of iron-hulled ships roamed the seven seas, all under the Union Flag. Some were naval vessels, most were merchant ships, but their captains knew, whenever they put into Singapore, Aden, Adelaide, Trincomalee, Malta, Calcutta, Cairo or Cape Town, that they could fill their holds with Durham or Yorkshire coal. Some dapper fellow from Aldershot or Gloucester, with a comically neat moustache, iron-pressed whites and an accounts book, would march out to supervise the refuelling. There might even be time to nip over to the yacht club for a sundowner and a hand of bridge.

It all led the English to develop a kind of swaggering confidence, a conviction of superiority, that not everyone found likeable. Some empire builders went so far as to suggest that this happy state of affairs was divinely ordained, or an expression of racial supremacy. Even at the height of the Empire's commercial lust, it imagined itself a civilising force. It was easy to overlook the extent to which global domination was due not to fine character, but simply to the coexistence of three basic natural resources: coal, iron and water. It was thanks to these that Britain was able to churn out not only half of the world's iron and steel, but half of its clothes. Who could gainsay such might? By 1883, it had half the world's battleships too.

Those thick seams of coal and iron were a geographical fluke every bit as unremarkable, and as telling, as the drizzly weather that had once made England so ideal for sheep and wheat.

Eighteen

Streets of Water

There was a problem with coal: it weighed a ton. Although in time it would come to enjoy a symbiotic relationship with the railway – trains needed coal to power their steam engines; coal needed trains to shunt it around the country – there was a period when the only way to ferry the stuff was via England's other great resource: water. Fortunately, there was no shortage of that. Millions of gallons fell from the sky most days.

It is impossible to nail down the exact moment when England's first canal was dug. The Romans were famous for their towering aqueducts, but in England, where water was so plentiful, they limited themselves to a few rough-and-ready ditches. The Foss Dyke was, in effect, a minor diversion of the River Trent, with the modest aim of giving Lincoln access to the sea; while the Car Dyke in the Lincolnshire Fens had as much to do with drainage as it did with transport.

Medieval England presided over a range of similar ventures: Dartmoor was criss-crossed with 'leats' – slim gullies cut by hand to deliver water to the tin mines. There were hundreds of miles of these channels, but they were too small to function as roads. Some early attempts to improve the flow of rivers involved a form of canalisation – the Lea and the Exe were both enhanced in this way, and something resembling a canal was dug at Exeter in 1566 – but it was the industrial demand for coal in the eighteenth century that gave England the push it needed to make full use of its abundant rainfall.

Coal plus water equalled steam. But they also made highways.

The campaign to improve the distribution system for coal enjoyed strong political backing. In 1755 Parliament passed an Act 'for making navigable the River or Brook called Sankey Brook' in Lancashire, with the intention of giving the area's coal mines easy access to Merseyside. Inspired by this modest watercourse, and by his experiences as a Grand Tourist on the Canal du Midi in the south of France, the twenty-three-year-old Duke of Bridgewater had a brainwave. He could see the merits of a new route connecting the mines on his Worsley estate to the coal exchange in Manchester. As things stood, it took a team of packhorses to drag the coal to the exchange, so the thought of shipping it at a fraction of the cost was mouth-watering.

The man Bridgewater entrusted with the task was James Brindley. Like Newcomen and Trevithick, he was neither high-born nor scholarly; indeed, he was semi-literate, and famously bad at spelling. But his father had been a yeoman farmer in the Peak District, so young James had grown up in sheep country; and since he had started out as a millwright, he had plenty of mechanical know-how. In Macclesfield he also gained insights into water power, building an engine for draining a mine in 1752, but he had little repute as an engineer when Bridgewater signed him up.

He proved an inspired choice, however. He had a subtle feeling for contours that allowed him to follow the lie of the land with uncanny accuracy. This was just as well, since he lacked the engineering wherewithal to cut through mountains. He was also quick to grasp that he should line his channels with puddling clay to stop them leaking. These were not ordinary gifts. Bridgewater gave him a budget of £168,000 (more than £20 million in today's money) and approved the construction of both underground tunnels and an aqueduct.

The English are often mocked for their supposed aversion

to flights of fancy. They are said to prefer practical skills to philosophical contemplation, and have a ruddy-faced impatience with abstract ideas. The absence of academic pedigree in great men like Newcomen, Trevithick and Brindley seems to bear out the point – superb industrial accomplishments do not always require much in the way of higher learning. George Stephenson did not study railway engines in books; he could not even read until he was seventeen. He was educated by the rustic wagonway that passed his window as it carried coal down the Tyne valley. Getting your hands dirty, having a bit of common sense, remaining down to earth ... these were the prized English characteristics. They run in parallel with a detectable suspicion of expertise.

The Bridgewater Canal, which included a spur to connect it to the Mersey at Runcorn, finally opened in 1764. It was a major gamble, and proof of the importance of capital in such endeavours. But it paid off. The thirty-ton barges could be towed by a couple of strong men, a mule and a thick rope. The waterway was only thirty-nine miles long (the Canal du Midi was nearly a hundred miles), but it slashed transport costs and consequently halved the price of Manchester coal.[1] It also enriched Bridgewater to a degree that England's other industrialists could hardly fail to notice.

An up-and-coming potter named Josiah Wedgwood was quick to see the merits of such a scheme. He had already established a ceramics factory at Etruria (named after the home of the Etruscans) on the Trent, near Stoke, and the idea of transporting his creamware by water was appealing, since it was too fragile for long cart journeys on the pitted roads of the day. A canal would not only deliver clay and coal to his kilns but serve as a distribution channel for his products.

Wedgwood and a group of other West Midlands magnates

1 The Grand Union Canal had an even greater impact. It cost fifteen pounds to transport a ton of coal from Birmingham to London by packhorse. By canal, the fee per ton was a few shillings.

contacted Brindley and set him to work. In 1776 the potter
hacked out the first clod of a new canal designed to link the
Trent and the Mersey (Brindley wheeled it off in a barrow).
In so doing, he launched what in time would be known as
'canal mania'. It generated a stock market bubble, but it was a
major infrastructural stride forward. The Thames and Severn,
the Kennet and Avon, the Leeds to Liverpool, the London to
Birmingham ... the key nodes of England's new manufacturing regions were all joined together. Brindley himself, with
epic ambition, envisioned a national network that would link
four great rivers – the Thames, Severn, Trent and Mersey – and
though he did not live to see it achieved, he laid the foundations. A 1767 letter to a London newspaper urged everyone to
see the Harecastle Tunnel, near Kidsgrove, Staffordshire, on the
grounds that it was 'the eighth wonder of the world'.

Britain was already blessed with a thousand miles of navigable rivers, but the canal-building frenzy quadrupled this
figure in no time: by 1850, it stretched for 4250 miles. Not
for the first time, there were advantages in being a small, wet
country. No one could call it superfast: the speed limit on the
canals was just two miles per hour. But there were fables about
this sort of thing, to do with tortoises and hares. The barges
that crawled around England carried enough freight to ensure
that the country would never be the same again. An industrial
power gained a brand-new set of arteries.

Many factors contributed to the emergence of the nation's
canals: the fat reserves of capital, some of it the piratical proceeds of Empire and slavery, but most of it the residual wealth
gathered in the Age of Wool; the engineering expertise that
grew out of the agricultural craft tradition; the mills' insistent
demand for coal; the thousands of workers ('navvies'), armed
only with picks and shovels, who were driven from the fields
by labour-saving machinery, or forced out of Ireland by famine;
the efficient legal and political structure; and the immeasurable
cultural hinterland, which included the ability to cooperate in

teams, the religious work ethic and the faith in progress. But nothing would have been possible without the water that fell from the sky. Now it was carrying goods around the country ... and on to the rest of the world. By the middle of the nineteenth century, a single drop of rain that fell on Seathwaite could trickle down the shires until, one day, it passed beneath London Bridge and out to sea.

And while it was a triumph of rational thought, the canal network had a magical side, too. One of England's most basic raw materials (rain) was being used to transport another (coal), which was converting more water into steam, in order to help miners dig up more coal. It was quite a trick. One plus one – in this strange land – really did equal three.

Canals turned out to be a short-lived answer to England's transport needs – steam trains rendered them obsolete – but the engineering riddles they forced England's entrepreneurs to solve (all those aqueducts, tunnels, locks and gates) gave the railways a terrific technological head start. Powered by coal and water, they raced across the countryside in a flash.

One of the first realms of English life to be affected by the new infrastructure was one of the oldest: wool. Canals made it possible for the wool-working mills to move away from the rivers and wolds they had always called home, and delivered the coal-fired steam engines that allowed them to develop on an extraordinary scale.

Just three years after Wedgwood had first dug his spade into Staffordshire soil, a new waterway appeared in Gloucestershire. Known as the Stroudwater Canal, it ran for only eight miles. But what it lacked in length it made up for in guile, because it conquered an incline of over a hundred feet, using a dozen locks to adjust the level of the water in its slender channel.

This major technical achievement was a long time in the planning. A proposal had been approved by Parliament way back in 1730, but the mill owners on the Frome had fretted over the potential impact on their river, and the scheme had foundered. Contrary to their fears, though, everything boomed when the canal opened in 1779 – employment, profits, productivity . . . and noise. It became an extensive textiles factory, set in lovely countryside. Before long, the canal was carrying 16,000 tons of coal to the mills every year.

The mills had been drawn to this area in the first place because it stood at the foot of the Cotswold escarpment and had the finest wool in the world on its doorstep. But the topography that made the Stroud valley picturesque had also made it inaccessible – until now. The arrival of the canal exposed a rural craft economy to the brutish wonders of coal and steam, and the mills started to turn out cloth on an industrial scale. It was Bridgewater all over again. Previously, eight packhorses had been needed to carry a ton of wool to market; now just one tough pony could lug a fully laden hundred-ton Severn 'trow' off to market. Some bargees even hoisted a sail and did away with the horse power altogether.

The architecture of the mills changed dramatically. The various cottage-based crafts associated with the trade – carding, spinning, weaving, fulling and dyeing – were brought under a single roof and driven by engines of unprecedented strength. The age in which people worked at home on hand looms was brought to an abrupt end as ever more workers were sucked into huge factories that looked – and felt – like prisons.

Some of the consequences were foreseeable – the concentration of workers in towns and cities, the drift away from the countryside and, most striking of all, the decline of the horse as a fact of English life. In Victorian England more than three million horses worked in the fields, transporting goods and toiling in pits; by the First World War, there were probably no more than 25,000 left, a sensationally abrupt alteration.

Some of the other effects were less easy to predict. It seemed a waste to send the barges that delivered the coal away empty, so they were loaded up with West Country products: wool, timber, rope, tools and fancy goods. As a result, many once-small businesses – basket-makers, milliners, brewers, farmers and so on – discovered that they could reach promising new markets in distant corners of the country. More important, perhaps, the canal brought things to the Cotswolds that had seemed impossibly remote. In 1789, while the *sans-culottes* of Paris were marching on the Bastille, navvies in Gloucestershire were engineering a different revolution on the Avon. Engineers cut a new channel linking the Severn and the Thames, and a new world opened up. Two great river basins were united, and a highway was forged between London, Bristol and the West Midlands.

No one called it the Southern Powerhouse, but they could have.

Only a generation earlier, Stroud had been a dozy shepherds' village. Now it became an inland port, even a capital of boat-building. Tropical luxuries like cocoa, coffee, sugar and vanilla started to drift into a neighbourhood whose inhabitants had rarely seen the next valley, let alone the islands where these things came from.

When England flexed its manufacturing muscles, it broadened its horizons too. A hunger for trade and travel was born.

The pretty valley west of Stroud changed fast. Dozens of new mills hummed to life along the route of the canal: according to one map, there were 150 textile enterprises on its banks by 1824.[2] Nineteenth-century paintings show the surrounding hillsides covered with vivid cloth – the best Stroud wool, dyed with brilliant red pigment extracted from the South American cochineal beetle (carmine) and destined for the uniforms of the British army. The material, known as 'Stroud Scarlet', was hung out to dry in the steep surrounding fields on special frames called tenters. Naturally, everyone involved had to keep a nervous eye on the sky in case a shower came along to ruin the drying process, so a new saying was born: both the cloth and the people who wove it were always on 'tenterhooks'.

2 Today only two remain. One of them is the imposing, historic home of Stroud District Council.

Caen Locks, near Devizes. At the height of canal mania, water could even be used to make staircases.

The biggest of the new ventures was Ebley Mill. Cloth had been woven here since the fourteenth century, but the scale of the enterprise was transformed by the arrival of the canal and the coal it carried. Several small factories appeared almost immediately, and then, in the 1860s, a vast structure rose up that would soon employ eight hundred workers within its six-storey stone walls. To emphasise its importance, the architect gave it the regal air of a French chateau.

The combination of canal-inspired industry and West Country rainfall had another interesting consequence. In 1830 a man named Edwin Budding – a mechanic in a Stroud mill – came up with a brilliant new way of cutting grass. Having studied the rotating drums that were used to shave nap off cloth, he adapted them into a device that could be used 'for cropping or shearing the surface of lawns, grass plots and pleasure grounds'. A local engineer named Ferrabee turned one of the old woollen mills on the London Road into an ironworks and he was soon turning out the first generation of Budding lawnmowers.

It may have been a modest invention compared to the grander technological leaps of the time, but in its own way it changed English life just as much. Gardens, parks, picnics, sports . . . the English weekend would have been very different without Budding. Mowing the lawn, along with washing the car, became an integral part of suburban English life.

The arrival of canal-borne coal, and the introduction of large-scale, steam-powered mills, represented something of a death knell for the wool villages of Suffolk and the Cotswolds – Lavenham, Long Melford, Lechlade and Castle Combe. They began to seem rather small, and their rushing streams of water were no longer needed. The industry began to migrate to locations closer to the coalfields – on the rain-swollen rivers of Yorkshire, for example, near Leeds, Bradford and Halifax, and not far from the Cistercian monasteries of the Middle Ages.

The same wet weather that had once made this region so

rich in grass (and all the lucrative animals that grazed it) now made it the natural home for heavier industry.

The biggest of the new factories was Armley Mill, on the River Aire, in Leeds. It had been a site for fulling since Tudor times, and by 1788 had five wheels driving eighteen separate textile works, making it the largest mill complex in the world. It was rebuilt after a fire in 1805, again with water wheels, and its owner, Benjamin Gott, became one of England's richest magnates. However, when steam power was installed in 1850 the factory roared into new life, using cheap wool from Australia's Botany Bay as its raw material and exporting finished cloth across the Empire.

The terrific scale of the new factories in this area inspired the digging of the Leeds to Liverpool Canal, which in time became the most important – and profitable – waterway in the kingdom: the principal route across the Pennines.

A different upheaval shook Mitton, near Kidderminster. The gentle topography of the Severn valley made this the perfect place to connect the Staffordshire and Worcestershire Canal with the river. Designed once again by James Brindley, it opened up a narrow – only seven-feet-wide – but effective cross-country route from the Trent to Mersey Canal. Mitton became the major interchange for traffic between Liverpool and Bristol – an especially lucrative position in the heyday of the slave trade.

Since the Severn's barges were much larger than Brindley's narrowboats, Mitton became a depot too, with wharves, warehouses and inns for travelling merchants. Whatever came up the river – wine, wool, grain or timber – had to be transferred to the narrowboats that squeezed up and down the canal. Thanks to its convenient location, a village in the middle of nowhere became an important freight hub.

Only a dozen people had lived in Mitton prior to the coming of the canal; swans drifted beneath willows barely disturbed by modern eighteenth-century life. Bewdley, a few miles to the north, was the riverside capital of the area. But the hilly terrain that inspired its name (Beau Lieu) made it unsuitable as a canal basin, so Mitton was chosen instead. Fine Georgian houses were built for the merchants, and numerous hostelries competed over the fashionable visitors who came simply to marvel at the bustling scene.

The town became the foremost transit lounge in the region when the Birmingham Canal was completed in 1772. It was renamed Stourmouth, then Newport and finally Stourport, by which time it was the second inland harbour in the country after Birmingham (which grew larger still once the Grand Union Canal gave it direct access to London).

Stourport's star fell when a new waterway – built to link Worcester and Birmingham – bypassed the Severn valley altogether. But for half a century it was a major junction for English water . . . and English commerce. After that, it became a town impregnated with the most English flavour of all – a sad sense that it had once been quite something.

As is so often the way, the next big thing – cotton – was already limbering up. But unlike wool, it was not indigenous – it had to be imported from the vast new plantations in North America. So it is not one of the native ingredients from which England is made. It did trigger a shift of emphasis in the entire textile industry, however, in that mills no longer needed to be close to the wool supply, but adjacent to the ports where cotton was unloaded.

A new industrial region came into being: the north-west. The trading capacity of Liverpool and Manchester, with their access to the Atlantic-facing coast – made this part of England the ideal place to build a factory or two . . . or three.

There was another stroke of geographical good fortune: the Lancashire climate turned out to be better for cotton than the region east of the Pennines. The soft Lancashire water was better for washing the raw material, and the damp air meant the finished fabric did not dry or crack. Most important of all, the cotton mills had no need for fast-flowing Pennine water. A loom wheel driven by a Yorkshire flood was no match for a coal-fired steam engine.

The wool industry wasn't helped by the fact that it was set in ways that dated back to the Middle Ages. The time-honoured guilds, so proud of their traditions, were slow to react to this new force in the land; indeed, they opposed it. Lancashire powered on regardless.

It was North West England's turn to become the leading driver of technical innovation and advance. First, James Hargreaves, a poetically minded spinner from a village near Blackburn, had a eureka moment when his daughter knocked over their hand-operated wheel. As he watched the spindle continue to whirr, he glimpsed a radical possibility: instead of using one upright wheel to draw a single thread, he could build a connected bank of *eight* spindles, all powered by the same rotating wheel. All of a sudden, the production of thread could be multiplied eightfold. He then added a useful feeder device, which meant there was no longer any need for a human hand to feed in the yarn. When he unveiled the finished contraption in 1764, it was obvious that it could do the work of a sizeable gang of men and women. According to legend, Hargreaves named his machine the 'spinning jenny' after the daughter whose clumsiness had helped to inspire it.[3]

Not everyone celebrated. Fearing, with reason, that the machine threatened their livelihoods, some of his neighbours broke into Hargreaves's house and smashed the prototype to pieces. Hargreaves fled to Nottingham to escape the outcry. But it is never easy to suppress new inventions, especially when they are so profitable, and the only impact of this uprising was to turn Nottingham into a textile capital.

The second giant step forward was taken by Richard Arkwright on the banks of the River Derwent in Derbyshire. His 'water

---

3 She was not called Jenny, but the story caught on regardless.

frame', patented in 1769, used rollers to improve the way in which yarn was fed into the spinner, multiplying the number of threads that could be teased out simultaneously. The great mill he built at Cromford two years later was powered by the river at first, but in time used steam to drive its many looms.

As at Coalbrookdale, a new factory planted a new industry in an area of outstanding natural beauty, where the Derwent flowed through a peaceful green dale on the edge of the Peak District. There were two interesting side-effects of this: due to its remote location, Arkwright was obliged to build housing for the two hundred workers he needed to operate his five-storey mill; and since the engines never stopped, he could run the factory all day and all night, in two twelve-hour shifts. Company housing and the Victorian factory system were born at the same time.

The third breakthrough followed soon afterwards. Back in Lancashire, a young cotton spinner (and amateur violinist) named Samuel Crompton, the son of a Bolton caretaker, was moved to make some improvements to Hargreaves's machine. Adding Arkright's new rollers, he produced an advanced hybrid which he called a 'mule', partly because it was so tough, partly because it was a cross-breed. Over a thousand spindles now worked together to produce much finer thread.

Influential as these three inventors were, we cannot ascribe the Cotton Revolution only to their ingenuity, because the single most important ingredient in the cotton industry was cotton itself. So this particular page in England's story was written not by something it possessed, but by something it lacked. A theme was emerging. England was starting to be governed by a desire for crops it could not grow: tea, coffee, tobacco and sugar cane – luxuries from warmer climates it could no longer do without. There was only one thing for it: it would have to conquer the world.

As demand grew, England made one of the most drastic decisions in its history: it started shipping African slaves to plantations in North America and the Caribbean, where they could be forced to grow exotic commodities.

This is not the place to tell the story of that horror. It remains the darkest stain on England's national character. Yes, the Arab slave market was already well established when England appeared on the scene. Yes, several other European nations – not to mention Scotland, Wales and Ireland – behaved just as cruelly. Yes, people were prisoners of their time. Yes, England played a leading role in the abolition of slavery. None of this blots out its culpability for a historic evil.

The past cannot always be counted on for a moral; history is not a parable. But this is not an ambiguous story. The dismal truth is that between 1662 and 1807 England – as the leader of the British federation – shipped nearly three and a half million Africans to the New World to harvest the treats it could not grow at home. And its leaders remained blind to the irony of it all. In 1740 an audience at Cliveden, a stately home on the River Thames, tapped its feet to a new musical masque titled *Alfred*. One of the songs – 'Rule Britannia' – celebrated an epic English hero and included the rousing idea that Britons 'never, never, never shall be slaves'.[4] That same year, England sent no fewer than thirty-three ships on the wicked triangular trade.

Cotton fuelled Britain's imperial ambition in another way, by funnelling profits from Indian textiles in the early days of its mercantile adventuring. As the years passed, however, the 'mother country' sought to discourage this rival textile industry. It wanted the colony to be no more than a cotton producer, growing the raw material for English and Scottish mills. Some of the stories about how this was achieved – one features British

---

4 Of course, the lyrics are untrue: England was conquered repeatedly for centuries. Indeed, the nation was formed by waves of Roman, Saxon, Viking and Norman assault. It may even be that this is where England's reflexive suspicion of foreigners originates. 'England for the English' was the battle cry of the thirteenth-century Barons' Revolt even though its leader, Simon de Montfort, was of Norman stock.

agents cutting off the hands or thumbs of Dacca's weavers – may or may not be untrue, but the intention was clear. India's development was deliberately held back to boost the profitability of Lancashire and Lanark. The 'Jewel in the Crown' was turned into a dependency – a low-cost producer of cotton, tea and spices for Britain – not to mention opium, for the Chinese market.

The British Empire had begun as a purely English gambit. In the first flush of its nautical strength, Elizabeth I's sea captains had jauntily raided Spain's Atlantic treasure fleet. Since the gold and silver in these galleons had been looted from the New World, England's pirates could convince themselves that they were latter-day Robin Hoods – all pluck and derring-do. But this was plunder on an international scale.

As was the next stage. In 1600 the Queen granted a charter to the East India Company to explore the commercial possibilities on the far side of the world – i.e. to secure new markets for the English textile industry. The scholar–traveller Richard Hakluyt declared that 'Our chief desire is to find out ample vent of our woollen cloth, the natural commoditie of this our Realme.' In these early days, the Empire was founded on the marriage of ships and sheep – two historic English resources. When cotton came on to the scene, the toolkit was already in place: the expertise needed to spin it into wealth; maritime strength; a culture of trade; a class of affluent people who liked to follow the latest fashions; the wherewithal required to finance the project; and a horde of greedy customers.

It has been estimated that if the world had not switched from wool to cotton in the nineteenth century it would now need 28 billion sheep to keep it clothed. But though the rise of cotton spelled trouble for England's wool industry, it triggered an urge to plant the nation's favourite pastoral activities – shepherding and weaving – in pastures new.

At first, these fresh fields were close to home. After the Battle of Culloden, in 1746, the English practice of transforming farmland into sheep runs – and evicting the people who lived there – was introduced north of the border. This marked the start of the infamous Highland Clearances.

The Scots fought back, just as their English predecessors had done, but when farmers in Ardross drove six thousand sheep off the land, the Black Watch came a-calling. Villagers were corralled into small crofts on desolate moors, or cold huts on the infertile, rocky coast. In the end, thousands of families were evicted in a bitter war of England against Scotland, Protestant against Catholic, rich against poor. A few racial theorists justified the process by arguing that the Anglo-Saxon was superior to the Celt – a grim argument that fires anti-English resentment to this day.

Many Scottish people took a deep breath and fled – as far as they could.

It was a long way to Australia, but when they arrived the Scots found the landscape quite familiar. The first fleet to arrive in Botany Bay in 1788 – eleven ships filled with British convicts – had also transported ninety sheep. They were soon eaten by the starving new arrivals, but Australia clearly had the potential to become a wonderful wool colony. That is indeed what it soon became. By 1855, there were twelve million sheep grazing on the colony; a century later, there were ten times as many.

One of the earliest settlers, Captain John Macarthur, arrived on the second fleet, a convoy of converted slave-ships that sailed to Sydney in 1790. The conditions on the six-month voyage were atrocious. The 1026 convicts were chained in a torment of malnourishment, lice and disease. A quarter died at sea, and the rest stumbled ashore like ghosts. A vicar who watched the scene unfold called it 'indescribable'.

Macarthur was the son of a Scottish mercer/draper who had been living near the Plymouth docks. After a spell in the Durham Light Infantry, he had signed up as a lieutenant in the New South Wales Corps, formed to police the new dominion. On that scandalous voyage south he had challenged the master of his original ship, the *Scarborough*, to a duel before transferring to another vessel. And he brought the same feisty approach to his new life in Sydney. Within two years he was a regimental paymaster – a well-connected man of influence. In 1793 he was granted a hundred acres of land which he named 'Elizabeth Farm' in honour of his wife. It was the least he could do: as the daughter of a Devon farmer, she was much better at managing the land than he was – indeed, her letters home are one of the most expressive records of colonial Australia.

A devout Christian, Elizabeth presided over the farm's ninety convict labourers with diligent calm. In time, she came to be known as 'Australia's first and greatest lady'. Her childhood had given her a clear sense that a sheep farm should resemble an English park, and that was what she created in New South Wales. Moreover, she achieved much of this alone: her husband returned to England in 1801 to face a court-martial for his part in a rum rebellion,[5] then remained there for almost a decade.

The years of exile in London proved to be the making of John Macarthur. Despite picking a fight with the estimable Joseph Banks, he befriended the Colonial Secretary and was granted a further five thousand acres on which to conduct research into sheep-rearing. He finally went back to Australia, in something like triumph, on a ship called the *Argo*. It was aptly named: that was the ship which carried Jason to the Golden Fleece.

The Macarthurs began with a herd of merino sheep from South Africa, and improved the stock with some top-notch rams from the royal holding in Kew Gardens. By 1818, their estate, now ten thousand acres and a major exporter of wool to Victorian England, was home to four thousand sheep. Three years later, John was awarded – mostly for his wife's work – the Royal Society's gold medal for the quality of his

5 When Macarthur sailed back to England, he took with him the first bale of wool ever exported from Australia.

wool. Thereafter, he diversified into racehorses and wine, creating Australia's first vineyard. At the time of his death, his estate covered nearly 25,000 acres. Along with his wife, he had founded a new agricultural power in the world. John appeared on a postage stamp, while Elizabeth became the face of the Australian two-dollar bill. She is also remembered in a painting, a high school and, appropriately, an agricultural college.

It is stating the obvious to say that the Macarthurs effectively planted England in the Australian countryside. When modern historians talk about 'ecological imperialism', they are merely using a new term for an old phenomenon. But while it was nineteenth-century commercialism that drove this process, something else was exported in its baggage: the unmistakable flavour of medieval England. Before long, rural Australia became a land in which sheep nestled beneath shady trees around the edges of green cricket fields, while church bells pealed from Gothic spires.

Elizabeth Farm still stands beside a river in Parramatta. The farmhouse is a poised colonial building (now a museum), with wide verandas looking out over rolling parkland. It manages to make an extraordinary feat – creating a wool economy from scratch on the far side of the world – seem natural, almost inevitable. And it hints at something else about the imperial adventure: the remarkable opportunities it offered to England's (and the rest of Britain's) bolder citizens. Some were scurrilous, some high-minded; some were crooks, some saints. Either way, they were all drawn to distant horizons. If Victorian England sometimes seems staid and ultra-conservative, it might be because its racier children could not wait to leave. It was a land peopled by stay-at-homes.

A good part of England's global Empire, then, was founded on the very ingredient that had fuelled its own ancient prosperity. The wool that had built Winchester and Lincoln did the same for Sydney and Melbourne. Not for nothing was the area around Botany Bay named New South Wales. And when the Steam Age arrived, the forces that were carrying English culture around the world fused. Wool, coal and boiling water were the rails on which English civilisation spread.

Karl Marx noticed the power of this cultural wave rippling from the English countryside: 'Land grabbing on a great scale, such as was perpetrated in England,' he wrote, 'is the first step in creating a field for the establishment of agriculture on a great scale.' He added that this also concentrated ownership in the hands of a tiny elite. The first farmers were also the first capitalists: 'The labourers are driven from the land, and then come the sheep.'

Is it fanciful to see similar ideological forces at play in the way that sheep have become emblems of dire stupidity? To be sheep-like is to be vacant, woolly, gullible, easily led. Farmers reinforce this notion with stories about the animal's idiotic, accident-prone nature. But sheep may attract such mockery for another reason. For centuries, the Western world has prized individual initiative – entrepreneurial energy – above herd-like conformity. The passive nature of sheep is the polar opposite of the self-reliant, independent, go-getting qualities that were lauded in Victorian England.

Nevertheless, sheep were an astonishing export. In 1929 there were 700 million in the world, and one-third of them were in the British Empire, producing half the world's wool. By then, the UK itself had only thirty million. The medieval shepherds of Norfolk and Wharfedale, the weavers of Kent and Essex and the merchants of Lechlade and Calais had rather a lot to answer for.

And as English people spread around the world, they carried their own cultures with them. David Fisher suggested, in *Albion's Seeds*, that the English migration to America had four strands: East Anglians planted puritanism in New England; refugee royalists from the shires took their florid manners to the southern states; tough border people from Cumbria and Northumberland (along with the Scots and Irish) carried a frontier mentality to the American West; and sensible folk from the Midlands built a conservative heartland in the Midwest.

As the Industrial Revolution advanced, England (and the rest of Britain, of course) became the world's workshop, turning out a vast tonnage of iron, steel and textiles. Its raw materials, on the other hand, were increasingly imported from elsewhere. England even began to look overseas for its grain: in the last decade of the nineteenth century, the national wheat field shrank by a million acres. But the transformation of the colonies into sheep farms was the really significant development. From then on, cotton – not wool – would be king.[6]

Lancashire was transformed. There were a hundred mills in the Salford area as early as 1805, and these clanking dynamos turned England on its head over the next half-century. Between 1800 and 1860 the value of Britain's cotton exports jumped from £5.4 million to £46.8 million. Manchester became the capital of weaving (taking over from Leeds or Spitalfields), while Preston, Burnley, Blackburn, Nelson, Accrington and Oldham all developed into major towns. By 1860, this one county boasted more than 2500 mills and half a million workers. They often lived and worked in squalid discomfort, but they produced eight *billion* yards of cloth every year – half the world's total output.

This was more woven cotton than the world either wanted or needed; and when the American Civil War disrupted the supply of raw cotton, the industry crashed. Lancashire became a byword not for enterprise and the modern way, but for destitution. However, it soon picked up, and by the early years of the twentieth century it seemed to be an unstoppable force once again.

It is hard to overstate the extent of the cultural change that

6 In 1938, when it was discovered that the Woolsack in the House of Lords was stuffed with horse hair rather than wool, everyone agreed that it must be restuffed properly this time. Naturally, the wool for the task was sourced from around the Commonwealth.

tore through English society in the wake of the cotton boom. It sucked people out of the countryside and into new conurbations. It pulled them out of the home and set them to work in brick factories, in a storm of noise and smoke, clocking them in and out like livestock. It obliged them to work with strangers rather than their own families, and created rigid divisions of labour: men operated heavy machinery; women wove. Everyone was subsidiary to the iron pulse of the engine that ruled their lives, and it created a fierce sense of injustice among some of them (such as the loom-smashing Luddites).

It was the birth of the proletariat as a force in English affairs, and all that this implied. The pitiful conditions in which industrial workers lived shook the hearts of Dickens, Engels and others. But it was double-edged. As Alexis de Tocqueville wrote: 'From this foul drain the greatest stream of human industry flows out to fertilise the whole world. From this filthy sewer pure gold flows. Here humanity attains both its most complete development and its most brutish; civilisation works its miracles, and civilised man is turned back almost into a savage.'

This was the world that inspired the ashen vision of L. S. Lowry – a bleak forest of drab chimneys with dispirited people shuffling along as if making their way to an abattoir. Yet it was also the world that gave rise to a new range of escapist English entertainments: football, drinking, bingo, dancing, gambling, comedy and days out in Blackpool.

Similar distractions form the basis of the nation's Saturday nights even today: *Strictly Come Dancing*, a quick pint down the pub, the National Lottery and *Match of the Day*. It all dates back to the time when mills first lined the banks of Lancashire's rivers and canals.

Nineteen

The English Underground

Saturday, 28 September 1844 looked like being a good day in the colliery village of Haswell, a few miles south-east of Durham. And not before time – it had been a difficult summer. The four-month strike had not ended well – the newly union-ised miners had been starved into submission – but at least they had proved they had the stomach for a fight. Of course, there was still some lingering rancour towards the 'scabs' who had kept the flow of coal going,[1] but there was also palpable opti-mism in the bright autumnal air. One lost battle was not the end of the war . . . not by a long shot.

Haswell was the first mine in England to have a steel cable in its shaft – a sight well worth seeing. One of the miners brought his ten-year-old son that day, to give him a taste of what lay in store when he grew up. Half a mile below their shoes was a five-foot seam of coal – easy pickings for a hungry workforce.

None of them had an inkling that fate had something else in mind for them that day.

Disaster struck in the middle of the afternoon. There was a loud crump far below the surface, then silence. No one above ground knew what had happened until four men crawled to the surface. All through that summer, lethal gas had been

---

1 The word for a nasty lesion on the skin had long since acquired a secondary defini-tion of scoundrel or creep, but in Victorian times it started to be used for anyone who betrayed his fellow workers. Clearly, such a turncoat was a blot on the body politic.

collecting in the crevices of the coal seam. One falling stone chip, the spark of an iron pick, a foolish candle, a gust of oxygen – any of these might have ignited the fireball. Ninety-five miners, some of them children, were trapped.

The ten-year-old who had gone down the shaft for the first time never came back. His father perished too. Some of the miners were burned beyond recognition, just blackened lumps. Others looked peaceful. One group of twenty men had held hands as they gave up their lives.

Haswell was one of England's newer coal villages – cheap workers' houses grouped around the mineshaft. It did not even have a church, so the coffins of the dead had to sit on empty bedsteads in their homes. In a particularly ghoulish twist, one household had four of those.

This awful tragedy was compounded by the fact that it was not even a shock. Everyone knew that mining was danger-ous work – accidents were not rare. Most pit villages had a memorial to a recent disaster. Haswell's was just another name on a tragic roll call. In Durham and Northumberland alone, a total of thirty explosions would eventually claim the lives of fifteen hundred men in the course of the nine-teenth century. The death toll read like a First World War casualties list: 204 at Blyth; 164 at Seaham (along with 181 pit ponies); 102 at Wallsend; 92 at Felling; 76 at Burradon; 74 at Trimdon; 72 at Jarrow. In the sparsely furnished coal towns of northern England, men and boys were choked, burned and crushed to death.

That didn't make Haswell easier to take, for anyone con-nected to the place.

Just over a decade earlier, Haswell had been nothing more than a farm, a 'hazel well' in the middle – or on the edge – of nowhere. But then, in 1833, engineers found a coal bed half a mile underground and the big money started to move in. The shaft that opened a year later was in one sense the world's first modern mine, thanks to that new steel winding mechanism, which was both an elevator cage for the men, and a bucket that could raise eight hundred tons of coal in one twelve-hour shift.

When the first load of Haswell coal was shipped from the nearby port at Seaham, the mine's owners celebrated with a slap-up dinner at the Ship Inn.

In the years that followed, Haswell attracted miners from all over Britain (not just England), and as its population swelled to five thousand it gained houses, shops, a school and even a railway station. The village was only one small cog in a very large machine. *The Times* put it bluntly in 1850 when it called Durham 'one huge colliery'. This north-eastern principality – once a land of monks and fishermen ruled by prince bishops who enjoyed the freedom of viceroys (an official 'Keeper of Coal' had been appointed since 1372) – was now providing the red-hot fuel for the imperial engine. The county's coal output jumped from 2 million to 40 million tons per year during the course of the nineteenth century, while the population grew from 160,000 to 1.5 million – a ninefold increase at a time when the national population 'only' tripled.

Coal was cheap because labour was cheap. Indeed, on the Victorian pay scale, it was so inexpensive (compared to the alternative, timber) that almost anyone could have a go at digging it out of the ground. In 1913 there were 1439 colliery companies in Britain, employing over a million men – 9 per cent of the total workforce. Scotland and Wales accounted for a significant part of that figure (the Rhondda valley alone had fifty collieries), but the majority were based in England. It was the high point of the national coal industry; seventy years later, a year-long strike proved to be its death spasm. By then, however, coal had changed England in more ways than can easily be counted.

And it had done so in double quick time. Between 1842 and 1856, the number of coal mines doubled, and their output increased many times more. The coal industry was the glowing heart of the Industrial Revolution; the red eye of the storm.

The rail network was increasing at a staggering rate – from 2000 to 4500 miles in five years. Iron, steel, ships: there seemed to be no end to it. Nothing like this had been seen before, and at the centre of the factories and foundries that were making it all possible was the glaring fact that England was sitting on a treasure chest of coal.

Meanwhile, in Haswell, the lethal ingredients of a catastrophe were gathering.

It is often said of terrible events that they 'bring the community together'. In most cases, this is no more than a routine expression of condolence. But Haswell had not had the chance to become a community before 1844. It did not have a thousand years of rural tradition to fall back on, and there were no deep local ties or affections from which to draw comfort. So, on this occasion, disaster really *did* bring a village together, probably for the first time. The survivors forged a community of shared sense of sorrow and anger. From that day onwards, tragedy – and grievance – were threaded into Haswell's very roots.

No one had to look far to find the villain. Charles Vane, 3rd Viscount of Londonderry and also Viscount Seaham, was one of the ten wealthiest men in the land. Dublin-born, he had fought with the Duke of Wellington in the Peninsular War, but he made a muddier name for himself in the North East, opposing the education of miners' children (no sense filling their heads with silly ideas) and rejecting requests for safety inspections.

The miners had only one card: collective power. They had played it before, with some success, and in the summer of 1844 they went on to strike again. It was a major stoppage. In March, twenty thousand miners attended a rally during which they pledged to send a petition to Westminster. They had, they wrote, 'by sad and manifold experience been subject to frequent disastrous explosions of inflammable gas'. They sought a promise from on high that an Inspector of Mines would be appointed to perform safety checks.

A month later an even larger assembly – some thirty-five thousand – vowed to strike until their complaints were addressed . . . for as long as it took. This time the mine owners responded. Replacement labour was recruited and thuggish teams of 'candymen' started to tour the coalfield – to 'persuade' the men to abandon the strike, or evict them if they refused.

In response to this intimidation, the Miners' Association composed a remarkable 'Letter to the Coal Owners of Great Britain and Ireland' requesting a meeting between the two sides to resolve the matter. In an arresting flourish, the authors borrowed one of Aesop's fables:

> The moral and physical consequences of a contentious warfare between capital and labour appear to us to be fully illustrated by the fable of two noble animals fighting for a piece of prey, and while the combat was going on, another animal of diminutive size and strength came and carried off the prize; while neither of the two, such was the state of exhaustion, could prevent him.

The language was arresting. Capital? Labour? This was 1844, long before such terms were in common use. Friedrich Engels, a German businessman shocked by the slums of Manchester, was writing *The Condition of the Working Class in England*, but it did not appear until the following year, and even then it was titled *Die Lage der Arbeitenden Klasse in England*. It was not translated into English until 1885. *The Communist Manifesto*, which Engels co-wrote with his friend Karl Marx, was published in 1848, while the first volume of the latter's *Das Kapital* appeared in 1867. So the authors of the Durham petition were years ahead of their time.

It is common knowledge that Marx's ideas gelled during his period of exile in England, but the extent to which his new home informed, rather than merely exemplified, those ideas is not so often acknowledged. Nor is it common to hear that

England's miners were the co-authors of his groundbreaking theses. But the Haswell letter suggests that this may have been the case.

Once again, though, nobody answered the miners' eloquent appeal. A country that prided itself on its decorum, sense of fair play and propriety sat on its hands and looked the other way while the owners stepped up their campaign of intimidation. After eighteen weeks of increasing hardship, the strike cracked.

It was an impressive show of strength, but it failed.

Then, in September, the mine at Haswell blew up.

In retrospect, it may be that the strike, and the conditions that gave rise to it, did more lasting damage even than the disaster itself. It cemented into place a divisive, tribal war at the heart of England's most important industry which became a profound national rift. From then on, the gap between capital and labour, boss and worker, exploiter and exploited – even south and north – would become the turbulent battleground of English politics and society. The emotions of 1844 would shake the country right up to the terminal strike of 1984. The rancorous England of us and them emerged from the smoke.

In this context, what happened next is even more surprising. Under pressure from William Roberts, a campaigning lawyer who took up the miners' cause and conducted an inquiry into the disaster, the powers-that-be finally sat up and took notice. The *Illustrated London News* printed a drawing of Haswell Colliery, and the Prime Minister, Robert Peel, appointed a committee of the great and the good to look into the explosion. It included two of the most senior scientists of the day: Michael Faraday, the great pioneer in gas and electromagnetism; and Sir Charles Lyell, whose principles of rock formation anticipated the work of Charles Darwin by suggesting that the earth had been shaped by snail's-pace evolutionary forces.

The pair co-authored a pamphlet that identified the two leading culprits as 'fire damp' (an inflammable form of hydrogen) and 'choke damp' (an asphyxiating carbon fume). They also emphasised the dangerous role played by 'coal dust', which in certain conditions could ignite in a lethal flash.

So far, so good ... for the authorities, who could still shrug Haswell off as a dreadful 'accident'.

But there was another, more controversial message. In the course of his inspection, Faraday had found himself sitting on a bag of gunpowder within reach of a naked candle flame. It made him jump to his feet in alarm. He mentioned the incident in the committee's report and issued a firm rebuke to the mine owners for their lax – or non-existent – safety regime.

This was not quite the whitewash the government had anticipated. It slipped the report through the House of Commons on a busy day in the hope that nobody would notice. Haswell noticed, though: there is a Faraday Terrace just off the main road to this day.

There are two morals to this story. The first – an easy one – is that the early coal bosses were greedy profiteers. But the second is that England now began, however briefly, to consider the interests of its workers. Liberty was a concept whose time was coming. Four years after Haswell, the revolutions of 1848 would light beacons across Europe. In England things took a less impassioned, more practical turn, but it was nevertheless a period of sharp social progress. In 1844 the Cooperative movement was born in Rochdale, taking the wheatsheaf, a sign of rural togetherness, as its emblem. Three years later, the Ten Hours Bill extended the scope of the Factory Acts of 1833 by limiting the working hours of England's mill workers (especially the women and children). Finally, in 1848, the Public Health Act confirmed that England at least aspired to travel in a more humane direction.

It would have been better for everyone if the mine owners and authorities had seen the light before the disaster at Haswell.

But this is often how progress is made: through shocks and tragedies. Though many hearts remained stony, some quarters of England did respond. The sector of society that was still celebrating the abolition of slavery was open to new humanitarian causes, and it found them in the mills, foundries and mines of northern England.

Once again we can see contradictory impulses coexisting in a characteristic way. Newcastle had some terrible slum conditions, but was also the first city in England to provide free school meals. The coal industry influenced England's political culture in another way: it inculcated the close working-class camaraderie that was essential for collective action to succeed. The mining families knew they could count on no one but each other, so they became one big family. In a sense, they were a distillation of the national temperament – strong and proud, but prickly and insular.

Ordinary people in other fields were beginning to test their strength, too. The signing, in 1838, of the 'People's Charter' by an unusual committee of six MPs and six working men established a movement that pledged to empower the common man: Chartism.[2] Four years later, it collected three million signatures for a petition demanding social justice, and while it was rejected by Parliament, it was clear that a new force had arrived.

England was changing, and Haswell was one of the places that inspired it to change.

The Haswell Colliery did not survive for long – it closed in 1895. Today, it is a lonely tangle of bungalows in the middle of open, treeless farmland, with not much to suggest that anything momentous ever happened here. But if you walk south, you come to the brick remnants of the old engine house. Guarded by low railings, it is a sombre memento of the 1844 disaster. A modern sculpture, installed on the

---

2 William Roberts, the lawyer who represented Haswell, was a prominent Chartist.

centenary of the pit's closure, shows the heads of trapped miners squashed between slabs of rock. It is a melancholy place. No one would call it a beauty spot, but it is an authentic stretch of England's coastal landscape. If you turn to the east you can *almost* see the North Sea. And it is one of many places that suffered such a blow. In 1862, for example, at Hartley Colliery, in Northumberland, a beam supporting a steam engine snapped and blocked the shaft, trapping 204 men. The wreckage was cleared after a round-the-clock, six-day effort, but by then it was too late. All the men perished.[3]

There was a national outcry. Queen Victoria sent her 'tenderest sympathy' to the bereaved families, and sixty thousand people attended the mass funeral, which became a four-mile procession of coffins. Parliament stipulated that each colliery must have at least two shafts, as a safety precaution.

A culture of political protest was well on the way to being fully formed. The old chivalric ideal of *noblesse oblige* had long been threadbare, but in the smoking world of heavy industry it disintegrated altogether. The industrial barons felt little obligation towards their social inferiors, regarding them with a mixture of suspicion and fear. Engels, for one, thought them every bit as high and mighty as their feudal predecessors.

In *The Road to Wigan Pier* (1937) George Orwell was forthright about the part coal played in English life. 'Practically everything we do,' he wrote, 'from eating an ice to crossing the Atlantic, and from baking a loaf to writing a novel, involves the use of coal, directly or indirectly.' He also had an intense and well-founded sympathy for the men whose job it was to hack the stuff out of the ground: 'Their lamp-lit world down there is as necessary to the daylight world above as the root is to the flower ... It is only because miners sweat their guts out that superior persons can remain superior.'

3 The names of the victims are inscribed on a column in the churchyard at Eardon. The oldest was seventy-one, the youngest just ten. A single family lost nine men.

The fact that this obvious truth was so easy to overlook reveals the depth of the class divide over coal. It first emerged as an aesthetic shiver. When Thomas Carlyle visited the Black Country in 1824, he called it 'a frightful scene ... a dense cloud of pestilential smoke hangs over it forever, blackening even the grain that grows upon it'. Dickens used similar terms when he spoke about 'miles of cinder-paths and blazing furnaces and roaring steam engines, and such a mass of dirt, gloom and misery as I never before witnessed'. Coal, and the industry it powered, opened up a chasm between those who got their hands dirty and those who banked the profits.

England would not be England without that chasm. One of its most famous features is the division of the country into an idle-rich south and a hard-suffering north – an officer class of donkeys and a pride of sweat-stained lions. It may not have been a coincidence that Disraeli's novel *Sybil* was published in 1845, only a year after Haswell. It highlighted the harrowing contrast, evident to anyone who visited an industrial town at the time, between the comfortable lives of the gentry and the hardships endured by its manual workers. In a speech that became very famous, one of the characters summarised the extent to which England was a ruptured society by calling it:

> Two nations; between whom there is no intercourse and no sympathy; who are as ignorant of each other's habits, thoughts and feelings as if they were dwellers in different zones, or inhabitants of different planets; who are formed by a different breeding, are fed by a different food, are ordered by different manners, and are not governed by the same laws.

The ready supply of coal in England's northern hills only widened this gulf. The awful fact that forty thousand people died in England's coal mines in the second half of the nineteenth century incubated fierce tribal emotions. One glance at the Labour vote in the 2015 General Election shows the extent to which it is rooted in the now-obsolete English coalfields (see illustration, page 318). The social and political culture that evolved in mining towns like Haswell turned them into Labour heartlands for ever.

At the other end of the country, a long way from the black world of coal, stand the white cliffs of Dover. Hardly anything seems so emblematically English. Scrubbed by English rain, for years they have put a gracious smile on the sunny south coast, while baring their teeth at would-be invaders. They thus embody both significant aspects of the divided national character – one rebutting, one welcoming. Forbidding in surly weather, they are warm on summer afternoons, casting a benign shadow over the Channel waves.

They have long been part of the national iconography: the only piece of England visible from the continent, and much fêted on celluloid. 'Look ... England,' sighed the Scarlet Pimpernel – played by Leslie Howard in the 1935 film – as he sailed home from his final mission in revolutionary France.[4] Many generations of returning servicemen have echoed this sentiment, not to mention hordes of holidaymakers on the ferry from Calais. And the chalk that gives the cliffs their dramatic colour, made of billions of crushed sea creatures, is the homely material that is still used on the blackboards of countless English schools.

The Straits of Dover were formed when some of that chalk – the land pavement that linked England to the continent – collapsed, turning the peninsular into an island. They are, then, another example of the way England has been produced by geographical forces. More recently, English sailors

---

4 Intriguingly, this celebration of English decency was the invention of four Hungarians. The original author (Baroness Orczy), the producer (Alexander Korda), the writer (Lajos Biró) and the star (Leslie Howard) all had roots in Eastern Europe.

harried the Spanish Armada in the waters that lap at their base, and the cliffs themselves came to symbolise the Battle of Britain, much of which was fought in the sky overhead. In the twenty-first century they stand on the front line of the attempt to stop migrants from Calais slipping into England.

They are to England what the Statue of Liberty is to America – a symbol of resilience. Charles II reclaimed the Crown here when he stepped ashore in 1660; the first international radio signal was received here; and radar masts guided the Spitfires and Hurricanes of 1940 from these heights. Gleaming in the morning sun, they are both a gateway and a door: they have kept the world out . . . and let it in.

Vera Lynn cheered up the troops by singing about bluebirds fluttering above the chalk cliffs of Kent, in a song that became a patriotic anthem, a declaration of what they were fighting for.[5] Modern ramblers along the cliffs come across a Battle of Britain memorial, stationed on a high point with wide views. It features a rumpled pilot gazing warily out to sea.

This evocative balcony is also the site of something very different. In 1882 geologists started probing the land beneath these cliffs in search of a route for the proposed Channel Tunnel. No one can say that the Victorians lacked ambition. Their plan, a century ahead of its time, was to drill a passage from Dover to the once-English town of Calais. The press was quick to denounce the scheme, whipping up fears that the dastardly French might soon pour into Tunbridge Wells. So the project, which had already bored a mile-long shaft into the cliff just west of Dover (and had been visited by Gladstone and other grandees), was cancelled.

But the surveyors had caught a whiff of something exciting during their excavations: coal. It seemed there were

5 It is often pointed out that there are no bluebirds in England. The best of several rival explanations is that it is an antiquated rural term for swallows, which arrive in the late spring and are therefore harbingers of summer, signalling better times ahead.

valuable deposits of the black stuff under England's famous landmark. Forty-five test bores later, it was confirmed that a large proportion of Kent – from Ramsgate and Canterbury in the north to Folkestone and Dover in the south – was a coal-field. It formed part of a great seam of carbon that ran all the way from South Wales to Belgium and Westphalia, passing beneath this ancient land of wool, hops and cathedral choirs. The fact that it lay deep underground did not stop a local chancer, Arthur Burr, from snapping up the mineral rights in a bid to become a coal tycoon. His Shakespeare Colliery opened in 1896.

Unfortunately for Burr and his miners, the Kent coal seam was thin and, worse, trapped in a warren of underground lakes. The first shaft struck water at just 366 feet; and eight men were drowned when the second attempt flooded at only 303 feet. The force of the flood was so strong it brimmed to the surface in minutes. In future, all tunnels in the area would have to be lined with iron to prevent them from cracking, and would need powerful pumps.

Nevertheless, an unusual railway station opened in the chalk face (Shakespeare Cliff Halt) to bring miners into the colliery and lug coal away. It never appeared on a timetable because no other passengers were invited, and there was no platform: the miners simply jumped down on to the gravel. It did not last long, either: there was simply not enough coal down there.

But that was by no means the end of the Kent coalfield. Over the next few years a dozen similarly speculative attempts were made, and some of them – the collieries at Chislet, Betteshanger, Snowdown and Tilmanstone – went on to thrive. The workings at Tilmanstone (they were actually at Eythorne, a mile to the west) continued to operate until 1986, while the mine at Betteshanger (which was just to the east of the village) employed over two thousand workers during the Second World War and operated until 1989. In all, some twenty million tons of coal were dug out of this gentle terrain.

It is worth remembering, when we think of mine owners as overfed, cigar-chomping tyrants, that they take risks too. They do not have to sweat and suffer underground – a particular problem in Kent, where the subterranean temperatures were unusually high – but they do put themselves on the line in other ways. Burr sank two decades and a small fortune into his coal dream, agitating for railway lines and other infrastructural necessities, and ended up with very little to show for it. The mine at Shakespeare Cliff never produced more than eight tons of coal a day ... and its drainage engines alone consumed more than that. And none of the other twenty-two collieries in which he had an interest came close to turning a profit until he finally hit pay dirt in 1913.

It was a few weeks after Christmas, and the earth stood hard as iron. But the miners at Snowdown Colliery – midway between Dover and Canterbury – were jubilant because they had finally struck a thick seam. The surveyors estimated that eight hundred tons could be hacked from the ground every week. Burr had triumphed at last.

It was enough to earn him the Freedom of Dover at a ceremonial dinner. The guest speaker, none other than Arthur Conan Doyle, agreed that this historic port would soon be the 'Liverpool of the South' and become one of Britain's six biggest cities.

But it came too late for Burr. There had always been an element of chicanery in his management style: he set up separate companies for owning, drilling, operating and maintaining his mines, making himself his own customer many times over. And there were an alarming number of accidents – three dead at Tilmanstone in 1909, twenty-two at Snowdown itself. He took risky short-cuts by installing second-hand drilling equipment, and the hard-living miners he imported from Wales, Yorkshire and Belgium were hardly welcomed with open arms by the genteel population of Deal. Having spent a million pounds on a largely fruitless quest, he was widely regarded as an unreliable con man, and a bankrupt one at that. He died, humiliated, a few months after the end of the First World War.

His project did not die with him, however. In 1921 the *Dover Express* dreamed of 'transforming the Garden of England into one vast coalfield'. It never happened because the coal seam was simply too flimsy and too far underground. A chance of geography meant that Kent did not turn into another Durham.

It is quite a thought. How different England would have been if the coal had been found in the south rather than the north. Dickens would have set *Hard Times* not in Preston but in Whitstable; Lowry might have painted Margate, not Salford; Kes could have soared over Sandwich; Broadstairs might have been a pit village. Gas flares might have burned over Guildford, while slag heaps cast ominous shadows over Hastings.

The north–south divide would have been turned on its head.

As early as 1872, Professor Joseph Prestwich, President of the Geological Society, published an intriguing map of the possible 'Thames Valley Coalfield', which showed the great seam of South Wales coal continuing east beneath Bristol, Devizes, Newbury, Aldershot and Wimbledon before burrowing under the Channel and emerging in the Pas-de-Calais.

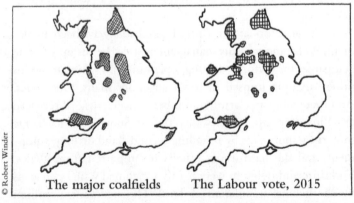

© Robert Winder

The major coalfields   The Labour vote, 2015

England's coalfields, and the Labour vote. Coincidence? Or geography as destiny?

Prestwich was something of a seer: he had already written enthusiastically about the geological possibilities of excavating a tunnel between England and France. But in this case his foresight was slightly off: the Thames valley never became a great mining region; and nor, in the end, did Kent. The county was shaped by older forces, on lines laid down by medieval weaving. When craftsmen from Flanders landed in England they set up their looms in Canterbury, Cranbrook, Tenterden and Tonbridge. This was the garden of England, and its proximity to the great drinking market of London made it an ideal location for hop fields too, so migrant brewers from the Low Countries also settled here. Kent is dotted with old oast houses and mills to this day. There can be few clearer signs that geography really is destiny.

Only a few glints of the Kentish coal industry survive. Miners' cottages form a neat circuit around a social club in Betteshanger, and there are similar terraces in Aylesham, where Snowdown's 650 miners were housed. A rusty sculpture of a local family pushing a couple of carts of coal patrols the entrance to the Miners' Way Industrial Park. And above the railway station that once took the coal to Dover, colliery buildings still lurk behind a security fence, waiting for the day when they are turned into a multi-million-pound heritage centre.

Even less remains at Tilmanstone: light-industrial sheds now occupy the site of the colliery. And when you leave the miners' houses at Betteshanger (now a community park) and walk up to the old farming village, the county's industrial story is swiftly forgotten. An ancient church stands in a quiet graveyard among sloping fields, shaded by oaks, near a manor house that is now a boarding school. It comes as no surprise that it was here, on a trip home from the Western Front, that Rupert Brooke wrote his celebrated expression of native English pride, 'The Soldier':

> *If I should die, think only this of me*
> *That there's some corner of a foreign field*
> *That is for ever England. There shall be*
> *In that rich earth a richer dust concealed;*
> *A dust whom England bore, shaped, made aware,*
> *Gave once her flowers to love, her ways to roam*
> *A body of England's, breathing English air*
> *Washed by the rivers, blest by suns of home.*

Brooke had no way of knowing that the scenery behind this touching evocation – which helped to stoke the patriotic fervour that was needed to endure the horrors of Flanders – was about to become a coal mine. But poetry, like England, moves in mysterious ways.

Not far from Haswell, on a cold cliff above the North Sea, stands the abandoned colliery of Easington, a once-mighty coal district that was the site of yet another subterranean explosion (it claimed eighty-three lives in 1951). Founded in 1899, its shafts once extended four miles beneath the sea, and at its peak it employed three thousand men who lived in a sizeable village, with shops, post offices and a brass band. It also gave England its youngest recipient of the Victoria Cross in the Second World War – Dennis Donini, the son of an Italian ice-cream maker. He was decorated for continuing to lead a charge when badly wounded near the Dutch border during the final advance on Germany in 1945.

The colliery closed in 1993, and Easington has yet to find a new *raison d'être*. It has the defeated air of many such townships, created by an industry that no longer exists. Indeed, it is one of the most economically deprived places in England. It also has one of the lowest immigration rates in the country: in the 2001 census it was 99.2 per cent white British. No one wants to move there any more.

A passer-by would not guess it was ever any sort of

powerhouse. A battered cage stands in a field in solitary ...
well, one could hardly call it splendour. If anything, it looks
as if it landed here by accident – a Tardis from another world,
another time. The coal mine is now a windswept nature
reserve, and the miners' houses stand in silent rows above a
wide, grey sea. This was where *Billy Elliot* was filmed, although
it was renamed Everington. The Elliots lived in a terraced
house with an outdoor toilet and a thin strip of grass out
front – a mock-village green which provided, even here in the
bruising world of the coal industry, a faint echo of medieval
English village life.

Easington was not quite the end, however. That came in
2015 when England's last remaining coal mine, at Knottingley
in North Yorkshire,[6] finally closed, bringing the curtain down
on the whole colossal industry. Yet English coal's final act
attracted less media attention than the death of a minor pop
star. This wasn't an example of polite English unflappability –
'Let's just get this over with, chaps.' It was simple forgetfulness.

Thousands of local mining families, many in tears, marched
behind the Knottingley Silver Band to mark the closure of the
mine known as Big K – once the largest deep-pit colliery in
Europe. At its peak, it had employed sixteen hundred workers,
who gouged millions of tons of coal from the Yorkshire earth.
By the end, only a few hundred remained.

They were given twelve weeks' pay and told to go home.

England still burns coal, in its fireplaces and power stations.
But all of it comes from abroad. Thirty million tons of the stuff
remains untouched in the land beneath our feet.

A hundred years ago, in Britain as a whole, there were three
thousand collieries, employing a million people. They did
not enjoy a comfortable life – every miner was familiar with
death and disaster. But coal was what wool had been for earlier
generations – *the* key to England's wealth and power. And it

6 Not far from Kirkstall Abbey, where a dozen Cistercians from Fountains had
tended their sheep in the Middle Ages.

was nothing more than a geographical fluke. A resource that had ripened for thirty million years had been hacked from the ground and burned to ashes in a century and a half, by men often thought of as 'unskilled', when in truth they merely possessed the kind of skills that politicians, lawyers (and authors) could never emulate. Now it was no more.

The miner's lamp went out for good.

Twenty

A New Kind of Town

C oal gave England a new urban face. As we know, the
traditional pattern of English land use was laid down in
the Middle Ages. But the nineteenth century boom in canals,
railways, mills, mines and factories – all fuelled by inexpensive
coal – changed the way the country lived and worked. England
became an urban jungle.

It happened fast. In 1750 only 15 per cent of the English
population lived in towns; by 1850, it was close to 50 per cent;
and thirty years later it was 80 per cent. Manchester grew
from 182,000 in 1831 to 250,000 forty years later. Birmingham,
whose prosperity was based not on textiles but on engineering,
swelled from 144,000 to 344,000 in the same period. Liverpool
rose from 202,000 to 493,000, Sheffield from 92,000 to 240,000,
and Newcastle from 54,000 to 128,000. By the end of the century, all of these places had nearly doubled in size again.[1]

One might have expected the old hierarchies of rural life
to dissolve in these new industrial towns, but if anything the
opposite happened: they became even more pronounced.
Village life permitted a surprising degree of independence:
even the smallest smallholder had to be self-reliant and adaptable. Factory life, in contrast, rendered workers passive. It

[1] In the course of the nineteenth century, Britain's total population jumped from nine
million to thirty-six million. This figure is even more remarkable when we consider
that more than ten million people left Britain between 1800 and 1900.

forced them together and gave them common grievances, but offered few opportunities to use their own initiative. In a village, the lord of the manor might attend the same church as his plough team, play for the same cricket club, drink the same beer and wink at the same milkmaid. But, in the collieries, where men were mere 'labour' – and disposable labour at that – a much more confrontational culture began to crystallise. The mine owners rarely lived anywhere near the slums in which their workers had to slave; on the contrary, they built fine villas elsewhere. Given England's prevailing wind, these were often situated to the west of the collieries, mills and factories, for who wanted to live downwind of all that soot? The East End became synonymous with poverty and graft. The owning class, which was also the ruling class, soon started to pride itself on its appreciation of 'nature', as if this were a mark of cultivated good taste, rather than mere affluence; as if the working class lived in their foul communities because of plebeian appetites, rather than simple desperation.

Coal ruled. But it also divided. And it changed the *way* people lived as well as where they lived. Coal was a terrific source of heat, but its grimy smoke turned England into a land of tall chimneys. In the Age of Wool only the grandest dwellings could afford their own stacks, so they became status symbols: witness the forest of 241 decorated pillars that rise over Hampton Court. But now even the humblest cottage had a coal fire and a chimney pot.

These chimneys needed cleaning. London alone produced four hundred tons of soot every day, and it took an army of hired hands to sweep it away. And since the chimneys were narrow, and orphans plentiful, boys as young as six, recruited from poorhouses, were sent up to do the (very) dirty work. Many contracted a disease known as 'chimney sweeps' cancer'. This attacked the scrotum and was a curiously English condition, caused by the fact that the sweeps often slept in their sooty sacks at night.

Parliament passed a Bill to outlaw the use of such children in 1834 – it formed part of a rush of liberal legislation in
that period – which was widely ignored. Several subsequent
attempts failed too. But Charles Kingsley's *The Water Babies*
(1863) significantly changed the public mood. The novel tells
the story of a sweep named Tom who escapes the misery of his
occupation by falling into a cleansing river.[2] It played a leading
role in inspiring the Chimney Sweepers Act of 1875, which
belatedly stamped out the hateful practice.

The chimney sweep was only one of many new characters created by English coal. But he remained a sufficiently
vivid idea to feature as a stock figure in comic-book depictions of Englishness, such as *Mary Poppins*. Meanwhile, other
by-products of coal became synonymous with the country's
daily life. Principal among these was the thick, noxious smog
caused by the collision of hot smoke and cold fog, known as
the 'peasouper'. At its worst – as in the Great Smog of 1952 –
it was lethal.[3] London became famous for it. All over the
world, people imagined Sherlock Holmes dashing through
a peasouper. In fact Conan Doyle never used the word. The
books contain lots of dun-coloured and yellow 'mists and
veils', but not so much as a sniff of proper London pea soup.

Coal also had a profound impact on the social texture of
English life. As we know, the whirling marriage of coal and
steam had created a new class of people: the urban proletariat.
Not every worker in the mills, mines and factories was a prisoner. Some were driven to enter the urban workforce by need,

2 Kingsley was probably inspired by William Blake's 'The Chimney Sweeper', in
which an angel releases another boy named Tom from his 'coffins of black' and washes
him clean in a river. Sadly, though, it is only a dream. When he wakes, Tom has to
gather up his brushes and climb back into the darkness.

3 The sulphurous peasouper of 1952 not only choked Londoners but caused numerous collisions and accidents on the roads. In total, it was said to have claimed twelve
thousand lives. On the bright side, it led to the Clean Air Act of 1956.

but rural life could be just as soul-destroying as factory toil, and thousands fled the fields willingly, eager to find easier work in one of the new towns. Yet, even if it was not quite a slave army, the emergence of a *working* rather than a *farming* class changed England markedly.

For one thing, it forced people into very close proximity with each other – both at work and at home. The back-to-back terraces – which were joined at the rear as well as the sides – gave people roofs over their heads, but very little elbow room. Out of Nottingham's eleven thousand houses in 1840, seven thousand were built in this crammed style. They had no toilets or running water, and the cess pits often leaked. Communal life in these squalid conditions engendered a form of determined solidarity that would eventually become a potent political force.

Perhaps surprisingly, urban living led to a weakening of religious faith in England's working poor. Despite a keen church-building programme, churchgoing itself declined,

© Pictorial Press Ltd/Alamy Stock Photo

Made in England. Gustav Doré's depiction of London's slum dwellings catches the urban lifestyle manufactured by the marriage of coal, steam and rail.

partly because the unremitting grind of factory life created an appetite for more active pleasures in the workers' rare moments of repose, and partly because attending church too closely resembled going to the factory. People needed a break from forming an obedient line, keeping silent and following orders.

Industrial working practices may even have increased the gap between the sexes. The division of labour was especially pronounced in the coalfields. Mining was deemed too tough (and too dangerous) for women, so a culture developed in which men put in long shifts down the pit, while their womenfolk did ... everything else: house, children, social life, neighbourhood obligations, often while doing paid work as well.

In so doing, they nurtured the tight bonds that are usually described as 'community'.

Domestic drudgery could be a prison, of course, even if in some ways it was preferable to – and safer than – the subterranean life of a miner. And men and women had long performed their own designated tasks in rural communities. But there was a degree of togetherness in the fields and barns that did not hold in the mills and mines, and in laying down regulations regarding the exploitation of women and children, the well-intentioned Factory Acts may have exacerbated this division. Masculinity was increasingly a matter of mere muscle power. On the spot where Easington Colliery once stood a plaque reads: 'A man is not really a man in Durham until he has been down the pit'. His job was to bring home the flitch of bacon; he happily abandoned the domestic realm to his wife. And if he felt like spending his evenings down the pub ... well, what of it?

In a 1929 essay on his Nottinghamshire childhood, D. H. Lawrence wrote: 'There was a big discrepancy, when I was a boy, between the collier who saw, at best, only a few brief hours of daylight – often no daylight at all during the winter weeks – and the collier's wife, who had all day to herself when the man was down the pit.' No one could ever have said such a thing in the England of sheep and corn.

The status of women in the Industrial Revolution is one of history's most contested arenas. It is certainly possible to see their 'relegation' to the domestic sphere as part of a patriarchal conspiracy to deny them independence. Either way, by enlarging the already wide gulf between men and women, coal mining laid down patterns which English life would follow for years.

Lawrence did not go along with the idea that mining was dehumanising. On the contrary, he felt it created intense bonds of togetherness ... but only between men. No one – not the boss, not the government, not even their women – could intrude upon these brotherhoods, although the military quickly saw that this was the stuff from which loyal soldiers could be made. Being a miner was a bit like being in the army – a world of marching bands, banners, and undying friendships.

For most people in England, even in the Victorian era, 'labouring at the coalface' was a mere figure of speech. But the men involved developed subtle codes and routines all their own. When safety legislation insisted that the wooden props supporting the coal tunnels must be replaced with strong metal struts, the miners' objections surprised many of those who had campaigned on their behalf. The men at the coalface had learned to interpret the creaks of the old timbers. There was music in these groans. They knew when a tunnel was about to collapse. The new metal props snapped without warning ... not so often, but much more dangerously.

The other ways in which coal changed England were side-effects of the urban jungle it spawned. The booming population placed unprecedented demands on the country's agriculture. Historians are undecided whether it was due to a rising birth rate or a falling death rate. Either way, there were a lot of extra mouths to feed. Steam engines boosted productivity in the shires, first in the form of stationary threshing machines, then through traction engines, which could plough the fields faster than any human-and-horse team. Moreover, one of coal's by-products – quicklime, released in the smelting of iron – proved to be a powerful fertiliser. Touch it and it would scald your skin, but it could turn a reclaimed marsh into a golden wheat field as if by magic. In time, lime kilns appeared beside canals all over the country.

That was not all. The need for cheap housing within walking distance of the mills, factories and collieries caused England to fill up with the overcrowded terraced housing that was now its hallmark. This in turn generated a widespread yearning for open space and clear blue sky. The result, thanks to a philanthropic impulse lurking in the industrial frenzy of Victorian England, was a vogue for civic parks and gardens. It began in Derby, where a public arboretum opened in 1840. Joseph Strutt, the owner of several textile mills in the area, donated ten thousand pounds to create this eleven-acre gift to the workers who had helped him prosper. Then he filled it with unusual trees from around the world: Turkish hazel, American magnolia, Chinese aïlanthus, Mediterranean lime. On the day it opened the entire population of the town went along to see it.

Something similar happened in London later that year. Victoria Park, in Hackney, opened in response to a petition signed by thirty thousand people which begged for action after the cholera crises of the 1830s. And in 1847 Birkenhead Park – planned along 'picturesque' lines, with lakes and woodland bringing a rural quality to the industrial scene – opened just over the Mersey from Liverpool.

Before long, every English town was following suit. And London, by no means the most beautiful city in the world, outdid all its rivals: its spacious parks became a glory of the world. It is estimated that there are some 200,000 acres of urban greenery in England today: going to the park, walking the dog, feeding the ducks, dozing in a deckchair and enjoying an ice cream beneath the shade of a tree all became routine aspects of English life. A new character (now almost obsolete) became a solid authority figure in the local community – the park keeper.

The creation of these parks, and the cosmopolitan array of trees and plants they planted in England's industrial landscape (and in Wales, Scotland and Ireland too), revealed the country's serene confidence in its power to mould the physical world to its will. With horizons expanded by imperial adventuring, plant hunters roved across China, South America and Alpine Europe in search of seedlings. They had already shuffled rubber from Brazil to Malaysia (two thousand filched seeds were germinated at Kew en route to Kuala Lumpur) and tea from China to India on an industrial scale. Now they brought roses, camellias, dahlias, tulips and lilies to England's public spaces.[4]

England began to believe it could do anything it liked. The world seemed to be its oyster.

Something else emerged in the new townscapes: mass-market leisure. Some of this took the form of larkish day trips to existing resorts such as Brighton, Broadstairs, Hastings, Scarborough, Weymouth and Whitby. But in 1845 Thomas Cook organised his first railway outing from Leicester to Liverpool, and the package holiday was born. The following year, the railway reached Blackpool and started to carry Lancashire mill workers to the seaside in their thousands. And when their factories took to closing for a week – to repair the machinery – Blackpool was more than able to accommodate the extra visitors. By 1890, it was entertaining a quarter of a million at a time.

Just as significant was the rise of the spectator sports: football, cricket and rugby. All grew out of this new urban world. It was quite easy to find a patch of relatively flat grass for a football pitch; Blackburn had twenty, some of which doubled up as cricket grounds in the summer. But the more important factors were the appetite for sport aroused by long working hours in unsavoury places and the predictability of those hours.

---

4 Plant hunting was by no means a sedate pursuit. When Ernest Wilson was carrying the first Regal lily (*Lilium regale*) out of the remote Chinese mountains, a boulder crashed on to his leg and broke it in two places. It was not an easy journey home, but it may have seemed a small price to pay for his seven thousand rare bulbs.

Factories worked to methodical timetables; and the Saturday afternoon game was born when the 1850 Factory Act ruled that mills must close at 2 p.m. on that day. By contrast, rural life was governed by the weather – nobody knew when they might be able to sneak some time off.

Compressed leisure time plus regular hours led to Burnley vs Preston.

A quick glance at the origins of professional football shows how quickly this upheaval happened. The first FA Cup Final, in 1872, was a predominantly amateur affair; as with cricket, there was the odd professional in northern clubs, but playing for money was much frowned upon in the corridors of power down south. The trophy was won by a public school eleven, the Wanderers, and was claimed by Oxford University and the Royal Engineers over the next few years. But in 1883, when Blackburn Rovers beat the Old Etonians, football changed. Five years later, a dozen clubs from Lancashire and the Midlands formed a professional league and the game never looked back.[5] Many of the early clubs had specific roots in industry. Those from Lancashire were all based in mill towns, but West Ham began as Thames Ironworks, Arsenal as a team of munitions workers in Woolwich, and Manchester United as Newton Heath Lancashire & Yorkshire Railway Company FC.

One ironic coda to this sporting story concerns the rise of rugby league. It often puzzles onlookers that English rugby divided not just into two codes – amateur and professional – but into two distinct sets of rules. There is a simple answer, however. Rugby league was launched as a professional breakaway after an 1895 meeting at a hotel in Huddersfield. Bradford, Oldham, Halifax, Rochdale, St Helens, Stockport, Hull, Wakefield, Warrington, Widnes and Wigan – all northern

---

5 The founding members of the Football League were: Accrington, Blackburn, Burnley, Bolton, Everton, Preston North End, Aston Villa, Derby, Notts County, Stoke, West Brom and Wolverhampton Wanderers. Nearly all of them are best known, today, for their glorious pasts.

industrial towns – seceded from the ruling rugby body on the obvious grounds that their players could not afford to play for nothing, unlike the pampered children of southern schools. The new rules – teams of thirteen instead of fifteen, no crashing mauls or lineouts, and a slight rebalancing of the scoring system to favour tries – were adopted even though the northern players prided themselves on being tougher than their soft union counterparts. But the fact was, they were much more fearful of injury. With no financial safety net, they simply could not afford to suffer the kind of injury that might be worn as a badge of honour by the son of a duke. Their game had to be made safer.

This was just one minor manifestation of the north–south divide embedded by the geographical distribution of England's coal and iron deposits. It is stretching a point to call rugby league a by-product of coal – like quicklime – but it was significantly shaped by the world that coal made. And as the next century unfolded, this political and cultural legacy would affect not just the nation's ball games, but its wealth, its industrial and class relations, its art, its music and its politics.

Nowhere is the connection between sport and coal-fired industry so obvious as it is in Ashington, just north of Newcastle. One of the first recorded football matches was played in nearby Ulgham in 1280 (where our story began), so this area's connection to the sport goes back a long way.[6] Almost seven centuries later, Ashington was famous for giving Newcastle United one legend, Jackie Milburn, and England two more: the World Cup-winning Charlton brothers (whose mother was a Milburn). It also produced the Durham and England fast bowler Steve Harmison, who completed the circle by becoming manager of Ashington Football Club when he hung up his cricket boots.

Ashington was a sporting powerhouse, in other words. But first it was a coal powerhouse. From small beginnings in 1867,

6 The national game was rough from the word go – one of the players in that match was stabbed, which may explain why someone felt the need to write a report on it.

it grew into one of the largest colliery towns in the region, employing over three thousand people by the time the First World War broke out. Thirteen of its miners were killed by an underground explosion in 1916, but the town continued to boom after the war. At its peak, 5500 men worked beneath its spreading streets.

Coal made Ashington, and everything in it. It became a town of brass bands, allotments, bowls, pigeon racing, ballroom dancing ... and more than a few football teams. Bobby and Jackie Charlton acquired the skills that would win them world renown on a public park laid out on an ash pit.[7] As in Lancashire, it wasn't smart facilities that drove the boys to succeed; it was hunger. The north-east had a reputation for 'shamateur' football. Fine old clubs like Bishop Auckland and Blyth Spartans were happy to pay 'expenses' to persuade the best players to abandon working down the pit and kick a ball around instead. But the Charlton brothers didn't need to fiddle anything. They had bigger fields to conquer.

One of the most famous photographs from their great 1966 season is the newspaper image of the day they returned to Ashington for the victory parade. Some fifteen thousand people (more than half the town's population) lined a route that ran from the family's house in Beatrice Street – one of several named after Shakespearean heroines, along with Portia Street, Rosalind Street and Juliet Street – to the town hall. A Lancashire magnate had lent the brothers a yellow Rolls-Royce, and in the picture they are sitting politely on the back seat with the roof down as they nudge through the crowd.[8] They are wearing their best

---

7 Hirst Park, described by Bobby Charlton as 'our very own Wembley', was rewarded in 2016 when it won a Heritage Lottery grant of £2.3 million. In his day, it featured a memorial to the 1916 pit disaster.

8 Two years earlier, a film titled *The Yellow Rolls-Royce* had featured an identical car, as driven by an English marquess (Rex Harrison), an American mobster (George C. Scott) and an heiress (Ingrid Bergman). Its romantic reputation was assured when Bergman smuggled Omar Sharif over the border to Yugoslavia in her elegant boot.

suits and neat ties, and their hair is well combed. If anything, they look slightly embarrassed by all the fuss. Not many images so perfectly capture the central place of sport in the imagination of working-class England – the pride swelling in a small town thanks to the heady achievements of two of its own. Had the boys done well, or what?

Local heroes. Bobby and Jack Charlton return in triumph to the colliery town of Ashington, near Newcastle, where their football journey began.

Even their father was in attendance. On the whole, he took little interest in his sons' football prowess; it was their mother who had pushed them to excel. According to friends, on his rare days above ground Charlton Senior was more attached to quieter pursuits – his pigeons and his allotment – than to silly games. As someone remarked at the time: 'Typical miner, really.'

But there is more to this image than a family story. The

brothers' smiles, as they wave from their carriage like returning Roman conquerors, evoke a tradition that is often overlooked. In the cartoon version of the national character, the English are routinely portrayed (not altogether unfairly) as top-hatted, toffee-nosed and stuck-up. But this photograph reveals another England, one in which people rise politely from ordinary origins and show the world what they are made of.

This is a more common, and older, English story than we sometimes think. From Dick Whittington to James Brindley to Bobby Charlton, England is full of such rags-to-riches tales. Shakespeare, the son of a Warwickshire glove-maker, ran off to become an actor in an age when this was a disgracefully low-rent calling; Dickens, the son of a bankrupt, was packed off to a boot-blacking outfit when he was twelve (helping to fire his vision of impoverished heroes who grow up to be fine young gentlemen); Joseph Conrad began life hauling rope on ships. Edward Elgar, perhaps the most English composer, is the epitome of the gifted local lad who won all the prizes. None was polished by universities or tutored in classical wit.

England could be snooty, but it was a country in which people could rise – and always had been. It was a land of severe class boundaries, to be sure. But it also delighted in mocking anyone born with a silver spoon in his mouth.

In 1805, when Nelson was ripping into the French fleet at Trafalgar, nothing stood at the mouth of the Tees aside from four small farms on an estuarine marsh amid colonies of seals and terns. Twenty-four years later, only forty people lived there. But the Quaker railwaymen behind the Stockton–Darlington line recognised the value of the riverside location and acquired the entire locality for thirty thousand pounds. It was a gamble, but they set about turning it into a staging post for Durham coal. Six miles of track were added to the existing line, and the place was initially named Port Darlington.

It was an immediate success: a gritty English Klondike. In

1831, its first full year of operation, it shipped 150,000 tons of coal; a decade later, it was handling ten times as much.

Its career as a coal station was short-lived, however. Newcastle soon regained its position as the region's premier port. Fortunately, though, there was something else in this landscape. A prospector named John Vaughan identified it as a good place to set up an ironworks. He brought in ironstone from Scotland and Whitby, and smelted it in his foundries. A few years later, in the summer of 1850, he was rambling in the nearby Cleveland Hills when he tripped over an unusual clump of glinting, red-coloured earth.

He knew exactly what it was: iron ore!

At this time, in this place, it was as good as gold.

That is how the story goes, anyway. The truth may be more prosaic: Vaughan did not stumble across that red clod by accident; he had been conducting a rigorous search for just this sort of thing. Nevertheless, his discovery was enough to give Middlesbrough a prosperous new *raison d'être*. And he knew just the man to make it work: a German friend from Newcastle named Heinrich Bölckow.

Bölckow had arrived in the north-east from Rostock as a corn merchant, but he soon found himself on the ground floor of the new iron industry. He and Vaughan built furnaces in Middlesbrough (on a road they named Vulcan Street), started to smelt the local red rock into pig iron, and set about rewriting the modern history of north-east England. They opened mines in the hills up at Eston (until then a frantic metropolis of just two cottages); yet when they finally formed themselves into a limited company in 1864, Bolckow Vaughan & Co.[9] was the biggest business in Britain. It was clear from a number of accidents – such as the Dee Bridge disaster of 1847 – that iron beams had structural weaknesses, but a solution was already on the horizon. In 1856 Henry Bessemer had realised that molten

9 By then, Bolckow had dropped the umlaut … and changed his name to Henry.

iron's impurities could be blown away with a swift blast of oxygen. His discovery gave the north-east a new lease of life.

If the railway invented Middlesbrough, Middlesbrough returned the compliment by delivering the means to expand the railway. By 1870, it was turning out one-third of Britain's iron: four million tons. A few decades later it was an 'ironopolis', a bustling city of nearly a hundred thousand people that would (along with Redcar) provide the steel for the Sydney Harbour Bridge, and many other far-flung projects. It was a sweaty, gold-rush sort of town; there was a frontier bustle about it. The roads were named after compass points (North Street, West Street and so on) or neighbouring towns (Stockton Street, Gosforth Street), and its population was strikingly cosmopolitan, since the foundries sucked muscle power from across Britain and beyond. And given that the work, by its very nature, attracted a preponderance of young men, Middlesbrough became a byword for a raucous new note in the hard-working, hard-drinking working-class culture for which England had been famous since its naval heyday.

Partly as a result of its success, Middlesbrough had the unhappy distinction of becoming the first English town to be bombed in the Second World War. In May 1940 a lone Luftwaffe plane dropped thirteen bombs not far from the steel plant. By then, the rest of England had forgotten how young the town was: it felt as though it had been there for ever.

Gladstone had famously described Middlesbrough as 'an infant Hercules' – a blast furnace for steel, with *en suite* terraced housing for the workers. It was apt, given its cosmopolitan make-up, that Henry Bölckow became the town's first mayor, its first (Liberal) MP in Westminster, and effectively the father of the town. He sponsored a school, a hospital, a working men's club and the seventy-acre Albert Park (named in honour of a fellow German, the Prince Consort).

The Latin motto on Middlesbrough's town crest was *Erimus* – 'We shall be'. It was a pithy statement of the obvious:

this was a town with its eye set firmly on the future, not the past. But the English past was hard to shake off. In 1889, when the imposing new town hall was officially opened by the Prince of Wales, it was a grand structure in the French Gothic style, designed to suggest ancient roots. It featured statues of muses – Painting, Literature, Music and Commerce – in medieval raiment, and a depiction of St George slaying the dragon, a quasi-Arthurian image. It also had a 170-foot clock tower which rose above the foundries like a cathedral spire.

In this it was imitating the style of the town's railway station, unveiled in 1877, which used local wrought iron to create the same sense of Gothic majesty. The future? The past? Why not seize the best of both worlds?

Middlesbrough was not the only new town thrown up by the dictates of industry: Swindon and Crewe grew as rail junctions; Liverpool and Hartlepool as ports; Newcastle and Barrow-in-Furness as centres of shipbuilding.[10] Consett, Corby and Sheffield were steel towns; Stoke was a ceramics factory.

Some settlements developed lighter forms of expertise. Walsall, like Northampton, specialised in leather (it was home to seven thousand saddlers), and made the footballs for the FA Cup Final. And York, somewhat implausibly, became a chocolate city. This had nothing to do with the availability of local raw materials – the cocoa and sugar were imported from thousands of miles away. Rather, York possessed citizens affluent enough to buy sweets, and a Quaker culture that wanted to promote delicious alternatives to alcohol. Two of the great names in English chocolate – Rowntree and Terry – established themselves in the city in the nineteenth century. Just as

10 There was a Cistercian abbey in medieval Barrow – second only to Fountains in wealth – and the village had smelted the odd bit of iron from time to time. But there was not much here in 1850 when another metalworker with German roots, Henry Schneider, found iron ore in the Cumbrian hills. The rest was shipbuilding history: Barrow-in-Furness became a steelworks, a naval yard and a jute mill.

Oxford became famous for marmalade, and Norwich for mustard, so York became synonymous with chocolate.

It still is. Rowntree eventually merged with Mackintosh (founded by John Mackintosh of Halifax, the home of Quality Street[11]), and was then bought by Nestlé, but York's factories continue to produce some of England's favourite indulgences: Kit-Kat, Milky Bar, the Terry's Chocolate Orange, Aero and – of course – Yorkie.

Something even busier was stirring on the edge of Bradford. And not before time, because of all the urban sprawls inspired by coal, steam and wool, nowhere could match this Yorkshire town for squalor. Here, more than anywhere else, England managed to put both its feet forward at once. It was simultaneously the richest place in the world and the filthiest.

In 1801 Bradford was a straightforward textile manufactory with a population just above 6000; by the 1870s, it was home to 200,000 people. And it was a notoriously dismal home, with two hundred chimneys belching out poisonous fumes twenty-four hours a day. There were attempts to pipe in fresh water from the Pennines, but it was hard to keep pace with the hygienic need. As a result, Bradford became the most unsanitary place in England. From the top of the Wool Exchange the patron saint of wool-combers, St Blaise, looked down Market Street – and it was not a pretty sight. Two statistics make all others redundant: only a third of the children born to textile workers reached the age of fifteen; and the average life expectancy was barely eighteen. Typhoid, cholera, anthrax ('wool sorter's disease') – Bradford had them all. Its people were bent out of shape by rickets. The town was a world capital of disability and malnourishment.

Forget four to a room – the children of Bradford slept four to a bed.

It was another city with shallow roots. In 1851 only half the population had been born there; the rest had flocked from

11 The famous selection box was named after a 1901 play by J. M. Barrie, but the sweets are still made in Halifax.

other parts of Britain and beyond. There were plenty of Jews, an Irish community, and enough Germans for one area to be christened 'Little Germany'.

One man decided that radical action was called for. Titus Salt was a native of west Yorkshire, the son of a wool merchant, apprentice to a stapler at the age of seventeen, and thoroughly imbued both with the trade and with this place. Early in his career, just married and looking for something new, he experimented with a bale of tangled Russian wool no one else wanted, shorn from sheep on the banks of the River Don (not the one that flows through Doncaster). When he found a way to process it, he opened his own mill in Bradford. A little later, in 1834, he took a punt on some foul-smelling fleece that was languishing in Liverpool's docks. It was alpaca wool from Peru, and Salt soon found that the fibres it produced were unusually smooth and fine. He bought the whole consignment, and was soon running five mills in his filthy home town.

Alpaca cloth was as smooth as silk. Queen Victoria liked it so much that she sent Salt fleece from her own pair of alpacas in Windsor Great Park. This prestigious endorsement helped him become the richest mill owner in Bradford and, in 1848, the town's mayor.[12]

By then, though, he was hungering for more than money and titles. The story goes that he read Disraeli's *Sybil*, which included a sketch of a utopian village built by a northern industrialist, and decided to turn fiction into fact. The result was Saltaire, a factory township that merged his own name with the river on which it stood.[13]

---

12 Queen Victoria was herself a keen spinner and knitter. A famous photograph shows her at a spinning wheel, like a medieval cottager, and there is a bust of her spinning at Osborne House, Isle of Wight.

13 Alas, we do not know for sure that Salt read *Sybil*. It may have been Disraeli who was inspired by Salt, rather than the other way round. Disraeli's sketch was on the syrupy side – 'The men were well clad; the women had a blooming cheek; drunkenness was unknown' – but the concept was a high-minded revelation.

Saltaire, Bradford. Half satanic mill, half Renaissance palace.

There were one or two precursors. Richard Arkwright had built housing for his Cromford Mill workers; and Edward Akroyd did something similar in Halifax. But Salt's dreams were on a much grander scale. He chose a scenic – and healthy – site in the hills a few miles to the north-west of Bradford. It was on the banks of the River Aire and the Leeds–Liverpool Canal, and close to the brand-new Midland Railway.

The first building to be completed was the mill. Shaped like a Renaissance monastery, it could hold 3000 workers and

1200 looms, and at full capacity it could produce 30,000 yards of fabric a day. It was the biggest such enterprise in the world: Tuscan palazzo meets satanic mill.

The village that Salt constructed around this centrepiece was equally visionary. Eight hundred houses (graded by seniority – managers had better gardens and views) were built in neat rows above the great mill complex, and the villagers were also provided with two churches, a school, a hospital, public baths, a social club, a fire station and a sports ground. Every house even had its own toilet, an unimaginable luxury at the time. Compared to Bradford, it was idyllic.

In one sense, Salt was a tyrant. A zealous non-drinker, he refused to permit a pub, and erected a sign on the road into the village that read: 'Abandon beer all ye who enter here'. He also banned smoking, gambling, pawn shops and swearing. But tyranny rarely came in such a benevolent guise. Saltaire was by far the best home a factory worker might hope to find in this polluted textile underworld. There was no police station because there was no crime. There were almshouses for retired mill workers (so long as they were 'of good moral character') and works outings to Salt's villa: in 1856 he chartered special trains so three thousand workers could enjoy tea and 'harmless frolics' in his pleasant garden.

Nothing could hide the fact that the workers' lives were being devoured by the puffing dragon that lay at Saltaire's heart – the ever-churning mill. But this village was a remarkable experiment which paved the way for many other such projects. In York, the Rowntrees developed the suburb of Earswick to house their chocolate workers; at Bournville, near Birmingham, the Cadburys created a town powered by Dairy Milk; and at Port Sunlight, on the west bank of the Mersey, the Lever brothers built a fairy-tale estate out of soap that now boasts nine hundred listed buildings. These may have looked like a break with the past, but in fact they were tributes to continuity.

Twenty-one

Arthur and Robin

We find it easy to see music as something that drifts out of the English countryside. Ralph Vaughan Williams's *The Lark Ascending*, often rated the country's favourite piece of music, sounds like a summer's day. And Vaughan Williams himself wrote: 'there, in the fastness of rural England, was the well-spring of English music'.

But can a nation's literature also be 'natural', expressing the setting and soil out of which it grew? It sounds unlikely. We are used to seeing regional scenery as a leading character: Hardy's Wessex; Wordsworth's Lakeland; Brontë and Herriot country; Kipling's Sussex; Du Maurier's Cornwall. But are there *national* trends or flavours we can ascribe to prevailing considerations of geography? Can art and literature be rooted in native things?

It would be easy to overstate the case. The influences on a literature are broader than a quick inspection of their roots can possibly explain. But if you live in a German forest, with wolves loping through the shadows, then the adventures of Hansel, Gretel and Little Red Riding Hood will seem hauntingly familiar. And if your home was a desert, you might feel a similar kinship with Sheherazade or Ali Baba. Indeed, it is often said that the narrative frame of *A Thousand and One Nights* – a story that never ends – suggests the infinite sands of Arabia. Norwegian legends feature mountain trolls and eagles; Greek myths tell of stormy islands; African folk

tales involve lions, crocodiles and hyenas; and Japanese stories tremble with rice farms, cherry blossom and bamboo.
Beowulf roams the North Sea wilderness as confident in his
icy setting as the volcanic Cyclops is in the Mediterranean,
where Vesuvius once roared.

It is hardly surprising, in this context, that many English
folk tales are grounded in their own rural landscapes: bogs,
owls, mistletoe, ravens, corn dollies, green men, May queens,
hares, will-o'-the-wisps, barnyard creatures and lost sheep. In
the very first fairy tale to be printed in England (in 1621) Tom
Thumb wears an oak leaf as a hat; Jack, meanwhile, exchanges
a sheep for enchanted beans on his way to market;[1] and the
pantomime babes in the wood are covered with leaves by good
old English robins.

In one of Suffolk's most celebrated stories, two green-
skinned children are discovered in a pit. They are clad in plain
woollen cloth (from Lavenham, at a guess) but do not seem to
understand English, French or Flemish. The boy soon dies,
but once the girl starts tucking into fresh beans and good local
bread, her skin loses its green tinge and her hair turns golden.
Before long, she is just like anyone else.

It is a rugged parable of migration and assimilation, but
rooted in Suffolk lore.

Native features of this sort are central to many children's
books. English animals do all the talking in *The Wind in the
Willows*, *Watership Down* and everything by Beatrix Potter.
Country ways also lie at the heart of *Swallows and Amazons*,
Ring of Bright Water, *Children of the New Forest*, and indeed *Three
Men in a Boat* – a classic tale from the riverbank. Tolkien's Shire
is an idealised English village set in a medieval fairyland not far
from Oxford[2], and in *Thomas the Tank Engine* and *The Railway*

---

1 In later years, the sheep morphed into a cow.

2 When the wizard Gandalf visits Bilbo Baggins, he is offered wine, and his host suggests the 1296 – 'a very good year'.

Children the Steam Age is woven into the rural scene. *The Secret Garden* promotes the restorative effect of growing roses (with a robin chirping in the background), while the Harry Potter series – with its wizards, witches, owls and dragons – is a shrewd re-creation of medieval Merrie England.

All of these works ferment the ordinary ingredients of English nature into literature. The muse doesn't live in a town; her home is a cave, a glade, a cliff, a river or a waterfall. Austen, Dickens and Thackeray may have brooded on civic society, but George Eliot, Hardy, Lawrence and many others grounded their work in country life. Nearly every major poet has celebrated green thoughts and natural wonders, and in the First World War nothing was more resonant, for those stranded in Flanders, than honey-still-for-tea dreams of daisies and hollyhocks. As Paul Fussell has pointed out, the horrors of trench warfare inspired thousands of Englishmen to cherish the memory of roses, foxgloves, church clocks and the lush green acres of Grantchester and Adelstrop.

It was a world worth fighting for.

Many of the landscapes that inspired English literature have become cultural monuments or visitor attractions in their own right. And England has been so well trodden for so long that relics of the past can be unearthed almost anywhere. Sometimes, with a fine sense of symmetry, they can write themselves back into the land that inspired them. They have even generated insights that deepen our sense of England as a brew of time-honoured memories and traditions.

This is certainly the case at Chipping Campden. Earlier, we saw that the monument marking the northernmost point of the long-distance footpath through the Cotswolds features a quotation from 'East Coker', the second of T. S. Eliot's *Four Quartets*. The lines were well chosen to celebrate a route that runs both ways, merging beginnings and endings. But there is a stronger allusion to this spot earlier in the poem, in 'Burnt Norton'. Eliot used to visit Chipping Campden in the interwar years, to stay with his friend Emily Hale and enjoy the country air. It was from her house, in 1934, that the pair strode over the ridge to the north and slipped into the grounds of a secluded manor. It was a private estate, not open to the public, so the ramblers were trespassers, lifting the latch on a secret world. An abandoned rose garden around a drained pool full of dead leaves triggered Eliot's heartfelt reflection on the present, the past, memories not disturbed and paths not taken.

He did not stay long, but he saw enough in that garden to glimpse the guttering candle of historic England – to catch the faint chimes of a distant era.

Other passages in *Four Quartets* range over the English countryside – the fields surrounding a village near Yeovil; a secluded chapel in Cambridgeshire – but it was this Cotswolds manor house which led Eliot to observe that history was ... *now*.

He was not wholly enamoured of the Cotswolds, claiming in letters that it carried the whiff of death and decay. But on this occasion he was inspired by whispers from another time. As it happened, there may well have been ghosts in the garden. The estate was once the scene of an infamous saga: its founder, Sir William Keyt, set the original house ablaze in 1741 in a hot burst of self-pity and romantic dismay. Since its name was Norton House, the building that rose from the ashes became known as 'Burnt Norton'.

Sometimes it seems as if the landscape itself generates such imaginings. They cling like honeysuckle, or a rambling rose.

Hardly anywhere is so quivering with such notions as the Somerset town of Glastonbury. Danny Boyle used its distinctive tor in the opening ceremony for the 2012 Olympic Games, and with good reason: its cricket fields, sheepfolds and crooked cottages encapsulate the long history of bucolic England. Of course, if you type the word 'Glastonbury' into a search engine you bump into something very different: a music festival: the midsummer gala in which a hundred thou-sand party animals gather in the West Country to get – in all senses of the word – soaked. It is a major national event, and every year the newspapers publish images of the English at play in its soggy acres: couples grinning as they splash through knee-deep mud; teenagers swaying arms in a downpour; gran-nies frowning over puddles. We have always loved messing about on the water.

It is intrinsically English in the way that it celebrates both modern life (music) and an ancient tradition (rain).

Glastonbury is the ideal place for such a fiesta, because this corner of Somerset throbs with echoes of England's pagan past. It is steeped in the foggy folklore of druids, witches, star signs, goddesses and healing rituals. But while these are crucial to the local economy – the town does a roaring trade in New Age knick-knacks – it owes even more to its natural attributes: the ancient wool that generated its wealth; and the fudge-coloured local stone from which its buildings were constructed.

This is why Glastonbury became such a rich node in English life. Edmund Ironside was crowned there in 1016, and it was sacred ground long before that: it boasted first a Celtic shrine and then a seventh-century Saxon church.

Yet Glastonbury's true fame rests on something that probably never happened, because this is also the cradle of England's favourite myth: the legend of King Arthur. Tintagel, on the rocky Cornish coast, may claim to be the birthplace, and the Round Table may hang in Winchester Cathedral,[3] but it was in Glastonbury that twelfth-century monks claimed to have discovered a stone tablet that read: 'Here lies Arthur, King'. The hill fort at nearby Cadbury was thus crowned the true site of Camelot, and Glastonbury Tor

3 Edward III awarded the Round Table to Winchester partly as a nation-building gimmick – to imply that he had rebuilt Arthurian Camelot. In 1348, he founded his own fellowship of knights, the Order of the Garter. A century later, Thomas Malory identified Winchester as the site of Camelot in *Le Morte d'Arthur*.

became the magical 'isle' of Avalon, rising above the marshy Somerset wetlands. On a misty November morning, with dew shining on the fields at its base, it does indeed seem to float above this earthly realm.

Glastonbury Tor. Close your eyes, and you can almost hear Sir Gawain.

Not much can equal the enduring power of these stories: they have shaped the way that generations of English people have thought about themselves. Arthur and his knights occupy centre stage in a thousand books, films, plays, poems and bedtime tales. Malory's *Morte d'Arthur* was one of the first books to be printed by William Caxton – in 1485, just nine years after the *Canterbury Tales* – so was one of the foundation stones of England's national literature.

Arthur is an idealised warrior, a beacon of chivalry, and also entwined with the birth of English Christianity since, in William of Malmesbury's fanciful account, it was to Glastonbury that Joseph of Arimathea brought the infant

Jesus. Years later, Joseph returned with the Holy Grail – the cup from which Jesus drank at the Last Supper. He buried the grail beneath Glastonbury Tor, and his staff turned into a flowering thorn tree, which became a famous site of pilgrimage.[4] Indeed, this is the fable behind William Blake's poem 'Jerusalem' – now a quasi-national anthem – which begins by asking if those holy feet, in ancient time, really did walk upon England's mountains green. It is an arresting idea, though, the probable answer (if we are honest) is: no.

Of course, the Arthurian tales may be equally fictitious. William of Malmesbury advanced the idea that Excalibur was forged in Avalon, but Glastonbury's monks also played a part in building the legend, since myths and miracles were good for the pilgrimage trade. (At the time, the shrine at Canterbury was making a killing out of martyr's blood.) The 'real' Arthur – the king who led the post-Roman Britons against invaders from the continent and united the British with his victory at Mount Badon, where he scattered his enemies like pigeons with Christ's Cross on his shoulder[5] – is much less captivating than the fallible Arthur, whose tragic love for Guinevere and Lancelot broke the fellowship.

But it doesn't matter if the stories are untrue. The point is that they *feel* true. They seem to grow out of the Somerset scenery, becoming dramatic expressions of its watery mists and promontories. It is hard not to feel a shiver when you climb past grazing sheep to reach the summit of Glastonbury Tor, with its ruined medieval tower. It is like the humped spine of a dragon, coiled in the English grass. If Arthur and Guinevere

---

4 The Glastonbury Thorn stood for centuries on the hill opposite the tor, beguiling visitors with the fact that it flowered twice a year, unlike native hawthorn. By tradition, a sprig was sent every Christmas to the royal household. Cromwell's evangelists cut it down as a symbol of monarchy, and in 2010 it was beheaded again. When a fresh sapling was planted in 2012, it was snapped in half two weeks later.

5 It is ironic that the most glorious king in England's history won undying fame by fighting *against* the Angles.

did not set up court in this evocative spot, they should have. The tor commands lordly views across the county – all the way to Cheddar Gorge and the Mendips, with Wiltshire in the opposite direction and Wells Cathedral to the north. At dawn, as the town slumbers in its deep shadow, the turret lights up like a glittering crown, silhouetted against the western sky.

At such times, it is as if this land generated not just superlative grass for sheep, but immortal myths. Although Arthur and Lancelot were filtered through a French sensibility, they emerged in Malory's epic in English clothing, with Merlin connecting them to a magical Celtic past. Camelot is a fairyland of bright pennants on tented pavilions, fluttering in the breeze, a world of soft mornings and owl-haunted woods, with the cluck and splash of moorhens, invisible in the mist, the rustle of dry leaves on tracks that meander past lonely chapels, and wells gleaming with silvery water. In the clashing antlers of tilting deer, we can almost detect the knightly crack of lances splintering on shields; and that drunken reveller lounging in the field looks awfully like Lancelot, fast asleep under an apple tree. The thud of horses' hooves in the distance is like a hunting horn: is that Sir Perceval spurring on, or Sir Galahad sallying forth after the grail? It is a wonderful place for unlikely visions. Modern visitors commonly report seeing unexplained saucer-shaped objects hovering in the sparkling sky.

Henry VIII – and his enforcer, Thomas Cromwell – clearly understood the importance of Glastonbury in the mythology of old England. His father had made a point of identifying Arthur – the great unifier of the ancient kingdom – as their ancestor (indeed, Henry VII had named his eldest son after the ancient king). So when the Catholic realm was dissolved during the Reformation, Cromwell took Glastonbury's last abbot, Richard Whiting, from the Tower of London to Somerset, where he was dragged up the hill by horses, then hanged, drawn and quartered. His head was taken to the abbey, while his infidel limbs were placed on public display in Bath, Bridgewater, Ilchester and Wells.

But it takes more than that to kill a good story. The legends of Glastonbury live on.

Every nation is selective with respect to the myths and legends it records and remembers – the stories it chooses to tell about itself. These may not paint a consistent or coherent picture – England produced both Iago and Galahad – but we can draw a few tentative conclusions from the neverending popularity of the Arthurian tales. Hardly anyone believes that the honourable and just society of Camelot actually existed, but lots of us wish it had. England has harboured an aching desire for such a realm ever since the Middle Ages. The tales also reflect the nation's enthusiasm for valorous violence; its weakness for male fraternities; its respect for family ties and lineage; its sneaking dread that every paradise contains a snake, raging to destroy it; its sense of love as something both ennobling and deadly; its undying respect for gallantry; and its conviction that treachery is the vilest of all sins.

Much the same could be said about England's other great mythical hero: Robin Hood. We have already seen how Sherwood Forest helped to put the oak tree at the centre of English culture, and Robin is one of its chirruping spirits. We should add that he was already old by the time he started to appear in medieval ballads – a gallant from former times. Even then, England sought inspiration in its past.

Like Arthur, Robin is imaginary. The sources are foggy. He might be no more than a fictional avatar of Hereward the Wake, an archetypal warrior against oppression, symbolising all the real outlaws who took to the forest in defiance of Norman rule. But just as with the Arthurian myths the din of knights' spurs and the silken scarves of distressed damsels seem to rise out of the marshy sunset in the West Country, so Robin seems to creep out of Nottinghamshire's dappled glades and clearings.

The ballads are hardly realistic. It is always summer; the air is always sweet; the oaks are copious; the deer practically charge towards arrows. We do not often hear Little John's teeth chattering, and Robin is rarely caught rubbing his hands against the frost. But he is still rooted in a specific place. Clad in Lincoln green (the local cloth), he is a spirit of the woodland, hopping from twig to twig like the bird after which he is named. So, even if he never existed in the glad-poaching, arrow-splitting form we know so well, the glee with which England embraced him – as a 'true' yeoman who defied the barons and redistributed their loot – is telling. The balladeers who sang his praises pretty much wrote the book on how to be a hero: ever since, thousands have mimicked Robin's quick-witted, man-of-the-people act. Poems, children's stories, plays, films ... he is even one of the few fictional figures to be granted an entry in the *Dictionary of National Biography*.

The plucky POWs who escape from German camps in the war stories are modern-day versions of bold Robin, standing up to the bad guys with nimble feet and ready grins. He planted in our culture an icon that could inspire socialists and libertarians alike: half dissident, half troubadour, roasting the king's venison in his secret camp.

Sherwood Forest echoes with his name to this day: there's Robin Hood's stable, Robin Hood's chair, Robin Hood's cave, Robin Hood's larder, the Robin Hood Festival, even a Robin Hood pie (full of venison, of course). We also have the village of Edwinstone, where he supposedly married Maid Marian, the grave of Will Scarlett, and the castle where Friar Tuck may (surely *this* one is true) have poisoned King John. His legend ranges all the way to the sea – to Robin Hood's Bay.

In remembering Robin, we are celebrating a verdant chip of old England.

Glastonbury and Sherwood Forest may be particularly well suited to the production of myth, but each and every aspect of

England's geographical inheritance helped to write the literature we now call 'classic'.

First there is the sea. In addition to forming our early trading instincts, and the pattern of our development, it has been a forceful presence in our imaginings. One of England's earliest poems, the Anglo-Saxon *Seafarer*, is a biting meditation on the spiritual lessons of oceanic voyages. On the one hand, the poem charts the sea's extremes, its stormy depths. On the other, it captures the sailor's enhanced appreciation of life on land – 'the woodland grows flowers, the cities seem sweet, the grass grows greener, the whole world seems fresh'.

Four of Shakespeare's plays begin with violent storms at sea – *The Merchant of Venice*, *Twelfth Night*, *Othello* and *The Tempest*. Perdita is lost on a sea voyage in *The Winter's Tale*, and King Lear is 'mad as the vex'd sea'. When Brutus murmurs about 'a tide in the affairs of men' in *Julius Caesar*, he is using a metaphor that would scarcely occur to a Roman, safe on his tide-free Mediterranean shore.

England's marine setting, famously invoked in *Richard II* (This precious stone, set in a silver sea'), informs rafts of English verse, from *The Rime of the Ancient Mariner* to the lonely seas and grey sky of John Masefield.

The English novel has also looked out to sea from its very beginnings. Daniel Defoe had only one model when he wrote *Robinson Crusoe* in 1719: John Bunyan's *Pilgrim's Progress*. Yet it seemed as natural for an Englishman to tell the tale of a castaway who turns a wilderness into a garden as it was for Chinese poets to describe mountains or Japanese writers to dwell on the samurai. Much has been said of *Robinson Crusoe*'s allegorical implications, and with good reason, for it certainly embodies the seafaring imperial impulse of the time. Crusoe colonises an island, then tames it. What could be more English than that, aside from recruiting Friday as his manservant? Crusoe's instinct is to make himself master of all he surveys, like one of Gainsborough's squires. He refers to his improvised shelter as 'my castle'.

The sea has been a powerful presence in English literature ever since. It is the presiding spirit of *Treasure Island*, *Coral Island* and *Lord of the Flies*; its perils inspired endless true stories of drama and disaster (the *Titanic*, the *Cutty Sark*, the *Hood*); and there are dozens of naval adventures from the days of oak and canvas (Hornblower, *Mutiny on the* Bounty, *Mr Midshipman Easy* and the novels of Patrick O'Brian) as well as the Steam Age (*Lord Jim*, *The Cruel Sea*, *Sink the* Bismarck! and *HMS* Ulysses).

Few novelists were so steeped in seafaring as the Polish-born Joseph Conrad. Works like *Nigger of the* Narcissus and *Lord Jim* were inspired by the drama of life on the ocean waves – in his case, the Indian Ocean. But no matter how far from London he sailed, he always addressed an English subject. In *Youth* (1902), he remarked that the main events of the story could have occurred nowhere else but England – 'where men and sea interpenetrate, so to speak'. And though he had seen tropical storms with his own eyes, he drew a typically English axiom from the central incident of *Typhoon*, written the same year: 'Facing it, always facing it. That's the way to get through.'

England's rivers have also beguiled everyone from Spenser ('Sweet Thames, run softly, till I end my song'), Shakespeare ('There is a willow grows aslant a brook') to Tennyson ('The broad stream bore her far away / The Lady of Shalott'), and Jerome K. Jerome. George Eliot set *The Mill on the Floss* at the mouth of the Trent – St Ogg's and Mudport are based on Gainsborough and Hull, respectively – to give the river a major place in the story. It precipitates the flood-surge climax, but mostly it is a metaphor – a symbol of freedom, the 'stronger presence' whose stream carries away the heroine 'without any act of her own will'. Her heart is 'borne along by the tide' to its sad fate.

The ceaseless coming and going of the sea may have left one more mark on the English temperament. The regularity of the tide, and its power to govern people's lives, made England a country of charts and timetables. In due course, when new means of transport arrived, the habit was already well entrenched. Life was measured by stopwatches and station clocks, and there was no sense rushing: best to form an orderly queue. The greatest of all England's national habits – standing in line – came to us early – and naturally.

And it still rules our lives today. Till number *nine*, please!

As for the role of the native weather in English literature, well, where to begin? Another aspect of *Robinson Crusoe* that marks it out as distinctively English is the attention it pays to rainfall and fresh water: Crusoe creates an ingenious drainage system, even fashions an umbrella out of animal skins.

Back in England, the rain never stops. It trickles through the literature like a babbling stream. William Langland's fourteenth-century ploughman harrowed the earth while praising the 'gentle' rain that falls on the just and unjust alike, while Portia, in *The Merchant of Venice*, suggested that merciful justice 'droppeth as the gentle rain from Heaven'. Chaucer's pilgrims set off for Canterbury just as April's 'sweet' showers are ending the 'drought' of March (a surprising idea to modern minds), while Lear raged against a deluge on his wild heath. Shakespeare so liked the song 'For the rain it raineth every day' that he used it twice – in *Twelfth Night* as well as *King Lear*.

Oddly, England fell even more in thrall to the weather as its citizens began to move from country to town. 'Our dispositions too frequently change with the colour of the sky,' wrote Dr Johnson, before urging his readers to 'struggle against the tyranny of the climate'. This was a rational view in an age that prized rational views, but a new generation of poets was starting to take a different stance.

The Romantic poets in particular turned this notion up a notch by depicting human life as a guttering flame, always at the mercy of the elements. Wordsworth's 'Resolution and Independence' (or 'The Leech Gatherer') is a reverie triggered by a storm – a 'roaring in the wind all night' that makes the morning grass 'bright with raindrops' – while *The Prelude* is full of airy blasts. Shelley devoted an ode to the west wind; Keats obliged us always to think of autumn as the 'season of mists and mellow fruitfulness'; and Browning longed for the sights and sounds of springtime in his homeland, the chaffinches singing on orchard boughs 'in England – now'.

One of Dickens's most famous passages is his description of the London fog at the beginning of *Bleak House*, but it is matched by a long riff about the downpour in Lincolnshire a few pages later: 'The shot of a rifle loses its sharpness in the moist air, and its smoke moves in a tardy little cloud ... The vases on the stone terrace in the foreground catch the rain all day, and the heavy drops fall – drip, drip, drip – upon the broad flagged pavement.' It is often raining in Jane Austen's novels, too: her eligible young women are permanently at risk of a dousing. Marianne Dashwood, in *Sense and Sensibility*, catches a chill after walking through wet grass; Jane Bennett has to take to her bed after riding in the rain.

These dainty showers might precipitate happy endings – a break in the clouds permits Emma and Mr Knightley to take another turn around the garden, which allows him to declare his love – but stormy weather is often more ominous. It is hard to imagine *Wuthering Heights* without its 'wild and windy' moor, while Pip, in *Great Expectations*, shudders at the 'violent blasts of rain' that threaten his fortunes.

The most dedicated chronicler of England's weather and the way it shaped English people was Thomas Hardy. The labourers in *Tess of the d'Urbervilles* are not just *in* the countryside; they are part of it, tuned to the natural world as if they were musical instruments. 'These denizens of the fields served vegetation, weather, frost and sun,' wrote Hardy, and he was even more explicit in *The Return of the Native*, a novel in which, as D. H. Lawrence noted, the characters seem less like individual souls than by-products of the Egdon ecosystem: 'spirits of the heath ... one year's accidental crop'.

The weather often plays a malevolent role in Hardy's tales. A squall might catch out unwary farmers and ruin their hay ricks; rain might sputter through a church gargoyle and on to some flowers, mocking a tender gesture; and what else could the hero of *Far From the Madding Crowd* be called, as an emblem of dependable rustic wisdom, than Farmer Oak? We cannot know whether Hardy was consciously evoking the satirical figure John Bull (created by a Scot, Doctor Arbuthnot, in 1712) when he suggested that an Englishman's mood 'rose and fell with the weather-glass'. But he certainly clung to the idea that characters moved through their landscapes and buffeting weather with only the illusion of free will.

Few would maintain that the emotional well-being of modern England is tethered to the sun, the wind, the health of the crops and the kindness of the skies. Modern life has moved indoors. But the legacy of all that sowing, reaping and animal husbandry lingers: all across the nation farmers, gardeners, cricketers, fishermen, sailors and ramblers – not to mention lifeboatmen, firefighters and flood engineers – lead lives still ruled by the sky. None of us can truly escape. Even in our hyper-engineered era of mains water, heating and air-conditioning, we still look to the clouds for advice and consolation.

This may be more obvious to foreign visitors than to home-grown writers. V. S. Naipaul's *The Enigma of Arrival*, set in Wiltshire, begins like a despondent postcard home to sunny Trinidad: 'For the first four days it rained.' Then it goes on to explain how unsettling the English seasons can be for a man born in the tropics: 'It was hard ... I didn't associate flowers or the foliage of trees with any particular month.'

This sense of endless seasonal change made England seem a land constantly lapped by time. When Naipaul went nosing around a dilapidated farm near Stonehenge he was struck by the feeling of ruin – 'fallen tiles, holed roofs, rusted corrugated iron, bent metal, a pervading damp, the colours rust and brown and black'. Among these 'superseded things' he came upon the man who lived there – a fellow called Jack – and admired the garden he had created: clipped hedge, trim flowers and neat vegetables. It reminded Naipaul of the reference to Salisbury Plain in *King Lear*, and soon he felt himself to be in a 'historical part of England'. Riding home on the bus, he thought of Jack and his garden as 'emanations [of] literature and antiquity', in much the same way as Eliot had contemplated England's history in the garden at Burnt Norton.

Something similar happened to the German-born author W. G. Sebald when he settled in East Anglia. In *The Rings of Saturn* he walks along the Suffolk coast to the drowned medieval town of Dunwich, and has this to say about the elemental power of the unruly North Sea: 'The East stands for lost causes. You can sense the immense power of emptiness.' Later, he sits in the Sailors' Reading Room in Southwold, a quaint old clubhouse overlooking the colourful huts on the sand below. It is crammed with mementoes from England's maritime past – models, photographs and logbooks – and Sebald cannot help but feel the shiver from an age of tar and salt.

The literary term for the tendency to give the weather human emotions – 'pathetic fallacy' – was coined by John Ruskin in 1856. But by then it was already an ancient practice. Ever since *Hamlet* had opened with the observation that 'the air bites shrewdly' with 'an eager and a nipping wind', hardly a writer had been able to resist conjuring up a ravenous gale, a cruel sea, merry sunbeams, a miserable downpour or a cheerful breeze. Mountains sang, forests groaned, willows wept, flowers nodded and the sun – when it was not hiding – peeped out of a lonely sky.

P. G. Wodehouse mocked this tradition by imagining that the weather shared the brainless mental outlook of his dukes and earls. *Service with a Smile* begins: 'The morning sun shone benignly down on Blandings Castle.' Other novels have titles like *Heavy Weather* and *Summer Lightning*, and root the whole bally plot in such things. One golf fable opens: 'It was a morning when all nature shouted "Fore!" The breeze, as it blew gently up from the valley, seemed to bring a message of hope and cheer.'

This sort of affectionate joshing highlights the extent to which weather runs through the veins of English culture. Rain is in our blood.

The green countryside created by all this water has been a recurring theme for poets. Ever since England could write, it wrote about fields, shepherds, and bread. As the pub song has it, there'll always be an England – a grainy realm of cottages and country lanes.

No sooner had French, German and Latin merged to form English than writers started to use the new language to discourse on shepherds and shepherdesses. Rural life fused with art: a poem was hardly a poem without a music-piping boy watching o'er his sheep. Thus was born English pastoral. From Spenser and Sidney to Herrick and Herbert, from Milton and Marvell to Clare and Blake, from Crabbe and Gray to Tennyson and Housman – all were inspired by the same green muse. It also breathed country air into many English hymns. What else could the Lord be but our shepherd, making us to lie down in green pastures?

John Gay could hardly help borrowing from this tradition for his satire of urban life – *The Beggar's Opera* is subtitled 'A Newgate Pastoral' – while Edward Thomas, Ted Hughes and many others kept it alive long into the twentieth century. It became 'nature writing' – rapt descriptions of the great outdoors – in the hands of Gilbert White and Richard Jefferies (and their modern descendants Robert Macfarlane, James Rebanks and Helen Macdonald). And it fostered the scientific work of Wallace, Lyell and Darwin as well as the practical walking guides of Alfred Wainwright and company.

The rural thrust of all this literature extended to a profound

identification with village life as the basis of English civilisation.
Thomas Gray's 'Elegy Written in a Country Churchyard' (1751)
and Oliver Goldsmith's 'Deserted Village' (1770) were forerunners of this tendency, with Gray sounding what turned out to be
one of the signature moods in English verse ('The lowing herd
winds slowly o'er the lea / The ploughman homeward plods his
weary way') while also providing Thomas Hardy with a memorable title ('Far from the madding crowd's ignoble strife'). But no
one did more to embed this feeling in the national consciousness
than Shakespeare. *A Midsummer Night's Dream* and *As You Like
It* are fairytale frolics set in woodland glades, and the collected
plays vibrate with country idioms. 'Leaf' through the pages and
English country life streams out:

> Now is the winter of our discontent / Made glorious
> summer ... Sweet lovers love the spring ... Youth
> like summer morn, age like winter weather ... Love
> comforteth like sunshine after rain ... Men are April
> when they woo, December when they wed ... I know
> a bank whereon the wild thyme grows ... There is a
> willow grows aslant a brook ... Where the bee sucks,
> there suck I / In a cowslip's bell I lie ... Blow, blow,
> thou winter wind ... But look, the morn, in russet
> mantle clad / Walks o'er the dew of yon high eastern
> hill ... Light thickens / And the crow makes wing to
> the rooky wood ... There's rosemary, that's for remem-
> brance ... There's fennel for you, and columbines ...
> Freeze freeze, thou bitter sky ... Out of this nettle,
> danger, we pluck this flower, safety ... A rose by any
> other name would smell as sweet.

Ever since, the heart of England has seemed to lie in its shires.

It was not a paradox that the pace of industrial change
provoked a yearning for nature. Isaac Newton had asserted
that every action has an equal but opposite reaction a couple

of decades before Newcomen built his first steam engine. So the Steam Age was always likely to inspire torrents of poetry devoted to the natural world.

The sea, the rivers, the weather, the farms, the rural life – all of these natural aspects of the English scene have seeped into its literature. So we might assume that the rock on which industrial England was built – coal – is in there too.

It should be, certainly. But the awkward truth is that there is little classic English writing inspired by coal. France can boast *Germinal* – a powerful depiction of life in the mines – which, as the title implies, nurtured or 'germinated' human suffering.[6] Wales has Richard Llewellyn's *How Green Was My Valley*, while Upton Sinclair made heroes of Colorado's miners in *King Coal*. For the most part, England seemed to prefer natural wonders.

There were exceptions, of course. Disraeli and Elizabeth Gaskell painted broad-brush pictures of the divisions created by industrial change, while Dickens's depictions of urban slums were even more memorable. In *Hard Times* he described 'Coketown' (based on Preston) as a place of dehumanising awfulness:

> It was a town of red brick, or of brick that would have been red if the smoke and ashes had allowed it; but as matters stood it was a town of unnatural red and black ... It had a black canal in it, and a river that ran purple with ill-smelling dye, and vast piles of building full of windows where there was a rattling and a trembling all day long, and where the piston of the steam engine worked continuously up and down like the head of an elephant in a state of melancholy madness.

Mechanisation could crush the human spirit, but not quite kill it. Indeed, as Dickens went on to note, it inspired a striking affection for life outside the factory:

6 France's miners were impressed – thousands turned up to attend Zola's funeral.

> Exactly in the ratio as they worked long and monoto-
> nously, the craving grew within them for some physical
> relief – some relaxation, encouraging good humour and
> good spirits, and giving them a vent – some recognised
> holiday, though it were but for an honest dance to a
> stirring band of music, some occasional light pie ...

Few followed Dickens's example, however. Yes, Nottinghamshire's coalfield served as the nursery for D. H. Lawrence's *The
White Peacock* and *Sons and Lovers*. Just as Hardy's characters were
made in Wessex, so Lawrence's were 'animals of coal', as he said
in *Lady Chatterley's Lover*. And yes, B. L. Coombes wrote: 'There
is blood on the coal, there will always be blood on the coal' in
Those Clouded Hills. But there is not much else. When George
Orwell went down a coal mine on his way to Wigan Pier, it felt
like a foreign land.

Only in its death throes did coal mining create the kind
of pathos that attracted writers' attention. David Almond
made the pit villages of the Tyne the setting for his children's
novel *Kit's Wilderness*, while the screenwriters of *Billy Elliot*
and *The Full Monty* used heavy industry as bleak backdrop for
their redemptive human dramas. It was left to the poet Tony
Harrison to find a seam of classic literature in the dying pits.
In his long poem 'v.' (1985 – the year of the miners' strike) he
inspected the expletive-riddled graffiti on his father's headstone
in Leeds, then, with a mock-heroic nod to Gray's 'Elegy', delivered a sermon on the sour effects of economic decline. He was
especially aware of the mine shafts below his feet.

A decade later, in his film-poem *Prometheus*, Harrison imagined mining as a Greek myth – an ancient, tragic flame. In so
doing he paid tribute to the violence of the coal world, be it the
hacking that the earth itself suffered or the agonies of the men
who wielded the picks.

But even if coal has not inspired as much grand literature
as one might expect, it has become an important part of

England's mental furniture – one of its fixtures and fittings. It has contributed the canary in the coal mine, the black eyes of snowmen and the ugly notion of 'slags'. The coal fire in the front room was the roaring centrepiece of the twentieth century's 'hearth and home' culture; and when England's soldiers went to war, those left behind were urged to 'keep the home fires burning'.

There is one other way in which the natural history of England entered its literature – and that concerns the pattern of landownership. We have seen how topography dictated the evolution of English agriculture – downland sheep farms, open fields, enclosures – and how this in turn shaped the development of inheritance and property rights. And this subject has gripped many English writers. Dickens saw it as the dead hand of the past: Miss Havisham's gloomy towers in *Great Expectations* are a cold relic; Bleak House is a blighted burden; and the forbidding homes of Ralph Nickleby and Scrooge are dusty prisons. Nearly all of Austen's novels turn on the status of some grand estate or other, be it Northanger Abbey or Mansfield Park, and this tradition was maintained by the 'men of property' who strode through the works of Thackeray, Trollope and Galsworthy.

English literature has continued to resemble a gazetteer of elite houses in modern times: Howards End, Blandings Castle, Manderley – it is a long list. Lady Chatterley's unfulfilled domestic life would have been of little interest to the censors if she had not been able to call upon the services of her own private gamekeeper, while the plot of *The Go-Between* was built on similar upstairs-downstairs tension. Later, Kazuo Ishiguro's *The Remains of the Day*, Ian McEwan's *Atonement*, Sarah Waters's *The Little Stranger* and Alan Hollinghurst's *The Stranger's Child* were all set in substantial country piles. In their own way, these comprise a national work of art. 'Of all the great things that the English have invented and made part of the credit of the national character,' wrote Henry James, 'the only one they have mastered completely in all its details, so that it becomes a compendious illustration of their social genius and their manners, is the well-appointed, well-administered, well-filled country house.' He may have been right. The number of novels that feature grand houses is exceeded only by those preoccupied by the making of a good marriage – and often this amounted to the same thing.

Not everyone reads Thomas Hardy and Jane Austen. But television programmes like *Countryfile*, *Springwatch* and *Coast* tap into much the same appetite for rural England, gripping an urban population that rarely takes to the hills, let alone shears a sheep or gathers in the harvest. Just as radio listeners are waylaid by *The Archers*, and readers drool over the unattainable balconies of the great houses in *Country Life*. One recent episode of *Countryfile* was watched by nearly ten million viewers – far more people than actually live in the English countryside. Similarly, the shepherd James Rebanks found a huge audience when he described life among Herdwick sheep in the Lake District. Traditional leanings still hang, like birdsong, in the English air.

Returning to the founding tales of Robin and Arthur, we can see the first stirrings of another English characteristic: manners. Two legends, both deeply rooted in the English landscape and drawing strength from it, produced chivalrous fruit. Arthur remains a byword for courtesy – his Round Table is a fantasia of civility. And while Robin may be up for a scrap, he is always loyal to the true King and happy to share a haunch of venison with a passer-by. He is even charming to his enemies.

As we have seen, neither of these fables was an accurate depiction of the early Middle Ages. So it should be stressed that the manners they espouse were superimposed on medieval life, not inspired by it. On the whole, people did not have the time to right a wrong or help a neighbour – they were too busy ducking witches, burning heretics and hanging thieves. In Robin's case the contrast is extreme. Medieval outlaws were a genuine menace – England's woods were full of poachers, few of them friendly – yet Robin is invariably polite, merrily tweaking the noses of the rich as he tosses their purses to the poor. He is also as honest as an oak tree.

Real-life knights were rarely perfect or gentle, either. Nor was the culture of courtesy in Arthurian legend native – troubadours imported the tales from France (the land of the chevaliers). But England was highly receptive to the notion. The tales of Lancelot, Gawain and Guinevere are saturated in the values of courtly love, in particular the novel idea that women should be treated with respect. In the fairytale world of courtly love, knights swore 'always to do ladies, damosels, and gentlewomen and widows succour; strengthen them in their rights, and never to enforce them, upon pain of death'.

This oath is one of Camelot's founding principles, and the knights are always mindful of it. And while it is hardly a realistic description of Arthurian gender politics, the fact that the idea of chivalry appealed to England as a concept is significant in itself. In contrast to the giant-slayers of the epic tradition (Beowulf and St George), Arthur did at least dedicate himself to noble causes.

Even this is not the most important implication of the Arthur and Robin stories. Their most powerful quality is the sense they transmit of a golden age as a lost paradise back at the beginning of England's story. Is anything more English than that? In the land of sheep, wheat, coal and iron, utopia was always in the past.

We have strayed some distance from the central proposition – that England's landscape shaped the nation's cultural character. But it is not landscape alone that performs this task. There is another essential ingredient: time. The depth of history embedded in England's hills and fields is what fertilised the soil in which civilised society developed. This is why a walk in an English field is also an exploration of the nation's background. The rural heritage is so rich that whenever we enter the countryside we are also travelling back in time.

Such journeys are also exercises in self-knowledge, because when we journey back in time we are also returning home. This is why literary nostalgia is not superficial. There is more to it than the simple sense that our best days are behind us. 'Nostalgia' is derived from the Greek for homesickness: it is the ache we feel to return to the place from which we came.

Of course, this notion of the past as a psychological hinterland is not unique to England. It has been one of the guiding myths of European culture since Odysseus went the long way home, or the writers of the Christian Gospels dreamed of returning to paradise. A thousand stories have been powered by that primal idea.

The same impulse lies behind the deeply-rooted English preoccupation with family trees.

Unsurprisingly, since the idea of returning home figures so prominently in our dreams, it also infests our daily conversation. We send happy returns on birthdays, believe that east, west, home's best, that there's no place like home, that we must keep the home fires burning (while our hearts are yearning) and that we should always cherish home thoughts from abroad. Moreover, chickens come home to roost and charity begins at home, which is also where the heart is. There is more to this than mere whimsy: all of these phrases betray the common belief that the past explains the present.

It may also connect to the Darwinian urge to pin down the origins of everything. And though it often seems that an interest in the past is escapist, it meshes with the widespread desire to cling on to the intensities of childhood – a time when the world seemed full of magic.

This is why nature is a muse. It is the place where our memories reside, the cradle in which we grew. In early times, when religious feelings ran strong, the unfathomable oceans, wild mountains and dark forests were unsettling rather than inspiring. They seemed godless and indifferent, and filled the devout with anxiety or dread: they were the lairs of dragons and trolls. Today, we feel the opposite: nature seems grand. The dragons have fled; and far from toying with us, the sea and the sky provide numinous glimpses of the eternal. Ever since the Romantic poets taught us to see it as sublime, we have been nature's willing disciples.

Not that we see it very often any more.

Twenty-two

We Shape our Houses

On Christmas Eve 1918, with the Great War over but half the army still in uniform, the Dean of King's College, Cambridge (the great monument to choristers founded by Henry VI in the age of monks and sheep) prepared to deliver a new order of service. His name was Eric Milner-White[1] and he had based the service on one held at Truro in 1888, when the intention was to tempt men away from the public house. He called it 'Nine Lessons and Carols' and wrote a bidding prayer that urged the festive congregation to spare a thought for fellow-worshippers 'on another shore'. He did not have to add any details; everyone knew he was referring primarily to the men who were still stuck in Flanders. A century later, that phrase has acquired a larger metaphorical sense: it now invokes all overseas personnel.

The following year, the running order was changed so that it began with 'Once in Royal David's City' and a powerful new tradition was born. Ever since – especially after the BBC began broadcasting the service in 1928 – the sound of a solitary treble voice floating up to the vaults of the lordly chapel has been an evocative emblem of English culture around the world: from Barbados and Bangladesh to Fiji and Zambia.

It remains a much-loved part of the national schedule, and

---

1 A graduate of the college, Milner-White had served as chaplain to the 7th Infantry Division on the Western Front.

feels timeless as it connects even faithless refugees from the festive shopping binge with England's earliest traditions. It strikes such a solemn note, rising above Cambridge's gracious lawns and pinnacles like a messenger from the age of bells and candles, that few think of it as a twentieth-century composition.

This is just one of many 'ancient' traditions that are more modern than we think. The Harvest Festival, which feels medieval, dates back only to the 1840s; decorated Christmas trees arrived in England only in the 1850s, courtesy of the Prince Consort; and many classic carols are Victorian, too. The King's College choir *is* a venerable institution, of course: in 1918 it included sixteen treble voices, as stipulated in the original statutes. But the people who gather around their televisions and radios to listen to the service today – some perhaps moved by the thought that it has remained unchanged for centuries – are actually hearing something relatively new.

The Christmas celebration of 1918 was inevitably solemn – it was no ordinary year – but in one way was paradoxical. For the prevailing spirit of the age lay not in an antique, medieval hush, but in the brash hiss of railways, factories, cities, slums, smoke, steam and smog. England was the humming imperial capital of the world, and modern science had already chipped away at traditional articles of faith. And yet, at the height of this progressive ardour, England could not help but glance back to its long-lost past – to the world of swords and prayerbooks, shepherds and weavers, when men were knights and damsels were dainty and God was in His Heaven and all was right with the world.

There could hardly have been a clearer sign that England's heart lay in the Middle Ages. In the age of Ypres, it seemed a time of peace.

England's enthusiasm for the medieval was best seen in the most public of the arts: architecture. And nowhere was it more forthrightly expressed than in the palatial seat of government at Westminster. But in the middle of the night, on 16 October

1834, a plume of smoke drifted through the floorboards of this proud palace. Workmen had been incinerating tally sticks – the wooden tokens used to keep score in the Exchequer – in stoves beneath the House of Lords. Then the stoves overheated, and the whole place went up.

There had been several such alarms in the past (in 1263, 1298 and most notably 1512 – when Henry VIII moved to Whitehall) as well as a few recent warnings that the building was unsafe. But no one imagined a conflagration like this. Before long, the palace was a ball of flames.

It was an extraordinary spectacle – a bonfire party for the whole of London. Half the luminaries of Victorian England witnessed it: Dickens, Carlyle, Palmerston, the Duke of Wellington. Even the young Princess Victoria could see the flames from her window twenty miles away, in Windsor. Constable and Turner grabbed their notebooks and hurried out to sketch the catastrophe.

After some hesitation, it was decided to hold a competition to design a replacement building. The Royal Commission swiftly determined that the winner would be in the Gothic style. Ostensibly, this was so the new building would blend harmoniously with Westminster Abbey, but there was more to it than that. The classical idiom, with its Italian Palladian flourishes, had been the favoured style ever since Christopher Wren's rebuilding of London's churches – most notably St Paul's – in the seventeenth century. By 1807, when Lord Elgin imported his Athenian marbles, the Parthenon's influence was evident all over London – especially in Admiralty Arch, the Royal Exchange, the National Gallery, the British Museum and Buckingham Palace.

Gothic, to many of the people who counted, was a derogatory term – a byword for oafish clumsiness.

The Commission, however, considered the Graeco-Roman aesthetic too pagan for Christian Britain's Parliament. The members wanted something more austere ... and less foreign.

The fact that Washington had recently dressed itself in classical white marble reinforced the feeling that the Roman style was not quite the thing.

The ninety-seven entries were assigned numbers and judged anonymously. Four made the shortlist; the winner was number 64. The architect turned out to be a local man, Charles Barry. Born within spitting distance of the proposed palace, he was keen to emulate the Tudor tracery of the Henry VII Chapel in the abbey. He had seen the wonders of Greece and Rome, and indeed had designed the Travellers' Club in Pall Mall on classical lines, but he preferred the domes of Constantinople and the cathedrals of France. And he was already well versed in the Gothic style, having used it for several churches in Lancashire.[2]

So far as the judges were concerned, he was singing from the right hymn sheet.

Barry's enthusiasm for the project was shared by his friend Augustus Pugin, a French-descended designer invited to help with the interior décor. The pair had already worked together on the King Edward VI Grammar School in Birmingham, and Pugin had been drawing Gothic churches since the age of nine. A confirmed believer in *anciens régimes* (his father was a refugee from the French Revolution), he had a fierce faith in the medieval style. He dismissed even St Paul's as 'revived pagan' and did not mourn when Westminster went up in flames. The old palace, he thought, was full of architectural 'heresies'. 'There is nothing to regret,' he wrote, 'and much to rejoice in.'

In the year of the conflagration he was working on a book – *Contrasts* (published in 1835) – which compared modern buildings unfavourably with their fifteenth-century forebears and advocated 'a return to the faith and the social structures of the Middle Ages'. In time, he would be more precise, dating the birth of the 'perfect' English style to the thirteenth century. His ideal building was an 'English parish church of the

2 Barry went on to design Highclere in Hampshire, the 'medieval' setting for *Downton Abbey*.

time of Edward I' – the period when Peter Corbet was hunting England's last few wolves, the Cistercians were tending sheep in Yorkshire and Newcastle was starting to ship coal.

The new Palace of Westminster was not completed until 1870, which gave Pugin plenty of time for other projects, such as the medieval court for Prince Albert's Great Exhibition in 1851.[3] By the standards of the old cathedral builders this was fast, but it still meant that his work at Westminster could be thorough. He left his signature all over the building – in the tiles, wallpaper, benches, chairs, candelabra, stained glass, railings, ceilings and bookcases . . . No detail was too small.

When a curtain trembled, it was as if the Lady of Shalott might swish through.

Pugin even invented the House of Commons' motif – the crowned portcullis that adorns its pencils, mugs, chairs and stationery to this day. The image is redolent of medieval fortresses and was intended to suggest ancient strength. But it was a Victorian design, to show that this was a legislative 'castle'. It was the emblem on a form.[4]

The telling point was that, in seeking an architecture to project imperial pride, the judges turned to the idiom of medieval England. If they had wanted to make the Scottish, Welsh and Irish Members feel ill at ease, they could hardly have done better. Under English leadership, Britain at this time was approaching the height of its domineering swagger: Darwin was aboard the *Beagle*; Faraday was writing up his electrical experiments; Morse was patenting the telegraph; gigantic mills were cranking out half the world's cloth; new trains were roaring through tunnels and into burgeoning cities; iron was pouring out of foundries; Parliament was being reformed;

3 Queen Victoria described the day it opened, 1 May, as 'the happiest, proudest day of my life'. An estimated six million visitors filed through the great Crystal Palace in Hyde Park in just six months.

4 It soon embedded itself in the national consciousness. The English cricket team and the Football Association both used it in their crests.

rotten boroughs and slavery were being abolished. But though it was a joint project, the 'Mother of Parliaments' chose to dress herself in the costume of bygone days.

Was it conservative of England to be so smitten with medieval imagery? Perhaps. But in another way it was logical. Victorian England was a powerhouse, but the pace of change was traumatic. It made sense to reach out for a comfort blanket.

The Palace of Westminster was not a one-off. The same impulse drove thousands of similar projects across the country. Nearly all of England's churches were ancient – dating from the sixteenth century and before – and the majority were in villages. But if the fortunes sheared from sheep financed the first great wave of church building, the coal-iron wealth of Victorian England subsidised the second. Almost four thousand new religious houses were built in the nineteenth century, most of them in the Gothic accent, with pointed arches and steepling spires. A soaring hint of Northamptonshire landed even in the slums of Lancashire.

Since the original churches had a ruined, melancholy air, it seemed only right that the new ones should, too. They were intended to symbolise the Empire, after all, so they were given the full and graceful depth of England's knightly past. Indirectly, the elemental forces – rain, grass and sheep – that generated the original built fabric now re-emerged as a defining expression of the nation's ancient character.

The Victorian fondness for Gothic gives us another glimpse of England's divided personality. The rivalrous nature of the country's politics – Whig versus Tory, Labour versus Conservative – is only one manifestation of the nation's either/or tendency. Other nations accommodate many voices and conduct their politics through many parties. England, impatient with such nuances, prefers a stark, polar opposition: yes/no, rich/poor, private/public, north/south, in/out. In the nineteenth century there was a resounding clash between the urge to look to the future, and

the desire to look to the past. Victorian England, with its surging industrial leaps, certainly had its eye fixed forwards; but its
architecture, perhaps to compensate, looked the other way. The
roar of its factories generated an equal and opposite ache for the
consolations of yesteryear.

The Middle Ages, went the thinking, with all its cruelties
conveniently forgotten, was the period when England had been
most truly itself. That is when this God-fearing, honour-loving
island had enjoyed its finest hour.

In fact, the medieval flame had never truly died. The Grand
Tour may have inspired a new reverence for classical forms
among the upper echelons of English society, but Gothic ideas
continued to flourish in their shade, even in the predominantly
neo-classical eighteenth century. In Blackheath, John Vanbrugh
created a fortified monster that was more like a twelfth-century
castle than a villa. Nicholas Hawksmoor followed suit when
designing his church turrets. And in 1764 Horace Walpole published what is usually deemed the world's first Gothic novel,
The Castle of Otranto, before going on to build a decidedly
'medieval' pleasure house in Twickenham: Strawberry Hill.

It was Arthurian chateau meets iced wedding cake. The white
battlements, pinnacles, vaults, tombs and chimneys brought to
mind the good old days, while the interior looked like the work
of someone who had rifled through Guinevere's dress-up box.
Walpole called it 'a little Gothick castle' and it attracted some
notable admirers, even though it was a touch too dandyish to be
placed alongside genuine Gothic. It now seems the work of an
eccentric – a shard of mad King Ludwig in the Thames Valley.

An even grander pile sprang up in Wiltshire countryside
1813, when William Beckford used the fortune from his father's
slave plantations in the West Indies to build a gigantic new
palace on the site of the ruined Fonthill Abbey. The entrance
hall alone was a cross between Windsor and Chartres; the
tower soared above the trees; and the door into the octagonal

main hall was thirty-five feet high. It was decorated in silver, purple and red, but unlike the ancient buildings on which it was modelled, not built to last. When the tower collapsed (for the third time) in 1925, the rest soon followed.

Both of these enterprises were aristocratic follies, but they were the forerunners of an energetic flowering. In 1818 Mary Shelley's *Frankenstein* struck a nerve thanks to its moral – science tempts humanity to create monsters – but also to its bat-haunted setting. The combination resonated with an audience that was already groaning beneath the twin burdens of rationality and the profit motive. The medieval atmosphere was frightening but also reassuring. It gave rise not just to an architectural movement but to a flowering of old-fashioned arts and crafts.

First, there was renewed interest in the antiquated field of stained glass. In 1811 a London plumber named Thomas Willement made a coloured window in the old way – by mounting tinted glass in a frame, like pieces in a jigsaw puzzle, rather than painting images directly on to a glazed panel. At any other time, in any other place, he might have been dismissed as a batty conservationist, but in Regency England he inspired an industry. The new churches needed windows – the more medieval, the better.

Willement went on to become the official 'artist in stained glass' to Queen Victoria.

Much of England's finest glass had been destroyed by Henry VIII, but now it was replaced: Lincoln Cathedral's east window was one of many to be restored in the nineteenth century. Just one workshop, William Kempe's in London, made four thousand new windows.

Barry and Pugin's Palace of Westminster gave official backing to this trend. It identified the Gothic style as grand yet earthy – honest, rough-hewn, patriotic and, as Pugin put it, 'true Christian'. In a word, English. The industrial towns and cities were given a chivalrous makeover, involving arches, turrets, ribbed vaults, pitched roofs, glowing imagery and hooded gables that resembled cowled monks.

It suggested – did it not? – that there was something divinely ordained about the old place, even with the chimneys and foundries belching soot over everything.

This is supposed to be an English story, but it is impossible to keep Scotland out of it. After all, it was a man from the Borders, Sir Walter Scott, who did more than anyone else to popularise the mood music of the Middle Ages in *Ivanhoe* (set in Newark) and *Lay of the Last Minstrel*. And few were as sold on such things as the 13th Earl of Eglinton – Archibald William Montgomery. In 1839, captivated by the drama and pageantry of the fourteenth century, he decided to host a three-day joust at his faux-medieval castle in Ayrshire.

Forty knights of various realms agreed to take part, commissioned new suits of armour (the surviving heirlooms were too tight for Victorian physique) and conducted an elaborate rehearsal in London's Regent's Park. Practice went perfect. Pennants fluttered in the breeze. But the event itself was a disaster. Maybe a hundred thousand people (in colourful raiment) beat a path to the estate – but the weather was grim. It took hours for the crowd to slog through the mud, and even longer for the knights and their entourages to stage the opening ceremony.

At which point the heavens gaped and it rained, quite literally, on Eglinton's parade. The tents flooded so badly that the banquet had to be cancelled.

We can hardly call it a farce, because in truth it was little more than a large-scale fancy-dress party in the first place. But Eglinton did invite some ridicule by commissioning an oil painting of himself astride a mighty charger, clad in golden armour, all tossing plumes and chivalrous glamour, as if he were the reincarnation of Sir Galahad himself.

The fact that Eglinton and others felt an urge to re-create

medieval England in the age of steam shows how power-ful was the aesthetic appeal of that first stir. The England of Edward I – a realm that sent knights out in search of wolves and glorified itself with majestic cathedrals – was a vision that glowed even in the heather-clad hills north of the Tweed. In an era of violent upheaval and mind-boggling change, it held out the promise that the centre could hold; that the spinning forces of the new world could be kept in check.

In the same year as Eglinton's rained-off tournament, 1839, a group of precocious students founded an architecture club to promote the Gothic style. The Cambridge Camden Society – named after the sixteenth-century traveller William Camden – soon boasted seven hundred members, includ-ing bishops and Members of Parliament. It was aligned with the Catholic revival in England[5] and looked to restore 'high' ceremony to the Anglican Church. In 1841 the Society urged architects to imitate the style of medieval England; and, as we have seen, they listened. It was a good time to be a church builder: new buildings were appearing across England at a rate of a hundred per year, and most of them were neo-Gothic.

This movement enjoyed high-level intellectual backing from one of the leading opinion-formers of the day: John Ruskin. In *The Seven Lamps of Architecture* (1849) he explained why 'north-ern Gothic of the 13th century' was 'the only proper style' for new work. He had in mind Lincoln and Wells, Chartres and Amiens, and he expanded on this in *The Stones of Venice* (1853), suggesting that Gothic architecture did not *resemble* nature; it *was* nature. Its excrescences and asymmetries were organic responses to the landscape itself. In a famous flight

---

5 The Catholic Emancipation Act of 1828 completed the liberation of Britain's Roman Catholics by lifting the restrictions that had barred them from Parliament and high positions in the law and the civil service. When Pugin became a Catholic seven years later, it was a natural extension of his enthusiasm for pre-Reformation architecture. It was also a shrewd career move, as he was invited to design dozens of churches in Ireland and Australia. It did, however, lead Ruskin, most ungratefully, to denounce him as a minor figure.

of fancy he imagined himself as a bird, flying north from the Mediterranean, inspecting and absorbing the changes in climate, terrain, flora, fauna and, most notably, the monumental labours of man:

> Let us watch with reverence as he ... smooths with soft sculpture the jasper pillars that are to reflect a ceaseless sunshine and rise into a cloudless sky: but not with less reverence let us stand by him when, with rough strength and hurried stroke, he smites an uncouth animation out of the rocks he has torn from among the moss of the moorland, and heaves into the darkened air a pile of iron buttress and rugged wall, instinct with a work of an imagination as wild and wayward as the northern sea; creatures of ungainly shape and rigid limb, but full of wolfish life; fierce as the winds that beat, changeful as the clouds that shake them.

Modern readers may be struck by the sheer emotional temperature of Ruskin's rhetoric. He was never slow to feel heat under his collar, so this was not unusual. But by emphasising the natural (geographical and geological) origins of Gothic buildings he was tacitly objecting to classical architecture, which aped the patterns of Greece and Rome to promote an anachronistic vision of elegant restraint.

Either way, he and his disciples were fervent promoters of the Gothic mood. It had certain practical advantages – the pointed arch was an excellent load-bearing device, allowing architects to design on the grandest scale. But more important, it represented a world based on faith rather than science, stability rather than progress. Darwin may have cracked the intellectual foundations of the Christian story, but that merely inspired some people to cling even harder to their old convictions. Ruskin's guiding lights (or 'lamps') were ethical rather than visual qualities – obedience, sacrifice, truth – so he saw

Gothic as a moral force. It dignified the labourer by letting him sculpt stone as if he were an independent artist. And its rough-hewn quality was political, implying respect for humble craft. This may have been fanciful – it certainly overlooked the extent to which medieval craftsmen struggled to ward off starvation. But we can see what he meant.

When Ruskin described industrial progress as a 'plague cloud', he insisted that this was no metaphor, but a meteorological fact. He included detailed drawings of cloud formations as evidence. The plague cloud was a 'dense manufacturing mist . . . a dry black veil which no ray of sunshine can pierce'. And it was 'made of dead men's souls'.

Again, the vehemence of his language sent his words ringing across England like a peal of bells. The more urban, industrial and modern England became, the more it enjoyed dreaming of former glories. Thomas Carlyle (who was much influenced by both Ruskin and Dickens – *Hard Times* was dedicated to him) begged England to return to 'the noble spirit of the Middle Ages'. Robert Browning took him at his word. His mighty poem *The Ring and the Book* was described as 'essentially Gothic' by Henry James, and Tennyson's *Idylls of the King*, an Arthurian epic, rose up in England's midst like a great cathedral. He averted his eyes from the contemporary scene, with its smoking chimneys and roaring engines.

It is ironic that England should have had such mixed feelings about its industrial heritage. Indeed, no other country in the world has quite so much of it, and any reckoning of what it is to be English must place the clanging memories of coal and steam – with its iron and steel, ships and trains, looms and canals, factories and slums, bridges and parks – high on the list of characteristic things. It may be that we take this for granted. Not everyone who goes to London's Round House knows that it was once a locomotive shed for the London and Birmingham Railway. And while most visitors to the Tate Modern glimpse the brutish power station behind the avant-garde art, few who hurry past Rotherham on the motorway pause to imagine what lies beneath: one of the most elaborate labyrinths of coal shafts in the world.[6]

Nor do we often notice the traces of Victorian industry at our feet. But our towns and cities are studded with iron remnants of the past – grilles, covers and plates over our drains, watercourses, telegraph cables, gas pipes and coal holes. These signed works of industrial artistry are inscribed with the names of the foundries that made them: in London alone we walk on Hayward Bros in Southwark, J. W. Carpenter in Earl's Court, Nettleton & Co. in Sloane Square and Pike & Co. in Pimlico. Some are plain; others are beautifully decorated with chevrons, grids, even the occasional *fleur-de-lis*. Wander across the lawns outside Westminster Abbey and you might spot one made by the sanitary engineer immortalised in our daily slang: T. Crapper of Chelsea.[7]

England is not alone in having a long industrial history. What marks it out as unusual is the fact that this coexisted with a deep urge to return to the medieval world. It is the combination that gives Englishness its unique flavour: the constant *pas-de-deux* of old and new, past and present, shire and factory.

Pugin and Ruskin inspired many other artists, most notably the Arts and Crafts disciples of William Morris and the pre-Raphaelite 'Brotherhood' – Edward Burne-Jones, William Holman Hunt, John Everett Millais and Dante Gabriel Rossetti. All sought to revive the medieval spirit, both in their paintings and in the domestic sphere: wallpaper, drapery, furniture, books, tapestries ... everything. The boom in church building

6 The miners at Manvers Colliery excavated a 3000-acre coalfield down to a depth of 648 yards. There was also a brick factory, a power station, a gas plant, coke ovens, railway sidings, smoking chimneys and slag heaps. In its heyday the place stank of soot and sulphur. It closed in 1988, and the area is now home to a business park.

7 In 2015 Jeremy Corbyn, the leader of the opposition, startled a television interviewer by confessing to an enthusiasm for these relics. His passion is shared by thieves, who pinch several hundred each year, motivated by the fact that collectors of vintage ironwork are willing to pay a hundred pounds or more for a good one.

led to a boom in associated trades: new workshops opened up to make thousands of altar rails, lecterns, kneelers, candelabra and polished oak pews. All of these items became part of the everyday texture of English life.

None of this is as contradictory as it seems. The enthusiasm for medieval values was not a counterpoise to the thunderous arrival of powerful machines in English life; it was *produced* by them. The Gothic revival was not the enemy of industry, but its child.

William Morris, the leader of this backward-looking army, called Ruskin's tract on Gothic architecture 'one of the very few necessary and inevitable utterances of the century'. And it was Morris, more than anyone else, who extended the same impulse to all aspects of interior design, giving hand-made craft the status of high art in the process. A keen dyer and silk weaver, he experimented with hand-knotted carpets and established a firm in Merton that employed a hundred crafts-men. Nine years later, in *News from Nowhere* (1890), he gave medievalism a political dimension by presenting Camelot as a socialist paradise – a world in which modernity receded into a cottage realm with no cities, no prisons, no machines, no gov-ernment and no class tension.

The Victorian medievalists stuck together, becoming that most English institution – a club. Morris and Burne-Jones had been friends at Oxford, admired the same paintings and were spellbound by the same book – *Morte d'Arthur* – which the Poet Laureate, Tennyson, recast as *Idylls of the King*.

The egalitarian purpose of Morris's enterprise meant that it was not a conservative project. But it was anti-progress on the technical level; and in 1877 he founded the Society for the Protection of Ancient Buildings, a forerunner of both the National Trust and English Heritage. Taking its lead from Ruskin (inevitably), the Society campaigned for the *preservation* of historic monuments, rather than their restoration, which it viewed as a form of tampering. This distinction continues to divide people today: some hope to revive heritage on original lines, while others prefer their ruins to stay ruined.

In Morris's hands the Gothic revival became a back-to-nature movement as much as an architectural style. It encouraged naturalists such as Richard Jefferies, who loved to vent his disgust at the ruinous impact of industrial life on England's ancient traditions. In *After London* (1885) he could hardly disguise his glee at the thought of nature conquering the urban landscape, drowning human 'civilisation' with bramble and briar, moss and fern: 'By the thirtieth year, there was not one single open place, the hills only excepted, where a man could walk, unless he followed the tracks of wild creatures or cut himself a path.' The passages describing London as a poisonous swamp are almost euphoric.

In their way, those stern, bearded Victorian moralists were also New Age hipsters.

At the end of his life, Morris published Ruskin's classic essay 'The Nature of Gothic' in a lavish new edition. This was method publishing: it took the argument of the text literally by using Gothic lettering and mimicking the look of an illuminated manuscript. It was, Morris seemed to be saying, what Caxton would have wanted.

There is plenty of truth in the charge that the Victorian love of Gothic was a nostalgic reaction against progress. And this was not the only way in which a modernising nation turned to the past. While Ruskin, Morris and Pugin hailed the beauty of the medieval world, Arnold, Browning and Pater were making an equally ardent case for the glories of Greece and Rome. Egyptian and Japanese forms had their admirers, too. But Gothic always retained the upper hand.[8] It was even visible in the latest technology, through the pioneering work

8 The taste endures to this day. In 2013, when the Tate Gallery conducted a poll to rank the nation's favourite paintings, the top two were Pre-Raphaelite: *The Lady of Shalott* by John William Waterhouse and *Ophelia* by John Everett Millais.

of the photographer Julia Margaret Cameron: she favoured Arthurian themes, and loved to dress her great friend Tennyson in Druidic robes.

It is in public design, however, that its most lasting impact was made. Thousands of Victorian buildings have medieval accents. Schools, universities, town halls, law courts, memorials, shops, private houses, banks, even pubs ... the new world wore Gothic make-up. Kenneth Clark later declared that industry 'changed the face of England' and while this was true, that face was often an antiquated one. When a new warehouse appeared at Coalbrookdale in 1840, it was done in the best Pugin-Gothic taste.[9] It wasn't only an Englishman's home that was his castle: his coal mine, his ticket office and his ironworks were fortresses, too.

It would take a very long time to list all of the notable buildings in the Gothic revival style, but here are some: the Martyrs' Memorial in Oxford (1841), the Scott Monument in Edinburgh (1844), the Crimea Memorial at Westminster Abbey (1858), the Pitt Rivers Museum of Natural History in Oxford (1861), Keble College, Oxford (1870), Charterhouse School (1872), the Albert Memorial (1876), St Pancras Station and the Midland Hotel (1876), London's Natural History Museum (1880), the Royal Courts of Justice (1882), the Oval Pavilion (1898), the Birmingham Law Courts (1891), Tower Bridge (1894) and the John Rylands Library in Manchester (1900). We could add innumerable wells, niches, gravestones, gates, porches and fonts to the roll-call.

It is not hard to understand why cultural institutions wanted an oak-aged gloss. But the Gothic impulse also clothed the pillars of industrial wealth. Far from celebrating their thrilling modernity, England dressed them as cathedrals. Bradford's Town Hall and Wool Exchange, the imposing civic buildings of Barrow-in-Furness, Manchester and Middlesbrough, most

9 It is now the Ironbridge Museum.

of the great railway stations, even new dams and water towers were given the full Arthurian treatment.

It was an extraordinary union of past and future things. Manchester's town hall, designed by Alfred Waterhouse, was conceived 'in the style of the thirteenth century suffused with the feeling and spirit of the present time'. When he visited, De Tocqueville described the city as 'a medieval town with the marvels of the nineteenth century in it'.

The Gothic style was global, spreading Englishness across the Empire like a flame. Adelaide, Calcutta, Shanghai, Melbourne, Bombay, Sydney and many other cities acquired civic buildings that reflected the backward-looking mood of a country thousands of miles away. It certainly made life easier for the colonial administrators. They did not need to close their eyes to think of England, wherever they were, because even in the midday sun it looked astonishingly like home.

Fresh from turning the clock back in the seat of government, Pugin set about doing the same for Alton Towers, Staffordshire, home of the 16th Earl of Shrewsbury. The estate's modest hunting lodge was transformed into a full-blown Gothic 'abbey': Pugin gave it an entrance hall, a banqueting chamber and a conservatory, then engaged Thomas Willement to create new – but old-looking – stained glass for the refurbished chapel.

He also lavished attention on the most prominent medieval feature of all: the moat. The Norman castle that once stood on this spot had needed a moat for defensive purposes, but by Victorian times it was a purely decorative feature. The river, lake and water gardens were added to give the appearance of fortified prowess.

England is rich in such moats – all of them picturesque. This is another way in which the architectural language of the Age of Wool threads into the present day. At Stokesay, Shropshire, where Laurence of Ludlow turned wool into wealth, at Little Moreton Hall, Cheshire, Birtsmorton Court, near Malvern, Baddesley Clinton, Warwickshire, Oxburgh in Norfolk,

Broughton in Oxfordshire, Kentwell in Long Melford, Lower Brockhampton in Herefordshire and Tattershall Castle in Lincolnshire ... in all these lavish homes, and many others, the pattern is repeated: a stone manor in a loop of ornamental water, on land that never saw hint of a siege.

Moats are wet-weather accessories, so they are delivered by England's climate (hotter lands tend to look to the hills for their security needs). As such, they are echoed in miniature by the ponds, rills, fountains and other water features that bubble away in England's suburban back gardens. Even these toy with an old and distinguished emotion. In his famous 'Sceptr'd Isle' speech, Shakespeare's John of Gaunt makes a point of comparing England to a castle of this sort, aloof and indomitable in its ring of bright water:

> *This fortress built by nature for herself . . .*
> *This precious stone set in a silver sea*
> *Which serves it in the office of a wall*
> *Or as a moat defensive to a house,*
> *Against the envy of less happier lands,*
> *This blessed plot, this earth, this realm, this England.*[10]

John Donne swore that no man was an island, but the idea that an Englishman's home is his castle has always been stronger ... and the English have gone to a lot of trouble to re-create the nation's island setting in their domestic landscapes.

This remains true, as does our fascination with the Gothic. The technological miracles of modern times have triggered a new hunger for medieval atmospherics. Just as Victorian England turned to the Gothic for its images of nature and faith in a period when both were under siege, so now – in Harry

10 This is usually quoted as a piece of patriotic bombast, but in fact it is the over-blown prelude to a sorrowful complaint (John of Gaunt is something of a windbag). Eventually he gets to his point, which is that England is a sinking ship – 'like to a tenement or a pelting farm ... bound in with shame'.

Potter, *The Lord of the Rings*, *Game of Thrones* and other fantasies of swords, sorcery and vampires – there is an urge to flee modern life and escape into a world of strong-blooded magic.

Ironically, for we pride ourselves on our superiority to those stiff Victorian patriarchs, we remain in thrall to very much the same ideas that melted nineteenth-century hearts. The next generation of England's elite continues to absorb – in the cloisters of Eton, Westminster, Oxford and Cambridge – the old monastic reflexes, which seep through the quadrangles, while younger children are drip-fed the spirit of medieval England in books, films and games about knights and wizards.

Rarely do they hear it so clearly as when, in the glimmering heart of the bleak midwinter, a candlelit child sings 'Once in Royal David's City' beneath a vault of old stones.

In our dreams, large, irrational parts of us still prefer faith to reason. It makes sense that Alton Towers is now a fun park operated by Merlin Entertainments.

Twenty-three

Herbaceous Borders

According to the usual geographical rules, England's most northerly town – Berwick-on-Tweed – should stand on the south bank of its river, not to the north. It is hard to imagine a more Scottish waterway. Everything about the Tweed smacks of salmon fishing, castles, shortbread, golf, whisky and the cloth from which those famous caps and suits are made – ideal for grouse moors and deer stalking. Berwick is *obviously* a Scottish town.

Once Scotland's second city, a pillar of North Sea trade, it retains a Caledonian flavour. A Saltire hangs proudly from the Bank of Scotland (and also from the Lebanese restaurant – 'Berwick's only'); the local accent makes Geordie seem southern; and the regimental band marching down Castlegate has bagpipes. The air tingles with sea fret and heather; the football and rugby teams both play in Scottish leagues; and it has all the smells and sounds of a Scottish harbour: the fresh chill in the air, the clouds of gnats, the clamorous seagulls squawking over kippers.

So how come Berwick is in England?

Even geography moves in inscrutable ways, and it is clear as soon as one arrives why the town is on the wrong side of the water – connected to England by a tall Victorian viaduct. It stands on a stony mound in a dramatic loop of the river – a near-impregnable defensive position. And, given its long history as a frontier post between two quarrelsome neighbours, that was its role. Medieval England, the wealthy wool producer, feared land invasion from only two quarters – the west and the north. So that was where it built its ramparts and castles.

The ancient gun emplacements give the town the air of a stout military garrison. They are a Tudor upgrade of the medieval walls, and are still a forbidding presence. It could hardly be otherwise, because this is a lonely outcrop. It is closer to Edinburgh than it is to Newcastle, and is even north of obviously Scottish landmarks such as Ayr, Dumfries, Hawick, Melrose, Kilmarnock and Troon.

Berwick has changed hands at least thirteen times in its history. Its contested status between England and Scotland damaged its development as a harbour, but it remained an important bridging point on the river – a customs post and administrative centre. And in 1707, thanks to the Act of Union, it became something new: British.

This is one of history's more inspiring stories – two enemies agreeing to merge as a united kingdom – but in recent years the ties have been fraying. In many minds, Berwick is a trophy of English imperialism that should be returned to its rightful owners at once, if not sooner.

Either way, it is a good place to sit upon the (damp) grass and wonder what it means to be English in the modern world. It was clear during the Scottish referendum that Scotland was energetically exploring what kind of country it wished to be. Perhaps England should do the same.

But around what might it cohere? Not race or religion – too late for either of those. And not the English language – half the world can claim that. Fair play? Tricky, given its history of workhouses and slavery. Moderation? From the people who led the scramble for Africa and sent children up fiery chimneys?

Liberty? Equality? Fraternity? Someone else has them.

Berwick itself hardly knows where to stand. A quarter of

the town sees itself as Scottish, another quarter as English. The remaining half claims to be both ... or neither. These are people of the Borders. Some of them cross the so-called frontier several times a day – to visit relatives, buy a pint of milk or walk the dog. Everyone knows that joining Scotland might trigger extra public spending (up to a thousand pounds per person, on average), and can see that Berwick does not figure much in the calculations of Westminster. But there is a lot of Englishness in Berwick, too. The military fortifications are of a piece with the Citadel at Plymouth, linking this northern outpost to a different war, a different time. And many of the buildings share the architectural style of the wool heartlands down south. Glance out of the old Queen's Head Hotel and you can see the golden stone and white windows of what used to be the corn exchange and the municipal baths. You could be in Cheltenham or Bath.

The air of shopworn grandeur also seems noticeably English: Berwick is a town awash with former glories. This grave ambience inspired L. S. Lowry to make frequent visits: 'I am attracted to decay,' he said. 'A derelict house gets me.' One house in particular captured his attention – a tall but dilapidated husk that stood in haughty splendour on the northern rampart, staring at the North Sea. He toyed with the idea of buying it, but in the end merely included it in a painting – *The Island*. He made it look like a beached ship in a desolate ocean of industrial ash and rubble. Now in the Manchester Museum, the blasted winterscape looks exactly like the Salford scenery Lowry painted so often. But this was a purely imaginary voyage: the house poses against a backdrop of shattered telegraph poles and smoking chimneys, a blighted outpost in a grey pit of wrecked boats.

It is a stereotype of industrial England, in other words.

In 1502 Berwick was declared to be *of* but not *in* England – a semi-independent city state along the lines of medieval Calais. In this diplomatic form it was a member of the alliance that fought the Crimean War, but nobody thought to add the town's name to the 1856 peace treaty. In theory, Berwick-on-Tweed is still at war with Russia.[1]

It goes without saying that Englishness is not uniform. No one could hold in their mind's eye images of the Yorkshire Dales, a Tower Hamlets housing estate, Dartmoor, Felixstowe, the suburbs of Leicester, Ullswater and Gatwick Airport without knowing that to be an incoherent notion. Windermere is nothing like Stevenage; Widnes would look decidedly out of place on the South Downs; you *can* tell the difference between Constable country and Wolverhampton. There may once have been a look, an air, an imperious glance that suggested Englishness, but this became intertwined with Britishness so long ago that it is now hard to disentangle it. And then it lost confidence altogether.

But we cannot content ourselves merely with the idea that Englishness is diverse, since there are bonds of nature, climate, language, culture, commerce, art, religion, industry and politics that have produced something very like a unified whole. Not all of this is endearing. Berwick has the same cloned feel as any other English town: chain stores, chain restaurants, chain pubs, chain banks, chain estate agents, chain garages. It has the same basic palette as Bristol, Canterbury or Solihull. Drive into the TweedBank Retail Park and you find Argos, Marks & Spencer, Homebase, Next and Curry's, all ranged around a car park, just as you would in Worthing. Walk further and you come to Morrison's, Ladbrokes, Travelodge, Sports Direct, McDonald's, Thomas Cook, Holland & Barrett, Barclays, a Shell garage and the inevitable barrage of pound and charity shops.

So it is possible, when you wander around Berwick's

---

1 It is said that a Soviet representative visited Berwick in 1960 and that a peace accord was signed between the warring parties. But by all accounts it was not a very high-level delegation. A good thing those ramparts still stand.

medieval walls – all grim bastions and gun emplacements, with a regimental barracks by the church – to feel that you could easily be at the other end of the country – in Dover, say, or the Scilly Isles – staring at cold waves buffeting seal-strewn rocks while seagulls circle on the wind.

The origins of this connective tissue or common ground lie in the facets of England we have touched on throughout this book. The compact size meant that all corners of the country – however different they were from one another – could become components of a single political and economic unit. The marine ring road and inland waterways allowed disparate regions to communicate and trade with one another from early on, which meant that innovations spread to all parts. Every part of the kingdom – beauty spots and dead ends alike – shared the ambiguous fruits of coal and steam as well as the vicissitudes of the Atlantic climate. These forces turned England into a sturdy mould in which marked variations could coexist. The accents might change, the intonations could vary, but everyone was English, one way or another.

What *is* Englishness, though? Is it enough to say that it is too broad and multi-faceted to be summarised?

At the outset we said that it could not be reduced to a simple set of values (democracy, equality, fair play etc). But having sought its origins in the things that are irrevocably its own – landscape and history – what have we learned about the national character? Perhaps we can conclude that it is a method, an approach, a set of habitual responses . . . a *knack*. The natural features of England's geography, and the twists and turns of its history, created a sensibility good at negotiating a path between extremes. Winter/summer . . . sun/rain . . . land/sea . . . north/south . . . hill/valley . . . night/day . . . high tide/low tide . . . field/factory . . . city/countryside . . . new/old . . . past/future . . . continuity/change . . . England learned how to navigate a course between these contrary pressures long ago. This in turn has produced the divided temperament we recognise and laugh at, the one torn between tradition and progress, wealth and poverty, mind and body, pleasure and duty, politeness and pugnacity, sobriety and drunkenness, pomposity and modesty, and so on. The English have always had to pick a path between warring impulses – the age of the refined country house was also the age of slavery, the monstrous mill lived alongside the stately home; the age of faith was also the age of savagery. Greed coexisted with saintly generosity.

This abrasive heritage helps explain why England rarely favours extreme positions, preferring to steer a sensible course between them. It is why Shakespeare is celebrated for mixing tragedy and comedy. It is why the nation's favourite poem is Rudyard's Kipling's 'If', a composed response to the 'twin imposters', triumph and disaster. It is why 'keep calm and carry on' became a favourite national expression. And it is why, when it comes to national emblems, we relish the bittersweet. Nelson's death came at the instant of his greatest victory; Victoria ruled half the world, but could not smile; and Lawrence of Arabia was never so English as when he went native in the Arabian desert.

In this context it is not surprising that there often seem to be two forces ruling English life – one seeking to pull things together, the other looking to tug them apart. That is one lesson of the 2016 Brexit vote. Just over half of the electorate wanted to withdraw; the other half voted for togetherness. Each side believed it stood for the 'true' national character.

Perhaps the answer is that the real break with tradition was to hold the referendum in the first place. This is not the usual English way: a yes/no vote did not come naturally to a people who liked being somewhere in between. In truth, the outcome was sufficiently close that either side could have won if the weather had been a little warmer, or cooler; or if the poll had been held a week earlier, or later. But asking the whole country to vote on a single issue ... *that* was left field. Softly, softly ...

gently does it ... no need to rock the boat ... don't frighten
the horses ... sweep it under the carpet ... kick it into touch
(or the long grass) ... let's not jump to conclusions ... muddle
through ... put it on the back-burner ... crisis – what crisis?
These, as we have seen earlier, have long been the traditional
components of English decision-making. We have never been
keen on either/or. An in/out choice didn't come easily to a
people who prided themselves on seeing both sides.

A few miles south of Berwick we find ourselves at one of the
places where our story began, in an early outpost of English
culture: Holy Island. St Aidan came to this remote rock as
a missionary from Ireland in the seventh century, and for
reasons we can scarcely imagine, built a monastery and kept
Christianity alive in England's dark, unpleasant land. It is not
far from Jarrow, where the Venerable Bede wrote the first
history of England; it is where tenth-century monks illuminated the Lindisfarne Gospels, using local plants to make
their brilliant inks. It is also where Cuthbert had his feet
miraculously washed by holy otters on his way to becoming
a Northumbrian saint.

The ruins that attract tourists to the island today date from
'only' the twelfth century – the original monastery was much
humbler – but they have survived long enough to dramatise
the volume of time that hangs over this lonely place. It stands
in a marvellous sweep of coast, with the hulk of Bamburgh
Castle – from whose walls Grace Darling rowed to rescue a
stricken ship – rising on its southern promontory like an enormous battleship. A few hundred yards in the other direction,
on the northern spur, stands another lofty castle. In the years
when this coast was open to Viking assault, and when England
and Scotland were tussling over Berwick, this needed to be a
heavily guarded spot. Indeed, beneath the hiss of the waves and
the squawks of the gulls one can hear the authentic voice of
early England.

© Robert Winder

Holy Island. Wild Northumbrian redoubt, Cotswold manor house . . . or both?

The castles that lord it over this stretch of coastline – there are others at Alnwick and Dunstanburgh – have an embattled air, as if they are hunkering down against a siege.[2]

They would be an effective metaphor for England as a whole – an isolated realm bristling with craggy pride – if

2 Alnwick, a day's march north of Newcastle, was one of the seats of the Percy family, including Hotspur, the reckless warrior in *Henry IV, Part I* ('Out of this nettle, danger, I pluck this flower, safety'). These days it is better known as one of several film sets for Hogwarts.

they were not such a striking exception to the rule. Because England, as we have seen, is by no means a land of hilltop forts and redoubts. Europe's roads and railways run below the stern gaze of castles built to command and terrify the local population. Most of England's monuments nestle in trees or next to placid rivers.

Not in Northumberland. The turrets in this windswept region evoke an England that once feared danger, an England where wolves still roamed free.

Yet when one scrambles up the twisting path to Lindisfarne Castle, on Holy Island itself, something different emerges. From a distance, this is a fairytale palace or a wizard's retreat – the great pile seems to grow out of the stone on which it perches, with broad views over the tide-washed bay. But inside the courtyard everything changes: this is no castle; if anything, it is a Cotswolds manor house.

The medieval antiquity of its towers was already an illusion when it was built in Tudor times, as part of Henry VIII's fortification of Berwick-on-Tweed (the masons used stones from the dissolved monastery at its foot). But it lost its military role after the union of England and Scotland and fell into disuse, so it owes its present incarnation to a very different, but equally typical, English impulse. In 1901 it was bought by Edward Hudson, the owner and editor of *Country Life* magazine. As such, he was the arbiter of an energetic reverence for cultivated country living, and he and his friend Edwin Lutyens wasted no time in turning this lonely garrison into the kind of idyllic weekend retreat one might find in Oxfordshire.[3]

That is how it still appears today, preserved in National Trust mothballs. Inside the front door, by the fireplace, stand a set of golf clubs, a tennis racket, fishing rods and a straw boater, propped insouciantly against the stone walls like a

---

3 According to legend, Hudson and Lutyens discovered the castle by accident when, rather like T. S. Eliot and Emily Hale at Burnt Norton, they trespassed over the surrounding wall. The role of gatecrashing in English culture may be underrated.

young viscount up from Sandhurst. The slender stone columns echo in miniature the nave of Durham Cathedral, while a mural above the fireplace depicts the English navy seeing off the Armada, with lavish and grateful references to the 'goodly towers' that guard this 'lordly strand of Northumberland'.

In the kitchen next door a wrought-iron range stands alongside a table daintily laid with Spode china, Frank Cooper's Oxford marmalade, and a Harrod's tea chest. Brass bedwarmers and copper cooking implements hang from the wall, and a well-thumbed edition of *Mrs Beeton's Everyday Cookery* lies open on the sideboard next to a wartime edition of the *Daily Telegraph* ('Fierce Fighting in the Polish Sectors') and some delivery boxes – Austin Reed of Regent Street and Sporting Hats of Piccadilly. The drawing room is in the best Victorian Gothic style, with stained-glass windows, a brick parquet floor and low pointed arches. It could almost be a crypt.

All of this makes for a jarring contrast with the world outside. The windy terrace on the top floor, with brick chimney stacks that would not look out of place in Surrey, offers a majestic vista of low islands in a grey sea, with crystal water in the sandy shallows and pale sunlight bouncing off the distant rocks.

Here is the odd part. Somehow, the aesthetic culture of Oxfordshire and Gloucestershire found it easy to insinuate itself in this most distant corner of the realm. Once again, we sense the rival tugs of familiarity and difference, all suspended on a cold salt wind.

A final oddity on Holy Island is the walled garden. Once a vegetable plot for the troops who were stationed here, it was converted into herbaceous beds by none other than Gertrude Jekyll, hardly a local girl. But, given the Home Counties flavour of the house, it is hard to imagine a more appropriate choice: Jekyll was a true child of south-east England. Just as the landscape gardeners of the eighteenth century found themselves imitating art, so Jekyll's first ambition was to be a painter. She travelled widely, befriending Ruskin and Morris in the process.

It was only later, when her eyesight started to fail, that she became a leading light in the Royal Horticultural Society.

She was famous not for grand parks but for billowing, cottage-garden profusion; and she especially loved wild flowers, planting them in drifts rather than geometric patterns to generate natural clouds of colour. In her way she was an impressionist – a grow-your-own Monet – and she soon joined London's arty set.

That is how she became a friend of both Hudson (she contributed a thousand articles to *Country Life*) and Lutyens, who designed her house in Surrey.

On Holy Island, behind four stone walls set well away from Hudson's house, like a tennis court in the suburbs, Jekyll created a tumble of sweet pea, rose, geranium, salvia, phlox, hollyhock, fuchsia, camomile, rhubarb, nasturtium, clematis, apple and lavender. It was the English country garden to a T. And while it took a great deal of planning to achieve such an unplanned look, this really was an improbable location for it. Stranded in a sea of windswept grass, open to the north-east's tides and gales, it had the gallant look of a frontier fort – a far pavilion, a resolute corner of old England keeping up standards far from home. Planting the medieval village fantasies of Hudson, Ruskin and Morris on this forbidding island, it was a floral tribute to the world built by wool.

Jekyll was by no means alone, but by creating gardens on a small scale she breathed life into what would soon become an enormous industry. 'Our England is a garden,' cried Kipling, and it needed constant upkeep. It is estimated that a million acres of England are devoted to gardening. It is *the* great national hobby. As we have seen, urbanisation only intensified the urge to potter about in the open air. The less we saw of the great outdoors, the lovelier it seemed. The more we moved into cities and towns, the more we dreamed of cornflowers and peonies. No one tended their seedlings more lovingly than the coal miners of Durham ... aside, perhaps, from Lancashire's mill workers, who were said to have no equal when it came to specimen plants. Slums bred an ache for flower beds.

And it was so easy! The rain that watered the pastures for sheep and created the fields for grass-hungry games also gushed into England's domestic lawns and borders. The meteorological conditions that allowed England to become a wool factory turned it into a nation obsessed with south-facing walls, sheltered spots, well-drained soil, ericaceous supplements, pest control, weather forecasts, compost, secateurs, water features, perennials, climbers, raised beds, rockeries, seeds, slugs, bulbs and hosepipe bans.

This is still true today. Every weekend, all across England, people fill their boots at garden centres before grooming their plots, yards, greenhouses, balconies and window boxes.

And how they *love* their lawns. Quite a few sounds define the English summer, but few are as expressive as the droning rhythms of lawnmowers on a Sunday afternoon.

A few miles up into the Cheviot Hills, which rear up along the Anglo-Scottish border,[4] stands another remarkable house: Cragside. Nestling in an ocean of pine woods, it may not be the oldest house in England, but it is one of the oddest. A rambling Victorian pile teetering on the edge of a cliff, with heather-clad moors above and a river gurgling through the forest, it was built by the great engineer of Tyneside, William Armstrong. He was famous for the hydraulic cranes he brought to Newcastle's waterfront, the swing bridge over the Tyne, and the machinery that powered London's Tower Bridge.

The latter was designed to resemble the portcullis of a medieval castle, so it followed the example of the Houses of Parliament by looking to the Middle Ages for inspiration and authority. Armstrong was one of the greatest engineers of his

4 These hills are home to one of Britain's toughest breeds of sheep – a white-faced animal that can live three thousand feet above sea level.

astonishing era – a scientist, inventor, manufacturer, mayor and philanthropist. In 1863 he was also Newcastle's leading employer, providing work for 3800 people in his Elswick factory, which turned out dock gates, pumps, hydraulic machinery and ships.[5] Yet even he had a weakness for the Arthurian glory days.

Is it a paradox that one of the engineering celebrities of the age – a man synonymous with a mighty industrial leap forward, the builder of ships and factories, cranes and bridges, pumps and mills – should pine for fresh mountain air? Not really. Cragside was only an hour from the chimneys and bridges of Newcastle, but when blue sky illuminated the pines and splashing water glistened in the sunlight, it must have seemed like virgin territory. It makes perfect sense that Armstrong should want to escape the roar of daily life. The more his factories grew, the more he was drawn to Cragside's invigorating river and hills.

As for the house itself, it is considerably more than a country cottage. Glimpsed from below, from the iron bridge that straddles the river, it feels Bavarian – a Wagnerian fantasy castle in the forest. On the other hand, it also looks very like a Surrey golf club. Sunshine pouring through pine woods on to green grass, colourful mounds of rhododendron, ponds and streams splashing over carefully arranged rocks – this was the Highland-estate look that Southern golf architects tried to re-create. And this was the look of Cragside too.

It thus embodies the double nature we have glimpsed in other Victorian buildings. On the one hand, it was England's first 'modern' dwelling: lit by electricity (generated by hydro-electric screws), supplied with running water from the same

---

5 He also helped to perfect the breech-loading field gun, and was knighted for his contribution to British artillery. When he lost his contract with the British government he continued to do well out of foreign powers, supplying both sides in the American Civil War, and pulling the same trick in the Franco-German conflict. As a result, several hundred thousand men were killed by bullets with Armstrong's name on them.

© Robert Winder

Cragside, Northumberland. A little touch of mad King Ludwig in the pines. A house with one eye on the future, and both feet in the past.

source, with the world's first automatic washing machine, central heating, lift, telephones, even spa (known then as a Turkish bath). It was a state-of-the-art, environmentally friendly showhouse, a century ahead of its time.

Yet all of its scientific, engineering and mechanical innovations were dressed (some would say tricked out) in the idiom of yesteryear. With the help of a little-known architect named Norman Shaw, Cragside became a steepling mish-mash of gables, arches, turrets and crenellations, finished off with tall chimneys, Tudor beams and broad Elizabethan windows. Ruskin would have approved. The stained glass, by William Morris, featured Arthurian knights in silver armour, and the walls were full of Pre-Raphaelite art.

It was not full-on Victorian Gothic in the Pugin manner, however; Shaw's vision was rather more eclectic than that. His first notable building was in Cranbrook, Kent, one of the villages in which Flemish weavers had boosted the local cloth trade, and it was that kind of quaint, olde worlde aesthetic – thatched, nook-strewn and very chocolate-box – that Shaw took to Northumberland. A high-profile monument to modernity, science and mechanical expertise was wrapped in a sugar-plum coating inspired by the wool-working heart of old England.

The antiquarian note in Victorian architecture had many eager supporters, as we have seen. But few lay so close to its heart as Norman Shaw. His client on that first commission in Cranbrook was a Victorian painter named John Horsley, who also happened to be Isambard Kingdom Brunel's brother-in-law. Horsley had contributed frescoes to Pugin's Palace of Westminster, and his style was what we would now dismiss as Victorian kitsch – apple-cheeked girls reading books by the fire, tubby peasants sharing a joke, young lovers draped in blossom, doe-eyed dogs – all rendered in bright colours and bold shapes, rather like a stained-glass window. In his house, this aesthetic emerged as a jumble of tiles, half timbers, chimneys, gables and dormer windows – like a higgledy-piggledy vicarage.

Horsley himself did much to promote this vision. In 1843, at the suggestion of his friend Henry Cole – later the founding director of the Victoria and Albert Museum – he created the world's first Christmas card. The jolly image of a well-fed family distributing largesse to the poor set a standard of brazen sentimentality to which Christmas cards have remained loyal ever since. One of his later cards had even more impact. Entitled 'It's About Time', it depicted Victoria and Albert dandling their children in front of a decorated tree – a German habit the royal family had recently imported to Britain. It swept the country off its feet, and a whole new way of celebrating Christmas was born.

This, filtered through Norman Shaw's magpie imagination, was the cultural inspiration for Cragside. Even the stark Cheviot setting was an illusion. Armstrong bought a patch of empty moorland, then filled it with millions of pines and other plants, not all of them native (he grew bananas there, too). It may have looked like a rugged slice of old Northumbria, but in truth it was a toyshop, with a gingerbread house perched up in its treetops. It is hard to say which part of the house's divided nature was more influential. Its novelties and new technologies certainly transformed the interior of the English house, and lit the way ahead. But the way in which the exterior embraced the ideals of earlier times had an equally marked impact on how England lived.

The backward glance was just as influential as the forward-looking gaze.

The gospel according to Cragside reached London in 1875. And its prophet was Jonathan Carr. The son of a Marylebone draper and a cloth merchant of no great renown (his brother, an art critic and devout Pre-Raphaelite, was more prominent) he lived in Turnham Green, a village near Chiswick. Central London was heading this way. Gilbert Scott designed a Gothic church, and then the Metropolitan Line linked the area directly to Paddington.

Sniffing an opportunity, Carr bought twenty-four acres of land near the station and invited Norman Shaw to create a range of dwellings that might lure Londoners away from the smog and grime of inner-city life.

The result was a logical extension of the work Shaw had already done: in the course of the coming decades 356 houses appeared, following a twisting pattern that was designed to look natural ... and old. The buildings shared similar antique styling – boarding school meets cricket pavilion – so they appeared related without being quite identical. Gothic and Tudor elements rubbed shoulders with Flemish motifs, pitched roofs, gables, cosy nooks, porches and bay windows. Dozens of mini-Cragsides popped up in the suburbs, like forest mushrooms.

Like the earlier industrial villages of Saltaire and Bournville, the new development boasted social amenities: parish halls, parks, lawns, leafy passages and back gardens. Unlike them, it also had pubs. What emerged was a new sort of settlement. Known as Bedford Park, it seemed ancient even when it was brand new, like parchment soaked in tea.

On the blueprint, the pub was named 'Ye Hostelry'. It was not even trying to be up-to-date.[6]

Hermann Muthesius, the German author of *The English House* (1904), called this the 'starting point' for modern suburban living. Sir John Betjeman thought it was 'the most significant suburb built in the last century'. But both would have been surprised at just how far its influence would ultimately extend. Similar garden suburbs soon appeared in nearby Brentham (where the young Fred Perry honed his forehand on the club courts) as well as in Hampstead, Sutton, Birmingham, Manchester, Oldham and Liverpool. They shared a strong idealist streak, and owed a good deal to the utopian principles of William Morris's Arts and Crafts movement. Residents were not obliged (this was England, after all) but expected to pursue some sort of morally improving hobby: wood engraving, marquetry, tapestry. And it would be perfectly splendid if they learned how to grow prize-winning

6 G. K. Chesterton parodied the whole concept in *The Man Who Was Thursday*, calling it Saffron Park: 'The stranger who looked for the first time at the quaint red houses could only think how very oddly shaped the people must be who could fit into them.'

marrows, formed an orchestra, or helped tidy the kneelers in the church. No one minded the emphasis on 'traditional' pastimes – ceremonies fondly imagined to have played a central role in village life in olden times. The future could wait.

In an echo of the open field system, residents took it in turns to mow the communal grass, light the bonfire and sweep up autumn leaves.

And this was only the beginning, because as England's population became ever more mobile, so the idea planted by Bedford Park took wing. An architect named Ebenezer Howard had the wild notion that *entire towns* could be conceived along similar lines, with a careful balance of housing, factory space, farming plots and cultural life folded in from the very beginning. If a garden suburb worked, why not a garden city?

Like the agricultural pioneers whose experiences on the Grand Tour inspired innovation at home, Howard's ideas ripened overseas, in Chicago, where he worked as a shorthand reporter and typewriter engineer. In his case, his stint in Illinois sharpened his love for the England of his youth. Born in London, and schooled in Suffolk and Hertfordshire, he had the urban man's love of the idea of country life. His book *Tomorrow: A Peaceful Path to Real Reform* (1898) laid out a detailed vision of a new sort of town, one that would enjoy the best of all worlds: industrial heft, social harmony and health-giving green lungs.

The illustrations could have been the work of a mad scientist, with their eerily precise arrangements of waterfalls, homes for waifs and inebriates, colleges, forests, allotments and 'epilectic farms'. But it was easy to satirise Howard's vision as a cute dictatorship – village life for the people, by the people, whether the people liked it or not. He was not thinking small: he wanted to usher in 'a new civilisation' and believed that all London could be rebuilt along his well-organised lines.

Before long, he caught the attention of town planners. With Howard as its patron saint, the Garden City Association was formed in 1899, and a conference was held, hosted by George Cadbury (of Bournville). The association then raised £156,000 to bring Howard's vision to life on some empty fields at Letchworth, near Hitchin, in Hertfordshire. Barry Parker and Raymond Unwin – the architectural duo behind the Rowntrees' factory village at Earswick, York – won the design competition that followed (Unwin was later credited with inventing the term 'town planning'). They imagined a 4000-acre town with 1300 houses, a full set of municipal buildings, a square, a tree-lined boulevard, a shopping precinct, a factory, a school, churches (one for each subsidiary 'village') and everything else an old-fashioned but ultra-modern family might want.

By 1914, Letchworth had 14,500 residents. Sometimes dreams do come true.

Thanks to its non-drinking, Quaker godparents, Letchworth had an alcohol-free pub called the Skittles Inn.[7] But in other respects it stayed true to the spirit of Shaw and Howard. The factory, which housed the corset-maker Spirella, was styled as a Georgian country mansion; the office block was disguised as a thatched barn; and the residents' houses looked like cottages that had eaten a handful of magic beans. Generously proportioned, they had large, beamed drawing rooms, like proper country houses. There was a cricket pitch, a lido and – an important innovation – a green belt. The houses were arranged in an irregular pattern, as if shards of Dorset and Kent had been scattered on Hertfordshire for a Merrie England get-together.

The experiment at Letchworth was repeated at nearby Welwyn Garden City, and soon its influence was felt more broadly. The Ideal Homes Exhibition, created by the *Daily Mail* in 1908, was quick to promote the 'Tudorbethan' style, and soon the whole of England was being restyled in a wistful melange of antique flavours. Residential estates and suburbs

7 John Betjeman later satirised Letchworth as a place inhabited by humourless health freaks and morris dancers.

boasted mock-Tudor beams, leaded windows, stained glass and thatched gables, all set discreetly behind hedges on swirling avenues, with painted wooden gates opening on to Jekyll-inspired banks of delphiniums and sweet peas.

The terrors of the First Word War intervened for a while, but afterwards the movement gathered pace, as England ached to turn the clock back to a happier time. At an after-dinner speech in 1924, the leader of the Conservative Party, Stanley Baldwin, looked to his childhood in rural Worcestershire for those features of England that seemed to him eternal: 'the tinkle of hammer on the anvil in the country smithy, the corncrake on a dewy morning, the sound of the scythe against the whetstone, and the sight of a plough team coming over the hill'. These visions of the English countryside 'strike down into the very depths of our nature, and touch chords that go back to the beginning of time'.

There was more to this than mere rural dreaming. It implied that the essence of England could only be found in a country village. And many people agreed with Baldwin. Although the great majority of the population now lived in much larger conurbations, the rural idyll could still be advanced as an invincible national myth.

So, as time wore on, commuter-belt estates (not just in new towns like Bracknell and Milton Keynes, but everywhere) were given Georgian columns and rustic names like The Pines or Mill View; car ports were dressed as a classical loggia; modern kitchens were given 'distressed' fireplaces and iron ranges. The idea was to make the urban fabric of England look as though it had been there for ever – or at least since the age of monks.

It was a domineering aesthetic. Suddenly, England's town-dwellers aspired to be members of rural communes. Other countries saved space by clustering their populations in apartments. That was not for England. There had to be trees, lawns, and forget-me-nots in the long grass by the bus stop.

The end result was a look that few other countries possessed;

or if they did, it was only because they were consciously copying the English style.[8] Cavernous supermarkets started appearing in the form of mock-Tudor granaries, with fake timber frames and tiled eaves. Modern shopping arcades – the retail 'villages' of Bicester and Gatwick – named themselves after medieval settlements clustered around greens, ponds and churches. At Burnage, in Manchester, the 'green' was a bowling green, but the idea remained the same.

Several generations of art critics have enjoyed attributing this to a defective artistic sense – they particularly disliked it when Prince Charles sponsored a 'village' of this sort at Poundbury, in Dorset – but it grew out of an understandable yearning for home to be a harmonious refuge. The past may have been brutish ... but so was the present. And the rustic look of olden times could be mimicked without importing its more blood-curdling qualities.

So, in modern England, huge areas of the inner cities were expensively 'restored' to their original characters. In 2016, the government announced plans to build 14 new garden villages and towns. No one wanted a complete return to the old days – what, no wi-fi? – but the emotion could not be restrained: the past was where the poetry was.

The same village dream filtered its way into many of the twentieth century's most popular fictions. The leading detectives of the period – Father Brown, Hercule Poirot, Miss Marple, Lord Peter Wimsey – spent much of their time popping in and out of church halls, or strolling across lawns and gravel drives. Sherlock Holmes was based in London, but even he was regularly summoned to solve mysteries in the depths of the English countryside.

Lark Rise to Candleford, Miss Read, Cider with Rosie, Swallows

---

8 Although, of course, this style was carried across the Empire, and still crops up unexpectedly: golf clubs in Sri Lanka and India; cottage-style bungalows in Kenya and New Zealand; railway stations and post offices in Canada and Barbados.

and Amazons, *Cold Comfort Farm*, *Peter Rabbit*, *Akenfield* – the bookshops groaned with village life. And television continued the tradition, using the same gentle settings to suggest timeless verities in shows like *Midsomer Murders*, *Emmerdale Farm*, *All Creatures Great and Small*, *Last of the Summer Wine*, *The Vicar of Dibley*, *Broadchurch* and many others. Children's programming leaned heavily on rural locales, too. Noddy drove his taxi (Parp! Parp!) through a toy village, while Postman Pat bumbled around Greendale. A specific kind of English culture, based on a modernised version of medieval village life, was dripped into the minds of many generations, buffing a cherished ideal that was rapidly disappearing in a sea of ring roads, supermarkets and enterprise zones.

A handful of these works tried to strike a note of realism. In *Cider with Rosie* (1949), for instance, Laurie Lee emphasised that rural life was 'a world of hard work and necessary patience, of backs bent to the ground'. But this was not enough to spoil the fantasy. The pages of England's property magazines, the brochures of its tourist industry and the imagery in its advertising all continued to push the idea that the true glory of the country was to be found in its countryside.[9]

The images often had shallow roots in the real world. Ridley Scott's famous advertisement for Hovis evoked a bygone time and, with its plaintive brass band, a distinct tone of northern England. But it was filmed in Shaftesbury, on Dorset cobblestones, and the soundtrack was by a Czech emigrant to New York.[10] Similarly, when Asda launched a cloudy lemonade in 2008, the label featured an image that seemed to be a cricket

9 Vintage labelling on packets of cheese and tins of tea sought to transmit discernible flavours: trees fringing a field of wheat, a welcoming pub, a crooked church, an ancient bridge.

10 In a clever twist, the idea was updated in 2008 in a two-minute commercial featuring a young boy running home through a collage of the last hundred years of English history: two world wars, suffragette marches, miners' strikes and World Cup celebrations. The twin idea, as so often, was that some things never change and the best things in life are old.

pitch in Southborough near Tunbridge Wells – a fine place, certainly, but hardly the home of the lemon.[11]

It didn't seem to matter that the rural population was dwindling. The dream was far more important, and it was more vivid than ever. Jane Austen had declared that 'three or four families in a country village is the very thing to work on', and that was now the standard view. 'The best of England is a village,' wrote C. Henry Warren in 1940. Even the urban population dreamed, along with Browning, of hawthorn hedges and chaffinches on the bough . . . in England, now.

Probably the best example of this village mentality appeared in 1929, when an accountant named Roland Callingham built a toy one in his back garden. He named it Bekonscot, and it was a tribute to the land he lived in. At the time, it was full of exciting novelties, but today it gives us a clear view of time-warp England, pre-electronic, all very cosy. A model train winds past fields full of sheep, a harbour, a windmill, a cricket pitch, a racecourse, and lots of miniature Cragsides. Ebenezer Howard would have swooned.

A handful of cottages around a village green, a church and a pub . . . now *that* was England.

The rest could go hang.

11 The drawing had exactly the same oak tree hanging over the boundary, the same Victorian church, the same flannelled fools at the wicket, but the company claimed that it was merely a design coincidence.

Epilogue

On the edge of a path on the South Downs Way, in the hills between Petersfield and Chichester, stands a small flint memorial. It is a rough and ready, home-made sort of thing, but well cared for: there are poppies at its foot and in the twigs above. The name on the tablet is 'Joseph Oestermann' and the dates are '1915–1940'. That is an eloquent clue, but in other ways the monument is mute: the stone offers no background story.

Oestermann was the very first casualty of the tumult in the clouds that became known as the Battle of Britain. He was flying his Junkers 88 back to France after a raid on Farnborough airfield on 13 August 1940, day one of the battle, when he was shot down by a Hurricane. Since the Hurricane itself went down over Portland that same day, the circumstances of Oestermann's disappearance were for a while mysterious.

The stone is unusual in that it commemorates a fallen enemy, but there is nothing strange about coming upon a war memorial in rural England. There is hardly a village that does not have a monument to the fallen – the official register lists 68,000 of them. The grandest – the cenotaphs of London, Liverpool and Southampton, the naval memorials in Chatham and Portsmouth, the Arch of Remembrance in Leicester – are historic, but it is the smaller crosses and tablets that decorate our greens, churches and schools, and are a distinguishing characteristic of English life.

Hardly anyone would claim actually to like war. It is a vale of suffering and tears. But the English certainly like the *idea* of it – the memory and the righteous drama of it all. Any estimate of the national character needs at least to notice this fact. Perhaps this is because the colossal wars of our recent past were played out, for the most part, on foreign soil – they are glamorised by distance. But the English are famous for dwelling on the subject: in films, books, plays, television programmes, and even (or especially) in sport. As a result, the sight of a list of names engraved in stone at a village crossroads is so familiar that we rarely bother to slow down for a closer look. It occasionally happens, in Switzerland, for example, that one feels a nagging sense of something missing. France's town squares have a similar air of sober remembrance to England's, but Swiss ones do not. There is a faint but detectable loss of gravitas.

It is so often remarked that the Second World War was England's finest hour, a time that brought out the best in us, five years when people stuck together, helped each other, kept calm and carried on – that we forget how unusual this is. The rest of Europe remembers the war years with a cold shiver. It is reasonable enough to congratulate ourselves for having faced down a deadly opponent, but doing so leads us to overlook the fact that the horrors of the war brushed us only lightly. Britain was not colonised and occupied; its citizens were not rounded up and massacred. We need to set the 40,000 English people who died in German raids against the 300,000 (a conservative estimate) who perished in the Allied bombing of Germany. At the height of the Holocaust, more people died in the gas chambers of Auschwitz–Birkenau every week. Then there was the destruction of Tokyo, Hiroshima and Nagasaki. In the scheme of these awful horrors, England escaped relatively unscathed.

The war appealed to something deep in England's nature, in part by tickling one of its most beloved myths, and urging people, both tacitly and explicitly, to return to the land. The Ministry of Agriculture struck a chord when it enjoined the nation to 'dig for victory' and assembled platoons of 'land girls' to grow food. England turned back to its rural roots in a way that felt healthy, thrifty and wholesome as well as patriotic. Government pamphlets – 'How to dig ... How to sow seeds' – reminded people of skills they had long forgotten.

While the military required the heavy industry of steel and coal, the home front delved into its agrarian subconscious. And there was something exhilarating about turning tennis courts into cabbage patches, or golf courses into onion fields. Perhaps this was why John Betjeman begged 'friendly bombs' to fall on Slough and blast it back to a time when it *was* fit for humans.

Ruskin and Morris would have applauded. War promised to rekindle the stolid folk values that the agitations of modern life had swept away – self-sufficiency, valour, self-sacrifice. England could hardly admit it, given the gravity of the situation, but it was *happy*. It had an opportunity to stiffen the upper lip, and was even given permission to grumble. What could be better?

One famous 'Dig for Victory' garden was planted in a bomb crater in the refined precincts of Westminster Cathedral – a low wall marked out a tidy circle of home-grown produce. How very English, to respond to a bomb blast with runner beans and Brussels sprouts. It was stoic. It cocked a snook.

Did something of this spirit come to the fore during the 2016 EU referendum? Did the poll reveal that familiar cocktail of pride and pugnacity simmering just beneath the urbane surface of English life?

At the risk of sounding 'metropolitan elite', a week after the fateful vote I was on a family holiday in Verona. As we drove into town from the airport the city was full of flags: Italy was playing Germany in Bordeaux that night in the quarter-finals of the Euros, and German banners fluttered alongside Italian pennants in roads that were also emblazoned with the blue-and-yellow European insignia.

It was a hot day, and Verona was having a party.

It was a city of medieval palazzos, villas, castles, churches, courtyards and gardens, many of them converted into internet cafés or designer boutiques – all chic clothes, sparkling wine and wi-fi hotspots. In ancient, narrow alleys bursting with delicious food, a mass of tourists hurried about in search of the balcony where Romeo supposedly serenaded Juliet (it was actually an old sarcophagus, added to a medieval building by an enterprising mayor). Some climbed up the tall campanile above the market square to admire the view, gasping at the red-tiled roof tops and the cold green river that gushes down from the Alps.

There were plenty of English accents. The Arena, a Roman coliseum that hosts an annual opera festival, was also honouring the four hundredth anniversary of Shakespeare's death. There were Chelsea shirts in the shop windows (the London club had just poached Italy's national team manager) and Kit-Kats on the sweet counters.

The visitors who gathered in the Arena that night to watch *La Traviata* were from all parts, but they shared a common passion ... and not only for opera. Verdi kicked off at the same time as the quarter-final, so the stadium was soon flickering with the glow of a thousand mobile-phones. When the match went to penalties, the ancient terracing – from which the Veronese had once watched gladiators hacking each other to bloody pieces – shook with groans, cheers and laughter.

The orchestra sat mute while the shootout was decided. Then, right on cue, a thunderstorm flared in the inky sky.

Lightning rippled. Italy lost. Violetta swooned. The crowd applauded.

It felt like a party all right, but it was a party that England, on Britain's behalf, had decided to leave. Why?

The air was thick with mixed feelings. It was possible to interpret the happy bustle in Verona as a joyful rebuke to the sour nationalisms that had almost destroyed Europe in the twentieth century. But it could also be seen – and was, by the England that wanted out of all this – as nothing more than a pampered elite spending its ill-gotten gains on an expensive holiday. Moreover, as it congratulated itself on its cosmopolitan fondness for foreign flavours, this 'elite' seemed to have forgotten that it was not above tribal feelings, but was itself a tribe. Oh, it imagined itself to be diverse, broad-minded, forward-looking and superior, but from the perspective of less fortunate fellow-citizens it looked like a smug and self-perpetuating aristocracy, robed in condescending airs and graces.

England was not unique in generating such dissident emotions: similar feelings were sweeping through most of the Western world that summer. According to this growling new critique, the modern elite had abandoned its own citizens. It might embrace a graduate engineer from Singapore or Sri Lanka and congratulate itself on its open-mindedness, but an out-of-work fisherman in Hull, a zero-hours haulier in Portsmouth or a single mother in Tewkesbury? The class-based modern definition of 'diversity' rarely extended to the likes of these. The elite was cosmopolitan only to the extent that it knew no borders and enjoyed foreign flavours (though even here, it seemed to prefer Afghan restaurants to Afghan refugees). Either way, it was all at sea in the glum back streets and housing projects of its own identity.

In the end, what the favoured class really valued was its own right to watch a musical version of a French play in a Roman amphitheatre, with Austrian wine, Dutch cheese, Spanish tortilla, Greek salad and Swiss chocolate, before driving a German car around an Italian lake and feeling faintly superior while it was about it. That was the take-back-control argument, anyway. It was about time the elite beneficiaries of globalisation listened to those who had been left behind, even if the vote ran the risk of leaving some of them further behind than ever.

These remarks may give the impression that I am pessimistic about England's future outside the EU. There is a reason for that. It's impossible to say what the future holds, but from the vantage point of Christmas 2016, we may have to hope that it will all end in tears, because that would be to get off lightly. At the very least, years of rancour and instability seem guaranteed.

One of history's best lessons is that people tend to forget history. In the 1930s, hardly anyone believed that a new war was possible. The last one had only just ended, so a repeat was unthinkable. Secure in this conviction, nobody took the steps that might have prevented the conflict from resuming.

In the summer of 2016, anyone who had the audacity to hint that Brexit was a modern equivalent of the nationalistic mood music of the 1930s was mocked as a moaning hysteric. Few paused to imagine the outcry if the referendum had gone the other way and (under the banner of 'hard remain') Britain had joined the euro, signed up to Schengen and opened its doors to a million Syrians. Yet the brand of populist, expert-hating nationalism was drawing from much the same well of grievance as the movements of that decade. Retreating behind national barricades ... a distrust of elites ... anti-foreigner sentiment ... a faith in simple 'solutions' – nearly all of history's bad patches had begun like this.

What did the result tell us about England, though? That it was insular? Brave? Wanted to retreat from the rest of Europe? Wanted to go forth boldly into new realms? Hated being tied down? Feared the rate at which the world was changing? All of the above? In reality, it showed us something we should have known already: that England was a land of many divisions. Most of these were familiar. Rich and poor, south and north, young and old, go ahead and left behind, town and country, white and not white. But the most powerful was the one between those who were animated by the future and those who were devoted to the past. The referendum did seem to have produced a vote in favour of the safety blanket woven by our long and twisting history.

This is an ancient English tradition, so perhaps the land was simply casting its old spell. And it wasn't only conservatives who were susceptible. The Levellers, Diggers, Puritans,

Chartists, Non-Conformists, Methodists, Jarrow marchers and striking miners of the 1980s all invoked their time-honoured right to dissent. Each of these proud progressive movements also drew on the well of feelings that preferred the old to the new, the familiar to the unknown. The simple message that won the day in June 2016 – take back control – successfully suggested that England had been mislaid, and that we only needed to retrace our steps to rediscover it.

Or perhaps something more subtle had been mislaid: the traditional English 'knack' of tip-toeing between contrary urges. Perhaps the two old Englands – one aching to turn the clock back to a past that might never have existed, the other with its eye fixed on the future – had lost their characteristic balance, and were teetering close to the brink, towards the stark and dangerous edge of yes and no.

I started thinking about these issues in Berwick; and I thought about them again as I stood at the other end of the country, on Dover's cliffs, looking across the water at the distant smudge of France. In one sense, these two outer tips of England are very different: one faces the vast Norwegian sky; the other looks south to a warmer world of sun, fruit and wine. But in another, they are very similar: choppy grey waters splash against a green shoreline that is streaked with coal and protected by castles.

Suddenly, that divided identity seemed to characterise almost every English location I had visited while brooding on this book. Holy Island was part isolated Northumbrian fortress, part Cotswolds nook; Coalbrookdale and Saltaire were smoke pits, but also tranquil beauty spots; the London parks were half metropolitan enclaves, half rural bowers; the monasteries were spiritual retreats and booming commercial enterprises; the coastal waters were half defensive moat, half gateway to the world; the landscape was natural and man-made; pretty Suffolk villages sought to secure their future by preserving their past.

Englishness, I had come to think, was the result of many compromises between opposite strands. A child of the abrasive marriage between the rough Teutonic world and Latin Christendom, it had a profound double nature right from the start, with a foot in both camps, a heart in neither. This was why English diplomacy, over many centuries, came to seem two-faced. Anything to avoid a Montagu-Capulet approach to such things: that was bound to end in tragedy.

Contradiction was the key. We did not sing from the same hymn sheet after all – or we did, but in different voices. The vote for Brexit did not indicate that we had finally made up our collective mind: it merely marked a slight – if telling – swing in the scales. And who could say it was not temporary? A year earlier, or a year later, and the outcome might have been different. Put another way, should a referendum have been held every decade since joining, England would have been in ... out ... in ... out ... and shaken all about.

It may be that this is where the national sense of humour has its origins. When England laughs at itself, it is sometimes no more than one side of its character having a chuckle at how the other half lives.

This was the thought that came to mind as I stood on the white cliffs, a blustery wind whipping a sharp shower into my face. England is no longer an island in any meaningful sense of the word. Modern technology – not to mention the tunnel that connects us to the once-English enclave of Calais – has put paid to that. But these cliffs still send an iconic message to the outside world: 'England is a fortress. Keep out.'

They carry other messages, too. Indeed, they have played more than a walk-on part in some of England's most distinguished literature. They are the setting for one of its finest scenes, in *King Lear*, when the Earl of Gloucester has his eyeballs gouged out and tries to fumble his way to the edge in order to throw himself off and end it all. 'There is a cliff,' he groans, 'whose high and bending head / Looks fearfully in the

'There is a cliff, whose high and bending head . . .' Dover's chalk ramparts have been an iconic English backdrop for writers, artists, pilots and coal miners alike.

confined deep.' His son Edgar escorts him not to the coast but to a minor dip in the ground, where he talks about the weight of space beneath their feet:

> *The crows and choughs that wing the midway air*
> *Show scarce so gross as beetles. Half way down*
> *Hangs one that gathers samphire, dreadful trade!*
> *Methinks he seems no bigger than his head.*
> *The fishermen that walk upon the beach*
> *Appear like mice.*

Fired by his son's rhetoric, Gloucester hurls himself forward, is miraculously unhurt, and resolves to bear his torments with greater fortitude.

The spot later became known as Shakespeare Cliff,[1] and

---

1 In 1994 a shelf appeared at the foot of the cliff, created by debris from the Channel Tunnel. A contest to name this reclaimed point, with its clear view of France, was won by an English teacher who merged Shakespeare with Francis Drake's Plymouth to produce Samphire Hoe.

many years later Dickens gave it a redemptive role in the life of his favourite son, David Copperfield. The tormented boy begins his climb towards happiness only when he walks from London to Dover and arrives at his aunt's cottage on this shore.

Finally, they also inspired Matthew Arnold's 'Dover Beach' (1867). In this case the broken hills, shining like teeth in the night, evoke a crouching serenity:

> *The sea is calm tonight.*
> *The tide is full, the moon lies fair*
> *Upon the straits; on the French coast, the light*
> *Gleams, and is gone: the cliffs of England stand,*
> *Glimmering and vast, out in the tranquil bay.*

These lines reinforced the image of Dover as a crowning glory of the landscape, one of the places where England's ghosts live. But nothing lasts for ever. Just as the moon gleams and is gone, so nations and empires rise and fall, ebbing and flowing like the tide.

That certainly seems to be the message of modern Coalbrookdale. At the height of its fame, when the valley was turning out the iron that built a superpower, it was hard to see anything dampening its fires and furnaces. Visitors flocked to gasp at the molten metal bubbling in a Wagnerian bonfire of despoiling greed. Indeed, the valley was often compared to the dark underworld in which Alberich forged his ring.

But the rapid development of England's canal and rail network soon exposed the drawbacks of Coalbrookdale's isolated location. Industry started to migrate to west Yorkshire, south Wales and the north-east, and this wild Shropshire valley, for a hundred years the furnace of England's industry and empire, fell into disrepair.

Anyone visiting today – and thousands do – may be forgiven for missing the irony that lurks in the trees. It is now an industrial heritage park, with a re-created Victorian village on top of the hill. But stroll along the river path, through the overhanging boughs, or follow the cinder trail of the disused railway, and it becomes clear that the natural power of England's landscape has reclaimed the old factory site and turned it back into what it was before: a natural dell. Its forges, mines, quarries and brickworks were only temporary blots on the landscape.

It might seem purely coincidental that this part of Shropshire played a vivid part at the start of this story, when it was the setting for Peter Corbet's final wolf hunt. But what are we to make of the fact that the same area is also home to Blandings Castle, the imaginary stately home in which P. G. Wodehouse's cast of earls, dukes, pigs, nephews, nieces, sisters and butlers play out their farcical plots in a swirl of old English rose gardens, lawns, dining rooms, pantries and battlements? Wodehouse described Blandings as 'a mixture of places', and there is no reason to think he was lying, but the books place it firmly in this part of Shropshire: Lady Constance is always nipping into Shrewsbury to do some shopping. The dust that falls on the flagged stone terrace can only be soot from the smokestacks of Coalport.

And that is the point. This dust falls no longer. The winds of change that cleared the land of wolves, and earls, has done for the ironworks, too.

Similarly, while most of modern Coalbrookdale celebrates its industrial heyday, some parts seem determined to pretend it never happened. A mile downriver from the famous bridge stands the Boat Inn – a pleasant spot to stop for a bite by the water's edge. Stencilled on the wall is a proud message: 'Unspoiled by Progress'. For a moment it does indeed feel like a haven of ancient charm, uncorrupted by hectic modern ways, but it soon dawns on the visitor that this charming hostelry has not escaped progress. It was *created* by it.

As if to cash in on the same myth, on the other bank stands another inn, this time called (none too realistically) Ye Olde Robin Hood. It serves all the traditional English dishes – tiger prawns in chilli, garlic and ginger, Cajun chicken wraps – and stands on Waterloo Street.

This is history as a melange of discordant sights, sounds and flavours, and it is why theorists have tended to pour scorn on English nostalgia. Tom Wolfe once compared England to a theme park – all thatched tea rooms, jolly Beefeaters and right-you-are-guv manservants. In 1986 Patrick Wright returned from Canada to find that the whole country had turned into 'some sort of anthropological museum'. A year later, Robert Hewison juxtaposed the closure of the steel works at Consett with the opening of a mock-Edwardian toy village at Beamish, and suggested that England was gripped by idle escapism. And as the Millennium Dome was nearing completion Julian Barnes imagined a cynical tycoon turning the Isle of Wight into an offshore Disneyland, with replica highlights from the pageant of English history mashed into a silly zoo, feet planted clumsily in the past.

Yet the heritage industry has boomed since then. The museums at Ashington, Bekonscot, Cragside, Coalbrookdale, Fountains, Wigan Pier, Jorvik, Portsmouth, Liverpool and a thousand other places preserve the past by packaging it into a visitor attraction. Thanks to the National Trust and a range of government agencies, England has half a million listed buildings, 17,000 protected monuments and 78 railway museums alone. It is a land in thrall to its origins, replacing its landmarks with pretend versions of themselves – castles with 'castles', factories with 'factories', mills with 'mills' and farms with 'farms'. This was why Hewison and his followers suggested that England needed not a prime minister but a curator, and enjoyed quoting Adorno's observation that a museum was only a few letters shy of being a mausoleum. The mines and mills have closed, the ironworks have disappeared, the canals might have been taken over by pleasure boats, and the railway branch lines may have been pruned, but the past ... ah, no one can take that away from us.

The nostalgic impulse does not express itself only in the urge to turn the country into a well-lit gallery of its former self. It can also be seen in the prime-time popularity of genealogy and in the way modern England likes to place its own past on trial – whether in the form of abusive priests, disc jockeys and care homes, tragedies like Bloody Sunday and Hillsborough, or other injustices from the bad old days. Even the apparently progressive anti-capitalist, anti-globalisation protest movement is rooted in nostalgia for a simpler time. In trumpeting its support for the little man against faceless fat cats, it echoes the Victorian desire to return to a 'natural' – that is, pre-industrial – culture peopled by stout yeomen who live off the land, darning socks by the light of tallow candles and boiling their own sweets.

Maybe the past really will be England's future, its best – or only – friend. History cannot read that future. It has enough trouble tracing the footprints of the past. But perhaps, to travel forwards, we need (as T. S. Eliot advised) to look back.

England is certainly full of old stories. Touch it anywhere and a memory falls out. And many of those memories are based on the humble ingredients with which we began, the basic geographical elements of the landscape and its climate.

Two examples: in Bristol in 1782, an alert plumber named William Watts realised that rain fell not in teardrops, but in round blobs. Suspecting that this was simple gravity doing its work, he conducted an experiment, dripping molten lead from the spire of St Mary's, Redcliffe (a lofty church financed, like so many others, by West Country wool), into a tank of water. Sure enough, the falling drops also formed themselves into perfect spheres. Watts had invented lead shot. He went on to invest in a purpose-built tower so that these two common ingredients – lead and water (combined with his own sharp eye) – produced an explosive advance.[2] Pheasant shoots were never the same again.

A century later, in what was then the small Hampshire village of Basingstoke, a shopkeeper had a comparable brainwave.

2 In 1799 an even taller shot tower – a cylindrical brick chimney – appeared on the banks of the Shropshire Union Canal in Chester. Long since obsolete, the fabric of the building is now listed, but there are plans to turn it into flats.

Noticing that the shepherds in his store were always snug in their home-made coats, he concluded that sheepskin had waterproof properties, put it to the test, and invented gaberdine. Again, two basic English substances – sheep and water – were used to produce something brand new. The coats sold so well that the shopkeeper was able to open a new store in London. Naturally enough, he traded under his own name: Thomas Burberry. He could not have foreseen that the emporium he founded would one day make headlines with a £28,000 coat made from alligator skin. That was not easy to come by, in Basingstoke.

There are so many historical threads of this sort. Leave the Northern Line at its southern terminus, Morden, and there is little to alert you to the fact that these were once lavender fields, or that the area was once owned by Westminster Abbey. But the street names soon reveal the truth: Canterbury, Crowland, Dorchester, Glastonbury, Malmesbury, Peterborough, Pipewell, Sherborne, St Albans, Tewkesbury, Woburn – they are all named after monasteries. Not that they are ancient: Morden was built in the garden suburb craze of the 1920s. There were cars on the roads. It must have felt grand, turning left at Waltham and parking in Tintern.

One last anecdote. Wandering through London not long ago, I was crossing one of the broad roads near Buckingham Palace when a troop of plumed and mounted cavalry jingled past. Maybe it was the weather, maybe it was the time of day, but for some reason the horses' rear ends were especially productive that morning. The road was soon littered with steaming piles.

As coincidence would have it, I had just learned that there were three million horses in the United Kingdom at the end of the nineteenth century. *Three million.* Delving further into the subject, I discovered that London then boasted ten thousand hansom cabs, several thousand horse-drawn buses and hundreds of brewery ponies and delivery carts. Since each of these produced several piles of manure every day, plus a fair few pints of urine, all of this horse power presented a major challenge to the city's sanitary engineers. In 1894, commenting on 'the great manure crisis', *The Times* predicted that the streets of London would soon be nine feet deep in horse dung.

It never happened. As so often with such extrapolations, the idea that things might change was overlooked. A racy innovation, the motor car was just about to make the horse virtually obsolete. The problem vanished – or was at least replaced by a different one.

The swift decline of the horse serves as a salutary reminder that change often comes fast. And also that one of the things which guarantees continuity is ... constant change.

So, before we wave the English countryside off into its modern incarnation as an interactive history experience, we should remember that there will almost certainly be more twists and upheavals than we can imagine in the future.

What happened to the pony, for instance, could just as easily happen to the car.

The signs are already there. According to a 2016 forecast by BP, the world can expect to have 100 million electric vehicles, a growing number of them driverless (mass production of which may be only a few years away) on its roads in the next two decades. The news has not yet sunk in, but they are coming round the mountain ... fast. The ramifications will be extreme. In the hands-free future, no one will need a car of their own: they will simply order one on their smartphone. It will be electric – slipping away overnight to recharge itself – quiet, cheap and pollution-free.

Our own nine-feet-thick traffic problem will evaporate like morning dew (or horse manure in Edwardian London). The driverless cars will not crash into bollards or each other, and the roads, drained of the stationary cars that used to park in them, will become roomy boulevards. After a tense phase in which the driverless vehicles are obliged to share the streets with accident-prone humans, they will grow calm. On long journeys we will smile about the bad old days when these car things actually had to be steered by hand, and we couldn't drink.

By the same token, we may be premature in imagining that people will continue to flock from the countryside into cities. There are signs that the long process of urbanisation may on the contrary be shifting into reverse. The combination of eye-watering property prices in city centres and quicksilver information technology is allowing people to move back to the shires, to the green acres where England began. Design consultancies are setting up on rural greens that once hosted fairs; internet whizz-kids are filling converted barns; travel agents are taking over rectories; printers are moving into mills, milliners into almshouses. Wireless data is reinventing England's green places, and virtual technology makes it simple for people to meet face-to-face from opposite sides of the world, let alone different parts of England.

Automation, meanwhile, looks set to make a thousand white-collar occupations obsolete in ways for which hardly anyone is prepared. Everyone knows that is on the cards; no one is quite sure what it means.

England, in short, is changing – again. Its abbeys have become schools, its halls hotels, its banks wine bars, its wharves art galleries, its pubs Thai restaurants, its vicarages care homes ... but that may be only the start of it. The land made by wool still stands,[3] and its ripples permeate English life every day. But in the synthetic modern world we are not so wool-dependent as we used to be, so they are growing weaker.

One thing is certain, however. Whatever the future holds, England will not be able to escape the oldest battle of all: the struggle to make sense of its own past.

3 Some fifteen million sheep still graze on England's hills and dales.

Historical Note

The notion that geographical factors shape national identity is unfashionable, but it has a pedigree. In *Spirit of the Laws* (1748), the French philosopher Montesquieu proposed climate as *the* decisive factor in the expansion of human civilisation. In his view, tropical weather produced 'hot-tempered' levels of conflict and misery, while frostier climates generated cooler personality types. It was no great trick to support this argument with reference to extreme locations – glaciers and deserts clearly gave rise to contrasting cultures – but he believed that even minor variations were similarly rooted. England's political system was more flexible than that of France, he suggested, because the former's gloomy weather obliged the citizenry to take nothing for granted.

The Enlightenment thinker Johann Herder agreed. He reminded his fellow-Germans that their *Volksgeist* resided not in language and literature but in their forests, mountains and rivers. A century later, the French historian Jules Michelet was sufficiently struck by England's weather – the persistent fog, the pale sun, the floating mist – to conclude that its influence on the natives must be immense. 'Under this absorbing climate,' he wrote, 'man, ever a-hungered, can only live by labour. Nature compels him to it ... All England pants with struggle.'

The English contribution to this literature has been more eccentric. In Victorian England, Henry Thomas Buckle attempted to do for cultural studies what Darwin had done for natural history (and Marx was attempting to do for economics) by laying down scientific 'laws' that governed 'the character and destiny of nations'. Prompted by an art-history question – was it a coincidence that sculpture and painting achieved perfection in the Mediterranean cultures of Greece and Italy? – Buckle sketched out a ten-volume work whose introduction alone ran to 854 pages. He had written barely a third of it when he died in 1862 ... and not everyone mourned the loss.

Given that he was trying to blend history, geography, religion, science and art into a single theory of everything, his project was probably doomed to remain unfinished. But his central argument was arresting: human societies were 'determined solely by their antecedents' – climate, soil, food and the 'General Aspect of Nature'.

It was not Christian virtue that led the English to wake early, he seemed to be saying – it was merely the pattern of their daylight hours. Maxims like 'Early to bed and early to rise /Makes a man healthy and wealthy and wise' had little to do with the Protestant work ethic; they were simply comments on the timing of dawn and dusk in England's shires.

This view was widely rejected as too radical by half. Just as Montesquieu was placed on the Catholic Church's list of proscribed authors – on the grounds that he gave too little credit to divine wisdom – so Buckle was damned for proposing that religion could possibly be junior to the weather. However, a handful of religious leaders offered their support. In a famous lecture delivered in Oxford in 1896, the Bishop of Peterborough, Mandell Creighton, argued that the English character *was* a product of the English soil, and correctly identified in it an inclination to distance itself from the main strands of European culture: 'In very early times it showed a tendency to withdraw cautiously from the general system in Europe, and go its own way. It had a notion that England's interests were not the same as those of the continent, and were not covered by any general system which there prevailed.'

This was not an opinion, or a recommendation. It was an observable fact.

Later philosophers found Buckle's theories sacrilegious for another reason, however. In arguing that society was determined by geography, he seemed to be suggesting that the races were different, and not necessarily equal – a scandalous proposition. If anything, it could be argued that he said the exact opposite: that the races *were* equal, and that any differences between them must therefore be due to variations in *terroir*. But this was insufficient to spare him condemnation. Was he seriously suggesting that the English were the product of nothing more than a fortunate geographical inheritance? Or daring to imply that they were *not* a cut above the rest? Either way, he was a damnable pagan. Send for the horsewhip!

One satirical rhyme went so far as to put words into Buckle's mouth:

> *I believe in fire and water,*
> *And in fate, dame Nature's daughter.*
> *I believe in steam and rice,*
> *Not in virtue or in vice.*

The religious position still had leverage in those days. A few historians were happy to concede that old Buckle might have had a point. Macaulay had already suggested that it was daily life down the ages which inspired the cultural spirit of Britain; J. R. Green called landscape 'the fullest and most certain of all documents'; R. H. Tawney (who famously urged his fellow-historians to wear 'stouter boots') and Maurice Beresford (with his 'emphasis on visual things') followed suit.

Walt Whitman Rostow – a devout American anti-communist – insisted that economic life was based on changes in material conditions, or what he called 'pre-conditions'. And in 1972 F. F. Mendels coined the phrase 'proto industry' to describe the fledgling steps in agricultural technology that paved the way for the industrial expansion that followed. A few years later, the Cambridge anthropologist Alan Macfarlane inspected marriage records and financial details from the Middle Ages, and concluded that medieval life in England was considerably more 'modern' than was usually thought.

The average smallholder, he suggested, had a home, a few animals, clothes, land, money, even a line of credit at the market, was 'no miserable subsistence peasant, but a small capitalist farmer'. In several English regions (East Anglia and Kent, for example), a surprisingly large number of people owned plots of land, traded on their own account, paid rent, used cash and lived 'open, mobile, market-oriented' lives.

Macfarlane did not conclude that medieval England was an equal-opportunities employer; far from it. But he did detect glimmers of liberation in the long-lost past – certainly enough to qualify the prevailing idea that industrial change ignited only in the eighteenth century.

Inevitably, a preoccupation with landscape and climate tends to give special weight to the most ancient expressions of a national culture. This also goes against the modern grain. When it comes to the Industrial Revolution, for instance, the received wisdom is that it burst on Georgian England like a thunderclap. In 1887 Arnold Toynbee argued that it took hold in 'the years after 1750' and marked a sharp break with the past: 'It destroyed the old world and built a new one.' Phyllis Deane – President of the Royal Economic Society – echoed this view in *The First Industrial Revolution* (1965), suggesting that England was 'essentially stagnant' until the middle of the eighteenth century. Linda Colley agreed, while France's Fernand Braudel took it as a given that 'change favourable to the peasants began in the eighteenth century'. In his view, all the significant European lands, including the insular British islands, resembled one another: they 'tackled the same major problems, in conditions and with solutions that were often alike'.

Most historians have taken the same view, and one would not wish to quibble too much. It is evident that the 'modern' world *did* grow largely out of the political upheaval in revolutionary France and the engineering surge in Britain. But though the big picture certainly changed, it did not change at the same pace for everyone. As Tawney noted, even at the start of the twentieth century people were living restricted lives, travelling only yards from the place where they were born, and meeting no more than a hundred human beings, if that, in their lifetime. They lived in their parents' house, used the same plough, tilled the same fields. In the same way, it might be that the world before the industrial convulsion was less stable, richer in small industrial glints and gleams, than we imagine.[1]

Several contemporary historians have adopted this anthropological approach. Jared Diamond argued that plain natural facts, operating like the random variations that drive evolution, created knock-on effects that over time were magnified into significant competitive advantages. The Arctic Inuit wore fur not because of any socio-cultural pressure or political insight, let alone random chance. Rather, their clothing was a simple response to the fact that the temperature outside their homes was forty degrees below zero: 'The human spirit won't keep you warm north of the Arctic Circle.'

David Landes was even more forthright in arguing that geography was formative. He pointed out that the world 'has never been a level playing field' and claimed that only a resolutely blinkered commentator could fail to notice the difference between its hot and cold regions. It was a sad truth that warm climates made human beings seek out others to do the heavy lifting: 'it is no accident that slave labour has historically been associated with tropical and semitropical climes'.

More recently, Robert Tombs gave religion and politics most

1 When Marx described England as a 'purely agricultural' land until the evil mills of capitalism drove a steam-powered wedge between worker and owner, it is possible that he was exaggerating the distinction in order to make his (powerful) point more vivid.

of the credit for nailing down the essential planks of nationhood. But he never forgot that England's island setting gave
it secure borders long before its European neighbours fortified theirs, which allowed the religious and political culture
to develop in relative peace. He was supremely alert, too, to
the ways in which the migratory habit of Europe's tribes was
prompted by simple considerations of climate and landscape.
One reason why the Vikings pressed south and west, he suggested, was that they coveted the milder weather – in particular
the long growing season for wheat – that their own icy fjords
could not provide.

On the whole, however, the suggestion that landscape might
shape human culture breaks too many modern rules: it seems
racist, because it implies that some characteristics are the preserve of pure-blooded natives, or that ancient inequalities
might be natural or preordained. Jared Diamond was accused
of 'environmental determinism' for hinting as much, and it
was not intended as a compliment. Buckle's world view was
mocked almost to death in the rush to find progressive new
ways of writing history.

There are plenty of these. History now presents itself sometimes as a science (weighing and measuring the past) and at
other times as literature (a chronicle). It may also be read in
different lights: Marxist, Freudian, feminist, post-feminist,
historicist, structuralist, post-structuralist, liberal, neo-liberal,
postmodern or sociological, to name but a few. It may follow
Vico, Hegel, Weber, Comte, Michelet, Macaulay, Oakeshott,
Carr, Spengler, Said, Foucault, Thompson or a hundred others,
all of whom have dedicated disciples. Since most of these con-
tradict at least some of the others, there are lots of intricate
disputes on arcane points. As a result, the modern past, if we
can call it that, has come to resemble a forest of criss-crossing
tracks, each one favoured by a different theoretical approach.
Some see it as a pageant of kings and queens; others as a war

between labour and capital. Some see it as a criminal conspiracy; others as an uplifting tale of progress and liberation; still others as an ongoing joust over sexual, religious or racial identity. Some look for change; others highlight continuity. Some search for difference; others hunt down similarities.

One way or another, history no longer presumes to be a single, universal story of the past. It is merely a critique of the sources that happen to have survived. Alas, these are patchy. Indeed, the prominence of ecclesiastical movements in the traditional version of English history owes much to the fact that monks and theologians were assiduous scribes who left detailed records, whereas shepherds and millers could rarely write their own names.

Nearly all of the modern ways of thinking agree that historic change is wrought not by individuals – kings, queens, princes, ministers and generals (the almost obsolete 'great men' theory) – but by ideologies: religious doctrines, economics, politics and class antagonism. And, given that the dominant class inevitably views the world through a prism that favours its own interests, history is not so much a reading of the past as an analysis of power. The duty of the historian is no longer to clean the rear-view mirror in order to gain a clearer vision of former times and glimpse new truths, but to agitate previous histories.

History, they say, is not the past. It is what historians make of the past. We do not expect musicians to produce identical performances of Mozart, so why should we expect historians to agree on a 'correct' view of events that occurred long ago?

This sort of thinking derives in part from literary theory, which takes it as read that all texts are tattered flags, shot through with tell-tale assumptions and absences. It is well known that the authorial voice is slippery and unreliable, and that storytelling obeys its own rules and conventions. Nor do historians enjoy universal authority – they merely interpret the past according to their own lights.

As a genre, history is evasive. By definition, even the most ardent revisionists suffer from the same blinkered view that sty-mies all the others. This can lead to some odd conclusions. In 2003 Krishna Kumar was happy to declare: 'It is not until the late 19th century, at the earliest, that we find a clear concern with the question of Englishness.'

At the earliest? Were we imagining all that patriotic breast-beating in *Henry V*?

It is hard to insist that the *ancien régime* is hidebound without conceding that the modern way of thinking might itself be subject to the same fluctuating laws of fashion.

History does not run on straight rails. The nation that oper-ated the slave trade also rose against it. Victorian capitalism produced greedy tycoons, but also tender philanthropists (and an anti-capitalist intelligentsia). So we should not dismiss envi-ronmental factors too hastily. If anything, the argument from geography helps to explain why human beings who are clearly equal have developed in different ways: the explanation for any variation lies not in *their* nature, but in the world that supports and nourishes them. The British did not colonise half the world because they were virtuous, or gifted. They were simply the beneficiaries of a remarkably favourable geographical wind.

As it happens, the idea that geography is fate accepts, in a way, the Marxist idea that material conditions create cultural superstructures, much as a tree generates blossom. Admittedly, this sort of argument can seem dismissive of today's cosmo-politan swirl – and silent on the fashionable fields of race, gender and identity. Some traditionalists have indeed argued that American and European conditions produced superior people. And the shriller sort of imperialist did fall for the idea that Western 'values' had a right to impose themselves on every corner of the world.

But the fact that a flag is waved in a bad cause does not entirely disfigure the flag.

It remains the case that there are not many fishermen in the Sahara Desert. And the Bedouin do not need five words for snow, let alone fifty. As David Landes says – with a sigh, as if resigning himself to an awkward fact – geography 'tells us an unpleasant truth, that nature, like life, is unfair, unequal in its favours'.

In this context it is fair to ask the question: what is history, if not the ramifications of geography over time?

Acknowledgements

In setting out to explore the subject of Englishness I faced a problem. I was not a professional historian: I had not devoted my life to manorial records. Abbey rolls, settlement patterns, marriage lists ... these had not been my home from home. And I was no sort of expert on industry, agriculture, geology, textiles, cathedral building, brewing, milling or any of the other fields that would feature prominently in this survey. I had also not worked the land, measured rainfall or analysed crop yields. I *had* delivered a lamb ... but only once. Would it be possible, given these failings, to describe so sweeping a terrain?

Nor did it escape my attention that I would be adding to an already significant shelf of works on this topic. Roger Scruton, Jeremy Paxman, Kate Fox, Harry Mount, Matthew Engel and many others have left bold footprints on this field. I would need to rummage through a compendious library of such works.

Finally, there was the challenge posed by the sheer size and weight of England's past. There is a reason why the nation's history books tend to be so long (Robert Tombs's recent *The English and Their History* runs to nine hundred pages – and feels compact). Even a routine run through the basic list of kings, queens and political leaders burns up several hundred pages, leaving little room for anything else. Fortunately, I intended to skip that sort of thing, or at least leave it in safer hands than mine. In the shadow of so much elevated scholarship, I resolved to write not so much a history as a historically minded excursion. It would dwell on England's past, but also get its feet muddy. It would inspect that past not to escape into it, but to seek early hints of modern attitudes beneath its mossy stones.

It would take the form of a chronicle, however, on the simple grounds laid down by Arthur Marwick: 'Without analysis, history is incomplete; without chronology, it does not exist.'

Thanks are due to Richard Beswick for provoking and shepherding the whole thing; to David Godwin for his expert support; to Hermione Davies for everything; to Tamsyn Berryman for sparing me a hundred blushes; and to the many libraries, librarians and custodians of places I visited. Thank you to the traffic app on my phone, which helped me dodge motorway jams in search of echoes.[1] And thanks to the generations of unnamed bakers, shepherds, masons, millers, farmers, tailors, monks, sailors, traders, musicians, soldiers, artists, merchants, miners, poets, philosophers and kings who have made England what it is today.

Most of all, though, I should thank the sudden squall that prompted me to pull over in Great Dunmow, and stumble upon the ancient folk tradition with which our tale began.

---

1 How different England might be had it stuck with its traditional road names. Instead of taking the A3 or the M40, we would follow the Portsmouth Road or Watling Street. For Lincoln, take the Great North and fly up Fosse Way. In this and countless other ways we have tried to annul history and geography, but much remains.

Bibliography

The following list of books is divided into thematic groups that inevitably overlap. Some titles may sit better elsewhere. My intention was only to make it a more useful guide to further reading in each of the fields on which I have trespassed.

There may be more out-of-date works than is usual. That is not because they contain neglected wisdom (although some do), but because they now form part of the story they once sought to tell. They may have been superseded by better-sourced analyses, but they have become literary works in their own right, exposing not just what people knew, but what they thought.

The list begins with studies of prehistory, on the assumption that what comes before history is . . . geography.

Prehistory
Bryant, Arthur, 'How Does Our Climate Reflect Our Character', *Listener* 623, 1933.

Buckle, Henry Thomas, *History of Civilisation in England*, Vols I and II, Grant Richards, 1903.

Creighton, Mandell, *The English National Character*, Romaines Lecture delivered at the Sheldonian, Oxford, 1896.

Darby, H. C., *A New Historical Geography of England Before 1600*, Cambridge University Press, 1976.

Elliott, Charles Boileau, *A Prize Essay on the Effects of Climate on National Character*, LOSE, 1921.

Hawkes, Jacquetta, *A Land*, Collins, 1951.

Huntington, Ellsworth, *Civilization and Climate*, Yale University Press, 1915.

Lewis, Samuel, *A Topographical Dictionary of England*, London, 1848.

Montesquieu, *The Spirit of the Laws*, Cambridge University Press, 1989.

Morris, Richard, *Time's Anvil: England, Archaeology and Imagination*, Weidenfeld & Nicolson, 2012.

Steel, Robert W., *British Geography 1918–1945*, Cambridge University Press, 1987.

Voltaire, *Morals, Manners and Character of Nations*, Paris, 1756.

Wood, Michael, *In Search of England: Journeys into the English Past*, Viking, 1999.

General History

Braudel, Fernand, *A History of Civilizations*, Penguin, 1995.

Burrow, John, *A Liberal Descent: Victorian Historians and the English Past*, Cambridge University Press, 1981.

Christopher, David, *British Culture: An Introduction*, Routledge, 1999.

Cohen-Portheim, Paul, *England: The Unknown Isle*, Duckworth, 1930.

Coombes, B. L., *Those Clouded Hills*, Cobbett, 1944.

Cornell, Martyn, *Amber, Gold and Black: The History of Britain's Great Beers*, The History Press, 2010.

Davies, Norman, *The Isles: A History*, Macmillan, 1999.

Diamond, Jared, *Guns, Germs and Steel: The Fates of Human Societies*, W. W. Norton & Co., 1997.

Easthorpe, Anthony, *Englishness and National Culture*, Routledge, 1998.

Green, J. R., *A Short History of the English People*, Macmillan, 1874.

Knight, Charles, *The Popular History of England*, London 1862.

Leader, Robert, *In Search of Secret Norfolk*, Thorogood, 2006.

Masterman, C. F. G., *The Condition of England*, Methuen, 1909.

Matless, David, *Landscape and Englishness*, Reaktion, 1998.

Mortimer, Ian, *The Time Traveller's Guide to Medieval England*, Vintage, 2008.

Morton, H. V., *In Search of England*, Methuen, 1927.

Pike, Luke Owen, *The English and Their Origin: A Prologue to Authentic English History*, London, 1866.

Rogers, David, and McLeod, John, *The Revisions of Englishness*, Manchester University Press, 2004.

Ruddick, Andrea, *English Identity and Political Culture*, Cambridge University Press, 2013.

Smith, Godfrey, *The English Companion*, Old House, 1987.

Stone, Lawrence, *The Family, Sex and Marriage in England 1500–1800*, Penguin, 1985.

Tawney, R. H., *The Agrarian Problem in the Sixteenth Century*, Longman's, Green, 1912.

Thomas, Keith, *Man and the Natural World: Changing Attitudes in England 1500–1800*, Penguin, 1991.

Thompson, E. P., *The Making of the English Working Class*, Gollancz, 1963.

Trevelyan, G. M., *English Social History*, Longman's, 1942.

Treves, Paulo, *England, the Mysterious Island*, Gollancz, 1948.

Vansittart, Peter, *In Memory of England*, John Murray, 1998.

Wood, Michael, *The Domesday Book*, BBC, 1996.

Wolves

Almond, Richard, *Medieval Hunting*, Sutton, 2003.

Griffin, Emma, *Blood Sport: Hunting in Britain since 1066*, Yale University Press, 2007.

Harting, James Edmund, *A Short History of the Wolf in Britain*, Whitstable, 1994.

Hatcher, Paul, and Batty, Nick, *Biological Diversity: Exploiters and Exploited*, Wiley, 2011.

Plukowski, Aleksander, *Wolves and the Wilderness in the Middle Ages*, Boydell Press, 2006.

The Middle Ages

Aberth, John Jordan, *From the Brink of the Apocalypse: Confronting Famine, War, Plague and Death in the Later Middle Ages*, Routledge, 2001.

Bailey, Mark, *The Decline of Serfdom in Late Medieval England: From Bondage to Freedom*, Boydell Press, 2014.

Bolton, J. L., *The Medieval English Economy 1150–1500*, Dent, 1980.

Bridbury, A. R., 'The Black Death', *Economic History Review* 26(4), 1973.

Burton, Janet, and Kerr, Julie, *The Cistercians in the Middle Ages*, Boydell Press, 2011.

Butler, Lionel, and Given-Wilson, Chris, *Medieval Monasteries in Great Britain*, Michael Joseph, 1979.

Coppack, Glyn, *The White Monks: The Cistercians in Britain 1128–1540*, The History Press, 2000.

Dyer, Christopher, *Standards of Living in the Middle Ages*, Cambridge University Press, 1989.

Dyer, Christopher, *Everyday Life in Medieval England*, Hambledon, 1994.

Foyle, Jonathan, *Lincoln Cathedral: The Biography of a Great Building*, Scala Arts & Heritage Publishers Ltd, 2015.

Fried, Johannes, *The Middle Ages*, Harvard, 2015.

Gimpel, Jean, *The Cathedral Builders*, HarperPerennial, 1993.

Given-Wilson, Chris, (ed.), *Fourteenth Century England*, Boydell Press, 2002.

Gottfried, Robert S., *The Black Death: Natural and Human Disaster in Medieval Europe*, Free Press, 1985.

Hislop, Malcolm, *Medieval Masons*, Shire Publications, 2009.

Holt, Richard, *The Mills of Medieval England*, Blackwell, 1988.

Huggett, Frank, *The Land Question in European Society*, Thames & Hudson, 1975.

Irvine, Helen Douglas, *The Making of Rural Europe*, Allen and Unwin, 1923.

Knoop, Douglas, and Jones, G. P., *The Medieval Mason: An Economic History of English Stone Building in the Later Middle*

Ages, Manchester University Press, 1967.

Le Goff, Jacques, *Medieval Civilisation*, Blackwell, 1988.

Lehfeldt, Elizabeth, *The Black Death*, Houghton Mifflin, 2005.

Maitland, Frederic William, *Township and Borough*, Cambridge, 1898.

Platt, Colin, *Medieval England: A Social History and Archaeology from the Conquest to A. D. 1600*, Routledge, 1978.

Platt, Colin, *King Death: The Black Death and its Aftermath*, University of Toronto, 1997.

Postan, M. M., *The Medieval Economy and Society*, Pelican, 1972.

Power, Eileen, *Medieval People*, Methuen, 1924.

Power, Eileen, *Medieval Women*, Cambridge University Press, 1975.

Richmond, Turlin, *The Brewing Industry*, Manchester, 1990.

White, Graeme, *The Medieval Landscape: 1000–1540*, Bloomsbury, 2012.

Whittock, Martin, *A Brief History of Life in the Middle Ages*, Robinson, 2009.

Williamson, Tom, *Environment, Society and Landscape in Early Medieval England: Time and Topography*, Boydell Press, 2013.

Ziegler, Philip, *The Black Death*, Penguin, 1987.

Wool

Bell, Adrian, Brooks, Chris, and Dryburgh, R., *The English Wool Market 1230–1327*, Cambridge University Press, 2007.

Bowden, P. J., 'Wool Supply and the Woollen Industry', *Economic History Review* 9, 1956.

Butler, Alan, *Sheep: The Remarkable Story of the Humble Animal that Built the Modern World*, John Hunt, 2013.

Donkin, R. A., 'Cistercian Sheep Farming', *Agricultural History Review* 6, 1958.

Fletcher, J. S., *The Cistercians of Yorkshire*, London, 1919.

Gossett, Adelaide, *Shepherds of Britain*, Constable, 1911.

Hanham, Alison, *The Celys and Their World*, Cambridge University Press, 1985.

Harnett, Cynthia, *The Woolpack*, Methuen, 1951.

Hurst, Derek, *Sheep in the Cotswolds: The Medieval Wool Trade*, The History Press, 2005.

Lloyd, T. H., *The Medieval Wool Sack: A Study in Economic History*, Cambridge University Press, 1977.

Lloyd, T. H., *The English Wool Trade in the Middle Ages*, Cambridge University Press, 2008.

Power, Eileen, *Medieval People*, Methuen, 1924.

Power, Eileen, *The Wool Trade in English Medieval History*, Oxford University Press, 1941.

Power, Eileen, *The Medieval English Wool Trade*, Oxford University Press, 1944.

Rebanks, James, *The Shepherd's Life: A Tale of the Lake District*, Allen Lane, 2015.

Ryder, M. L., *Sheep and Man*, Duckworth, 2007.

Thomas, J. F. H., *Sheep*, Faber & Faber, 1944.

Walling, Philip, *Counting Sheep: A Celebration of the Pastoral Heritage of Britain*, Profile, 2014.

Wheat

David, Elizabeth, *English Bread and Yeast Cookery*, Allen Lane, 1972.

Deane, P. M., *The First Industrial Revolution*, Cambridge University Press, 1965.

Ernle, R. E. P., *English Farming Past and Present*, Longman's, 1927.

Goody, Jack, *Food and Love: A Cultural History of East and West*, Verso, 2010.

Jefferies, Richard, 'The Future of Farming', *Fraser's Magazine*, 1873.

Kerridge, Eric, 'The Agricultural Revolution Reconsidered', *Agricultural History* 43(4), 1969.

Kerridge, Eric, *Farmers of Old England*, Allen and Unwin, 1973.

Massingham, H. J., *The Wisdom of the Fields*, Collins, 1945.

Overton, Mark, *The Agricultural Revolution in England 1500–1850*, Cambridge University Press, 1996.

Ritchie, Carson I. A., *Food in Civilization*, Beaufort, 1981.

Rubel, William, *Bread: A Global History*, Reaktion, 2011.

Thirsk, Jan, (ed.), *The Agrarian History of England and Wales*, Vol. IV, Cambridge University Press, 1967.

Unger, Richard, *Beer in the Middle Ages and the Renaissance*, University of Pennsylvania, 2004.

Williams, Anthony, (ed.), *Breadmaking: The Modern Revolution*, Hutchinson, 1975.

Williamson, Tom, *The Transformation of Rural England: Farming and the Landscape 1700–1870*, University of Exeter, 2002.

Water

Bates, David, and Liddiard, Robert, (eds), *East Anglia and its North Sea World in the Middle Ages*, Boydell Press, 2015.

Blair, John, (ed.), *Waterways and Canal Building in Medieval England*, Oxford University Press, 2007.

Cathcart, Brian, *Rain*, Granta, 2002.

Edwards, J. F., *The Transport System of Medieval England and Wales*, University of Salford, 1987.

Fort, Tom, *Under the Weather: Us and the Elements*, Century, 2006.

Hadfield, Charles, *The Canal Age*, David and Charles, 1968.

Kohn, Marek, *Turned out Nice: How the British Isles will Change as the Weather Heats Up*, London, Faber & Faber, 2010.

Markham, S. F., *Climate and the Energy of Nations*, Oxford University Press, 1942.

McKnight, Hugh, *The Shell Book of Inland Waterways*, David and Charles, 1981.

Pye, Michael, *The Edge of the World: How the North Sea Made Us Who We Are*, Viking, 2014.

Coal

Brimblecombe, Peter, *The Big Smoke*, Routledge, 1977.

Dennis, Norman, Henriques, Fernando, and Slaughter, Clifford, *Coal is Our Life*, Eyre and Spottiswood, 1956.

Freese, Barbara, *Coal: A Human History*, Perseus, 2003.

Glancy, Jonathan, *Giants of Steam: The Great Men and Machines of Rail's Golden Age*, Atlantic, 2002.

Hatcher, John, *The Oxford History of the Coal Industry*, Oxford University Press, 1993.

Heinemann, Manny, *Britain's Coal*, Gollancz, 1944.

Martin, E. A., *Coal and its Story: What it is: Whence it Comes and Whither it Goes*, Hodder & Stoughton, 1926.

Nef, J. U., *The Rise of the British Coal Industry*, Routledge, 1932.

Pounds, Norman, and Parker, William, *Coal and Steel in Western Europe: The Influence of Resource and Techniques on Production*, Faber & Faber, 1957.

Ritchie, A. E., *The Kent Coalfield: Its Evolution and Development*, The Iron and Coal Trades Review, 1920.

Webb, Sidney, *The Story of the Durham Miners: 1662–1921*, Fabian Society, 1921.

Wilson, Harold, *New Deal for Coal*, Contact, 1945.

National Identity

Anderson, Benedict, *Imagined Communities: Reflections on the Origin and Spread of Nationalism*, Verso, 2006.

Aslet, Clive, *Anyone for England: A Search for English Identity*, Little, Brown, 1997.

Barker, Ernest, *The Character of England*, Oxford University Press, 1947.

Belloc, Hilaire, *An Essay on the Nature of Contemporary England*, Constable, 1937.

Blake, Robert, *The English World: History, Character and People*, Abrams, 1982.

Bowle, John, *England: A Portrait*, Readers Union, 1968.

Briggs, Asa, *Saxons, Normans and Victorians*, Historical Association, 1966.

Bryant, Arthur, *The National Character*, Longman's, Green, 1934.

Capek, Carel, *Letters from England*, Geoffrey Bles, 1925.

Chenevix, Richard, *An Essay upon National Character*, London, 1832.

Chesterton, G. K., *Explaining the English, Collected Works*, Vol. 20, Ignatius, 1986.

Colley, Linda, *Britons: Forging the Nation, 1707–1837*, Yale University Press, 1992.

Colls, Robert, *Identity of England*, Oxford University Press, 2002.

Creighton, Mendell, *The English National Character*, 1896.

Dewey, Robert F., *British National Identity and Opposition to Membership of Europe 1961–3: The Anti-Marketeers*, Manchester University Press, 2009.

Haseler, Stephen, *The English Tribe: Identity, Nation and Europe*, Palgrave Macmillan, 1996.

Hueffer, Ford Madox, *England and the English: An Interpretation*, McClure, Philips & Co, 1907.

Kumar, Krishan, *The Making of English National Identity*, Cambridge University Press, 2003.

Macfarlane, Alan, *The Origins of English Individualism: Family, Property and Social Transition*, Blackwell, 1978.

Mackenzie, J. S., *Arrows of Desire: Essays on Our National Character and Outlook*, Allen and Unwin, 1920.

Mandler, Peter, *The English National Character: The History of an Idea from Edmund Burke to Tony Blair*, Yale University Press, 2006.

Nevinson, Henry, *Ourselves: An Essay on the National Character*, BBC, 1933.

Paxman, Jeremy, *The English: A Portrait of a People*, Penguin, 1998.

Tombs, Robert, *The English and Their History*, Allen Lane, 2014.

Economic History

Bridbury, A. R., *The English Economy from Bede to the Reformation*, Boydell Press, 1992.

Briggs, Milton, and Jordan, Percy, *Economic History of England*, University Tutorial Press, 1964.

Carus-Wilson, E. M., and Coleman, O., *England's Export Trade 1275–1547*, Oxford University Press, 1963.

Clapham, Sir John, *Economic History of Britain*, Cambridge University Press, 1949.

Cunningham, William, *The Growth of English Industry and Commerce*, Cambridge, 1922.

Faith, Rosamund Jane, 'Peasant Families and Inheritance Customs in Medieval England', *Agricultural History Review* 14(2), 1966.

Faith, Rosamund, *English Peasantry and the Growth of Lordship: Studies in the Early History of Britain*, London, 1999.

Goody, Jack, Thirsk, Joan, and Thompson, E. P., (eds), *Family and Inheritance: Rural Society in Western Europe 1200–1800*, Cambridge University Press, 1976.

Jamoussi, Zouheir, *Primogeniture and Entail in England: A Survey of Their History and Representation in Literature*, Cambridge Scholars Publishing, 2011.

Landes, David, *The Wealth and Poverty of Nations*, W. W. Norton & Co., 1998.

Postan, M. M., *The Medieval Economy and Society*, Penguin, 1972.

Rose, Susan, *Calais: An English Town in France*, Boydell Press, 2008.

Thirsk, Joan, and Bowden, Peter, *The Agrarian History of England*, Vol. I, Cambridge University Press, 1990.

White, Lynn, *Medieval Technology and Social Change*, Oxford University Press, 1962.

Whittle, J., *The Development of Agrarian Capitalism: Land Labour in Norfolk, 1440–1580*, Oxford University Press, 2000.

Wrighton, Keith, *Earthly Necessities: Economic Lives in Early Modern Britain 1470–1750*, Penguin, 2002.

Cultural History

Attenbury, Paul, and Wainwright, Clive, (eds), *Pugin: A Gothic Passion*, Yale University Press, 1994.

Barnes, Julian, *England, England*, Vintage, 1998.

Briggs, Asa, *Victorian Cities*, Penguin, 1963.

Buruma, Ian, *Voltaire's Coconuts: Or Anglomania in Europe*, Weidenfeld & Nicolson, 1999.

Davidson, Jenny, *Hypocrisy and the Politics of Politeness: Manners and Morals from Locke to Austen*, Cambridge University Press, 2007.

Durrell, Lawrence, 'Landscape and Character', in *Spirit of Place*, Faber, 1969.

Engel, Matthew, *Engel's England: Thirty-nine Counties, One Capital and One Man*, Profile, 2014.

Fox, Kate, *Watching the English: The Hidden Rules of English Behaviour*, Hodder & Stoughton, 2005.

Girouard, Mark, *The English Town: A History of Urban Life*, Yale University Press, 1995.

Hewison, Robert, *The Heritage Industry*, Methuen, 1987.

Hill, Rosemary, *God's Architect: Pugin and the Building of Romantic Britain*, Allen Lane, 2007.

Hoyles, Martin, *The Story of Gardening*, Journeyman Press, 1942.

Hutton, Ronald, *The Rise and Fall of Merry England: The Ritual Year 1400–1700*, Oxford University Press, 1994.

Langford, Paul, *Englishness Identified: Manners and Character 1650–1850*, Oxford University Press, 2000.

Laslett, Peter, *The World We Have Lost: Further Explored*, Routledge, 2004.

Leavis, Queenie, 'The Englishness of the English Novel', in *Collected Essays*, Vol. I, Cambridge University Press, 1983.

Lessing, Doris, *In Pursuit of the English*, Sphere, 1968.

Macfarlane, Robert, *The Wild Places*, Granta, 2008.

Moran, Dr Joe, *Queuing for Beginners: The Story of Daily Life from Breakfast to Bedtime*, Profile, 2008.

Mount, Harry, *How England Made the English: From Why We Drive on the Left to Why We Don't Talk to Our Neighbours*, Penguin, 2013.

Naipaul, V. S., *The Enigma of Arrival*, Viking, 1986.

Orwell, George, *The Road to Wigan Pier*, Penguin, 1937.

Orwell, George, 'The Lion and the Unicorn: Socialism and the English Genius', Secker and Warburg, 1941.

Osborne, Richard, *Music and Musicians of Eton*, Cygnet, 2012.

Pevsner, Nikolaus, *An Outline of European Architecture*, Thames & Hudson, 1943.

Priestley, J. B., *An English Journey*, Heinemann, 1934.

Priestley, J. B., *The English*, Gollancz, 1973.

Read, Herbert, *The English Vision: An Anthology*, Routledge, 1939.

Rogers, Ben, *Beef and Liberty: Roast Beef, John Bull and the English Nation*, Chatto & Windus, 2003.

Scruton, Roger, *England: An Elegy*, Chatto & Windus, 2000.

Thurley, Simon, *Men from the Ministry: How Britain Saved Its Heritage*, Yale University Press, 2014.

Verey, David, *et al.* (eds), *The Buildings of England: Pevsner Architectural Guides*, Yale University Press, 1951–1974.

Watson, Merlin, *The National Trust: The First 100 Years*, National Trust/BBC, 1994.

The Countryside

Allem, Robert C., *Enclosure and the Yeoman*, Clarendon Press, 1992.

Aston, Margaret, 'English Ruins and English History', *Journal of the Courtauld Institute*, 1973.

Bailey, Brian, *The English Village Green*, Robert Hale, 1985.

Beresford, Maurice, *The Lost Villages of England*, Sutton, 1951.

Driver, Leigh, *The Lost Villages of England*, New Holland, 2006.

Hall, David, *Medieval Fields*, Shire, 2010.

Hardin, Garret, 'The Tragedy of the Commons', *Science* 162, 1968.

Homans, George Caspar, *English Villagers of the Thirteenth Century*, W. W. Norton & Co., 1960.

Hoskins, W. G., *The Making of the English Landscape*, Hodder, 1955.

Irvine, Helen Douglas, *The Making of Rural Europe*, Allen and Unwin, 1923.

Muir, Richard, *The Lost Villages of England*, The History Press, 2009.

Rackham, Oliver, *History of the English Countryside*, Weidenfeld & Nicolson, 2000.

Thirsk, Joan, 'Industries in the Countryside', in F. J. Fisher (ed.), *Essays in the Economic and Social History of Tudor and Stuart England*, London, 1961.

Thirsk, Joan, 'The Common Field', *Past and Present* 29, 1964.

Thirsk, Joan, (ed.), *The English Rural Landscape*, Oxford University Press, 2000.

Wainwright, Martin, *The English Village: History and Traditions*, Michael O'Mara, 2011.

Williamson, Tom, *The Transformation of Rural England*, Exeter University Press, 2002.

Index